Lecture Notes in Computer Science 14390

Founding Editors

Gerhard Goos
Juris Hartmanis

Editorial Board Members

The series Lecture Notes in Computer Science (LNCS), including its subseries Lecture Notes in Artificial Intelligence (LNAI) and Lecture Notes in Bioinformatics (LNBI), has established itself as a medium for the publication of new developments in computer science and information technology research, teaching, and education.

LNCS enjoys close cooperation with the computer science R & D community, the series counts many renowned academics among its volume editors and paper authors, and collaborates with prestigious societies. Its mission is to serve this international community by providing an invaluable service, mainly focused on the publication of conference and workshop proceedings and postproceedings. LNCS commenced publication in 1973.

Jan Kofroň · Tiziana Margaria ·
Cristina Seceleanu

Editors

Engineering of Computer-Based Systems

8th International Conference, ECBS 2023
Västerås, Sweden, October 16–18, 2023
Proceedings

 Springer

Editors
Jan Kofroň 🆔
Charles University
Praha, Czech Republic

Tiziana Margaria 🆔
University of Limerick
Limerick, Ireland

Cristina Seceleanu 🆔
Mälardalen University
Västerås, Sweden

ISSN 0302-9743   ISSN 1611-3349 (electronic)
Lecture Notes in Computer Science
ISBN 978-3-031-49251-8   ISBN 978-3-031-49252-5 (eBook)
https://doi.org/10.1007/978-3-031-49252-5

This Springer imprint is published by the registered company Springer Nature Switzerland AG
The registered company address is: Gewerbestrasse 11, 6330 Cham, Switzerland

Paper in this product is recyclable.

Preface

As General and Program Chairs, we would like to welcome you to the proceedings of ECBS 2023, the 8th International Conference on Engineering of Computer-Based Systems, which took place in Västerås (Sweden) on October 16th–18th, hosted by Mälardalen University in cooperation with ACM SIGSOFT.

The special theme of this year was "Engineering for Responsible AI", which permeates many of its keynotes and technical contributions.

ECBS 2023 was an in-person event that integrated software, hardware, and communication perspectives of systems engineering through its many facets that include system modelling, artificial intelligence, requirements specification, simulation, architectures, safety, security, reliability, system integration, verification and validation, and project management. As such, the conference provided a bridge between industry and academia, blending academic research and industrial development. It provided an interdisciplinary forum for discussing the impact of the recent AI developments on research and industrial systems' development, but also education, and society.

The program of ECBS 2023 comprised:

- three keynotes:

- **How To Be An Ethical Technologist**, by Moshe Vardi, Rice University, USA, on Oct 16th
- **Dynamic Logics for Computer-Based Systems**, by Wolfgang Ahrendt, Chalmers University of Technology, Sweden, on Oct 17th
- **Toward Responsible Artificial Intelligent Systems: Safety and Trust-worthiness**, by Francisco Herrera, University of Granada, Spain, on Oct 18th

- presentation of 11 regular papers, 7 short papers, and 6 posters in eight sessions over the three days.

ECBS 2023 received 26 submissions from 10 countries (Romania, Germany, UK, Denmark, Ireland, Serbia, Sweden, Israel, China, USA), and we accepted 24 papers (regular, short, and poster papers). Each paper was reviewed by 3–4 program committee members; a single-blind review process was used. We sincerely thank the three distinguished keynote speakers, Prof. Moshe Vardi, Prof. Wolfgang Ahrendt, Prof. Francisco Herrera, all the authors, speakers, and session chairs for their excellent scientific contributions to the conference, the members of the program committee and external reviewers for their time and thoroughness in selecting the papers to be presented, and the local Organization Chair, Susanne Fronnå, and local organization team, Leo Hatvani, Peter Backeman, Rong Gu, Eduard Paul Enoiu, Mikael Salari, Hawa Diouf for their continuous precious support during the entire period preceding the event. We thank Springer Nature for being, as usual, a very reliable partner for the proceedings production. We are also grateful to the Steering Committee of ECBS whose support has been invaluable.

Special thanks are due to Mälardalen University for sponsoring and hosting the event in the R building on the Västerås Campus.

We wish all the ECBS 2023 participants lively scientific discussions, ideally leading to new cooperation and ideas to be presented at future ECBS instances.

October 2023

Jan Kofroň
Tiziana Margaria
ECBS 2023 PC Chairs

Cristina Seceleanu
ECBS 2023 General Chair

Organization

Program Committee

Bernhard Aichernig	TU Graz, Austria
Marija Antić	University of Novi Sad, Serbia
Peter Backeman	Mälardalen University, Sweden
Ilija Bašičević	University of Novi Sad, Serbia
Constanta Nicoleta Bodea	Bucharest Academy of Economic Studies, Romania
Costas Busch	Augusta University, USA
Mihai Carabas	Universitatea Politehnica din Bucureşti, Romania
Maria-Iuliana Dascalu	University Politehnica of Bucharest, Romania
Eduard Enoiu	Mälardalen University, Sweden
Christian Erfurth	EAH Jena, Germany
Predrag Filipovikj	Scania Group, Sweden
Mohammad Foughali	IRIF/Université Paris Cité, France
Silvia Ghilezan	University of Novi Sad, Mathematical Institute SASA, Serbia
Moshe Goldstein	Hebrew University, Israel
Stevan Gostojić	University of Novi Sad, Serbia
Rong Gu	Mälardalen University, Sweden
Gabor Karsai	Vanderbilt University, USA
Ivan Kaštelan	University of Novi Sad, Serbia
Jan Kofroň	Charles University, Czechia
Tibor Krajčovič	STU in Bratislava, Slovakia
Ján Lang	Slovak University of Technology in Bratislava, Slovakia
Tiziana Margaria	University of Limerick, Ireland
Elena Navarro	University of Castilla-La Mancha, Spain
András Pataricza	Budapest University of Technology and Economics, Hungary
Ivan Polášek	Comenius University in Bratislava & Gratex International, Slovakia
Libor Polčák	Brno University of Technology, Czechia
Elvira Popescu	University of Craiova, Romania
Miroslav Popović	University of Novi Sad, Serbia
Marek Rychlý	Brno University of Technology, Czechia
Ondřej Ryšavý	Brno University of Technology, Czechia

Johannes Sametinger	Johannes Kepler University Linz, Austria
Cristina Seceleanu	Mälardalen University, Sweden
Tiberiu Seceleanu	Mälardalen University, Sweden
Gokarna Sharma	Kent State University, USA
Goran Sladic	University of Novi Sad, Serbia
Miroslaw Staron	University of Gothenburg, Sweden
Milo Tomasević	University of Belgrade, Serbia
Dragos Truscan	Åbo Akademi University, Finland
Istvan Vajk	Budapest University of Technology and Economics, Hungary
Valentino Vranić	Slovak University of Technology in Bratislava, Slovakia
Min Zhang	East China Normal University, China
Huibiao Zhu	East China Normal University, China
Miodrag Đukić	University of Novi Sad, Serbia
Jiří Šafařík	University of West Bohemia, Czechia

Additional Reviewers

Tanwir Ahmad
Pavle Dakic
Imre Kocsis
Peter Lacko
Lukas Radosky
Bernhard Steffen

Contents

How to Be An Ethical Technologist

Moshe Y. Vardi$^{(\boxtimes)}$

Rice University, Houston, TX, USA
vardi@rice.edu

Abstract. Many of us got involved in computing because programming was fun. The advantages of computing seemed intuitive to us. We truly believed that computing yields tremendous societal benefits; for example, the life-saving potential of driverless cars is enormous! Recently, however, computer scientists realized that computing is not a game–it is real–and it brings with it not only societal benefits, but also significant societal costs, such as labor polarization, disinformation, and smart-phone addiction.

A common reaction to this crisis is to label it as an "ethics crisis" and talk about "corporate responsibility" and "machine ethics". But corporations are driven by profits, not ethics, and machines are built by people. We should not expect corporations or machines to act ethically; we should expect people to act ethically. In this talk the speaker will discuss how technologists act ethically.

1   Social Responsibility

I think often of Ender's Game these days. In this award-winning 1985 science-fiction novel by Orson Scott Card (based on a 1977 short story with the same title), Ender is being trained at Battle School, an institution designed to make young children into military commanders against an unspecified enemy Ender's team engages in a series of computer-simulated battles, eventually destroying the enemy's planet, only to learn then that the battles were very real and a real planet has been destroyed.

I got involved in computing at age 16 because programming was fun. Later I discovered that developing algorithms was even more enjoyable. I found the combination of mathematical rigor and real-world applicability to be highly stimulating intellectually. The benefits of computing seemed intuitive to me then and now. I truly believe that computing yields tremendous societal benefits; for example, the life-saving potential of driverless cars is enormous!

Like Ender, however, I realized recently that computing is not a game—it is real—and it brings with it not only societal benefits, but also significant societal costs. Let me mention three examples. I have written on the automation's adverse impact on working-class people—an impact that has already had profound political consequences—with further such impact expected as driving gets automated[1]. It has also become clear that "friction-less sharing" on social media has given rise to the fake-news phenomenon. It is now widely accepted that this had serious impact on both the 2016 U.K. Brexit referendum and the 2016 U.S. Presidential election. Finally, a 2017 paper in Clinical

---

[1] (http://bit.ly/2AdEv8A.

J. Kofroň et al. (Eds.): ECBS 2023, LNCS 14390, pp. 1–6, 2024.
https://doi.org/10.1007/978-3-031-49252-5_1

Psychological Science attributes the recent rise in teen depression, suicide, and suicide attempts to the ascendance of the smartphone[2].

A dramatic drop in the public view of Tech, a term that I use to refer both to computing technology and the community that generates that technology, has accompanied the recent recognition of the adverse societal consequences of computing. This decline was well exemplified by Peggy Noonan, a Wall Street Journal columnist who wrote a few years ago about trying to explain (dubiously, IMHO) why Americans own so many guns: "Because all of their personal and financial information got hacked in the latest breach, because our country's real overlords are in Silicon Valley and appear to be moral Martians who operate on some weird new postmodern ethical wavelength. And they'll be the ones programming the robots that'll soon take all the jobs!"[3]

The question I'd like to pose to us in Tech is as follows: We have created this technology; What is our social responsibility? Of course, not all of us sit in Silicon Valley, and not all of us make product-deployment decisions. But much of the technology developed by high-tech corporations is based on academic research, by students educated in academic institutions. Whether you like it or not, if you are a computing professional, you are part of Tech!

Computer Professionals for Social Responsibility (CPSR), founded in the early 1980 s, was an organization promoting the responsible use of computer technology. The triggering event was the Strategic Defense Initiative (SDI), a proposed missile-defense system intended to protect the U.S. from attack by ballistic strategic nuclear weapons. CPSR argued that we lack the technology to develop software that would be reliable enough for the purpose of SDI. Later, CPSR expanded its scope to other tech-related issues. The organization was dissolved in 2013[4]. With the benefit of hindsight, the issues that CPSR pursued in 1980 s appear remarkably prescient today.

One could argue that CPSR is not needed any more; there are now numerous organizations and movements that are focused on various aspects of responsible use of technology. But our society is facing a plethora of new issues related to societal impact of technology, and we, the people who are creating the technology, lack a coherent voice. The Association for Computing Machinery (ACM), the leading professional society in computing, is involved in many of these organizations and movements, by itself or with others, for example, ACM U.S. Public Policy Council, ACM Europe Policy Committee, the ACM Code of Professional Ethics, the Partnership on AI, and more. Yet, these efforts are dispersed and lack coordination.

I believe ACM must be more active in addressing social responsibility issues raised by computing technology. An effort that serves as a central organizing and leadership force within ACM would bring coherence to ACM's various activities in this sphere, and would establish ACM as a leading voice on this important topic. With great power comes great responsibility. Technology is now one of the most powerful forces shaping society, and we are responsible for it!

---

[2] http://bit.ly/2zianG5.

[3] https://www.wsj.com/articles/the-culture-of-deathand-of-disdain-1507244198.

[4] http://bit.ly/2zvZsZb.

2   Technology and Democracy

The past decade has been a decade of ACM milestones. In 2012, ACM celebrated the Turing Centenary.[5] In 2017, ACM celebrated 50 Years of the ACM A.M. Turing Award.[6] On June 10 of this year, ACM celebrated ACM's 75th Anniversary (ACM75).[7] But the differences in tone were palpable. The 2012 and 2017 events celebrated the achievements of computing and its remarkable ascendance as a technology. While the 2017 event did end with a panel on "Challenges in Ethics and Computing," such challenges were a major focus in 2022, and a participant found "the whole thing a little . . . depressing."

The somber tone of ACM75 cannot be separated from concurrent events. On June 9, 2023, a U.S. House of Representatives select committee opened public, televised hearings investigating the Jan. 6, 2021 attack on the U.S. Capitol, laying out evidence of an attack on U.S. democracy orchestrated at the highest level of U.S. government. The school shooting in Uvalde, TX, on May 24, 2022, was also on many minds, remembering that an 18-year-old gunman fatally shot 19 students and two teachers and wounded 17 others. Brian Bennett wrote in Time magazine, "Even as America's firearm massacres provoke profound shock, change seems out of reach."[8]

U.S. society is in the throes of deep polarization that not only leads to political paralysis, but also threatens the very foundations of democracy. The phrase "The Disunited States of America" (tracing back to Harry Turtledove's 2011 novel with this title) is often mentioned. "The U.S. is heading into its greatest political and constitutional crisis since the Civil War," wrote Robert Kagan in the Washington Post,[9] raising the specter of mass violence. How did we get here? What went wrong? Historians will probably spend the next 50 years trying to answer such questions, but the crisis is upon us. We need some answers now!

The last 40 years have launched a tsunami of technology on the world. The IBM Personal Computer – Model 5150, commonly known as the IBM PC, was released on Aug. 12, 1981, and quickly became a smashing success. For its Jan. 3, 1983 issue, Time magazine replaced its customary person-of-the-year cover with a graphical depiction of the IBM PC – "Machine of the Year." A computer on every work desk became reality for knowledge workers within a few years. These knowledge workers soon also had a computer at home. With the introduction of the World Wide Web in 1989, many millions could access the Web. The commercialization of the Internet in 1995, and the introduction of the iPhone in 2007, extended access to billions.

The socioeconomic-political context of this technology tsunami is significant. There was a resurgence of neoliberalism marked by the election of Margaret Thatcher as Prime Minister of the U.K. in 1979, and of Ronald Reagan as President of the U.S. in 1980. Neoliberalism is free-market capitalism generally associated with policies of economic liberalization, privatization, deregulation, globalization, free trade, monetarism, austerity, and reductions in government spending. Neoliberalism increases the role of the

---

[5] https://turing100.acm.org/index.cfm?p=home.

[6] https://www.acm.org/turing-award-50/conference.

[7] https://www.acm.org/75-celebration-event.

[8] https://time.com/6182996/biden-uvalde-guns-new-zealand/.

[9] https://www.washingtonpost.com/opinions/2021/09/23/robert-kagan-constitutional-crisis/.

private sector in the economy and society and diminishes the role of government. These trends have exerted significant competitive pressure on the economies of the developed world. To stay competitive, the manufacturing sector automated extensively, with the nascent distributed-computing technology playing a significant role. The implications are still with us.

A 2014 paper by MIT economist David Autor provided evidence that information technology was destroying wide swaths of routine office and manufacturing jobs, while creating new high-skill jobs.[10] The result of this labor polarization is a shrinking middle class. Autor's data showed that this pattern of shrinkage in the middle and growth at the high and low end of the labor-skill spectrum occurred in the US as well as in 16 European Union countries. The immediate outcome of this economic polarization is growing income and wealth disparities.

On top of this, information technology is flooding Internet users with more information than they can digest, so tech companies engage in mass personalization, and now we mostly read information that confirms our preconceived opinions. This exacerbated further the "filter bubbles" that were created earlier in the broadcast media, following the abolition, in 1987, by the U.S. Federal Communications Commission under President Reagan, of the "Fairness Doctrine," which required holders of broadcast licenses both to present controversial issues of public importance and to do so in a manner that reflected differing viewpoints fairly. Economic polarization was thus followed by cognitive polarization, creating political polarization.

Computing has become highly important in everyday life during the past 75 years. In addition to its numerous benefits, however, it has also played a major role in driving societal polarization. The somber tone of ACM75 appropriately recognized this.

3   Ethics and Corporate Behavior

Everyone in computing is promoting ethics these days. The Vatican has issued the Rome Call for AI Ethics, which has been endorsed by many organizations, including tech companies. Facebook (now Meta) has donated millions of U.S. dollars to establish a new Institute for Ethics in Artificial Intelligence at the Technical University of Munich, since "ensuring the responsible and thoughtful use of AI is foundational to everything we do"[11]. Google announced it "is committed to making progress in the responsible development of AI"[12]. And last, but not least, ACM now requires nominators and endorsers of ACM award candidates attest that "To the best of my knowledge, the candidate ... has not committed any action that violates the ACM Code of Ethics and ACM's Core Values."

But AI technology is the fundamental technology that underlies "Surveillance Capitalism," defined as an economic system centered on the commodification of personal data with the core purpose of profit-making. Under the mantra of "Information wants to be free," several tech companies have turned themselves into advertising companies. They have also perfected the technology of micro-targeted advertising, which matches

---

[10] https://www.nber.org/papers/w20485.

[11] https://about.fb.com/news/2019/01/tum-institute-for-ethics-in-ai/.

[12] https://ai.google/responsibilities/responsible-ai-practices/.

ads with individual preferences. In Silicon Valley lingo, this business model is described as, "If you're not paying for it, you're the product." Shoshana Zuboff argued[13] eloquently about the societal risk posed by surveillance capitalism. "We can have democracy," she wrote, "or we can have a surveillance society, but we cannot have both." Internet companies have mastered the art of harvesting the grains of information we share with them, using them to construct heaps of information about us. And just as the grains of information are turned into a heap of information about us, the grains of influence that Internet companies give us result in a heap of influence we are not aware of, as we learned from the Cambridge Analytica scandal. All of this is enabled by machine learning that maps user profiles to advertisements. AI is also used to moderate content for social-media users with a primary goal of maximizing user engagement, and, as a consequence, advertising revenues.Surveillance capitalism is perfectly legal, and enormously profitable, but it is unethical, many people believe[14], including me.

The tension between an unethical business model and a façade of ethical behavior creates unsustainable tension inside some of these companies. In December 2020, Timnit Gebru, a computer scientist who works on algorithmic bias, was the center of a public controversy stemming from her abrupt and contentious departure from Google as technical co-lead of the Ethical Artificial Intelligence Team, after higher management requested she withdraw an as-yet-unpublished paper, which detailed multiple risks and biases of large language models, or remove the names of all Google co-authors. This management request was described by many Googlers as "an unprecedented research censorship"[15]. In the aftermath of Gebru's dismissal, Google fired Margaret Mitchell, another top researcher on its AI ethics team. In response to these firings, the ACM Conference for Fairness, Accountability, and Transparency (FAccT) decided to suspend its sponsorship relationship with Google, stating briefly that "having Google as a sponsor for the 2021 conference would not be in the best interests of the community."

The biggest problem that computing faces today is not that AI technology is unethical—though machine bias is a serious issue—but that AI technology is used by large and powerful corporations to support a business model that is, arguably, unethical. Yet, with the exception of FAccT, I have seen practically no serious discussion in the ACM community of its relationship with surveillance-capitalism corporations. For example, the ACM Turing Award, ACM's highest award, is now accompanied by a prize of US$1 million, supported by Google.

Furthermore, the issue is not just ACM's relationship with tech companies. We must also consider how we view officers and technical leaders in these companies. Seriously holding members of our community accountable for the decisions of the institutions they lead raises important questions. How do we apply the standard of "have not committed any action that violates the ACM Code of Ethics and ACM's Core Values" to such people? It is time for us to have difficult and nuanced conversations on responsible computing, ethics, corporate behavior, and professional responsibility.

---

[13] https://nyti.ms/3u8IT4I.

[14] https://bit.ly/3g4rD8v.

[15] https://n.pr/3INYw5A.

4 In Conclusion

The ACM Code of Professional Ethics[16] starts with "Computing professionals' actions change the world. To act responsibly, they should reflect upon the wider impacts of their work, consistently supporting the public good." So how should one be an ethical technologist? One should reflect upon the wider impacts of one's work, consistently supporting the public good.

---

[16] https://www.acm.org/code-of-ethics.

Toward Responsible Artificial Intelligence Systems: Safety and Trustworthiness

Francisco Herrera[✉]

Department Computer Sciences and Artificial Intelligence, Andalusian Research
Institute on Data Science and Computational Intelligence, University of Granada,
Granada, Spain
herrera@decsai.ugr.es

Abstract. This short paper associated to the invited lectures introduces two key concepts essential to artificial intelligence (AI), the area of trustworthy AI and the concept of responsible AI systems, fundamental to understand the technological, ethical and legal context of the current framework of debate and regulation of AI. The aim is to understand their dimension and their interrelation with the rest of the elements involved in the regulation and auditability of AI algorithms in order to achieve safe and trusted AI. We highlight concepts in bold in order to fix the moment when they are described in context.

Keywords: Responsible AI · Trustworthy AI · AI safety

1 Keynote Talk: Extended Abstract

Artificial Intelligence (AI) has matured as a technology, AI has quietly entered our lives, and it has taken a giant leap in the last year. Image generative AI models such as Stable Diffusion, Midjourney or Dall-E 2, or the latest evolutions of large language models such as GPT-4 or Bart, have meant that AI has gone, in just a few months, practically from science fiction to being an essential part of the daily lives of hundreds of millions of people around the world.

This emergence goes hand in hand with a growing global debate on the ethical dimension of AI. Concerns arise about its impact on data privacy, fundamental rights and protection against discrimination in automated decisions, or the continued presence of fake videos and images. While some risks of AI, such as the potential for automated decisions harmful to certain vulnerable groups, are relatively well known, there are other less obvious risks, such as hidden biases that may arise from the data used in its training or the vulnerability of AI systems to adversarial attacks.

This whole scenario raises the need to establish responsible, fair, inclusive, trustworthy, safe and transparent frameworks. Before defining precisely these concepts, let's delve into the current state of the AI regulation.

The AI Act draft proposal for a Regulation of the European Parliament and of the Council laying down harmonized rules on AI [2] is the first attempt to enact

J. Kofroň et al. (Eds.): ECBS 2023, LNCS 14390, pp. 7–11, 2024.
https://doi.org/10.1007/978-3-031-49252-5_2

a horizontal AI regulation. The proposed legal framework focuses on the specific use of AI systems. The European Commission proposes to establish a technology-neutral definition of AI systems in EU legislation and defines a classification for AI systems with different requirements and obligations tailored to a "risk-based approach", where the obligations for an AI system are proportionate to the level of risk that it poses.

In this context, a technical approach to AI emerges, called trustworthy AI [3]. It is a systemic approach that acts as prerequisite for people and societies to develop, deploy and use AI systems. It is composed of three pillars and seven requirements: the legal, ethical, and robustness pillars; and the following technical requirements: human agency and oversight; technical robustness and safety; privacy and data governance; transparency; diversity, non-discrimination and fairness; societal and environmental wellbeing; and accountability.

On top of this, it is necessary to consider a holistic view of trustworthy IA, as outlined in [3], by bridging the gap between theory and practice. This holistic view offered aims to ultimately highlight the importance of all these elements in the development and integration of human-centered AI-based systems into the everyday life of humans, in a natural and sustainable way. We introduce shortly the two fundamental sides, theory and practice:

- Theory: ethical principles, philosophical approach to AI ethics, and key technical requirements (explainability, privacy-based algorithms such as federated learning with multiple private information sources, algorithmic fairness, among others),
- Practice: that revolves around regulation based on risk levels, and the design of intelligent systems that follow this regulation from a legal and ethical point of view. These systems are called "responsible AI systems", and we focus our attention on them in this reading.

It should be noted that the adoption of trustworthy AI [7,8] in the form of practical frameworks is not yet a reality. Trustworthy AI is still very underdeveloped and conceptual. Moreover, models to materialize this concept are just being born, and are far from common practice (see, for example, the TAII framework [1] and Wasabi conceptual model [9]).

The term responsible AI has been widely used quite as a synonym of trustworthy AI. However, it is necessary to make an explicit statement on the similarities and differences that can be established between trustworthy and responsible AI. The main aspects that make such concepts differ from each other is that responsible AI emphasizes the ethical and legal use of an AI-based system, its auditability, accountability, and liability, whereas trustworthy IA also consider technological requirements such as explainability, robustness, algorithmic fairness...

To fix the concepts, when referring to responsibility over a certain task, the person in charge of the task assumes the consequences of their actions/decisions to undertake the task, whether they result to be eventually right or wrong. When translating this concept of responsibility to AI-based systems, decisions issued by the system in question must be accountable, legally compliant, and ethical.

Responsible AI is an area of AI governance, developing AI from both an ethical and legal point of view. The key element in this context is the concept of "Responsible AI system":

> *"It is an AI systems that requires ensuring auditability and accountability during its design, development and use, according to specifications and the applicable regulation of the domain of practice in which the AI system is to be used* [3]."

The implementation of responsible AI can help reduce AI bias, create more transparent AI systems and increase end-user trust in those systems. We introduce shortly the two fundamental features:

- Auditability is becoming increasingly important when standards are being materialized regarding all trustworthy AI technical requirements. In terms of particular tools for auditing, especially when the AI system interacts with the user, grading schemes adapted to the use case are needed to validate an intelligent system.
- Accountability establishes the liability of decisions derived from the AI system's output, once its compliance with the regulations, guidelines and specifications imposed by the application for which it is designed has been audited. Again, accountability may comprise different levels of compliance with the requirements for trustworthy AI defined previously.

It is important to pay attention to auditability (ex-ante) versus accountability (post-hoc) in intelligent systems analysis. The challenge is in the design of auditability methodologies and metrics and accountability monitoring methodologies.

In parallel to the technical requirements, we have to pay attention to the regulation, with an approach based on levels of risk. In Europe, regulatory requirements in force for the deployment of AI systems are prescribed based on the risk of such systems to cause harm. Indeed, the AI Act agreed by the European Parliament, the Council of the European Union, and the European Commission, is foreseen to set a landmark piece of legislation governing the use of AI in Europe and regulating this technology based on the definition of different levels of risks: minimal, limited, high-risk and unacceptable risk. In these categories different requirements for trustworthy AI and levels of compliance are established [3].

It is important to note that auditability refers to a property sought for the AI-based system, which may require transparency (e.g. explainability methods, traceability), measures to guarantee technical robustness, etc. Note that the auditability of a responsible AI system may not necessarily cover all requirements for trustworthy AI, but rather those foretold by ethics, regulation, specifications and protocol testing adapted to the application sector (i.e., vertical regulation).

We talk about risk levels, and we must also talk about high-risk scenarios. The AI Act introduces the High-risk AI systems (HRAIs) as similar concept of responsible AI systems for high-risk scenarios, as systems that can have a significant impact on the life chances of a user (Art. 6); they create an adverse impact on people's safety or their fundamental rights. Eight types of systems fall into this category (that is, eight high-risk scenarios). These are subject to stringent obligations and must undergo conformity assessments before being put on the European market, e.g. systems for eligibility for public benefits or assistance, or law enforcement or access to education. They will always be high-risk when subject to third-party conformity assessment under that sectorial legislation.

A complete discussion on Responsible AI systems for a high-risk scenario leads us to stablish a set of auditability requirements and metrics to design the mentioned methodologies. Key attributes such as robustness, explainability, transparency and traceability, sustainability, fairness are essential among others. See [4,5] for an initial analysis in two different contexts, financial services and autonomous driving domain respectively. This is an area that requires a great deal of attention and is a great challenge to establish compliance requirements and metrics, and tailored to each high-risk scenario.

We should delve into another essential aspect for responsible AI systems, safe AI. AI safety is an interdisciplinary field concerned with preventing accidents, misuse, or other harmful consequences that could result from AI systems. It encompasses machine ethics and AI alignment, which aim to make AI systems moral and beneficial, and robustness technical problems, including monitoring systems, adversarial robustness, detecting malicious use, attacks and backdoors, ... Beyond AI research, it involves developing norms and policies that promote safety [6].

Last but not least in the holistic view, any analysis must be accompanied by another critical aspect dedicated to ethics and all its social implications. It is necessary to consider the social acceptance or economic and legal implications, thus analysing the ELSEC aspects of AI-based systems (ethical, legal, socioeconomic and cultural).

Finally, we would like to conclude by stressing that safe and trustworthy AI is a critical area to meet upcoming regulations, the necessary auditability metrics for their analysis and compliance, address ethical issues, manage risk analysis in human-AI system interaction, and ensure the technical soundness of responsible AI systems.

This is the beginning of a fascinating path that enables the development of technology for the development of responsible AI systems. The goal of a responsible AI system is to employ AI in a safe, reliable and ethical manner. The journey is just beginning and in the next few years we will have auditable AI systems and auditability methodologies in all the necessary high-risk scenarios.

Acknowledgement. I would like to thank the co-authors of the paper [3] and the members of the Spanish STAIRS (Safe and trustworthy AI) network proposal for the enriching discussions. These have allowed me to come up with the present lecture and a global view of the topic.

References

1. Baker-Brunnbauer, J.: TAII framework for trustworthy AI systems. ROBO-NOMICS: J. Autom. Econ. **2**, 17 (2021)
2. Commission, E.: Artificial intelligence act (laying down harmonised rules on artificial intelligence and amending certain union legislative acts) (2021). https://artificialintelligenceact.eu/the-act/
3. Díaz-Rodríguez, N., Del Ser, J., Coeckelbergh, M., de Prado, M.L., Herrera-Viedma, E., Herrera, F.: Connecting the dots in trustworthy artificial intelligence: from AI principles, ethics, and key requirements to responsible AI systems and regulation. Inf. Fusion **99**, 101896 (2023)
4. Fernandez-Llorca, D., Gómez, E.: Trustworthy artificial intelligence requirements in the autonomous driving domain. Computer **56**(2), 29–39 (2023)
5. Giudici, P., Centurelli, M., Turchetta, S.: Artificial intelligence risk measurement. Expert Syst. Appl. **235**, 121220 (2024)
6. Hendrycks, D., Carlini, N., Schulman, J., Steinhardt, J.: Unsolved problems in ml safety. arXiv preprint arXiv:2109.13916 (2021)
7. Kaur, D., Uslu, S., Rittichier, K.J., Durresi, A.: Trustworthy artificial intelligence: a review. ACM Comput. Surv. (CSUR) **55**(2), 1–38 (2022)
8. Li, B., et al.: Trustworthy AI: from principles to practices. ACM Comput. Surv. **55**(9), 1–46 (2023)
9. Singh, A.M., Singh, M.P.: Wasabi: a conceptual model for trustworthy artificial intelligence. Computer **56**(2), 20–28 (2023)

Ambient Temperature Prediction for Embedded Systems Using Machine Learning

Selma Rahman[1], Mattias Olausson[1], Carlo Vitucci[1,2(✉)],
and Ioannis Avgouleas[1]

[1] Ericsson AB, Stockholm, Sweden
{selma.rahman,mattias.olausson,carlo.vitucci,
ioannis.avgouleas}@ericsson.com
[2] Mälardalens Univeristy, Västerås, Sweden
carlo.vitucci@mdu.se

Abstract. In this work, we use two well-established machine learning algorithms i.e., Random Forest (RF) and XGBoost, to predict ambient temperature for a baseband's board. After providing an overview of the related work, we describe how we train the two ML models and identify the optimal training and test datasets to avoid the problems of data under- and over-fitting. Given this train/test split, the trained RF and XGBoost models provide temperature predictions with an accuracy lower than one degree Celsius, i.e., far better than any other approach that we used in the past. Our feature importance assessments reveal that the temperature sensors contribute significantly more towards predicting the ambient temperature compared to the power and voltage readings. Furthermore, the RF model appears less volatile than XGBoost using our training data. As the results demonstrate, our predictive temperature models allow for an accurate error prediction as a function of baseband board sensors.

Keywords: Predictive Maintenance · Temperature prediction · Radio Access Network

1 Introduction

The development of fifth-generation telecommunications, the so-called 5G, was not driven by technological evolution but by a commercial necessity. In fact, with the advent of smartphones, the value of the network has progressively shifted from connectivity to the data. 5G represents the opportunity for the operators to enter the rich market of services, making their business model and investment in network infrastructure sustainable. The core business shifts from connectivity to service deployment, and operators can generate profits by hosting a broad set of services in their infrastructure, close to the end user. However, 5G has led to increased infrastructure complexity due to:

– increased throughput and delay requirements [1],

© The Author(s), under exclusive license to Springer Nature Switzerland AG 2024
J. Kofroň et al. (Eds.): ECBS 2023, LNCS 14390, pp. 12–25, 2024.
https://doi.org/10.1007/978-3-031-49252-5_3

- widespread computing capacity deployment (especially for dense urban areas) [9], and
- intelligent self-monitoring and easily-maintained configuration system to decrease CAPEX and OPEX [2].

Consequently, the need for a fault management framework that is strongly oriented towards the centrality of the recovery action has also grown in tandem with the complexity of the infrastructure [24]. Fault prediction [8,11] and predictive maintenance [12] derive from the need of increasing the infrastructure sustainability.

1.1   Context Description

Our research focuses on the ability to do predictive maintenance for products in the Radio Access Network (RAN) domain. The "cloudification" of the network suggests a technological convergence with data center hardware products, but the environmental conditions are very different. A RAN solution, for example, must rely on something other than the cooling systems available for data centers due to cost, space, and noise constraints. Furthermore, RAN products should work under very different circumstances, e.g., their operating temperature spans a more demanding range than the typical for data center products. The above scenario exemplifies how research results that investigate the correlation between environmental parameters and system reliability depend on the domain of interest. Another characteristic of RAN products is that they poorly tolerate disturbances and interruptions. The data acquisition process must be unique regarding environmental and work parameters, i.e., the use of system resources. Furthermore, data collection is crucial for network access systems since they are often called for hosting soft real-time systems. The latter exhibit stringent requirements in terms of the reaction time and execution of a particular task such as the reception and decoding of traffic packets. The collection of data must therefore be as least intrusive as possible so as not to compromise the functionality of the node and the availability of bandwidth when transmitting the collected data.

1.2   Problem Statement

The more distributed computing and high data traffic capacity also involve a considerable workload. The evolution of hardware design on the nanoscale has been the response to this growth in data processing for both the latest generation processors and memory devices (DDR5). The reliability of hardware components has indeed increased in recent years [21], but it is equally valid that the complexity of the design has also increased. And, with the nanoscale hardware design, the probability of temporary or permanent fault conditions is higher due to power fluctuations, excessive operating temperatures, or cosmic radiation. Eventually, the hardware will end its life due to aging issues, and the system reliability will enter a critical phase where the failure rate will increase exponentially. The hardware repair process is costly: maintenance activities on-site, packaging, transportation, board troubleshooting, and test to confirm the failure condition diagnosis for the component, and faulty hardware replacement, if applicable. In telecommunication networks, multi-chip packages, robotics, automotive, and, more generally speaking, in an increasingly widespread distributed system, the hardware devices must work and inter-work properly, react to external disturbances promptly, and operate as long as possible. However, it must use an appropriate error prediction action by analyzing the data available from the system. Without this fundamental prediction action, the maintenance costs could be relatively high. Thus, it is essential to know how to identify a possible failure condition before it happens. Understanding how the state and use of resources affect their life cycle allows planning appropriate recovery actions in time, whether an actual replacement of the component or preventive isolation to enable an operational state in full or degraded function mode. Predicting the hardware fault is, therefore, fundamental for the sustainability of the future network. Without it, the unsustainable maintenance cost would compromise developing innovative services for industry 5.0 [10]. Machine learning and Artificial Intelligence can be the technology enabler for a fault prediction based on system data [5].

1.3   Research Objective

The paper assumption is that the likelihood of a system error depends on the environmental parameters, like temperature and humidity. Those environment parameters drive the entire life cycle of the hardware devices: board working continuously under stressful environment condition will have a shorter lifetime. Our research objective is to devise a model capable of predicting the ambient temperature of the board, i.e., the temperature of the immediate surroundings of the board. The latter has a direct impact on the board's operating temperature so an accurate ambient temperature model will allow for:

– implementing operations e.g., thermal throttling, that maintain the temperature of the device below a critical threshold, and
– forecasting the component's life cycle according to the ambient temperature for optimal maintenance planning.

1.4   Research Methodology

The paper is a quantitative engineering study [14] that aims to examine the relationships between environment parameters and resource usage using machine learning approach. For the evaluation of temperature prediction algorithms, the research used two types of data: environmental (i.e.: temperature and humidity) and resource use (number of cores used and their load). The data refer exclusively to industrial baseband boards, and this paper used them in respect of a confidential agreement. We have also used a thermal chamber to simulate different temperature working environments. We have verified the temperature prediction algorithms' validity by comparing them with other solutions proposed in the literature. Baseband board designers have reviewed the research outcomes and evaluated implementation feasibility and sustainability in the radio access network domain. With this approach, the advantage for the industrial partner is the possibility of reducing OPEX and the maintenance cost in the next generation of telecommunications systems.

2   Related Works

The ability to have a thermal model for any system is a well-known need because it is clear that, as the operating temperature increases, the reliability of the CMOS-based ICs decreases exponentially [23]. Yang et al. [27], for example, provides an interesting analysis of all those factors that negatively influence both the aging and the reliability of electronic components, such as the effects of voltage (Hot carrier injection) and temperature (Bias Temperature instability). Even considering the system as a non-divisible entity, the system's failure rate doubles for every ten Celsius degrees increase above twenty-one Celsius degrees [18]. Research on the thermal model mainly focuses on two types of algorithms [25]: those based on the thermodynamic laws and the physical characteristics of the components to find a thermodynamic model of the device [16, 19, 26] and those which, recognizing the limited capacity of a thermodynamic physical model to be representative for different types of installations, prefer algorithms that have data-driven solutions [15, 22]. The latter has received more attention from researchers recently, especially concerning the progress of AI/ML as a mechanism for evaluating predictive models. AI/ML methods have stood the test of time concerning temperature prediction by providing very accurate models for applications such as weather forecasting and temperature control in industrial environments, among others. For example, Ma et al. study demonstrates a spatiotemporal correlation for fault prediction algorithms using graph convolutional recurrent neural networks (GCRNN), which seems promising to replicate beyond the meteorological domain. In the networking domain, only a few researchers have dealt with temperature prediction in the RAN domain. On the contrary, most research works considered temperature prediction in data centers and High-Performance Computers (HPC). Therein, temperature prediction allows the intelligent implementation of energy saving utilizing workload management [17,28], effective heat dissipation [13], and improved cooling efficiency [20]. Previous works considered the operational data of the board, such as the number of cycles per CPU or the cache metrics, and the physical characteristics of the system, such as the number of CPUs, the size and type of memory or traffic devices [15,29]. One of the used algorithms is the long short-term memory-based temperature prediction (LSTM), an improved version of the more traditional recurrent neural network (RNN), more suitable for solving time series prediction problems. In the most significant works that have used LSTM, we point out the work of Cheng et al. [7] in the multicore and Network on Chip (NoC) domain. Neural networks are computationally demanding, and our research focuses on temperature prediction through less complex algorithms and less costly solutions to meet the requirements described in the context description section. There is an inevitable divergence in the research results we have considered. XGBoost is the algorithm frequently used in applied machine learning for structured data due to its fast speed compared with other gradient-boosting implementations [6].

3   Temperature Prediction Process

3.1   Design Description

This chapter presents the design description of a machine-learning model that predicts ambient temperature, i.e., the target value based on lab measurements. We train the model using board temperature, rail, and board power sensors as independent variables while controlling computing load, environment humidity, and fan speed to simulate different board operating conditions. We evaluated XGBoost Regressor (XGB) [6] and Random Forest Regressor (RF) [4] (with and without cross-validation [3]) models to determine the most suitable for the RAN domain. We performed hyperparameter optimization for both the tree-based models to fine-tune their performance and promote better generalization. By searching for the optimal hyperparameter values, our approach is to effectively regularize the models to mitigate the risk of overfitting and enhance their ability to generalize to unseen data. We placed the radio access network boards inside a climate chamber in the lab. The climate chamber allows the simulation of all possible humidities and temperature levels that the baseband is likely to encounter in the field. We collected data for different computing loads by simulating no network traffic, minimal activity, or peak traffic conditions. Since the baseband board is a multiprocessor system, we have modified the active processing units' number and computing load to simulate different working conditions. Additionally, to simulate the environmental conditions of the installation site on the baseband board, we varied the fan speed of the cooling system. Following the well-established ML principles, we split the data into two distinct data sets:

1) the **training set** that is used to train the ML model. The input features include temperature sensors, watts and power levels measured at different points of the baseband board, the relative humidity and the ambient temperature of the climate chamber, among others, and
2) the **test set** that is used to assess the model's performance.
   The training set is assigned a splitting ratio of 80%, while the test set receives 20%. Consequently, the collected data sets encompass the distinctive patterns that characterize the baseband board in various environmental and radio traffic conditions. We trained the ML model using the training data set to create an accurate and scalable model, making it possible to use the model for future versions of RAN boards without compromising its validity. Our evaluation metric regarding which ML model to use for environmental temperature prediction is based on the mean absolute error (MAE) i.e., the absolute value of the difference between the predictions and the targets, and R-squared (R^2).

Residual analysis between the predicted and the measured ambient temperatures is considered as well.

3.2 Execution

Table 1. The distribution of the dataset, for each setting of the controlled variables.

Variable	Value	Distribution [X/Total]
DSP	Low	9/18
	Mid	7/18
	High	2/18
CPU load [%]	0	1/18
	20	1/18
	30	8/18
	100	8/18
Fan speed [%]	30	2/18
	40	1/18
	50	1/18
	70	4/18
	100	10/18
Relative Humidity [%]	0	8/18
	20-80	2/18
	30-80	8/18
Temperature Ranges [°C]	0-35	8/18
	20-55	8/18
	50-60	2/18

As described in the previous section, we continuously test the baseband in the climate chamber. Thus, the training runs with a new data set after each successful run. The current training for the ML models contains 18 datasets, each collected from their respective laboratory tests. Table 1 shows the data distribution of the various combinations of the controlled variables (DSP, fan speed, CPU load, relative humidity, and ambient temperature). For example, out of eighteen datasets, nine have DSP set to "Low", seven have DSP set to "Mid", and two have DSP set to "High", etc. The data collected is then explored and handled appropriately for the models to process. We also analyzed how to impute missing values and decided to use linear interpolation after investigating a few other methods, such as rolling mean or dropping entire rows containing at least one missing value. For the training of the models, we randomly divided the whole dataset into a training and testing set using the train-test split-function in Python ($train\_test\_split()$[1] by specifying the splitting ratio to be $80-20\%$ respectively. The purpose of the testing set is to assess and evaluate the performance of the trained model by comparing the model's predictions with the actual values from the testing set. The performance evaluation described above allows us to measure metrics such as accuracy and residuals, which provide insights into how well the model generalizes to unseen data and, thus, performs in real-world scenarios. For the sake of presentation and to provide an efficient way to compare the predicted with the measured ambient temperature values side by side, we decided to introduce a data set referred to as unseen data. The unseen dataset contains a continuous baseband run in the climate chamber i.e. with the temperatures increasing with every measurement and it is completely excluded from the training and testing phase of the ML models. The data from the features (all variables except the target variable) is then used as an input to the models to acquire their predictions. This allows us to further evaluate the models' predictive ability of new and unseen data.

3.3   Results

We set the CPU and the fan speed maximum value (100%) as the test set of the baseband unit under evaluation. The prediction outcomes of this unseen data can be observed in Fig. 1a and Fig. 1b for both the Random Forest Regressor (with and without cross-validation) and the XGBoost Regressor, respectively. The reason to why cross-validation was not applied for the XGBoost regressor was because XGBoost generally performs well with smaller datasets where on the contrary Random Forest would benefit from cross-validation. The blue graph in both Fig. 1a and Fig. 1b shows the measured ambient temperature values obtained from an ambient temperature sensor during laboratory tests. It is the target value we want to predict successfully. The primary objective of the models is to predict this value accurately. Note that the Random Forest regressor with and without cross-validation overlays each other i.e., it did not matter whether we performed cross-validation on the training set or not. A well-performing model should exhibit residuals, i.e., the difference between the measured (actual) value and the predicted value, scattered randomly around the horizontal line at zero on the y-axis, with no apparent patterns or trends. The absence of patterns or trends indicate that the model effectively captures the relationship between the features and the target variable and that there is no further information that it could employ to enhance its predictions. On the other hand, if the residual plot displays patterns or trends, such as a U-shape or a curve, the model fails to satisfactorily capture the underlying relationships between the features and the target variable.

Including additional information could improve the models' predictions avoiding underfitting or overfitting. Underfitting occurs when a model or algo-

---

[1] sklearn.model_selection.train_test_split,
   https://scikit-learn.org/stable/modules/generated/sklearn.model_selection.train_
   test_split.html).

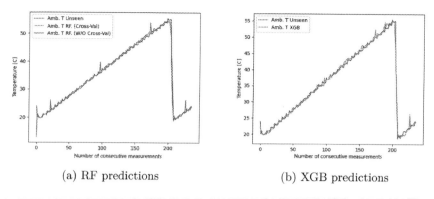

(a) RF predictions   (b) XGB predictions

Fig. 1. Ambient Temperature Predictions, CPU = 100% and fan = 100%

rithm fails to capture the underlying trend of the data, resulting in poor performance on training and testing data. Underfitting occurs when the training dataset is too small, the model needs to be more complex, or the data needs to be more precise. Overfitting happens when a model is too complex and learns from noise or inaccurate data entries in the training set, leading to poor performance on testing data. An over-fitted model indicates the need to explore the reduction of the model complexity, use early stopping during training, or implement regularization, among others. Upon observing the graphs in Fig. 2a and Fig. 2b along with the graphs in Fig. 1a and Fig. 1b, it is evident that the Random Forest and XGBoost regressors are capable of making predictions with a high degree of accuracy, without under- or overfitting and exhibiting errors between the range of $\pm 1\,°C$.

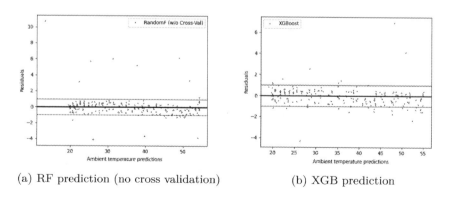

(a) RF prediction (no cross validation)   (b) XGB prediction

Fig. 2. Scatter plot of residuals between predictions and the measured value for a baseband with CPU=100%, fan=100%, and $\pm 1\,°C$ threshold displayed

To further evaluate the accuracy of the predictions, we calculated and compared the mean absolute error (MAE) and R-squared (R^2) between the model's prediction and the measured ambient temperature of either the testing or the unseen set. These metrics provide insight into how well the model is performing and how much of the variation in the data can be explained by the model. For instance, a low MAE suggests that the average difference between the predicted and actual values is small. In contrast, a high R^2 value indicates that the model explains a large proportion of the variance in the target variable - and vice versa. Table 2 shows the result. The models are trained successfully with relatively low error and high accuracy based on the metrics' values for the testing data, suggesting that the model fits the test data well and can make reliable predictions. Moving on to the metrics for the unseen data, it suggests that the model can generalize well and make accurate predictions on data that it has not seen before. The fact that the MAE value is lower for the unseen data than the testing data suggests that the model has not overfitted to the testing data and is not capturing noise or irrelevant information. Overall, these metrics indicate that the model has high accuracy and can be considered a reliable model for predicting ambient temperature.

Table 2. MAE and R^2 values for different models when predicting baseband ambient temperature at CPU=100% and fan=100%

Metric	Random Forest (CROSS-VAL)	Random Forest (w/o CROSS-VAL)	XGBoost
Test MAE	0.795	0.791	0.613
Test R^2	0.984	0.984	0.987
Unseen MAE	0.654	0.687	0.595
Unseen R^2	0.987	0.988	0.994

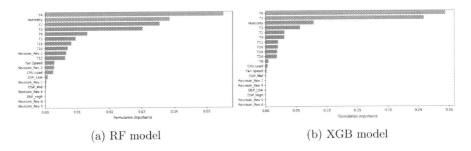

(a) RF model   (b) XGB model

Fig. 3. Top and bottom 10 features based on permutation importance, predicting baseband ambient temperature at CPU=100% and fan=100%.

The results available in our paper show temperature prediction using baseband temperature sensors and the controlled variables as features, excluding

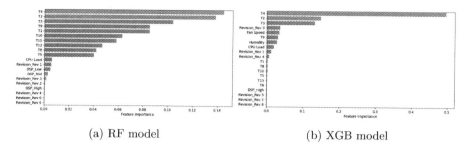

Fig. 4. Top and bottom 10 features based on importance, predicting baseband ambient temperature at CPU=100% and fan=100%.

temperature as it is the target variable. The permutation (Figs. 3a and 3b) and feature importance (Figs. 4a and 4b) indicate that our features' choice is correct. Permutation importance is a technique for evaluating feature importance based on a model's performance decrease during the permutation of a feature. It measures how much each feature contributes to the model's accuracy on the training set. On the other hand, feature importance is a metric that ranks features according to their importance for making predictions on new, unseen data. Figures 3a, 3b, 4a, and 4b indicate that it is the temperature sensors that primarily contribute to the model's performance and, hence predictions' accuracy. Moreover, they show that power and voltage readings can be excluded without any loss of prediction accuracy.

3.4   Predictions on Under-Represented Training Data

To assess the performance of our trained model on data that is under-represented we tested our models' predictions on a dataset for which the unseen data are: CPU load = 30%, fan speed = 70%, DSP = Low, ambient temperature range = $0-35°$C and relative humidity range = 0%. The predictions can be seen in Figs. 5a and 5b. Insufficient dataset refers to a situation where the prediction test case lacks adequate representation in the training dataset concerning the parameter settings. Note that the increased number of "triangles" in the Figures only indicates consecutive test execution at the same temperature. Figures 5a and 5b clearly show a case of overfitting. Possible reasons for overfitting could be:

- Insufficient training data: When the training dataset is small, the model may learn the noise or specific patterns present in the limited data. Increasing the amount of training data can help alleviate this issue.
- Feature overfitting: When the model has access to irrelevant or noisy features with no predictive power for the target variable, it may overfit by learning patterns specific to the training data. Feature selection or dimensionality reduction techniques can help address this issue.

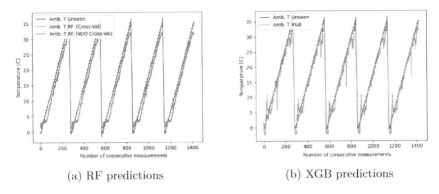

(a) RF predictions   (b) XGB predictions

Fig. 5. Ambient Temperature Predictions, CPU=30% and Fan=70%

– Complex model architecture: Models with high complexity, such as those with a large number of parameters, have a higher tendency to overfit. Simplifying the model architecture, reducing the number of parameters, or using regularization techniques can mitigate overfitting.

Table 3 shows how the value of MAE in the case of prediction based on an insufficient training dataset is higher than that obtained with an adequate number of variables in the training dataset (compare with Table 2) for both test and unseen data. An MAE greater than two indicates that, on average, the model's predictions deviate from the actual temperature by more than two degrees Celsius. This level is unacceptable; the goal is to keep the error below one degree Celsius. An R^2 of 0.94 indicates that the model is still explaining 94% of the variance in the data, which is still relatively high, but not as high as the previous value of 0.98.

Table 3. MAE and R^2 values for different models when predicting baseband ambient temperature at CPU=30% and Fan=70%

Metric	Random Forest (CROSS-VAL)	Random Forest (w/o CROSS-VAL)	XGBoost
Test MAE	0.919	0.897	0.633
Test R^2	0.985	0.985	0.986
Unseen MAE	2.252	2.144	1.524
Unseen R^2	0.942	0.947	0.959

4   Conclusion and Future Works

In this paper, we use two well-established machine learning algorithms to predict the ambient temperature of a baseband board; Random Forest and XGBoost

Regressors. The hypothesis is that we can achieve accurate ambient temperature prediction for baseband boards without using neural-network-based solutions. In fact, tree-based models are considered more suitable for regression tasks involving the prediction of continuous numerical values, and produces accurate result for the baseband domain described in 1.1. These models capture the relationships and patterns within the data to make accurate temperature predictions. Both tree-based models were hyperparameter optimized. Additionally, we performed cross-validation for the Random Forest regressor to evaluate its performance. The trained Random Forest and XGBoost models provide temperature predictions with an accuracy lower than one degree Celsius, i.e., far better than any other approach we used in the past. We observe MAE of at least 0.59 and R^2 values of around 0.99 on completely unseen data. The evaluation of our metrics (see Tables 2 and 3) indicate accurate predictions. Based on the generated permutation and feature importance measurements, we can further conclude that the temperature sensors are the most critical contributors to the model's performance. At the same time, the power and voltage readings don't contribute significantly, and the prediction can safely ignore them. When evaluating the models on unseen data where the test case is not well-represented, the MAE increases to approximately 2, and the R^2 decreases to around 0.95. The robustness of the models is underscored by the enhanced value for MAE and R^2, indicating their high confidence levels. This signifies that the models have successfully captured the intricacies of the data and minimized the potential for overfitting. Moreover, the comprehensive examination of the prediction graphs will not only yield further valuable insights but also solidify the overall findings of the study. Finally, predicting the ambient temperature is the first step to putting into practice those thermal throttling and preventive maintenance policies that we have indicated as the primary objective of our research (compare with Sect. 1.3). Pursuing the research's goals requires future study in two different but parallel domains:

- Use the ambient temperature prediction along with system resources (computer, networking, and memory) to obtain a hardware fault prediction.
- Use the prediction of ambient temperature as a critical variable in the runtime product's life cycle evaluation as a function of the environmental parameters.

References

1. 3GPP: TS 22 261–v19.1.0 - 3rd generation partnership project; technical specification group services and system aspects; service requirements for the 5G system; stage 1 (release 19) (2022)
2. Al-Dulaimi, A., Wang, X., Chih-Lin, I.: 5G networks: Fundamental requirements, enabling technologies, and operations management (2018). https://doi.org/10.1002/9781119333142
3. Bates, S., Hastie, T., Tibshirani, R.: Cross-validation: what does it estimate and how well does it do it? (2022). https://doi.org/10.48550/arXiv.2104.00673
4. Breiman, L.: Random forests. Mach. Learn. **45**(1), 5–32 (2001). https://doi.org/10.1023/A:1010933404324

5. Camps-Mur, D., et al.: AI and ML - enablers for beyond 5G networks (2021). https://doi.org/10.5281/zenodo.4299895
6. Chen, T., Guestrin, C.: XGBoost: a scalable tree boosting system. In: Proceedings of the 22nd ACM SIGKDD International Conference on Knowledge Discovery and Data Mining, pp. 785–794 (2016). https://doi.org/10.1145/2939672.2939785
7. Cheng, T., Du, H., Li, L., Fu, Y.: LSTM-based temperature prediction and hotspot tracking for thermal-aware 3D NoC system. In: 2021 18th International SoC Design Conference (ISOCC), pp. 286–287 (2021)
8. Chigurupati, A., Thibaux, R., Lassar, N.: Predicting hardware failure using machine learning. In: 2016 Annual Reliability and Maintainability Symposium (RAMS), pp. 1–6 (2016). https://doi.org/10.1109/RAMS.2016.7448033
9. Chih-Lin, I., Kukliński, S., Chen, T., Ladid, L.L.: A perspective of O-RAN integration with MEC, SON, and network slicing in the 5G era. IEEE Netw. **34**, 3–4 (2020). https://doi.org/10.1109/MNET.2020.9277891
10. Cotta, J., Breque, M., Nul, L.D., Petridis, A.: Industry 5.0 towards a sustainable, human-centric and resilient European industry. European Commission Research and Innovation (R&I) Series Policy Brief (2021). https://doi.org/10.2777/308407,https://ec.europa.eu/eurostat/statistics-
11. Das, A., Mueller, F., Rountree, B.: Aarohi: making real-time node failure prediction feasible. In: 2020 IEEE International Parallel and Distributed Processing Symposium (IPDPS), pp. 1092–1101 (2020). https://doi.org/10.1109/IPDPS47924.2020.00115
12. Das, M.K., Rangarajan, K.: Performance monitoring and failure prediction of industrial equipments using artificial intelligence and machine learning methods: a survey. In: Proceedings of the 4th International Conference on Computing Methodologies and Communication, ICCMC 2020, pp. 595–602 (2020). https://doi.org/10.1109/ICCMC48092.2020.ICCMC-0000111
13. Durgam, S., Bhosale, A., Bhosale, V., Deshpande, R., Sutar, P., Kamble, S.: Ensemble learning for predicting temperature of heat sources for minimizing electronic failures (2021). https://doi.org/10.1109/ICNTE51185.2021.9487663
14. Escudero-Mancebo, D., Fernández-Villalobos, N., Óscar Martín-Llorente, Martínez-Monés, A.: Research methods in engineering design: a synthesis of recent studies using a systematic literature review. Res. Eng. Design **34**, 221–256 (2023). https://doi.org/10.1007/s00163-022-00406-y
15. Ilager, S., Ramamohanarao, K., Buyya, R.: Thermal prediction for efficient energy management of clouds using machine learning. IEEE Trans. Parallel Distrib. Syst. **32**(5), 1044–1056 (2021). https://doi.org/10.1109/TPDS.2020.3040800
16. Lyu, N., Jin, Y., Xiong, R., Miao, S., Gao, J.: Real-time overcharge warning and early thermal runaway prediction of li-ion battery by online impedance measurement. IEEE Trans. Industr. Electron. (2021). https://doi.org/10.1109/TIE.2021.3062267
17. Nisce, I., Jiang, X., Vishnu, S.P.: Machine learning based thermal prediction for energy-efficient cloud computing (2023). https://doi.org/10.1109/ccnc51644.2023.10060079
18. O'connor, P.D.: Arrhenius and electronics reliability. Qual. Reliab. Eng. Int. **5**, 255 (1989). https://doi.org/10.1002/qre.4680050402
19. Ozceylan, B., Haverkort, B.R., Graaf, M.D., Gerards, M.E.: Improving temperature prediction accuracy using Kalman and particle filtering methods (2020). https://doi.org/10.1109/THERMINIC49743.2020.9420535
20. Peng, Y.H., Lee, C.M., Tung, K.Y., Chen, R.: Rack inlet temperature prediction based on deep learning (2022). https://doi.org/10.1109/ICMT56556.2022.9997747

21. Phuyal, S., Bista, D., Bista, R.: Challenges, opportunities and future directions of smart manufacturing: a state of art review. Sustain. Futures **2**, 100023 (2020). https://doi.org/10.1016/J.SFTR.2020.100023
22. Prisacaru, A., Gromala, P.J., Han, B., Zhang, G.Q.: Degradation estimation and prediction of electronic packages using data-driven approach. IEEE Trans. Ind. Electron. **69**(3), 2996–3006 (2022). https://doi.org/10.1109/TIE.2021.3068681
23. Spory, E.M.: Increased high-temperature IC packaging reliability using die extraction and additive manufacturing assembly (2016). https://doi.org/10.4071/2016-hitec-18
24. Vitucci, C., Sundmark, D., Jägemar, M., Danielsson, J., Larsson, A., Nolte, T.: Fault management framework and multi-layer recovery methodology for resilient system. In: Proceeding IEEE 6th International Conference on System Reliability and Safety (ICSRS), pp. 32–39 (2022)
25. Wang, N., Li, J.Y.: Efficient multi-channel thermal monitoring and temperature prediction based on improved linear regression. IEEE Trans. Instrum. Measur. **71**, 1–9 (2022). https://doi.org/10.1109/TIM.2021.3139659
26. Wang, N., et al.: An enhanced thermoelectric collaborative cooling system with thermoelectric generator serving as a supplementary power source. IEEE Trans. Electron Devices **68**(4), 1847–1854 (2021). https://doi.org/10.1109/TED.2021.3059183
27. Yang, X., Sang, Q., Wang, C., Yu, M., Zhao, Y.: Development and challenges of reliability modeling from transistors to circuits. IEEE J. Electron Devices Soc. (2023). https://doi.org/10.1109/JEDS.2023.3253081
28. Yao, X., Omori, M., Nishi, H.: Load balancing method using server temperature prediction considering multiple internal heat sources in data centers (2021). https://doi.org/10.1109/ICM46511.2021.9385604
29. Zhang, K., Ogrenci-Memik, S., Memik, G., Yoshii, K., Sankaran, R., Beckman, P.: Minimizing thermal variation across system components (2015). https://doi.org/10.1109/IPDPS.2015.37

A Federated Learning Algorithms Development Paradigm

Miroslav Popovic[1]([⊠]) [iD], Marko Popovic[2] [iD], Ivan Kastelan[1] [iD], Miodrag Djukic[1] [iD], and Ilija Basicevic[1] [iD]

[1] Faculty of Technical Sciences, University of Novi Sad, Trg Dositeja Obradovica 6, Novi Sad, Serbia
{miroslav.popovic,miodrag.djukic,
ilija.basicevic}@rt-rk.uns.ac.rs, miroslav.popovic@rt-rk.com,
ivan.kastelan@uns.ac.rs
[2] RT-RK Institute for Computer Based Systems, Narodnog Fronta 23a, Novi Sad, Serbia
marko.popovic@rt-rk.com

Abstract. At present many distributed and decentralized frameworks for federated learning algorithms are already available. However, development of such a framework targeting smart Internet of Things in edge systems is still an open challenge. A solution to that challenge named Python Testbed for Federated Learning Algorithms (PTB-FLA) appeared recently. This solution is written in pure Python, it supports both centralized and decentralized algorithms, and its usage was validated and illustrated by three simple algorithm examples. In this paper, we present the federated learning algorithms development paradigm based on PTB-FLA. The paradigm comprises the four phases named by the code they produce: (1) the sequential code, (2) the federated sequential code, (3) the federated sequential code with callbacks, and (4) the PTB-FLA code. The development paradigm is validated and illustrated in the case study on logistic regression, where both centralized and decentralized algorithms are developed.

Keywords: Distributed Systems · Edge Computing · Decentralized Intelligence · Federated Learning · Python

1 Introduction

McMahan et al. [1] introduced Federated Learning (FL) as a decentralized model learning approach that leaves the training data distributed on the mobile devices and learns a shared model by aggregating locally computed updates. From the very beginning, Google provided TensorFlow Federated (TFF) [2, 3] as a framework for developing federated learning applications. Many researchers and companies embraced this approach and soon after federated learning became a de facto standard for decentralized model learning in the cloud-edge continuum.

At present many distributed and decentralized frameworks for federated learning algorithms are already available (a short overview is given in Sect. 1.1). However, according to a comparative review and analysis of open-source federated learning frameworks

J. Kofroň et al. (Eds.): ECBS 2023, LNCS 14390, pp. 26–41, 2024.
https://doi.org/10.1007/978-3-031-49252-5_4

for Internet of Things (IoTs), made by Kholod et al. [4], the application of these frameworks in the IoTs environment is almost impossible. Besides, these frameworks typically have many dependencies, which makes their installation far from trivial, and they are not supported on all the platforms (e.g., TFF and BlueFog are not supported on OS Windows). Therefore, to the best of our knowledge, development of such frameworks is still an open challenge.

Recently, Python Testbed for Federated Learning Algorithms (PTB-FLA) [5] was offered as a a framework for developing federated learning algorithms (FLAs) i.e., as a runtime environment for FLAs under development, on a single computer (and on edge systems in the future). PTB-FLA was written in pure Python to keep application footprint small (to fit to IoTs) and to keep its installation simple (with no external dependencies).

PTB-FLA programming model is a restricted programming model, which imposes the following two restrictions: (1) using the Single Program Multiple Data (SPMD) pattern, and (2) specifying code for server and client roles in form of callback functions. Enforced by these restrictions, a developer writes a single application program, which is instantiated and launched by the PTB-FLA launcher as a set of independent processes whose behaviour depends on the process id. During processes execution, the callback functions are called by the generic federated learning algorithms hidden inside PTB-FLA. PTB-FLA supports both centralized and decentralized federated learning algorithms, and its usage was validated and illustrated in [5] by three simple algorithm examples.

The main limitations of the paper [5] are that it falls short on providing: (1) a more systematic approach to development of FLAs and (2) an example of a commonly used ML algorithm. This paper is a follow up paper on [5], which is motivated by the desire to overcome the previously mentioned limitations.

At this point, a short digression on exemplification of the utilization of the whole platform could help to understand, in a more specific way, the motivation and the achieved results of this paper. PTB-FLA is being developed within the ongoing EU Horizon 2020 project TaRDIS, which aims to create a toolbox for easy programming of innovative applications, such as: (1) multi-level smart electrical vehicles charging, (2) privacy-preserving learning through decentralised training in smart homes, (3) distributed navigation concepts for LEO satellite constellations, and (4) highly resilient factory shop floor digitalization to be implemented in a real factory comprising several production lines, a warehouse, an intralogistics fleet of robots, etc. These systems must use some ML/AI algorithms and be trustworthy and responsible.

We are living in a world where there are a lot of open-source software implementations of various ML/AI learning algorithms are freely available in various online repositories, such as Microsoft GitHub, Google Colab, etc. But how can software developers reuse this software to develop FLAs for the applications mentioned above? The ad hoc approach may work well for simple algorithms like the three examples in [5], but for more complex algorithms some development paradigm is needed.

In this paper, we present the federated learning algorithms development paradigm based on PTB-FLA, which is used by software developers as a systematic guideline to transform a given sequential source code into the semantically equivalent target PTB-FLA code. Here semantically equivalent means that the codes produce the same output data (also called the results). We define the target code to be *correct* if it is semantically equivalent to the source code. We define the target code to be *correct by construction* if the way how it was constructed (here the way is by using the paradigm) guarantees that it is correct. Finally, we define development *easier* than ad hoc development, or just *easier*, if it is governed by some paradigm (or methodology, etc.) that provides developers' instructions, typically as a series of steps in a natural language.

The main goals of PTB-FLA development paradigm are: (1) to aid the development of FLAs that are correct by construction and (2) to make the development of FLAs easier. In the next three paragraphs we argue that we achieved these two goals.

To achieve both goals mentioned above, PTB-FLA development paradigm is devised as a series of program code transformation phases where each transformation phase consumes its input code and produces the semantically equivalent code that is closer to the target PTB-FLA code. By convention, the phases are named according to their output codes. Altogether, the PTB-FLA development paradigm comprises the four phases: (1) the sequential code, (2) the federated sequential code, (3) the federated sequential code with callbacks, and (4) the PTB-FLA code.

The first goal (*correct by construction*) is achieved because each phase produces correct output code (according to the above-mentioned definition of correctness), therefore the whole pipeline of the four phases produces the correct PTB-FLA code by the way how this code was constructed through the four phases.

The second goal (*easier development*) is achieved because the PTB-FLA development paradigm (see Sect. 2) is defined as a series of phases, and phases as series of steps, which are explained in English language.

The PTB-FLA development paradigm is validated and illustrated in the case study on logistic regression, which is one of the simplest and at the same time one of the most used Machine Learning (ML) algorithms. In this case study, we train the logistic regression model that can make predictions on clients' orders based on their profiles. In the case study, we apply the PTB-FLA development paradigm to construct both centralized and decentralized logistic regression FLAs.

In summary, the main contributions of this paper are: (1) the PTB-FLA development paradigm, (2) the case study on logistic regression, and (3) the developed centralized and decentralized logistic regression FLAs.

The rest of the paper is organized as follows. The Sect. 1.1 presents related work, the Sect. 2 presents the PTB-FLA development paradigm, the Sect. 3 presents the case study on logistic regression, and the Sect. 4 presents the paper conclusions.

1.1 Related Work

This section presents a brief overview of the most closely related research that was conducted before this paper.

Back in 2017, *federated learning* was introduced by McMahan et al. [1] as a decentralized approach to model learning that leaves the training data distributed on the mobile devices and learns a shared model by aggregating locally computed updates. They presented FedAvg, a practical method for the federated learning of deep networks based on iterative model averaging (see algorithm FederatedAveraging in [1]). The main advantages of federated learning are: (1) it preserves local data privacy, (2) it is robust to the unbalanced and non-independent and identically distributed (non-IID) data distributions, and (3) it reduces required communication rounds by 10–100x as compared to synchronized stochastic gradient descent (FedSgd).

Immediately after the McMahan's seminal paper [1], federated learning got its traction. Widespread research in both industry and academia resulted in many researchers' papers, and in this limited space we mention just few of them. Not long after [1], Bonawitz et al. [6] introduced an efficient secure aggregation protocol for federated learning, and Konecny et al. [7] presented algorithms for further decreasing communication costs. More recent papers are more focused on data privacy [8, 9].

TensorFlow Federated (TFF) [2, 3] is Google's framework supporting the approach introduced in [1], which provides a rich API and many examples that work well in Colab notebooks. However, TFF is a framework for applications in the cloud-edge continuum, with a heavyweight server executing in the cloud, and therefore not deployable to edge only. Besides, TFF is not supported on OS Windows, which is used by many researchers, and TFF has numerous dependencies that make its installation far from trivial.

BlueFog [10, 11] is another federated learning framework with the same limitations as TFF: (1) BlueFog is cloud dependant because BlueFog authors consider deep training within high-performance data-centre clusters, see note on page 5 in [11] and (2) BuleFog has many dependencies on external software packages and is not supported on OS Windows.

Recently, Kholod et al. [4] made a comparative review and analysis of open-source federated learning frameworks for IoT, including TensorFlow Federated (TFF) from Google Inc [6], Federated AI Technology Enabler (FATE) from Webank's AI department [12], Paddle Federated Learning (PFL) from Baidu [13], PySyft from the open community OpenMined [14], and Federated Learning and Differential Privacy (FL&DP) framework from Sherpa.AI [15]. They concluded that based on the results of their analysis, currently the application of these frameworks on the Internet of Things (IoTs) environment is almost impossible. In summary, at present, developing a federated learning framework targeting smart IoTs in edge systems is still an open challenge.

TensorFlow Lite [16] is a lightweight solution for mobile and embedded devices, which enables both on-device training and low-latency inference of on-device machine learning models with a small binary size and fast performance supporting hardware acceleration [17]. So, TensorFlow Lite is not a federated learning framework, but it is an orthogonal AI framework for mobile devices, which might be combined with a federated learning framework such as PTB-FLA and this is one of the possible directions of our future work.

PyTorch Mobile [18] (formerly PyTorch Lite) is another AI framework very similar to TensorFlow Lite, which provides an end-to-end workflow, from training a model on a powerful server to deploying it on a mobile device, while staying entirely within the PyTorch [19] ecosystem. This simplifies the research to production and paves the way for federated learning techniques. Luo et al. [20] made a comprehensive comparison and benchmarking of AI models and AI frameworks (PyTorch Mobile, Caffe2 which is now part of PyTorch Mobile, and TensorFlow Lite) on mobile devices, and concluded that there is no one-size-fits-all solution for AI frameworks on mobile devices (see remark

2 on page 8 in [20]), because TensorFlow Lite performs better for some AI models or devices whereas PyTorch Mobile performs better for other AI models or devices.

Finally, we would like to clarify what PTB-FLA is not and why it is called a "testbed". PTB-FLA is neither a complete system such as CoLearn [21] and FedIoT [22] nor a system testbed such as the one that was used for testing the system based on PySyft in [23]. By contrast, PTB-FLA is just a FL framework, which is seen by ML&AI developers in our project as an "algorithmic" testbed where they can plugin and test their FLAs.

The PTB-FLA programming model is based on the SPMD pattern [24] like other well-known programming models: MapReduce, MPI, OpenMP, and OpenCL. For those who know the MapReduce programming model it doesn't take long to realize that the PTB-FLA and MapReduce are rather similar – the client callback function in PTB-FLA is like the map callback function in MapReduce, whereas the server callback function in PTB-FLA is like the reduce callback function in MapReduce.

Logistic regression is an important ML technique for analyzing and predicting data with categorical attributes, and in our case study (see Sect. 4) we took the simple implementation of the logistic regression at [25] as the source for our referent sequential code. In our future work, we plan to consider more advanced models, such as the generalized linear model, see [26].

2   Development Paradigm

In this section we present the PTB-FLA development paradigm. The next two subsections present the general concept and the development phases, respectively.

2.1   Concept

The PTB-FLA development paradigm is primarily intended to serve as a FLA developer guide through the process of developing a target FLA using PTB-FLA, which we call the FLA development process. The input to this process is the Python sequential program code of target AI/ML algorithm, whereas the output from this process is the PTB-FLA code with the same semantics, which means that for given input data it produces the same output data with some tolerance e. The tolerance e is typically some small error value (ideally zero).

Of course, the output PTB-FLA code must be compliant with the PTB-FLA programming model which is a restricted programming model that imposes the following two restrictions: (1) using the Single Program Multiple Data (SPMD) pattern, and (2) specifying code for server and client roles in form of callback functions. Obviously, there are many ways to define such a development process. Our intention was to prescribe it as a paradigm which is much more disciplined than ad hoc development, but also not too rigid to keep it attractive and creative.

The main idea of the PTB-FLA development paradigm was to follow the principle of correct-by-construction, which when applied in this context meant to define the development process that would for a given referent code yield the output PTB-FLA code with the equivalent semantics. Following the approach used by program compilers, we devised the PTB-FLA development paradigm as the series of program code transformation phases where each transformation phase consumes its input code and produces the semantically equivalent code that is closer to the target PTB-FLA code.

2.2 Development Phases

There are altogether four development phases, called phase 1, phase 2, phase 3, and phase 4, which are by the convention named by their output code i.e., (1) the referent sequential code, (2) the federated sequential code, (3) the federated sequential code with callbacks, and (4) the PTB-FLA code, respectively.

The input to phase 1 is the row sequential code and the output is the referent sequential code. The input row sequential code may come from various sources and may have various forms. Nowadays, many AI/ML algorithm solutions in Python are available online in Colab notebooks, where snippets of textual mathematical explanations, code snippets, and graphs plots dynamically created by code play (i.e., execution) are interleaved. Typically, these solutions are primarily intended for learning/understanding the solutions through interactive experimentation, where readers are even encouraged to tweak the code and play with it.

To make the output referent sequential code, a PTB-FLA developer essentially must select only the necessary code snippets (leaving out the alternative or redundant snippets), to tweak them if needed, and to integrate them into a standalone Python module(s) that they could preferably run on their PC (localhost), typically in a terminal of some IDE. The important requirement for the referent sequential code is that for a given input dataset it must deterministically produce some output data e.g., learned (trained) model coefficients and/or some quality indicators like accuracy, because this output data is used as the referent data by the next development phases, which they must produce (with some small error) to be semantically equivalent. To that end, a PTB-FLA developer should use asserts that automatically compare whether the output data is (approximately) equal to the referent data, and if not, report the corresponding assertion error.

In phase 2, a PTB-FLA developer makes the federated sequential code by the following three steps: (1) partition the input dataset into partitions (that could be distributed across clients), (2) split the monolithic computing of the complete input dataset into a series of computing on individual partitions (that could be collocated with corresponding partitions) such that they produce the set of partition models, and (3) add the computing for aggregating the set of partition models into the final model and for computing quality indicators (that could be located on a server), as well as for comparing output and referent data. For example, a single function call (calling the function f) to process the complete dataset could be split into a series of function calls (calling the same function f with different arguments) to process individual dataset partitions. Note that this is still one sequential program that runs on a single machine (developer's PC).

In phase 3, a PTB-FLA developer makes the federated sequential code with callbacks by the following four steps: (1) copy (and tweak) the computing on an individual partition (say a partition number i) into the client callback function, (2) replace the series of computing on individual partitions with the series of client callback function calls (with the arguments corresponding to the partition j in the call number j), (3) copy (and tweak) the computing for aggregating the set of partition models to the final model into the server callback function, and (4) replace the former computing with the server callback function call (the code for computing quality indicators should remain in its place). In the running example, the series of function calls (calling the same function f with different arguments) to process individual dataset partitions should be replaced with the corresponding series of client callback function calls, which lead to indirect calls to the function f (each call to the client callback function maps to the corresponding call of the function f).

In phase 4, a PTB developer makes the PTB-FLA code by the following two steps: (1) add the code for creating the instance *ptb* of the class *PtbFla* and for preparing local and private data for all the instances, and (2) replace the code for calling callback functions (both the series of client callback function calls and the server callback function call) with the call to the function fl_centralized (in case of a centralized FLA) or fl_decentralized (in case of a decentralized FLA) on the object *ptb*.

Generally, a PTB-FLA developer should first develop the centralized FLA and then develop the decentralized FLA, because the centralized FLA is simpler and easier to comprehend. As the next case study shows, when developing the decentralized FLA after the centralized one, a PTB-FLA developer may reuse the code from the first three phases, and then just tweak the server callback function for the last phase if needed – for example, to get the same output data (i.e., results) by both centralized and decentralized FLAs.

3   Case Study: Logistic Regression

In this section we validate and illustrate the PTB-FLA development paradigm by the case study on logistic regression. The input code for phase 1 was the Colab notebook by Adarsh Menon [25], which uses the Social Network Ads (SNA) dataset. SNA dataset comprises 400 samples (or rows) corresponding to user profiles and each record comprises the following features (or columns): (1) User ID, (2) Gender, (3) Age, (4) Estimated (yearly income), and (5) Purchased. Note that in the case study only features Age and Purchased are used.

The main steps in the input code for phase 1 are: (1) split SNA dataset into training and test datasets (320 and 80 samples, respectively), (2) train the linear logistic regression model comprising two coefficients, namely $b0$ and $b1$, (3) using the trained model, make predictions whether users in the test dataset would make purchase or not (i.e., whether the predicted probability p per user is above the threshold 0.5 or not), and (4) calculate the prediction *accuracy* as the ratio of test users for whom the predictions were correct.

In the next two subsections we apply the PTB-FLA development paradigm to first develop the Centralized Logistic Regression FLA (CLR-FLA, see Sect. 3.1) and then to develop the Decentralized Logistic Regression FLA (DLR-FLA, see Sect. 3.2). Note that algorithms in the following tables are given in a Pythonic pseudocode.

3.1   Centralized Logistic Regression

In the next four subsections we describe the four phases of the PTB-FLA development process that we conducted to develop the centralized logistic regression FLA.

Phase 1. As already mentioned, the input code for phase 1 is taken from [25]. The output code for phase 1 (called the referent sequential code) comprises the main function seq_base_case and two supplementary functions: logistic regression and evaluate, see Table 1 (note: the supplementary functions normalize and predict were not changed and therefore are not included to save space).

Table 1. CLR-FLA phase 1 output code

```
// pd is representing the Pandas library
01: seq_base_case()
02:    data = pd.read_csv("Social_Network_Ads.csv")
03:    X_train, X_test, y_train, y_test = train_test_split(data['Age'],
          data['Purchased'], test_size=0.20, random_state=42)
04:    b0, b1 = logistic_regression(X_train, y_train)
05:    y_pred, accuracy = evaluate(X_test, y_test, b0, b1)
// The supplementary function logistic_regression
06: logistic_regression(X, Y, b0=0., b1=0., L=0.001, epochs=300)
07:    X = normalize(X)
08:    for epoch in range(epochs)
09:       y_pred = predict(X, b0, b1)
10:       D_b0 = -2 * sum((Y - y_pred) * y_pred * (1 - y_pred))
11:       D_b1 = -2 * sum(X * (Y - y_pred) * y_pred * (1 - y_pred))
12:       b0 = b0 - L * D_b0
13:       b1 = b1 - L * D_b1
14:    return b0, b1
// The supplementary function evaluate
15: evaluate(X_test, y_test, b0, b1)
16:    X_test_norm = normalize(X_test)
17:    y_pred = predict(X_test_norm, b0, b1)
18:    y_pred = [1 if p >= 0.5 else 0 for p in y_pred]
19:    accuracy = 0.
20:    for i in range(len(y_pred)):
21:       if y_pred[i] == y_test.iloc[i]:
22:          accuracy += 1.
23:    accuracy = accuracy / len(y_pred)
24:    return y_pred, accuracy
```

The main function seq_base_case (lines 1–5) takes the following four steps. Step 1 (line 2): load the dataset SNA into the variable *data* of the type Pandas DataFrame. Step 2 (line 3): split the dataset from the variable *data* into the variables X_train, X_test, y_train, and y_test of the type Pandas Series, such that test size is 0.2 (or 20%) of the complete dataset (i.e., 80 test samples and 320 training samples), and random splitting always start from the random state 42 (to provide reproducibility of the splitting result and to enable comparing the output data in the next phases with the referent data). Step 3 (line 4): train the model by calling the function logistic_regression on the training data pair (X_train, y_train) – the return values are the resulting model coefficients: (b0, b1). Step 4 (line 5): evaluate the model (b0, b1) on the test data pair (X_test, y_test) by calling the function evaluate – the return values are the predictions y_pred made on X_test and the achieved accuracy.

The function logistic_regression (lines 6–14) has four default arguments: $b0 = 0.$, $b1 = 0.$, $L = 0.001$, $epochs = 300$. The default arguments ($b0$, $b1$) were introduced to enable the so-called incremental training in case when the initial model is given, say by the server; otherwise, the function starts from the default initial model $(0., 0.)$. The default arguments (L, $epochs$) are the learning rate and the number of epochs, respectively. The function takes three steps: (1) normalize X i.e., X_train (line 7), (2) train the model for given number of epochs (lines 8–13), and (3) return the trained model (line 14). The for loop (lines 8–13) comprises three steps: (1) make predictions (line 9), (2) calculate the gradient (D_b0, D_B1) (lines 10–11), and (3) update the model coefficients ($b0$, $b1$) (lines 12–13).

The function evaluate (lines 15–24) takes four steps: (1) normalize X_test (line 16), (2) make predictions (lines 17–18), (3) calculate accuracy (lines 19–23), and (4) return the predications and the accuracy (line 24).

The correctness of the output code for phase 1 was manually tested by comparing the results ($b0$ and $b1$) of the output code with the results of the input code.

Phase 2. The output code for phase 2 (called the federated sequential code) comprises the main function seq_horizontal_federated (see Table 2) and the supplementary functions from phase 1, and it targets the system with three instances (two clients and one server). We constructed the federated sequential code by following the three general steps for phase 2 in Sect. 2.2, which when applied to the case at hand became: (1) split the training data horizontally (i.e., sample/row-wise) into two partitions with 160 samples each, (2) split a single function call to the function logistic regression into two function per-client function calls, and (3) add the server code for aggregating the two client trained models.

Table 2. CLR-FLA phase 2 output code

```
01: seq_horizontal_federated()
02:    data = pd.read_csv("Social_Network_Ads.csv")
03:    X_train, X_test, y_train, y_test = train_test_split(data['Age'],
       data['Purchased'], test_size=0.20, random_state=42)
04:    X_train_0 = X_train.iloc[:160]
05:    X_train_1 = X_train.iloc[160:]
06:    y_train_0 = y_train[:160]
07:    y_train_1 = y_train[160:]
08:    b00, b01 = logistic_regression(X_train_0, y_train_0)
09:    b10, b11 = logistic_regression(X_train_1, y_train_1)
10:    b0 = (b00 + b10)/2.
11:    b1 = (b01 + b11)/2.
12:    y_pred, accuracy = evaluate(X_test, y_test, b0, b1)
13:    return [b0, b1]
```

The function seq_horizontal_federated takes six steps. The first two are the same as in the function seq_base_case (lines 2–3). Next steps follow. Step 3 (lines 4–7): split training data into two partitions, more precisely, split X_train into X_train_0 and X_train_1 (lines 4–5) and y_train into y_train_0 and y_train_1 (lines 6–7) where suffixes

0 and 1 are indices of client 1 and 2, respectively. Step 4 (lines 8–9): train client models by calling the function logistic_regression on the corresponding training data partitions i.e., (*X_train_0*, *y_train_0*) and (*X_train_1*, *y_train_1*), respectively – the return values are the corresponding model coefficients i.e., (*b00*, *b01*) and (*b10*, *b11*), respectively, where the first index is the model coefficient index and the second index is the client index. Step 5 (lines 10–11): calculate the aggregated model coefficients (*b0*, *b1*). Step 6 (line 12): evaluate the aggregated model by calling the function evaluate on the test data (*X_test*, *y_test*) and the aggregated model coefficients (*b0*, *b1*) – the return values are the predictions *y_pred* made on *X_test* and the achieved accuracy. Finally, return the result [*b0*, *b1*] (line 13), which is used by the asserts in the output codes for phases 3 and 4.

The correctness of the output code for phase 2 was manually tested by comparing the results (*b0* and *b1*) of the output code with the results of the input code.

For both phase 1 and 2, the achieved accuracy is the same and is equal to 0.9, but the values for the coefficients (*b0*, *b1*) are not equal. Here we use the relative error (absolute value of the difference divided by the true value) as the metric for the quality of the phase 2 output data. The relative error for the phase 2 model coefficients *b0* and *b1* is 8.89%, and 3.75%, respectively. Since the output model accuracy is the same (0.9), these relative errors are acceptable, and therefore we adopted the phase 2 output data (the model coefficients) as the new referent data for the next two phases i.e., phase 3 and phase 4.

Phase 3. The output code for phase 3 (called the federated sequential code with callbacks) comprises the main function seq_horizontal_federated_with_callbacks (see Table 3) and the supplementary functions from phase 1. We constructed the federated sequential code with callbacks by following the four general steps for phase 3 in Sect. 2.2, which when applied to the case at hand became: (1) copy one of the logistic_regression function calls that operate on an individual training data partition into the client callback function, (2) replace the series of logistic_regression function calls with the corresponding series of client callback function calls, (3) copy the computing for aggregating the set of partition models to the final model into the server callback function, and (4) replace the former computing with the server callback function call (the evaluate function call should remain in its place).

The function seq_horizontal_federated_with_callbacks (lines 1–18) takes 8 steps. The first three are the same as in the function seq_horizontal_federated (lines 2–7). Next steps follow. Step 4 (lines 8–9): prepare the arguments *localData* and *msgsrv* for the following client callback function calls – the former is the client initial model whereas the latter is the message from the server carrying the server initial model. Step 5 (lines 10–11): make the series of two client callback function calls (which replaced the original logistic_regression function calls in lines 8–9 in the phase 2 function seq_horizontal_federated). Note that training data partition is passed through the client callback function argument *privateData* (see line 19). The return values *msg0* and *msg1* are the messages from the clients to the server that carry client updated models that were trained on the client private data. Step 6 (line 12): prepare the argument *msgs* for the following server callback function call – this is the list of messages received from clients carrying their respective updated models (or more briefly called updates). Step 7 (line 13): the server callback function call (which replaced lines 10–11 in the phase 2

Table 3. CLR-FLA phase 3 output code

```
01: seq_horizontal_federated_with_callbacks()
02:    data = pd.read_csv("Social_Network_Ads.csv")
03:    X_train, X_test, y_train, y_test = train_test_split(data['Age'],
       data['Purchased'], test_size=0.20, random_state=42)
04:    X_train_0 = X_train.iloc[:160]
05:    X_train_1 = X_train.iloc[160:]
06:    y_train_0 = y_train[:160]
07:    y_train_1 = y_train[160:]
08:    localData = [0., 0.]
09:    msgsrv = [0., 0.]
10:    msg0 = fl_cent_client_processing(localData, [X_train_0, y_train_0], msgsrv)
11:    msg1 = fl_cent_client_processing(localData, [X_train_1, y_train_1], msgsrv)
12:    msgs = [msg0, msg1]
13:    avg_model = fl_cent_server_processing(None, msgs)
14:    b0 = avg_model[0]
15:    b1 = avg_model[1]
16:    y_pred, accuracy = evaluate(X_test, y_test, b0, b1)
17:    refbs = seq_horizontal_federated()
18:    assert refbs[0] == b0 and refbs[1] == b1
19: fl_cent_client_processing(localData, privateData, msg)
20:    X_train = privateData[0]
21:    y_train = privateData[1]
22:    b0 = msg[0]
23:    b1 = msg[1]
24:    b0, b1 = logistic_regression(X_train, y_train, b0, b1)
25:    return [b0, b1]
26: fl_cent_server_processing(privateData, msgs)
27:    b0 = 0.; b1 = 0.
28:    for lst in msgs:
29:       b0 = b0 + lst[0]
30:       b1 = b1 + lst[1]
31:    b0 = b0 / len(msgs)
32:    b1 = b1 / len(msgs)
33:    return [b0, b1]
```

function seq_horizontal_federated) – return value *avg_model* is the aggregated model. Step 8 (lines 14–18): unpack the model coefficients *b0* and *b1*, call the function evaluate (line 16), call the function seq_horizontal_federated (line 17), and assert that the result is the same as the result of the phase 2 output code (line 18).

The function fl_cent_client_processing (lines 19–25) takes 3 steps. Step 1 (lines 20–23): unpack the arguments *privateData* and *msg* into the local variables *X_train*, *y_train*, *b0*, and *b1*, which are needed for the following logistic_regression function call. Step 2 (line 24): make the logistic_regression function call (which is a copy-tweak of the line 8 in the phase 2 function seq_horizontal_federated). Step 3 (line 25): return the client updated model trained on its private data i.e., the client update.

The function fl_cent_server_processing (lines 26–33) takes 2 steps. Step 1 (lines 27–32): aggregate the client models from the list *msgs* (carrying the models from the clients) – the result is the server aggregated model coefficients *b0* and *b1*. Step 2 (line 33): return the final server aggregated model as the list [*b0, b1*].

The correctness of the output code for phase 3 was automatically tested at runtime by the assert in line 18, which compares the results (*b0,* and *b1*) of the phase 3 output code with the results of the phase 2 output code.

Phase 4. The output code for phase 4 (called the PTB-FLA code) comprises the main function ptb_fla_code_centralized (see Table 4), the supplementary functions from phase 1, and the main and the callback functions from phase 3. We constructed the PTB-FLA code by following the two general steps for phase 4 in Sect. 2.2, which when applied to the case at hand became: (1) add the code for creating the instance *ptb* of the class *PtbFla* and for preparing local and private data for all the instances, and (2) replace the code for calling callback functions with the call to the function fl_centralized on the object *ptb*.

Table 4. CLR-FLA phase 4 output code

```
01: ptb_fla_code_centralized(noNodes, nodeId, flSrvId)
02:    data = pd.read_csv("Social_Network_Ads.csv")
03:    X_train, X_test, y_train, y_test = train_test_split(data['Age'],
       data['Purchased'], test_size=0.20, random_state=42)
04:    X_train_0 = X_train.iloc[:160]
05:    X_train_1 = X_train.iloc[160:]
06:    y_train_0 = y_train[:160]
07:    y_train_1 = y_train[160:]
08:    ptb = PtbFla(noNodes, nodeId, flSrvId)
09:    lData = [0., 0.]
10:    if nodeId == 0
11:        pData = [X_train_0, y_train_0]
12:    else if nodeId == 1
13:        pData = [X_train_1, y_train_1]
14:    else
15:        pData = None
16:    ret = ptb.fl_centralized(fl_cent_server_processing,
       fl_cent_client_processing, lData, pData, 1)
17:    b0 = ret[0]; b1 = ret[1]
18:    y_pred, accuracy = evaluate(X_test, y_test, b0, b1)
19:    if nodeId == flSrvId:
20:        refbs = seq_horizontal_federated()
21:        assert refbs[0] == b0 and refbs[1] == b1
22:    del ptb
```

The function ptb_fla_code_centralized (lines 1–22) takes 8 steps. The first three are the same as in the function seq_horizontal_federated_with_callbacks (lines 2–7). Next steps follow. Step 4 (8–15): create the object *ptb* (line 8) i.e., start-up the system, and prepare the local data (line 9) and the private data (lines 10–15) for all the instances. Step 5 (line 16): call the API function fl_centralized on the object *ptb* – the arguments are the callback functions, the local and private data, and the number of iterations (here set to 1 i.e., one-shot execution), whereas the return value is the updated model (client model for client instances and aggregated model for the server instance). Step 6 (lines 17–18): unpack the model coefficients *b0* and *b1*, and call the function evaluate – the return values are the predictions *y_pred* and the achieved *accuracy*. Step 7 (lines 19–21): if the instance is the server, call the function main phase 3 function seq_horizontal_federated to get the referent output values, and assert that they are equal with the output values produced by this PTB-FLA code. Step 8 (line 22): destroy the object *ptb* i.e., shutdown the system.

The correctness of the output code for phase 4 was automatically tested at runtime by the assert in line 21, which compares the results (*b0*, and *b1*) of the phase 4 output code with the results of the phase 2 output code.

This concludes the development of the centralized logistic regression FLA.

3.2 Decentralized Logistic Regression

Once we developed a centralized FLA for the system with *n* instances (where $n > 2$), developing its decentralized counterpart for the system with $(n - 1)$ instances (note that the server is excluded because it's not needed anymore), which has the same semantics (i.e., it is producing the same output data), is rather straightforward. Obviously, since in the decentralized system, the server is excluded, the remaining peers need to do some extra work to get the same result that the missing server was producing. What is the missing part?

To see the answer, let's focus on the third phase of the generic decentralized FLA, where each peer receives $(n - 2)$ updated models from its clients. When compared with the third phase of the generic centralized FLA, where the server receives $(n - 1)$ updated models from its clients, we realize that one updated model is missing, and that is the updated model of the peer (in the role of a server) itself. Therefore, the server callback function first must update its local model by training it on its private data (here we can reuse the centralized client callback function), add it at the end of the received list of client models, and then aggregate all the client models, including its own (here we can reuse the centralized server callback function).

This means that we can simply reuse the first three phase of the development process we conducted for the decentralized logistic regression FLA, and then in the fourth phase we need to write the new server callback function and adapt the main function accordingly (see the next subsection on phase 4).

Phase 4. The output code for phase 4 (i.e., PTB-FLA code) comprises the main function ptb_fla_code_decentralized and the new server callback function fl_decent_server_processing (see Table 5), as well as the supplementary functions from phase 1 (in Sect. 3.1) and the callback functions from phase 3 (in Sect. 3.1) of the previous CLR-FLA development.

The main function ptb_fla_code_decentralized was constructed from the function ptb_fla_code_centralized (Sect. 3.1) by the following four changes: (1) the argument *flSrvId* is deleted (see lines 1 and 8), (2) the preparation of private data is reduced to preparation for two instances (lines 10–13), (3) the server callback function is changed to fl_decent_server_processing (line 14), and in contrast to the centralized FLA the assert must be satisfied for both instances (line 18).

Table 5. DLR-FLA phase 4 output code

```
01: ptb_fla_code_decentralized(noNodes, nodeId)
02:    data = pd.read_csv("Social_Network_Ads.csv")
03:    X_train, X_test, y_train, y_test = train_test_split(data['Age'],
       data['Purchased'], test_size=0.20, random_state=42)
04:    X_train_0 = X_train.iloc[:160]
05:    X_train_1 = X_train.iloc[160:]
06:    y_train_0 = y_train[:160]
07:    y_train_1 = y_train[160:]
08:    ptb = PtbFla(noNodes, nodeId)
09:    lData = [0., 0.]
10:    if nodeId == 0
11:        pData = [X_train_0, y_train_0]
12:    else
13:        pData = [X_train_1, y_train_1]
14:    ret = ptb.fl_decentralized(fl_decent_server_processing,
    fl_cent_client_processing, lData, pData, 1)
15:    b0 = ret[0]; b1 = ret[1]
16:    y_pred, accuracy = evaluate(X_test, y_test, b0, b1)
17:    refbs = seq_horizontal_federated()
18:    assert refbs[0] == b0 and refbs[1] == b1
19:    del ptb
20: fl_decent_server_processing(privateData, msgs)
21:    myData = fl_cent_client_processing(None, privateData, [0., 0.])
22:    msgs2 = msgs + [myData]
23:    myData2 = fl_cent_server_processing(None, msgs2)
24:    return myData2
```

The function fl_decent_server_processing takes the following three steps: (1) call the centralized client callback function fl_cent_client_processing – the return value is the local model that was updated by training on the private data (line 21), (2) add the updated local model at the end of the list of all client models (line 22), (3) call the centralized server callback function fl_cent_server_processing – the return value is the aggregated model (line 23), and (4) return the aggregated model (line 24).

The correctness of the output code for phase 4 was automatically tested at runtime by the assert in line 18, which compares the results ($b0$, and $b1$) of the phase 4 output code with the results of the phase 2 output code.

4   Conclusions

In this paper, we present the PTB-FLA development paradigm. The paradigm comprises the four phases dubbed by the code they produce: (1) the sequential code, (2) the federated sequential code, (3) the federated sequential code with callbacks, and (4) the PTB-FLA code. The PTB-FLA development paradigm is validated and illustrated in the case study on logistic regression, where both centralized and decentralized algorithms are developed.

The main original contributions of this paper are: (1) the PTB-FLA development paradigm, (2) the case study on logistic regression, and (3) the developed centralized and decentralized logistic regression FLAs.

The main advantages of PTB-FLA development paradigm are: (1) it aids the development of FLAs that are correct by construction and (2) it makes the development of FLAs easier. These advantages are achieved by devising the PTB-FLA development paradigm as a series of four program code transformation phases, where each phase produces code semantically equivalent to its input code, and for each development phase its main steps are clearly described.

The potential limitations of the PTB-FLA development paradigm may depend on developers' subjective development experience: (1) for some developers it may be too restrictive, whereas (2) for some other developers it may be too informal. This is because we tried to create a paradigm that is more disciplined than the pure ad hoc approach but not too rigid to let it be attractive and creative. Yet another limitation of the PTB-FLA development paradigm is that it is still in its infancy, so it still has not been tested during the development of a real application.

The main directions of future work are: (1) use the PTB-FLA development paradigm to develop other more complex FLAs and real applications, (2) continue improving the PTB-FLA development paradigm based on the feedback from developing more complex FLAs and real applications, and (3) research adapting and specifying the PTB-FLA development paradigm for AI tools, such as GPT-4, ChatGPT, and alike.

Acknowledgements. ▓▓Funded by the European Union (TaRDIS, 101093006). Views and opinions expressed are however those of the author(s) only and do not necessarily reflect those of the European Union. Neither the European Union nor the granting authority can be held responsible for them.

References

1. McMahan, H.B., Moore, E., Ramage, D., Hampson, S., Arcas, B.A.: Communication-efficient learning of deep networks from decentralized data. In 20th International Conference on Artificial Intelligence and Statistics, vol. 54, pp. 1273–1282. PMLR (2017)
2. TensorFlow Federated: Machine Learning on Decentralized Data. https://www.tensorflow.org/federated. Accessed 01 Sept 2023
3. Federated Learning from Research to Practice. https://www.pdl.cmu.edu/SDI/2019/slides/2019-09-05Federated%20Learning.pdf. Accessed 01 Sept 2023
4. Kholod, I., et al.: Open-source federated learning frameworks for IoT: a comparative review and analysis. Sensors **21**(167), 1–22 (2021). https://doi.org/10.3390/s21010167
5. Popovic, M., Popovic, M., Kastelan, I., Djukic, M., Ghilezan, S.: A simple Python testbed for federated learning algorithms. In: 2023 Zooming Innovation in Consumer Technologies Conference, Piscataway, New Jersey, USA, pp. 148–153. IEEE Xplore (2023). https://doi.org/10.1109/ZINC58345.2023.10173859
6. Bonawitz, K., et al.: Practical secure aggregation for privacy-preserving machine learning. In: 2017 ACM SIGSAC Conference on Computer and Communications Security, pp. 1175–1191. ACM, New York (2017). https://doi.org/10.1145/3133956.3133982

7. Konecny, J., McMahan, H.B., Yu, F.X., Suresh, A.T., Bacon, D., Richtarik, P.: Federated Learning: strategies for improving communication efficiency. arXiv, Cornell University (2017). https://arxiv.org/abs/1610.05492

8. Bonawitz, K., Kairouz, P., McMahan, B., Ramage, D.: Federated learning and privacy. Commun. ACM **65**(4), 90–97 (2022). https://doi.org/10.1145/3500240

9. Perino, D., Katevas, K., Lutu, A., Marin, E., Kourtellis, N.: Privacy-preserving AI for future networks. Commun. ACM **65**(4), 52–53 (2022). https://doi.org/10.1145/3512343

10. Ying, B., Yuan, K., Hu, H., Chen, Y., Yin, W.: BlueFog: make decentralized algorithms practical for optimization and deep learning. arXiv, Cornell University (2021). https://arxiv.org/abs/2111.04287

11. Ying, B., Yuan, K., Chen, Y., Hu, H., Pan, P., Yin, W.: Exponential graph is provably efficient for decentralized deep training. arXiv, Cornell University (2021). https://arxiv.org/abs/2110.13363

12. An Industrial Grade Federated Learning Framework. https://fate.fedai.org/. Accessed 01 Sept 2023

13. An Open-Source Deep Learning Platform Originated from Industrial Practice. https://www.paddlepaddle.org.cn/en. Accessed 01 Sept 2023

14. A world where every good question is answered. https://www.openmined.org. Accessed 01 Sept 2023

15. Privacy-Preserving Artificial Intelligence to advance humanity. https://sherpa.ai. Accessed 01 Sept 2023

16. Deploy machine learning models on mobile and edge devices. https://www.tensorflow.org/lite. Accessed 01 Sept 2023

17. David, R., et al.: TensorFlow lite micro: embedded machine learning on TinyML systems. arXiv, Cornell University (2021). https://arxiv.org/abs/2010.08678

18. PyTorch Mobile. End-to-end workflow from Training to Deployment for iOS and Android mobile devices. https://pytorch.org/mobile/home/. Accessed 01 Sept 2023

19. Paszke, A., et al.: PyTorch: an imperative style, high-performance deep learning library. In: 33rd International Conference on Neural Information Processing Systems, Article 721, pp. 8026–8037. ACM, New York (2019). https://doi.org/10.5555/3454287.3455008

20. Luo, C., He, X., Zhan, J., Wang, L., Gao, W., Dai, J.: Comparison and benchmarking of AI models and frameworks on mobile devices. arXiv, Cornell University (2020). https://arxiv.org/abs/2005.05085

21. Feraudo, A., et al.: CoLearn: enabling federated learning in MUD-compliant IoT Edge Networks. In: 3rd International Workshop on Edge Systems, Analytics and Networking, pp. 25–30. ACM, New York (2020). https://doi.org/10.1145/3378679.3394528

22. Zhang, T., He, C., Ma, T., Gao, L., Ma, M., Avestimehr, S.: Federated learning for Internet of Things. In: 19th ACM Conference on Embedded Networked Sensor Systems, pp. 413–419. ACM, New York (2021). https://doi.org/10.1145/3485730.3493444

23. Shen, C., Xue, W.: An experiment study on federated learning testbed. In: Zhang, Y.D., Senjyu, T., So-In, C., Joshi, A. (eds.) Smart Trends in Computing and Communications. LNNS, vol. 286, pp. 209–217. Springer, Singapore (2022). https://doi.org/10.1007/978-981-16-4016-2_20

24. Mattson, T.G., Sanders, B., Massingill, B.: Patterns for Parallel Programming. Addison-Wesley, Massachusetts, USA (2008)

25. Logistic Regression. https://colab.research.google.com/drive/1qmdfU8tzZ08D3O84qaD1 1Ffl9YuNUvlD. Accessed 01 Sept 2023

26. Cellamare, M., van Gestel, A.J., Alradhi, H., Martin, F., Moncada-Torres, A.: A federated generalized linear model for privacy-preserving analysis. Algorithms **15**(243), 1–12 (2022). https://doi.org/10.3390/a15070243

Machine Learning Data Suitability and Performance Testing Using Fault Injection Testing Framework

Manal Rahal[1], Bestoun S. Ahmed[1,2(✉)], and Jörgen Samuelsson[3]

[1] Department of Mathematics and Computer Science, Karlstad University, Karlstad, Sweden
manal.rahal@kau.se

[2] Department of Computer Science, Faculty of Electrical Engineering, Czech Technical University in Prague, 16627 Prague, Czech Republic
bestoun@kau.se

[3] Department of Engineering and Chemical Sciences, Karlstad University, Karlstad, Sweden
jorgen.samuelsson@kau.se

Abstract. Creating resilient machine learning (ML) systems has become necessary to ensure production-ready ML systems that acquire user confidence seamlessly. The quality of the input data and the model highly influence the successful end-to-end testing in data-sensitive systems. However, the testing approaches of input data are not as systematic and are few compared to model testing. To address this gap, this paper presents the Fault Injection for Undesirable Learning in input Data (FIUL-Data) testing framework that tests the resilience of ML models to multiple intentionally-triggered data faults. Data mutators explore vulnerabilities of ML systems against the effects of different fault injections. The proposed framework is designed based on three main ideas: The mutators are not random; one data mutator is applied at an instance of time, and the selected ML models are optimized beforehand. This paper evaluates the FIUL-Data framework using data from analytical chemistry, comprising retention time measurements of anti-sense oligonucleotide. Empirical evaluation is carried out in a two-step process in which the responses of selected ML models to data mutation are analyzed individually and then compared with each other. The results show that the FIUL-Data framework allows the evaluation of the resilience of ML models. In most experiments cases, ML models show higher resilience at larger training datasets, where gradient boost performed better than support vector regression in smaller training sets. Overall, the mean squared error metric is useful in evaluating the resilience of models due to its higher sensitivity to data mutation.

Keywords: Mutation testing · Data mutation · Fault injection · Machine Learning Testing · Responsible AI · Chromatography data

J. Kofroň et al. (Eds.): ECBS 2023, LNCS 14390, pp. 42–59, 2024.
https://doi.org/10.1007/978-3-031-49252-5_5

1   Introduction

The world is experiencing rapid evolution in using artificial intelligence and machine learning (ML) in almost every domain. This trend has raised questions about the resilience of ML systems to data faults, most importantly in safety-critical applications such as autonomous driving, cyber security, and healthcare [30]. In light of these concerns and the serious consequences of failure in ML systems, testing methods have gained much attention in the research community and industry [18]. Furthermore, the resilience of ML systems has become an important requirement to gain users' trust [9]. Given its unpredictable behavior, testing ML systems is more complex than classical software since inspecting the ML algorithm alone is not sufficient [2,20]. The behavior of the ML system does not depend solely on the algorithm but also on the training and testing data, the choice of hyperparameters, and the optimizer. All these factors impact the performance of the system [23]. The influence of data on the performance of the ML system is not negotiable. Therefore, performing tests to evaluate the suitability of the data is equally critical to achieving a production-ready ML system.

In the literature, various systematic testing methods are effective in testing the ML model, such as mutation testing (MT) and black-box testing tools [19]. However, not as many systematic methods were investigated to evaluate the training data as stated by Narayanan *et al.* [19]. Having an important impact on the performance of the ML, major faults in the input data could lead to incorrect outcomes by the system. In some cases, not faults, but drifts in the real-time data lead to undesirable outcomes. Fault injection is one of these few available methods that aim to intentionally inject faults into the data, as described by [23] as data sensitive faults, in an attempt to change the behavior of the system [6]. The more an ML system is resilient to data-sensitive faults, the better a system can learn from incomplete data and unexpected observations. Therefore, models that have high resilience generally generalize better to far-from-perfect real-world data.

ML systems based on supervised learning algorithms often assume the input data is static. However, this assumption does not necessarily hold when the system is deployed in the real world [11]. Therefore, unexpected events are likely to occur and can cause risks to the performance of the ML system. But a resilient ML system, as described in [28], has the capacity to absorb data fluctuations without performance degradation. According to [28], a resilient system can monitor, learn, anticipate, and respond to adversity. This means that the system should be able to maintain good performance when the input data are disrupted, to a certain extent. The sources of data disruption are many and could be classified as natural, system-related, or human errors, and can also include external factors [28]. The diversity in the types of faults raises questions such as are some ML models more resilient to data faults than others and which faults have the biggest influence?

Like any ML system, multiple fault sources can influence the data collected from a chromatography system. Consistent records of data could be attributed to the performance of the chromatographic instruments, experimental conditions, and other external factors. Such variations and errors are common in any real-world application and lead to degradation in the performance of the ML system. Therefore, there is a need for ML models that can predict under complicated uncertainty, yet perform efficiently when used in decision-making [16]. To address this gap, we present the Fault Injection for Undesirable Learning in input Data (FIUL-Data) testing framework to evaluate the resilience of an ML system to common faults. The design intends to introduce likely-occurring faults through artificial mutators before applying the ML model. The proposed framework is generalizable, explainable, feasible on a scale, and applicable in multiple domains. The main ideas behind designing the FIUL-data framework are (1) the mutators are not random; they are formulated based on previous knowledge about the data, (2) it is a single fault application; so that at any instance of time only one fault is applied, and (3) the ML models used in the evaluation phase are selected based on their suitability to the dataset. FIUL-Data empirically validates the resilience of ML systems by introducing data faults to the ML input data in scenarios that might otherwise be rarely considered. FIUL-Data framework is evaluated on a case study from the analytical chemistry domain. The data set includes antisense oligonucleotide sequences (ASOs) and their experimentally observed retention time (t_R). These text-coded sequences are transformed into numeric features before applying any ML system [31]. The data set is collected through a sequence of chromatography experiments from the Chemistry Department of Karlstad University. The evaluation of FIUL-Data consists of two steps; first, each ML model is evaluated individually. In the second step, the models are compared with each other to have a comparative view of the vulnerabilities of each model against the different fault injections. We are mainly considering supervised ML models in our case study. However, the proposed framework could apply to other types of ML systems.

In this paper, we propose and evaluate the FIUL-Data framework usable in multiple domains against likely occurring data faults. As a result, this paper makes the following contributions:

- Propose FIUL-Data as a data-mutation-based framework integrated with ML to evaluate the resilience of ML systems to data faults.
- Design and implement two data-level mutators applied to introduce likely-occurring faults to ML input data.
- The proposed FIUL-Data framework is evaluated on a dataset from the analytical chemistry field to demonstrate the usefulness of the framework in a real-world application.
- Propose and perform a multi-metric evaluation of the FIUL-Data framework to enable quantitative evaluation of the metrics and generation of insights.

The remainder of this paper is structured as follows: Sect. 2 summarizes the relevant background concepts and lays out the necessary terminologies to understand the paper. Section 3 details the research questions and the experimental setup to apply and evaluate the proposed framework. The evaluation results from the use case and the answers to the research questions are presented in Sect. 4. Finally, Sect. 5 concludes the paper with a summary of the findings.

2   Background

This section provides a selected overview of relevant MT definitions and applications in the literature.

2.1   ML in Chromatography Applications

Chromatography is an important separation method that is used in all chemistry fields [5]. Chromatography is considered powerful in separating mixtures of compounds even with similar physical properties due to the large number of partitioning steps involved [5]. The output of the separation is gaussian-shaped peaks for each eluted compound in the mixture. ML is commonly used in chromatographic separation applications to predict experiments before they are conducted in the laboratory. This is possible by predicting important parameters, such as t_R, which is the time a compound spends in the system from injection to elution. One of the most important goals in chromatographic separation is to achieve a sufficiently high resolution between the eluted peaks within a reasonable experimental time and resources [13]. Therefore, optimizing the experiment conditions to achieve this goal requires much effort. However, the optimization task can be complicated and time-consuming, given the large space of experimental variables and the possibilities of interaction among them [29]. The accurate performance of ML predictive models allows analytical chemists to reduce the costly and time-consuming experiments needed to achieve optimal separation conditions. In such cases, peak resolutions or t_R could be predicted as the output. Once the space of chemical conditions is controlled, more efficient separation experiments can be conducted in the laboratory. In the literature, various ML models have been tested in this context, including artificial neural networks (ANN) and traditional models such as in [4,12,25], which have shown promising results.

Another important application of ML in chromatography is to use it to analyze the chromatographic data that result from the experiments. Regardless of the type of chromatography system, data analysis is time-consuming and often requires manual human intervention [24]. Therefore, researchers actively investigate the potential of ML to reduce human-dependent steps in the analysis stage using mainly ANN, as in [3,22,24,27]. For example, [24] tested an approach based on convolutional neural networks to automatically evaluate the modeled elution profiles of the gas-chromatographic data. In [3], a multilayer neural network (NN) was applied to predict the retention behavior of amino acids in reversed-phase liquid chromatography. The authors concluded that NNs are powerful in modeling the influence of various gradient elution modes. ML offers great potential to advance the separation tasks toward more efficient handling of chromatographic data from collection to analysis. In this paper, we provide another example of the usefulness of ML with a focus on building more resilient separation pipelines in chromatography.

2.2   Common Faults in Chromatography Data

The reliability of the data generated by chromatography experiments has been investigated greatly in the literature. Although modern instruments used in laboratories have user-friendly interfaces, some types of variation and errors are inevitable [15]. Multiple approaches have been proposed to classify and quantify the errors in an attempt to understand their influence on the certainty of the measurements. In general, variations can be seen as person or system caused. Guiochon *et al.* [1] discuss the different sources of errors and their influence on chromatographic measurements. Kuselman *et al.* [14] identify nine human-related errors while performing experiments. The most common sources of common systematic errors in chromatography were also investigated in [10]. The causes of systematic errors ranged from errors in sample handling to wrong evaluation and interpretation of results. In the case of ASO chromatography experiments, errors are reflected in the output data in the form of skewness in the detected peaks, low signal-to-noise ratio, and high variation of the outcome across replicates of the sample. The inevitability and recurrence of errors in chromatography, demand handling before data are used for analysis or ML purposes [8]. MT methods integrated with ML are one of the approaches used to simulate likely-to-happen errors and study their influence on the performance of the models.

2.3   Data Mutation

To ensure the systems work as intended in real but uncertain conditions, we must understand and consider the faults in our input data [20]. There is no doubt that different types of faults would have a different influence on the performance of the ML system. Many approaches deal with the different faults, such as changing the input data, changing the model, or building a resilient system to faults [20]. One of the approaches to understand the influence of certain errors is the application of designed artificial mutations to the input data.

Originally, MT is a popular software engineering (SE) technique widely used in academia and industry [21]. The concept of MT is based on using artificial faults for system testing purposes. In other words, MT for evaluation is used to measure the effectiveness of a system in finding faults [32]. Traditionally, MT application involved inserting individual faults into the software, but later approaches tested higher-order mutations in which multiple faults are injected at once, which was shown to be expensive [7]. Although MT is a proven technique in SE, it recently started gaining attention in the field of ML, specifically in the subfield of deep learning (DL) [26]. However, MT for ML systems is still considered to be in the early stages [17]. The interest in adopting established methods such as MT is triggered by the willingness to improve the trustworthiness of DL systems [26]. It should be noted that by concept, MT has been most commonly used to test models, but rarely at the data level, which is our paper's focus.

Motivated by the success of MT in classical software systems and recently in DL models, the FIUL-Data framework applies mutation at the data level. In the literature, the tools used to evaluate the input data for ML are limited [19]. To address this gap, we propose the FIUL-Data framework to assess the responsiveness of multiple ML models to input data mutations. The framework is applied to ASO chromatographic data where the designed data mutations represent common faults in the field.

3   Methodology

In this section, we describe the systematic approach followed to study the resilience of ML models to data faults, including the specific research questions that guided the experiments. The dataset used to evaluate the FIUL-Data framework and the methods used for the evaluation are also described in detail.

3.1   Research Questions

This paper aims to answer the following research questions (RQs):

- **RQ1: How does the reduction in training data influence the resilience of the ML model?**
- **RQ2: How does the selection of the size of a certain class of data influence the resilience of the ML model?**
- **RQ3: How to evaluate the resilience of different ML models in response to different data mutators?**

3.2   Use Case Dataset

The data used in our use case are obtained by means of a chromatography experiment aimed at separating impurities from an ASO compound. The experiments were carried out under two different chemical conditions, therefore resulting in two different datasets G1 and G3. During the separation process, an aqueous-organic mixture is continuously pumped into the chromatography column, where the amount of organic solvent in the mixture increases over time (gradient time); this is called the gradient. The first dataset (G1) is collected from experiments in which the gradient equals 11 min. The second dataset (G3) is collected at a gradient of 44 min. The change in gradient results in a new t_R for each unique compound entering the chromatography system. At higher gradients, ASO compounds are retained longer in the system. Therefore, data collected at higher gradients are considered more sensitive to slight changes in experimental conditions.

In chemistry, the ASO compound is represented in a combination of four different nucleotide bases, adenine (A), thymine (T), cytosine (C), and guanine (G), forming a sequence. In this case study, non-phosphorothioated known as native and phosphorothioated ASO sequences are collected in a dataset with their respective t_R as the target variable. The t_R is always recorded as the separated compounds individually exit the system.

After pre-processing the datasets and removing the incomplete records, the clean G1 dataset included 876 data points and G3 dataset had 870 data points. Both datasets have compounds that do not include sulfur (non- phosphoroth-ioated), partially phosphorothioated compounds, and others fully phosphoroth-ioated. Both datasets have more than 79% of the compounds partially or fully phosphorothioated. As part of the data preparation methods before applying ML, the nucleotide sequences are encoded into numeric values, referred to as features, such as the frequency of each nucleotide and di-nucleotide (ordered and unordered) in a sequence, the total length, and the number of sulfur atoms present. Figure 1 shows the frequency range for the encoded features in the G3 training dataset. The same encoding system is applied to the testing data. As seen in Fig. 1, the ASO sequence can reach 20 nucleotides long, whereas, the number of sulfur atoms in the sequences varies between 0 and 19 atoms. The occurrence of A, C, T, and G nucleotide bases is relatively similar, while, in di-nucleotide occurrence, TT and CC are the most frequent.

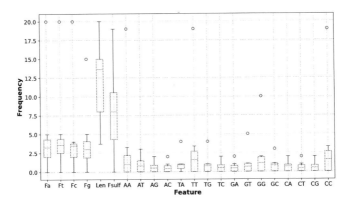

Fig. 1. Frequency of features in G3 training data. The features representing unordered di-nucleotides were removed for visualization purposes.

3.3   The FIUL-Data Framework

The FIUL-Data framework is built on four key phases, as illustrated in Fig. 2. In the first phase, the data mutators are designed and coded. The operation of the data mutators is application-specific and relies on the common faults encountered during implementation. The execution of data mutators comes next, where pre-trained ML models and the programmed data mutators are imported and performed on clean data. Once the mutated data are ready, the ML cycle starts, including typical training and evaluation of the models based on consciously selected metrics. The results are integrated into useful visualizations in the last phase, and insights are concluded. In our case study, Python language is selected to implement the data mutators' functions and run the experiments.

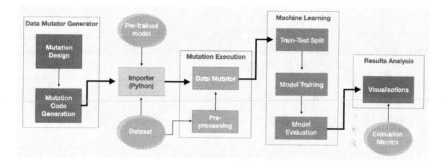

Fig. 2. Conceptual illustration of the FIUL-Data framework

The application of FIUL-Data framework consists of two general-purpose data mutators, the reduce_data_mutator and the select_data_mutator. The operation of both data mutators is described in detail in the following section. We note that the same data mutators are expected to behave differently in different applications. In this application, 10% of the data is repeatedly removed in every iteration until only 10% of the original data is left. The selected step-size induces small changes in the data that allows to record results and visualize behavioral trends from 10 data mutation iterations. In other words, the 10% iterative variation ensures that we have a sufficient number of instances from small yet sensitive changes that allows to monitor the behavior of the models. We note that the records in the dataset are randomly shuffled before applying the FIUL-Data framework. This is an important step, as compounds and impurities could share similar characteristics in the case of chromatography data. Data shuffling ensures representative distribution of the different compounds in the partitions of the training and testing sets.

– **Reduce_data_mutator** The reduce_data_mutator reduces the training data by 10% in each iteration. In some applications, where collecting data for ML is expensive and time-consuming, it is critical to know the size of training data that is sufficient for a good-performing model. Large data are a relative term and depend on the application being studied. In the case of chromatography data, laboratory experiments are expensive, the products used to perform the experiments are costly, and the experiments run for a long time. Therefore, collecting sufficient data could significantly reduce time and cost burdens. In our experiment, the data is first split into train and test datasets, 80% and 20%, respectively. The testing data remains unchanged, while the training data is reduced iteratively by 10%. For every iteration, the model is fitted to the training data and t_R is predicted on the unseen data. At the end of each iteration, the coefficient of determination (R^2) train, R^2 test, and the mean squared error (MSE) are recorded. The design and operation of reduce_data_mutator is illustrated in Fig. 3.

– **Select_data_mutator** The select_data_mutator iteratively reduces a certain class in the data. In this case, the records of the compounds that lost one or more sulfur atoms from their sequence are removed at a rate of 10% per iteration, while the other class (native compounds) remains unchanged. However, the percentage of the target class in the training and testing data after splitting is controlled for consistency purposes. The sulfur atom(s) loss is denoted by "-P=O" at the end of an ASO sequence. The models are then fitted to the new version of the training data and evaluated on the testing data. The operation of select_data_mutator is illustrated in Fig. 4. This mutator aims to reveal the influence of a certain class of data on the performance of the ML system. In this case study, the class of sequences having a -P=O suffix is subject to data mutation.

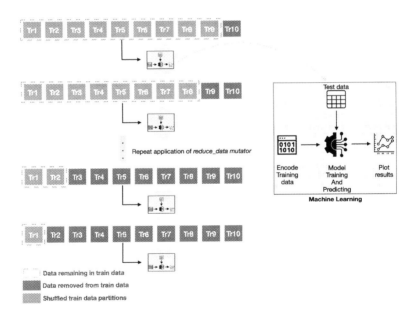

Fig. 3. The operation of reduce_data_mutator

4   Results and Analysis

After implementing the reduce_data_mutator and the select_data_mutator functions in a Python (3.9) supported framework, the G1 and G3 datasets along

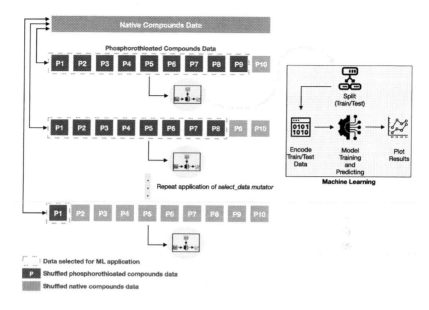

Fig. 4. The operation of select_data_mutator

with the corresponding pre-trained and hypertuned ML models, were imported. Then, the FIUL-Data framework was applied to both datasets, where the performances of the Gradient boost(GB) and support vector regression (SVR) models in response to the type of fault injected were compared. The evaluation metrics used in monitoring the performance of individual models and when comparing models to each other were the MSE, the R^2 train, and the R^2 test. The MSE is chosen to observe the variation in the average squared difference between the predicted values and the observed values of t_R.

4.1   Effect on G1 Dataset

In Fig. 5, the reduce_data_mutator is applied to the G1 dataset at a decreasing rate of 10% in each iteration. For each of the mutation iterations, the accuracy of the train and the test are recorded in addition to the MSE values. The performance of the SVR and GB models on G1 data yields relatively good results. The accuracy on unseen data for the GB model ranges from 0.80 to 0.82, showing relatively stable performance against reducing the size of the training data. For the SVR model, the R^2 test remained relatively stable until 60% of the training data were removed, and the performance began to degrade, reaching a minimum R^2 test of 0.74. Both models were shown to generalize reasonably well to unseen testing data when the training data is relatively large; however, GB performed better with a smaller training datasets. The same trend applies to MSE, which increased significantly for the SVR model with decreasing training data.

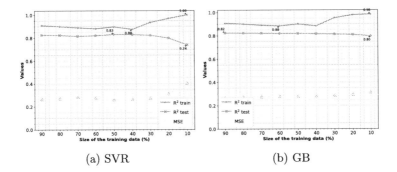

Fig. 5. The application of reduce_data_mutator in G1 dataset using SVR and GB models. Maximum and Minimum values are annotated.

The results of the application of select_data_mutator to input data are shown in Fig. 6. For the GB model, we can observe that the highest R^2 test is achieved with a 30% (0.98) subset size of the -P=O class. The R^2 test ranges from 0.86 to 0.98 and the graph shows a trend of increasing R^2 test with a decrease in the subset size of the -P=O data class. The GB and SVR models performed relatively similarly, with GB showing slightly better performance across iterations. However, high fluctuations are observed in the performance of both models in the case of select_data_mutator. The same trends are observed in the MSE values, ranging from 0.017 to 0.203 in GB and 0.018 to 0.029 in SVR. MSE is a measurement of error, so the lower the MSE value, the better the performance of the model. Both models achieved the lowest performance at the sizes of the subsets 90% and 30% of the -P=O class.

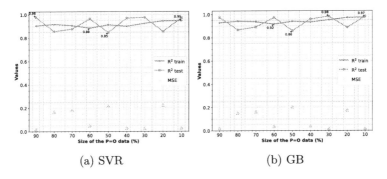

Fig. 6. The application of select_data_mutator in G1 dataset using SVR and GB models. Maximum and Minimum values are annotated.

4.2   Effect on G3 Dataset

Across both mutation applications and in almost all iterations, GB outperformed SVR as shown in the MSE trend line in Figs. 7 and 8. Starting with the results of reduce_data_mutator, both GB and SVR models showed relatively high performance on unseen data, with the R^2 test reaching a maximum value of 0.92 and 0.91 respectively. The R^2 train for both models is consistently high, indicating effective learning during the training process. After 60% of the training data is reduced, both models start to show over-fitting behavior where the training performance is exceptionally high, unlike the degrading R^2 test values. The R^2 test in both models remains stable until 70% of the training data is removed, where the R^2 test begins to show a downward trend. This trend is also reflected in the behavior of MSE, where it first shows a consistent trend, then a significant increase is observed after the 7th iteration of the data mutation.

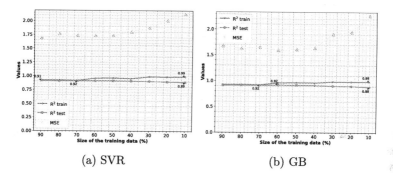

(a) SVR   (b) GB

Fig. 7. The application of reduce_data_mutator in G3 dataset using SVR and GB models. Maximum and Minimum values are annotated.

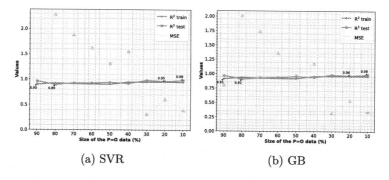

(a) SVR   (b) GB

Fig. 8. The application of select_data_mutator in G3 dataset using SVR and GB models. Maximum and Minimum values are annotated.

Figure 8 illustrates the results of the application of the select_data_mutator in G3 dataset. The values of R^2 train and R^2 test in the GB and SVR models are relatively similar and show stable behavior. However, a significant decrease in MSE is observed after the 2nd iteration, reaching 1.31 and 0.9 in SVR and GB, respectively. Another steep decline is observed after the 6th iteration where the error value decreases by 79.7% and 73.7% in SVR and GB, respectively.

4.3   Effect Analysis

For a coherent comparison of the results among data mutators and models, the fluctuation trends in the R^2 test and the MSE values are visualized in Figs. 9, 10. Section 4.3 is structured to answer the RQs 1–3 presented in Sect. 3.1

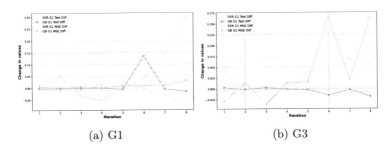

(a) G1   (b) G3

Fig. 9. Reduce_data_mutator comparison results in G1 and G3 datasets. Iterations of data mutation is on x-axis, and relative change in values of R^2 test and MSE on y-axis.

RQ1: How does the reduction in training data influence the resilience of the ML model?

Despite some similarities in the behavior of GB and SVR, in both datasets G1 and G3, GB performed better and showed greater resilience to the reduction in the mutation of the training data. The highest R^2 test and lowest MSE were attained at the 6th iteration indicating that, for ASOs data, collecting a large training dataset does not necessarily improve the performance of the ML model. In this case, 30% of the available data were sufficient to achieve the best performance.

In the case of G3 dataset, which is a more noisy and volatile dataset, the GB model showed high resilience in the predicted R^2 test; however, after the 5th iteration, the MSE fluctuations recorded slightly higher changes. Both models performed closely until the 5th iteration, where 50% of the training data was removed. In subsequent iterations, the models showed an increase in MSE and a spiking pattern in the case of the SVR model, as shown in 9. The obtained results are expected since the ML model needs more data to be able to sustain good performance in noisy data and generalize without fitting the noise.

RQ2: How does the selection of the size of a certain class of data influence the resilience of the ML model?

In response to the select_data_mutator both models seem to have identical fluctuating behavior in the MSE values. The change in the R^2 test values is nearly negligible. As a result, in the G1 dataset, both models show similar unpredictable performance in response to the decrease in one class of the data.

Despite the fluctuating performance in response to the reduction of a specific class from the ASOs data, GB model showed slightly better resilience corresponding to the MSE pattern across iterations in G3 data. The resilience of the models during the first four iterations shows relatively stable behavior, contrary to smaller datasets.

RQ3: How to evaluate the resilience of different ML models in response to different data mutators?

The fluctuations in MSE values in response to the reduce_ and select_data_ mutators were more significant than that of the R^2 test as shown in Figs. 9 and 10. Therefore, MSE shows higher sensitivity to data mutation changes compared to other investigated metrics.

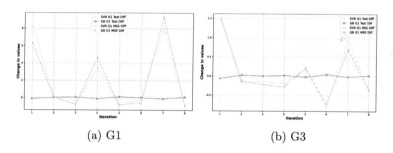

(a) G1   (b) G3

Fig. 10. Select_data_mutator comparison results in G1 and G3 datasets. Iterations of data mutation is on x-axis, and relative change in values of R^2 test and MSE on y-axis.

5   Conclusion

To test the resilience of ML models to multiple intentionally triggered faults, we present a Fault Injection for Undesirable Learning in the input data (FIUL-Data) testing framework. The proposed framework is evaluated on a case study of ASOs data where the performance of GB and SVR models is compared for each data mutator. In response to reduce_data_mutator, both models show relatively high resilience in larger datasets with GB outperforming SVR. We observe that 30% of the available data were sufficient to achieve the best performance.

Regarding the second type of mutation, the models show greater resilience in the G3 dataset with a decreasing trend of MSE compared to G1, which had unpredictable performance. This shows that when the size of the -P=O data is smaller, an ML model performs better. The highest R^2 test and lowest MSE were achieved at the sixth iteration of the reduced data mutation. Thus in the case of ASOs data, collecting a large training dataset does not necessarily improve the performance of the ML model. Regarding the evaluation metrics, MSE is considered as a sensitive metric since small data mutation significantly changed the MSE behavior. Therefore, we recommend monitoring the MSE metric when testing the resilience of ML models to data mutations.

For generalization purposes, the FIUL-Data framework could apply to any ML system where the researcher has pre-trained models and can define data mutators. The flexibility of the proposed framework comes from the ability to customize multiple steps depending on the application under study. The FIUL-Data framework can be used in many interesting applications, such as studying how a trained model responds to different kinds of data faults, quantifying and evaluating the trade-off between model resilience and prediction accuracy, and investigating tuning models based on the type of fault in the data.

6   Threats to Validity

External Validity

In any research, generalization of results is important to contribute to the field of study. Despite the application of FIUL-Data on a use case from the analytical chemistry field, the general and flexible design of the proposed framework allows its application in many domains. At every stage of the framework, the user could customize the steps to suit the use case. For example, the data mutators designed in this paper could be modified as the user sees convenient. The ML models applied were trained and optimized for these ASOs datasets; in other applications, other ML models could be studied and compared.

Reproducibility of Results

To ensure the reproducibility of the results, we provide a detailed description of the methodology and the experimental setup. The controlled random split of the train and test sets supports reproducibility.

Selection of Datasets

The evaluation results of the FIUL-Data framework depend on the datasets used. The datasets are generated based on specific and controlled experiments conducted in the Chemistry Department of Karlstad University. Therefore, the ASO compounds are limited to the sequences purchased for the purpose of the experiment. This kind of data has a special characteristic: up to 3 compounds could be derivatives from the same original compound sequence. Therefore, an ASO compound and the derivative compounds resulting from the separation process share similar characteristics, such as phosphorothioation and the frequency of nucleotide bases in the sequence. Since these characteristics are transformed into features, the underlying similarity could impact the models' performance during the mutation process despite the data's shuffling and random split before the ML application.

Acknowledgements. This work has been funded by the Knowledge Foundation of Sweden (KKS) through the Synergy project - Improved Methods for Process and Quality Controls using Digital Tools (IMPAQCDT) grant number (20210021). In this project, we acknowledge Gergely Szabados, Jakob Häggström, and Patrik Forssén from the Department of Engineering and Chemical Sciences/Chemistry at Karlstad University for their contribution to the acquisition and preprocessing of data.

References

1. Chapter 16 quantitative analysis by gas chromatography sources of errors, accuracy and precision of chromatographic measurements. In: Guiochon, G., Guillemin, C.L. (eds.) For Laboratory Analyses and On-Line Process Control, Journal of Chromatography Library, vol. 42, pp. 661–687. Elsevier (1988). https://doi.org/10.1016/S0301-4770(08)70088-5

2. Breck, E., Cai, S., Nielsen, E., Salib, M., Sculley, D.: The ml test score: a rubric for ml production readiness and technical debt reduction. In: 2017 IEEE International Conference on Big Data (Big Data), pp. 1123–1132 (2017). https://doi.org/10.1109/BigData.2017.8258038

3. D'Archivio, A.: Artificial neural network prediction of retention of amino acids in reversed-phase HPLC under application of linear organic modifier gradients and/or pH gradients. Molecules **24**(3), 632 (2019). https://doi.org/10.3390/molecules24030632, https://www.mdpi.com/1420-3049/24/3/632

4. Enmark, M., Häggström, J., Samuelsson, J., Fornstedt, T.: Building machine-learning-based models for retention time and resolution predictions in ion pair chromatography of oligonucleotides. J. Chromatogr. A **1671**, 462999 (2022). https://doi.org/10.1016/j.chroma.2022.462999

5. Fornstedt, T., Forssén, P., Westerlund, D.: Basic HPLC theory and definitions: retention, thermodynamics, selectivity, zone spreading, kinetics, and resolution. Anal. Sep. Sci. 5 Vol. Set **2**, 1–22 (2015). https://doi.org/10.1002/9783527678129.assep001

6. Gangolli, A., Mahmoud, Q.H., Azim, A.: A systematic review of fault injection attacks on IoT systems. Electronics **11**(13), 2023 (2022). https://doi.org/10.3390/electronics11132023, https://www.mdpi.com/2079-9292/11/13/2023

7. Ghiduk, A.S., Girgis, M.R., Shehata, M.H.: Higher order mutation testing: a systematic literature review. Comput. Sci. Rev. **25**, 29–48 (2017). https://doi.org/10.1016/j.cosrev.2017.06.001

8. Hellier, E., Edworthy, J., Lee, A.: An analysis of human error in the analytical measurement task in chemistry. Int. J. Cogn. Ergon. **5**(4), 445–458 (2001). https://doi.org/10.1207/S15327566IJCE0504_5

9. Jha, S., Banerjee, S.S., Cyriac, J., Kalbarczyk, Z.T., Iyer, R.K.: AVFI: fault injection for autonomous vehicles. In: 2018 48th Annual IEEE/IFIP International Conference on Dependable Systems and Networks Workshops (DSN-W), pp. 55–56. IEEE Computer Society (2018). https://doi.org/10.1109/DSN-W.2018.00027

10. Kaiser, R.E.: Errors in chromatography. Chromatographia **4**, 479–490 (1971). https://doi.org/10.1007/BF02268820

11. Katzir, Z., Elovici, Y.: Quantifying the resilience of machine learning classifiers used for cyber security. Expert Syst. Appl. **92**, 419–429 (2018). https://doi.org/10.1016/j.eswa.2017.09.053

12. Kohlbacher, O., Quinten, S., Strum, M., Mayr, B.M., Huber, C.G.: Structure-activity relationships in chromatography: retention prediction of oligonucleotides with support vector regression. Angew. Chem. Int. Ed. Engl. **45**(42), 7009–7012 (2006). https://api.semanticscholar.org/CorpusID:33345638

13. Korany, M.A., Mahgoub, H., Fahmy, O.T., Maher, H.M.: Application of artificial neural networks for response surface modelling in HPLC method development. J. Adv. Res. **3**(1), 53–63 (2012)

14. Kuselman, I., et al.: House-of-security approach to measurement in analytical chemistry: quantification of human error using expert judgments. Accred. Qual. Assur. **18**(6), 459–467 (2013). https://doi.org/10.1007/s00769-013-1020-9

15. Kuselman, I., Pennecchi, F., Fajgelj, A., Karpov, Y.: Human errors and reliability of test results in analytical chemistry. Accred. Qual. Assur. **18**, 3–9 (2013). https://doi.org/10.1007/s00769-012-0934-y

16. Lotfi, R., Gholamrezaei, A., Kadłubek, M., Afshar, M., Ali, S.S., Kheiri, K.: A robust and resilience machine learning for forecasting agri-food production. Sci. Rep. **12**(1), 21787 (2022). https://doi.org/10.1038/s41598-022-26449-8

17. Lu, Y., Sun, W., Sun, M.: Towards mutation testing of reinforcement learning systems. J. Syst. Architect. **131**, 102701 (2022). https://doi.org/10.1007/978-3-030-91265-9_8

18. Ma, L., et al.: DeepMutation: mutation testing of deep learning systems. In: 2018 IEEE 29th International Symposium on Software Reliability Engineering (ISSRE), pp. 100–111. IEEE Computer Society, Los Alamitos, CA, USA (2018). https://doi.org/10.48550/arXiv.1805.05206

19. Narayanan, N., Pattabiraman, K.: TF-DM: tool for studying ml model resilience to data faults. In: 2021 IEEE/ACM Third International Workshop on Deep Learning for Testing and Testing for Deep Learning (DeepTest), pp. 25–28. IEEE Computer Society, Los Alamitos, CA, USA (2021). https://doi.org/10.1109/DeepTest52559.2021.00010

20. Nurminen, J.K., et al.: Software framework for data fault injection to test machine learning systems. In: 2019 IEEE International Symposium on Software Reliability Engineering Workshops (ISSREW), pp. 294–299 (2019). https://doi.org/10.1109/ISSREW.2019.00087

21. Papadakis, M., Kintis, M., Zhang, J., Jia, Y., Traon, Y.L., Harman, M.: Chapter six - mutation testing advances: an analysis and survey. In: Memon, A.M. (ed.) Advances in Computers, Advances in Computers, vol. 112, pp. 275–378. Elsevier (2019). https://doi.org/10.1016/bs.adcom.2018.03.015

22. Petritis, K., et al.: Use of artificial neural networks for the accurate prediction of peptide liquid chromatography elution times in proteome analyses. Anal. Chem. **75**(5), 1039–1048 (2003). https://doi.org/10.1021/ac0205154

23. Riccio, V., Jahangirova, G., Stocco, A., Humbatova, N., Weiss, M., Tonella, P.: Testing machine learning based systems: a systematic mapping. Empir. Softw. Eng. **25**(6), 5193–5254 (2020). https://doi.org/10.1007/s10664-020-09881-0

24. Risum, A.B., Bro, R.: Using deep learning to evaluate peaks in chromatographic data. Talanta **204**, 255–260 (2019). https://doi.org/10.1016/j.talanta.2019.05.053
25. Sturm, M., Quinten, S., Huber, C.G., Kohlbacher, O.: A statistical learning approach to the modeling of chromatographic retention of oligonucleotides incorporating sequence and secondary structure data. Nucleic Acids Res. **35**(12), 4195–4202 (2007). https://doi.org/10.1093/nar/gkm338
26. Tambon, F., Khomh, F., Antoniol, G.: A probabilistic framework for mutation testing in deep neural networks. Inf. Softw. Technol. **155**(C), 107129 (2023). https://doi.org/10.1016/j.infsof.2022.107129
27. Tran, A., Hyne, R., Pablo, F., Day, W., Doble, P.: Optimisation of the separation of herbicides by linear gradient high performance liquid chromatography utilising artificial neural networks. Talanta **71**(3), 1268–1275 (2007). https://doi.org/10.1016/j.talanta.2006.06.031
28. Vairo, T., Pettinato, M., Reverberi, A.P., Milazzo, M.F., Fabiano, B.: An approach towards the implementation of a reliable resilience model based on machine learning. Process Saf. Environ. Prot. **172**, 632–641 (2023). https://doi.org/10.1016/j.psep.2023.02.058
29. Webb, R., Doble, P., Dawson, M.: Optimisation of HPLC gradient separations using artificial neural networks (ANNs): application to benzodiazepines in postmortem samples. J. Chromatogr. B **877**(7), 615–620 (2009). https://doi.org/10.1016/j.jchromb.2009.01.012
30. Zhang, J.M., Harman, M., Ma, L., Liu, Y.: Machine learning testing: survey, landscapes and horizons. IEEE Trans. Software Eng. **48**(1), 1–36 (2022). https://doi.org/10.1109/TSE.2019.2962027
31. Zheng, A., Casari, A.: Feature Engineering for Machine Learning. O'Reilly Media, Inc. (2018)
32. Zhu, Q., Panichella, A., Zaidman, A.: A systematic literature review of how mutation testing supports quality assurance processes. Softw. Test. Verification and Reliab. **28**(6), e1675 (2018). https://doi.org/10.1002/stvr.1675

IDPP: Imbalanced Datasets Pipelines in Pyrus

Amandeep Singh[1,2]($\boxtimes$) (iD) and Olga Minguett[1,3] (iD)

[1] University of Limerick, Limerick, Ireland
`amandeep.singh@ul.ie, olgaminguett@gmail.com`
[2] Centre for Research Training in Artificial Intelligence (CRT-AI), Dublin, Ireland
[3] Optum,Eden Prairie, USA

Abstract. We showcase and demonstrate IDPP, a Pyrus-based tool that offers a collection of pipelines for the analysis of imbalanced datasets. Like Pyrus, IDPP is a web-based, low-code/no-code graphical modelling environment for ML and data analytics applications. On a case study from the medical domain, we solve the challenge of re-using AI/ML models that do not address data with imbalanced class by implementing ML algorithms in Python that do the re-balancing. We then use these algorithms and the original ML models in the IDPP pipelines. With IDPP, our low-code development approach to balance datasets for AI/ML applications can be used by non-coders. It simplifies the data-preprocessing stage of any AI/ML project pipeline, which can potentially improve the performance of the models. The tool demo will showcase the low-code implementation and no-code reuse and repurposing of AI-based systems through end-to end Pyrus pipelines.

Keywords: Low-code · imbalanced medical datasets · data resampling techniques · Pyrus · AI/ML-systems · Responsible AI

1 Introduction

The combination of Artificial Intelligence (AI), Machine Learning (ML) and Deep Learning (DL) algorithms has uncovered enormous potential and unprecedented problems in the ever-changing environment of software engineering. Software engineering principles need to adapt to developing and evolving AI-based systems. Our work addresses the need of responsible AI engineering and by leveraging the strengths of the Pyrus tool. Pyrus [17] is a Python-based, web-based, graphical modelling environment for ML and data analytics applications.

A particular aspect of fairness and access to advanced AI is to increase its accessibility to domain experts that are non-coders. This is increasingly important in medicine, health and natural science context. Prior work successfully used low-code/no-code approaches to address workflow in bioinformatics [4,5], computational science [1] and paired with computational thinking, in education [8]. Those approaches share similar abstraction, encapsulation and coordination mechanisms to ours, however, their underlying tools were desktop or server

© The Author(s), under exclusive license to Springer Nature Switzerland AG 2024
J. Kofroň et al. (Eds.): ECBS 2023, LNCS 14390, pp. 60–69, 2024.
https://doi.org/10.1007/978-3-031-49252-5_6

oriented, the system used Java for the low-code part, and modelling was single user. Choosing Pyrus, we now support Python as implementation language, the system is cloud-based, and it supports distributed collaborative modelling, three core characteristics for the ease of adoption in modern interdisciplinary and distributed teams of natural and medical scientists and practitioners.

Tools like Tines[1] and H2O.ai 's*Hydrogen Torch*[2] are specifically low-code/no-code or support ML applications. Tines is a web-based no-code tool that uses workflows in the domain of cybersecurity. The workflows can be automated using different no-code snippets of generic components called 'actions' within automated workflows called 'stories'. Although Tines has a robust and easy to use interface, it lacks the ability to code specific 'actions' required for any complex data analysis or ML application. H2O.ai Hydrogen Torch is a ML/DL-specific, web-based, low-code/no-code tool that can be used by non-coders for their big-data needs. This platform can also be used to deploy ML pipelines and models, and it has API functionality for remote use. In comparison, Pyrus supports the features offered by Hydrogen Torch, and it is open source, thus it can be used without subscription fees. For a business/organisation looking to develop its own in-house AI models using their own proprietary data, sharing data with a third party and model training costs are the biggest issues.

From an application point of view, the AI/ML models, workflows and pipelines need to be explainable and reusable to allow for ease of future development and collaboration. The low-code/no-code paradigm helps by presenting the end user transparent, explainable and reusable ways to implement the AI/ML models in a reliable and fair way. We demonstrate how IDPP is a good solution to these problems on a real-world use-case where we show how to deal with the data imbalance problem for a selection of popular ML models, applied to the medical domain. To resolve class imbalance, data resampling techniques are used and all the IDPP modelling pipelines are developed in Pyrus using the low-code/no-code paradigm. This research extends the M.Sc. thesis of Olga Minguett [12], who chose the datasets and resampling methods. The new contribution is the IDPP tool: it concerns the restructuring of the code for the data analytics and the new model driven approach with ML pipelines in Pyrus[3].

In this paper, Sect. 2 describes the IDPP framework used in this research, Sect. 3 demonstrates the IDPP framework using a case study of imbalanced datasets from the medical domain, Sect. 4 concludes the paper.

2   Framework Description

Pyrus is a Python-based, web-based, graphical modelling environment for ML and data analytics applications. Pyrus is also part of the larger CINCO family

---

[1] https://www.tines.com/product.

[2] https://h2o.ai/platform/ai-cloud/make/hydrogen-torch/.

[3] All code, information on datasets used and the results are published on GitHub at: https://github.com/singhad/class_imbalance_pyrus.

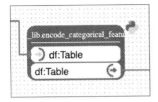

(a) The SIB in Pyrus

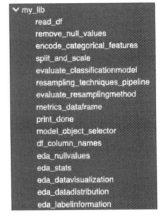

(b) Python implementation and body annotation

Fig. 1. Pyrus: SIB representation of the encode_categorical_features() function from the pre-processing and transformation pipeline

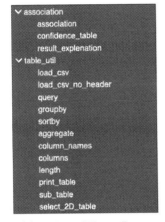

(a) Default SIBs in Pyrus   (b) IDPP: New Custom SIBs

Fig. 2. IDPP and Pyrus: List of SIBs in the Ecore palette

of low-code/no-code development tools [13], and it is integral part of a Digital Thread solution [9] that enables inter-accessibility and reusability of the code-base for different applications and objectives. Pyrus models are data-flow models, they are the no-code graphical equivalent to programming workflows that orchestrate reusable Python functions. The Python functions are implemented in the renowned programming platform Jupyter[4] following the OTA (One Thing Approach) paradigm [10]. Special signature annotations added to these functions enable their identification by the Pyrus web-based orchestration tool. The code generated by Pyrus from the pipelines is also stored and executed in Jupyter. This separation of the low-code development of functionalities and no-code orchestration via modelling is based on MDE principles [11].

Figure 3 shows a screenshot of the Pyrus web-based development environment. Each Python function implemented in Jupyter is represented in Pyrus as a collection of taxonomically grouped Service Independent Building blocks (SIBs) in its Ecore section, containing the SIBs palettes. Figure 1 shows the

---

[4] https://jupyter.org.

annotated code in Jupyter in Fig. 1b and its representation as a SIB in Pyrus, see Fig. 1a. A summary of the SIBs available in the Ecore section of IDPP is shown in Fig. 2.

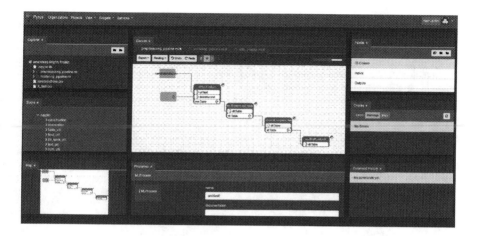

Fig. 3. Pyrus: View of the web-based development environment

3 Use Case and Demonstration

ML classification algorithms assume that the classes are balanced, but this is rarely the case in any real-life data. Class imbalance happens when one or more of the classes/categories in a dataset are not well represented and hence are thought to be outliers, noise or anomalies by the ML algorithms during their training process. This is a challenge for the ML algorithms, as the underrepresented categories will be ignored or misclassified. The problem is exacerbated when these algorithms are used as applications in real-life settings and produce biased or wrong results. According to [16], most ML classification algorithms assume that the classes are balanced and that the cost of miscalculation is the same for any class. However, for diagnosing conditions, improving prognostics, accurate patient monitoring and in personalised medicine, the cost of misdiagnosing a patient is significantly higher. For example, for the classification of tumours as malignant or not-malignant [2], the cost of miscalculation is very different. To resolve class imbalance, resampling techniques are used, such as data-resampling techniques that modify the training dataset in order for the ML models to have equal representation of the minority class.

3.1 Python Pre-requisites

We chose Python as the programming language. The two central packages used for the programming tasks are scikit-learn [14], used for data cleaning, modelling and evaluation, and imbalanced-learn [6], used to apply the different data-driven resampling techniques on the datasets.

3.2 Datasets

We chose these three datasets for this study:

1. Cerebral Stroke Dataset [7]: This dataset was created to aid in detection of a stroke using classification algorithms. It has 12 features containing 43.4K observations out of which 783 observations are labelled to be stroke.
2. Diabetes Dataset [15]: This dataset was extracted from the Behavioral Risk Factor Surveillance System (BRFSS) 2014 dataset that was published by the CDC[5]. The BRFFS 2014 dataset contained survey collected responses from over 400,000 people on health-related risk behaviours, chronic health conditions, and the use of preventative services, conducted since 1984. The extracted Diabetes dataset has 22 features, 254.6K observations with the target variable having 2 classes - 0 for no diabetes, 1 for diabetes.
3. Sepsis Dataset [3]: This dataset was created in the Computing in Cardiology Challenge from Physionet 2019 with the goal of early detection of sepsis. The data was sourced from ICU patients in three separate hospital systems.

3.3 Data Pre-processing and Transformation

To remove missing values and encoding of categorical variables, different approaches are employed for the three different datasets.

1. Cerebral Stroke dataset: only two features have missing values - *BMI* and *Smoking Status*. For the *BMI* feature, the missing values are imputed with the modal value, and for the *Smoking Status* feature, the missing values are categorised into a new label named 'Unknown'. The categorical features in this dataset are encoded using the Pandas package.
2. Diabetes dataset: it has no missing values or categorical features. The dataset has 253680 rows and 22 columns with an imbalance of target label of 16.19%. Since the dataset is very large for this study, a subset of the dataset is taken by keeping the imbalance percentage constant. The subset dataset we use has 41075 rows and 22 columns.
3. Sepsis dataset: the features with more than 70% missing values are deleted. The remaining missing values in the features are imputed using the median values. There are no categorical features in this dataset.

The datasets are split into a ratio of 80:20 for training and testing respectively. The stratified splitting method is used. For outliers, the RobustScaler() transform function is used for feature scaling to remove the median values and perform scaling of data between the 1st and 3rd quartile.

---

[5] https://www.cdc.gov/brfss/annual_data/annual_2014.html.

3.4   Experiments

Five classification algorithms were chosen: 1) Support Vector Machine (SVM), 2) Decision Tree (DT), 3) Gaussian Naïve Bayes (GNB), 4) K-Nearest Neighborhood (KNN), 5) Logistic Regression (LR).

Three types of data-driven resampling techniques were applied on the datasets: undersampling, oversampling, and hybrid techniques. The following specific data-driven resampling techniques were selected in the experiments:

1. Oversampling: RandomOverSampler, SMOTE, SMOTENC, BorderlineSMOTE, SVMSMOTE, KMeansSMOTE, ADASYN
2. Undersampling: RandomUnderSampler, ClusterCentroids, NearMiss, InstanceHardnessThreshold, TomekLinks, CondensedNearestNeighbour, AllKNN, EditedNearestNeighbours, RepeatedEditedNearestNeighbours, OneSidedSelection, NeighbourhoodCleaningRule
3. Combined/Hybrid: SMOTEENN, SMOTETomek

3.5   Pyrus Pipelines

The original code was transformed according to the OTA paradigm for modularization and reuse, and each SIB was annotated with special signature comments for the Pyrus orchestrator to recognise the functions in the pipelines. The code was then stored and implemented on Jupyter, and GUI-based pipelines were modelled in Pyrus. The Pyrus pipelines are depicted in Figs. 4, 5 and 6.

The performance of the algorithms on the datasets before and after resampling was evaluated using the metrics accuracy, precision, recall, f1 score, number of occurrences, predictions count, confusion matrix and area under the curve. The precision, recall and f1 score metrics were plotted, and the results were stored as a CSV file for each classification algorithm.

3.6   Results

Experiments were conducted on the three selected datasets. Figure 4 shows the exploratory data analysis (EDA) pipeline to get the overview and basic statistics of the datasets. Figure 5 shows the pre-processing and transformation pipeline used to clean the datasets and segment them into training/testing sets for ML models. Figure 6 shows the modelling and evaluation pipeline used to apply and evaluate ML models on the selected datasets.

The highest and lowest scoring results for each of the datasets based on the f1 score metric are shown in Table 1. The results are summarised as follows:

1. The Cerebral Stroke dataset has the most imbalanced class ratio. The best results were obtained by the KNN and DT models when undersampling and oversampling techniques were used. Although overall, oversampling techniques performed better. The worst results were obtained when a set of undersampling techniques were used.

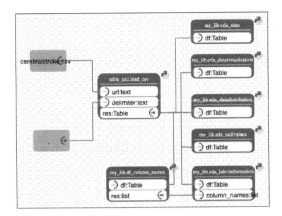

Fig. 4. Pyrus: Exploratory Data Analysis (EDA) Pipeline

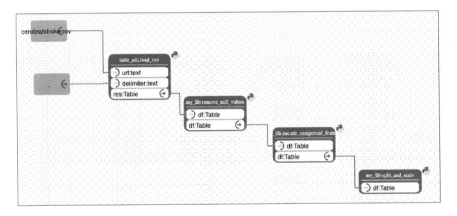

Fig. 5. Pyrus: Pre-processing and Transformation Pipeline

2. The Diabetes dataset had a mild class imbalance ratio and here too oversampling techniques performed better overall than undersampling techniques. For this dataset, the best algorithms were KNN and DT. The worst results were obtained when a set of undersampling techniques were used.
3. The Sepsis dataset had a moderate class imbalance ratio. Here the undersampling and oversampling techniques performed equally well. For this dataset, the best algorithm was DT. The worst results were obtained when a set of undersampling techniques were used.

Across all three datasets, the hybrid techniques had the best overall performance, with the least variance in f1 scores for different models. The best model for hybrid techniques was DT.

Across all datasets, specifically the TomekLinks/OneSidedSelection (undersampling), RandomOverSampler/KMeansSMOTE (oversampling) and SMOTE-Tomek (hybrid) methods performed the best.

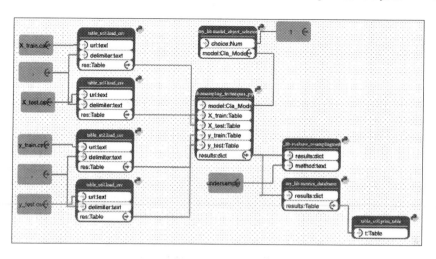

Fig. 6. Pyrus: Modelling and Evaluation Pipeline

Table 1. Results for all datasets - sorted by f1 Scores

Dataset	Technique	Model	Method	f1 Score	Accuracy	Precision	Recall
Cerebral Stroke Dataset	Undersampling	KNN	TomekLinks	**0.9906**	0.9812	0.9820	0.9992
		KNN	OneSidedSelection	**0.9906**	0.9813	0.9820	0.9992
		DT	NearMiss	*0.3702*	0.2376	0.9798	0.2282
	Oversampling	DT	RandomOverSampler	0.9831	0.9668	0.9821	0.9842
		DT	KMeansSMOTE	0.9760	0.9532	0.9832	0.9689
		GNB	ADASYN	0.8247	0.7057	0.9934	0.7049
	Hybrid	DT	SMOTETomek	0.9736	0.9486	0.9829	0.9645
		GNB	SMOTEENN	0.8264	0.7082	0.9937	0.7073
Diabetes Dataset	Undersampling	KNN	TomekLinks	**0.9111**	0.8422	0.8843	0.9596
		KNN	OneSidedSelection	**0.9111**	0.8421	0.8844	0.9393
		DT	ClusterCentroids	*0.3769*	0.3221	0.9020	0.2382
	Oversampling	SVC	KMeansSMOTE	0.8963	0.8220	0.8992	0.8934
		DT	RandomOverSampler	0.88	0.7945	0.8737	0.8737
		GNB	ADASYN	0.7596	0.6567	0.9558	0.6303
	Hybrid	DT	SMOTETomek	0.8768	0.7910	0.8900	0.8639
		KNN	SMOTEENN	0.7570	0.6526	0.9508	0.6289
Sepsis Dataset	Undersampling	DT	OneSidedSelection	**0.9736**	0.9510	0.9736	0.9736
		DT	TomekLinks	**0.9730**	0.9499	0.9734	0.9725
		SVC	ClusterCentroids	*0.4018*	0.2993	0.9634	0.2539
	Oversampling	DT	RandomOverSampler	**0.9736**	0.9510	0.9727	0.9745
		LR	ADASYN	0.8549	0.7601	0.9734	0.7620
	Hybrid	DT	SMOTETomek	0.9601	0.9270	0.9736	0.9470
		KNN	SMOTEENN	0.8399	0.7390	0.9738	0.7384

Overall, hybrid techniques perform the best with the least variance in f1 scores, oversampling techniques ranked second-best: with many higher f1 scores than hybrid techniques, but with more variance. Undersampling techniques ranked the lowest of the three types, with some high scores but a lot of variance in f1 scores. This result is in agreement with the established understanding that more data points are always better than fewer data points even when the resulting dataset is completely balanced. By design, undersampling techniques remove data points, which generally results in loss of information compared to oversampling/hybrid techniques that append more data points.

4   Conclusions

With IDPP we demonstrate that the low-code/no-code pipelines for imbalanced datasets in Pyrus serve as an embodiment of 'Responsible AI' concerning transparency, fairness, explainability, reliability and reusability of the AI/ML models and IDPP pipelines themselves. IDPP uses the web-based, low-code/no-code graphical modelling environment of Pyrus for AI/ML applications. We applied IDPP to imbalanced datasets, showing on 3 imbalanced medical datasets the performance of different data-driven resampling techniques in combination with a selection of ML classification algorithms.

The low-code Pyrus pipelines were easy to create and reuse. The development time of the pipelines was greatly reduced by using a web- and GUI-based tool. Pyrus was used to build the data-flow pipelines using SIBs generated from annotations in the Python code. With this low-code/no-code approach, future users can reuse the existing IDPP pipelines and SIBs by simply selecting them from the Ecore palette section in Pyrus, without the prerequisite of proficiency in programming. This ensures superior understandability of the logical steps in the pipeline w.r.t. the code based approach. IDPP's end-to-end Pyrus pipelines offer a variety of techniques, models and methods to rectify data imbalance in different scenarios without the need for redeveloping custom pipelines and AI/ML models from scratch for each use-case.

A challenge faced by IDPP and any low-code/no-code approach is the dependency of Python libraries on the Python kernel version. If the version of Python required by the libraries does not match the version of Python kernel used by Jupyter for the IDPP or Pyrus orchestration, the pipeline will not execute. It may help to re-deploy Pyrus framework using the most recent versions of Python and other supported packages. Ultimately, software obsolescence is inevitable, and it is essential to keep pace with newer versions, tools and technology.

Acknowledgments. This research was partially funded by Science Foundation Ireland (SFI) under Grant Number 18/CRT/6223 - SFI Centre of Research Training in AI.

References

1. Al-Areqi, S., Lamprecht, A.-L., Margaria, T.: Constraints-driven automatic geospatial service composition: workflows for the analysis of sea-level rise impacts. In: Gervasi, O., et al. (eds.) ICCSA 2016. LNCS, vol. 9788, pp. 134–150. Springer, Cham (2016). https://doi.org/10.1007/978-3-319-42111-7_12
2. Devarriya, D., Gulati, C., Mansharamani, V., Sakalle, A., Bhardwaj, A.: Unbalanced breast cancer data classification using novel fitness functions in genetic programming. Expert Syst. Appl. **140**, 112866 (2020), https://www.sciencedirect.com/science/article/pii/S0957417419305767

3. Kuo, N., Finfer, S., Jorm, L., Barbieri, S.: Synthetic acute hypotension and sepsis datasets based on mimic-iii and published as part of the health gym project, https://physionet.org/content/synthetic-mimic-iii-health-gym/1.0.0/

4. Lamprecht, A.-L., Margaria, T., Steffen, B.: Seven variations of an alignment workflow - an illustration of agile process design and management in Bio-jETI. In: Măndoiu, I., Sunderraman, R., Zelikovsky, A. (eds.) ISBRA 2008. LNCS, vol. 4983, pp. 445–456. Springer, Heidelberg (2008). https://doi.org/10.1007/978-3-540-79450-9_42

5. Lamprecht, A.L., Margaria, T., Steffen, B., Sczyrba, A., Hartmeier, S., Giegerich, R.: Genefisher-p: variations of genefisher as processes in Bio-jETI. BMC Bioinformatics 9(4), 1–15 (2008)

6. Lemaître, G., Nogueira, F., Aridas, C.K.: Imbalanced-learn: a python toolbox to tackle the curse of imbalanced datasets in machine learning. J. Mach. Learn. Res. 18(17), 1–5 (2017), http://jmlr.org/papers/v18/16-365.html

7. Liu, T., Fan, W., Wu, C.: Data for: A hybrid machine learning approach to cerebral stroke prediction based on imbalanced medical-datasets 1 (2019), https://data.mendeley.com/datasets/x8ygrw87jw/1

8. Margaria, T.: From Computational Thinking to Constructive Design with Simple Models. In: Margaria, T., Steffen, B. (eds.) ISoLA 2018. LNCS, vol. 11244, pp. 261–278. Springer, Cham (2018). https://doi.org/10.1007/978-3-030-03418-4_16

9. Margaria, T., Schieweck, A.: The Digital Thread in Industry 4.0. In: Ahrendt, W., Tapia Tarifa, S.L. (eds.) IFM 2019. LNCS, vol. 11918, pp. 3–24. Springer, Cham (2019). https://doi.org/10.1007/978-3-030-34968-4_1

10. Margaria, T., Steffen, B.: Business process modeling in the jABC: the one-thing approach. In: Handbook of research on business process modeling, pp. 1–26. IGI Global (2009)

11. Margaria, T., Steffen, B.: Continuous model-driven engineering. Computer 42(10), 106–109 (2009)

12. Minguett Pirela, O.M.: Evaluation of machine learning classification techniques for handling class imbalance in medical datasets. M.Sc. in Artificial Intelligence, University of Limerick (2022)

13. Naujokat, S., Lybecait, M., Kopetzki, D., Steffen, B.: Cinco: a simplicity-driven approach to full generation of domain-specific graphical modeling tools. Int. J. Softw. Tools Technol. Transfer 20, 327–354 (2018)

14. Pedregosa, F., Varoquaux, G., Gramfort, A., Michel, E.A.: Scikit-learn: machine learning in Python. J. Mach. Learn. Res. 12, 2825–2830 (2011)

15. Xie, Z.: Building risk prediction models for type 2 diabetes using machine learning techniques. Prev. Chronic Dis. 16, e130 (2019)

16. Xu, Z., Shen, D., Nie, T., Kou, Y.: A hybrid sampling algorithm combining m-smote and ENN based on random forest for medical imbalanced data. J. Biomed. Inf. 107, 103465 (2020)

17. Zweihoff, P., Steffen, B.: Pyrus: an online modeling environment for no-code data-analytics service composition. In: Margaria, T., Steffen, B. (eds.) ISoLA 2021. LNCS, vol. 13036, pp. 18–40. Springer, Cham (2021). https://doi.org/10.1007/978-3-030-89159-6_2

Learning in Uppaal for Test Case Generation for Cyber-Physical Systems

Rong Gu[(⊠)] (iD)

Mälardalen University, Västerås, Sweden
`rong.gu@mdu.se`

Abstract. We propose a test-case generation method for testing cyber-physical systems by using learning and statistical model checking. We use timed game automata for modelling. Different from other studies, we construct the model from the environment's perspective. After building the model, we synthesize policies for different kinds of environments by using reinforcement learning in Uppaal and parse the policies for test-case generation. Statistical model checking enables us to analyse the test cases for finding the ones that are more likely to detect bugs.

1 Introduction

Cyber-physical systems (CPS) are becoming pervasive in modern society. Such systems are not pure software or hardware but consist of cyber components (i.e., software controllers) and physical components. With the development of artificial intelligence, autonomous systems, a recent example of CPS, are becoming more and more realistic. Such systems, e.g., self-driving cars, run autonomously by perceiving the environment via sensors, making decisions via controlling software and interacting with the environment, such as moving and carrying goods. CPS are often designed to accomplish specific tasks that are repetitive and tedious for humans. On some occasions, CPS have to work alongside humans, such as on construction sites. In this case, the safety guarantee of CPS are crucial as a subtle fault in the system can lead to casualties.

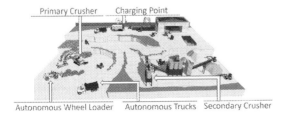

Figure 1 depicts an example of CPS working in an autonomous quarry. The quarry contains various autonomous CPS such as trucks and wheel loaders. In this example, the mission for the CPS are transporting stones in a quarry, where wheel loaders dig and load

Fig. 1. An example of CPS: an autonomous quarry

stones, and trucks transport stones. First, the wheel loaders need to move to stone piles, dig stones, and load them into trucks. Then, the trucks carry on to transport the stones to the primary crushers, where stones are crushed

© The Author(s), under exclusive license to Springer Nature Switzerland AG 2024
J. Kofroň et al. (Eds.): ECBS 2023, LNCS 14390, pp. 70–74, 2024.
https://doi.org/10.1007/978-3-031-49252-5_7

into coarse fractions before they are carried to the secondary crushers. When working in the quarry, the CPS must transport a certain amount of stones within 24h to keep a high level of productivity. They also must avoid obstacles such as rocks and other machines and visit the charging point periodically. To achieve the goal, the CPS must be able to find safe trajectories, track the trajectories closely to avoid obstacles and be ready to handle unexpected situations, such as animals suddenly appearing in the field.

When testing such systems, knowing whether the control software is functioning correctly is not enough. For example, when a wheel loader is putting stones in a truck, even if its controller sends the correct signals to the arm and bucket, the collaboration may still fail because the truck, which is part of the environment from the wheel loader's perspective, may be parking at the wrong position or turning to a wrong orientation. Therefore, testing must consider not only the system itself but also its working environment. Additionally, the wheel loader must be unloading stones preciously at the right moment when the truck's position is under its bucket. Hence, the correctness of the system depends on its own functions, the working environment, and the temporal order and timing of performing actions.

Another factor that makes the problem even more difficult is that the environment can be uncertain. In the example of the autonomous quarry, all machines are collaborating, so we can assume the environment to be friendly, which means every system is working toward the same goal. However, in some situations, the environment is neutral or even antagonistic. For example, from a self-driving car's perspective, pedestrians and other drivers are hard to predict. Some of them are friendly but some of them are aggressive, e.g., suddenly turning their direction without using the indicator. To test CPS working in such an environment, we need to cover all the possible situations so that the system is ready for emergencies. However, the environment is hard to model, and some even contain rare events that are very unlikely to happen but once they appear, accidents occur. In summary, testing such systems is extremely difficult and we need to consider not only the system but also the environment.

In this paper, we propose a method that uses reinforcement learning [9] to train various traffic agents such that the combination of their behaviour can form different types of environments. Based on the design of the reward function for reinforcement learning and the primitive behaviours of the environment, we can train the environment to behave in different ways, and the training is carried out in Uppaal Stratego[1] [4]. The tool enables us to not only perform the training but also verify the results by using its statistical model checker (SMC) [3]. The trained environment provides the test cases for the CPS and we use the quantitative answers of verification to evaluate the quality of the generated test cases. Most importantly, as the modelling, training, and verification are all done by using formal methods, the unreliable results of reinforcement learning are now strengthened by the rigour of formal methods, and the automatically generated test cases can be used for finding sophisticated bugs, like the ones concerning

---

[1] Uppaal Stratego is now integrated into Uppaal 5: uppaal.org.

the temporal order of task execution and the timing constraints, which is not achievable by other automatic testing techniques, such as fuzzing [8].

2   Test-Case Generation by Learning in Uppaal

In this section, we introduce the method for the generation of test cases for cyber-physical systems. In this method, we use the modelling language *timed game automata* to build the model of CPS and environment. Timed game automata (TG) are special timed automata (TA). The latter is finite-state automata extended with real-valued variables that increase at the same rate one [1]. TG further extends TA by partitioning actions into *controllable* and *uncontrollable* ones.

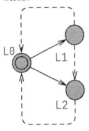

Fig. 2. TG example

Figure 2 depicts an example of TG, in which solid arrows represent controllable actions of the system and dotted arrows are uncontrollable actions of the environment. In Uppaal, circles are called *locations* and arrows are called *edges*, whose formal definitions are in the literature [4]. However, readers are not required to understand these concepts for reading this paper. Intuitively, when the TG example is at location L0, it has three options of controllable actions. Two are explicit, that is, going to location L1 and going to location L2. The third option is waiting at L0 until an uncontrollable action takes place, which is implicit as it is shown in the automaton. In Fig. 2, since there is no uncontrollable action at location L0, to choose to wait there means to stay at L0 for an unbounded time. At location L1, the uncontrollable actions may lead the model back to L0 or further to L2, whereas at location L2, there is only one uncontrollable action getting back to L0. Policy synthesis means calculating a set of state-action pairs that shows the TG which controllable actions to choose at each of the states such that the model satisfies some properties, e.g., eventually coming back to the initial location L0 within two steps or five time units.

TG have been applied in many real-world case studies [5] [2] [7]. In these studies, CPS are modelled as TG where controllable actions belong to the system and uncontrollable actions belong to the environment. Then they use reinforcement learning in Uppaal to synthesize policies for guiding the controllable actions of the system and analyse the results by using SMC or exhaustive model checking. In this paper, we construct the model in the opposite way. We model the environment's behaviour as controllable actions and the system's behaviour as uncontrollable actions. Then we use reinforcement learning to synthesize policies for the environment such that it knows how to *win* the game. If we switch the controllable and uncontrollable actions in the TG example and train an *unfriendly* environment, the resulting policy could tell the environment to go to location L2 when the model is at L1, which makes the system lose the game, i.e., coming back to L0 within two steps.

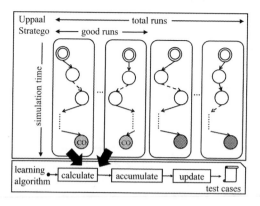

Fig. 3. The process of test-case generation. adapted from the literature [6].

We proposed a method for generating test cases by parsing the policies learned in Uppaal previously [6]. In this paper, we leverage the tool for test-case generation. Figure 3 shows the process of the method. First, we randomly simulate the model for a number of episodes and gather the runs of the model. Some of them are *good runs* that satisfy our property (i.e., environment winning the game) and some of them are *bad runs* that are abandoned for learning. After a certain amount of learning episodes, the policy becomes stable and we generate test cases, which represent the environment's behaviour. Further, we can use SMC in Uppaal to analyse those test cases for finding the ones that are more likely to detect bugs in the CPS.

In summary, our method is able to train different kinds of environments, which is crucial for testing CPS. Although the training is via reinforcement learning, because of the formal techniques in our method, we can generate test cases that are proven to be more likely to detect bugs in the systems, and the bugs can be sophisticated such as temporal-logic-based ones.

References

1. Alur, R., Dill, D.: Automata for modeling real-time systems. In: Paterson, M.S. (ed.) ICALP 1990. LNCS, vol. 443, pp. 322–335. Springer, Heidelberg (1990). https://doi.org/10.1007/BFb0032042
2. Dai, S., Hong, M., Guo, B.: Synthesizing power management strategies for wireless sensor networks with UPPAAL-STRATEGO. Int. J. Distrib. Sens. Netw. (2017)
3. David, A., et al.: Statistical model checking for stochastic hybrid systems. arXiv (2012)
4. David, A., Jensen, P.G., Larsen, K.G., Mikučionis, M., Taankvist, J.H.: UPPAAL STRATEGO. In: Baier, C., Tinelli, C. (eds.) TACAS 2015. LNCS, vol. 9035, pp. 206–211. Springer, Heidelberg (2015). https://doi.org/10.1007/978-3-662-46681-0_16
5. Eriksen, A.B., et al.: Uppaal stratego for intelligent traffic lights. In: 12th ITS European Congress (2017)
6. Gu, R., Enoiu, E.: Model-based policy synthesis and test-case generation for autonomous systems. In: 2023 IEEE International Conference on Software Testing, Verification and Validation Workshops (ICSTW). IEEE (2023)
7. Gu, R., Seceleanu, C., Enoiu, E., Lundqvist, K.: Model checking collision avoidance of nonlinear autonomous vehicles. In: Huisman, M., Păsăreanu, C., Zhan, N. (eds.) FM 2021. LNCS, vol. 13047, pp. 676–694. Springer, Cham (2021). https://doi.org/10.1007/978-3-030-90870-6_37

8. Li, J., Zhao, B., Zhang, C.: Fuzzing: a survey. Cybersecurity **1**(1), 1–13 (2018). https://doi.org/10.1186/s42400-018-0002-y
9. Sutton, R.S., Barto, A.G.: Reinforcement Learning: An Introduction. MIT Press, Cambridge (2018)

A Literature Survey of Assertions in Software Testing

Masoumeh Taromirad[1,2]($\boxtimes$) and Per Runeson[1]

[1] Lund University, 221 00 Lund, Sweden
{masoumeh.taromirad,per.runeson}@cs.lth.se
[2] Jönköping University, 551 11 Jönköping, Sweden

Abstract. Assertions are one of the most useful automated techniques for checking program's behaviour and hence have been used for different verification and validation tasks. We provide an overview of the last two decades of research involving 'assertions' in software testing. Based on a term–based search, we filtered the inclusion of relevant papers and synthesised them w.r.t. the problem addressed, the solution designed, and the evaluation conducted. The survey rendered 119 papers on assertions in software testing. After test oracle, the dominant problem focus is test generation, followed by engineering aspects of assertions. Solutions are typically embedded in tool prototypes and evaluated throughout limited number of cases while using large–scale industrial settings is still a noticeable method. We conclude that assertions would be worth more attention in future research, particularly regarding the new and emerging demands (e.g., verification of programs with uncertainty), for effective, applicable, and domain-specific solutions.

Keywords: assertions · testing · literature survey

1 Introduction

While there is abundance of research regarding the selection of test inputs and execution conditions, the assessment of expected results is less covered. Research on the expected results of test cases is often framed as "the oracle problem", with Weyuker as an early contributor, observing 1982 that "[a]lthough much of the testing literature describes methodologies which are predicated on both the theoretical and practical availability of an oracle, in many cases such an oracle is pragmatically unattainable" [82].

Barr et al. [6] surveyed the research literature related to oracles and classified oracles into specified, derived, implicit, and no automatable ones. Among the concepts identified in their survey are 'assertions', defined as "a boolean expression that is placed at a certain point in a program to check its behaviour at runtime". Despite being dated back to Turing and integrated into programming languages, testing tools and practices of today, they only found a few pieces of work specifically focused on assertions [16]. As our current research develops

© The Author(s), under exclusive license to Springer Nature Switzerland AG 2024
J. Kofroň et al. (Eds.): ECBS 2023, LNCS 14390, pp. 75–96, 2024.
https://doi.org/10.1007/978-3-031-49252-5_8

around assertions, we decided to survey the existence of assertions, for testing purposes, in more recent research.

Our research goal is to provide an overview of existing research literature on assertions in software testing, to provide a basis for further research. As our research "aims to improve an area of practice", we choose the design science paradigm as a lens for this literature survey, as proposed by Engström et al. [25]. We search for literature that uses assertions or addresses problems with assertions in software testing. In line with design science elements, we catalogue the *problems* addressed in relation to assertions, the *solutions* designed to address the problems with or using assertions, and the types of *evaluation*, assessing the strength and relevance of the contributions.

We present existing literature surveys on testing in Sect. 2. Our methodology is outlined in Sect. 3, followed by the main results – the literature overview and synthesis in Sect. 4. We discuss our findings in Sect. 5, report limitations in Sect. 6, and conclude the paper in Sect. 7.

2   Background and Related Work

Assertions are used to check program's behaviour at runtime: when an assertion evaluates to true (false), the program's behaviour is regarded "as intended" ("as erroneous") at the point of the assertion. They have gained significant attention and been used as a measure for code quality. Most dominantly, *program assertions* are used either to check the behaviour of the program, e.g., Blasi et al. [8], or to specify and check the contracts within the design by contract development.

Test oracle assertions (test assertions for short) are also used to specify and check the expected output of test cases [6]. Test assertions differ from program assertions as they check the expected output for one specific test case, while program assertions are typically located in the source code of the program, predicate on its variables, and return true or false throughout all its executions. Nevertheless, in many studies, program assertions and test oracle assertions are considered very closely or even interchangeably, e.g., Terragni et al. [74].

Specification assertions are also used to document programmers intent [16], i.e. modules are annotated with pre/post-conditions or invariants, e.g., JML. Specification assertions are basically non-executable and hence are inherently different from the other two types of assertions, although they seamlessly can be exploited at various stages of development for verification [54]. Our study basically focuses on test oracle assertions, yet designed to be inclusive of other types of assertions when they relate or contribute to testing.

Assertions (and their application) in software testing have been mostly studied under surveys on the test oracle problem, e.g., [6,55,61]. Among the 101 secondary studies, identified by Garousi and Mäntylä [32], only one is related to assertions, namely the one by Barr et al. [6] which reports on the roots of assertions, and existing support in languages and tools to use them for testing purposes. Surveys on automatic test generation techniques also consider assertions. Patel and Hierons [59] discuss the effectiveness and usability of assertions –

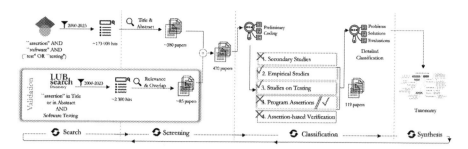

Fig. 1. Overview of the research method.

among others – in testing non-testable systems. In a mapping study on software test-code engineering, Garousi et al. [29] identify oracle assertion adequacy as a criterion of test-code quality assessment. In a survey on software testability [30], adding assertions is identified as an approach to improve testability. Winkler et al. [83] identify assertions as one of the factors affecting test code readability and understandability.

In summary, there are many secondary (and even tertiary) studies on software testing, but to our knowledge, there is no study specifically focusing on assertions used in software testing, and thus our survey fills a gap here.

3   Research Method

This study provides an overview of research involving (different types of) *assertions* used in the context of software testing. We follow similar research procedures as used in the literature surveys conducted by Harman et al. [4,6], namely a term–based search in Google Scholar, followed by a filtering process, and finally synthesized in a qualitative analysis. This type of reviews, i.e., *semi-systematic reviews*, is proposed by Snyder [69], in particular, for a non-homogeneous concept (similar to the target of our survey), where systematic literature reviews would be too strict, and a narrative approach is more feasible. Kitchenham et al. [38] label a similar process *mapping study* that "may be auditable but not necessarily complete"; that they should have transparent procedures but the search scope may be limited. In this paper, we aim to "map a field of research, synthesize the state of knowledge, and create an agenda for further research" [69].

This survey was conducted in four major steps which were iterated in several cycles (demonstrated in Fig. 1). The first author was the main driver of the work, while the second author primarily took a validation role at each step.

1. **Search** To include also grey literature, Google scholar was used as the primary search engine [31], with a query defined as: "assertion" AND "software" AND ("test" OR "testing"). We limited the search in time to the 2000–2023 to get an overview of modern research on assertions, still partially overlapping with earlier surveys to ensure consistency (e.g. Barr et al. covered 1978–2012 [6]). The initial search rendered about 173 000 hits.

2. **Screening** The titles and abstracts were screened to find papers on assertions, although being inclusive when in doubt. After about 5 000 titles, no more relevant papers where found among the last dozens of titles. The screening resulted in a set of about 380 papers before further classification of the papers. To validate the search and screening, we used the same query in our university's library search portal, limiting the search to title and abstract within the context of software testing. The results were further screened for relevance and overlap resulting in 86 additional papers, and hence, the initial pool of about 470 papers.

3. **Classification** We then performed a preliminary coding of the papers, based on the type of the study and then the type of assertion, resulting in five categories: 1) secondary studies, 2) empirical studies, 3) studies explicitly on testing, 4) studies involving program assertions, and 5) studies on assertion-based verification. Firstly, we filtered out category 1 studies, as they were already considered under the related work. We also excluded the papers in category 5, since they are fundamentally related to hardware. Moreover, throughout the preliminary coding, we found out that the studies in category 4 are divided into two groups of 1) studies totally separate from testing, and 2) studies that are related to testing, and hence, we excluded the first group from the further classification. Accordingly, we came up with 119 papers on assertions related/contributing to testing. We further classified the remaining papers according to the design science elements of *problem*, *solution*, and *validation*.

4. **Synthesis** Finally, we synthesised the research from the perspectives of 1) the *problems* addressed, 2) the *solutions* presented, and 3) how they are *evaluated*. The design science perspectives are motivated by earlier research, concluding that this frame is feasible for software engineering research [25]. The results are presented in Sect. 4 accordingly. The complete listing of the synthesis (including 119 papers) is available as complementary material at https://shorturl.at/ruCHL.

4   Results

This section presents the results of reviewing the studies through characterising three aspects of each study: the addressed *problem* (Sect. 4.2), the main proposed *solution* (Sect. 4.3), and how the proposal was *evaluated* (Sect. 4.4). It also outlines the *type* of assertions considered in the studies (Sect. 4.1). Throughout a few iterations over the studies, these aspects were narrowed down using more fine-grained and consistent taxonomy (presented in Fig. 2), that provides a comprehensive picture of the existing research on assertions in testing.

4.1   Assertion Types

Among our collection of studies, the three types of assertions are identified, which are considered for different purposes in the context of testing. Evidently, most of the studies deal with *test assertions*, where assertions are manipulated as the

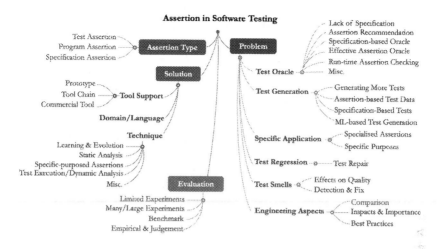

Fig. 2. Overview of the resulting taxonomy of the literature synthesis.

result of performing other tasks, such as automatically generating assertions [90] or improving their effectiveness [18]. Empirical studies (e.g., [41,68]) also focus on test assertions investigating them from different perspectives. *Program assertions* are also found among the studies for testing purposes – rather than just program verification. In such studies, program assertions are employed as part of the *solution* in order to fulfill a goal, such as generating test data (e.g., [87,92]). *Specification assertions* are also employed for generating tests (e.g., [23,43]).

4.2   Assertion Problems

The *problem* aspect looks into the principal focus of the research. The problems, addressed by the collected studies, include test oracle, test generation, test regression, test smells, specific applications (e.g., Mobile Apps, GUI, ML), and test improvements. Note that these classes recognize the most distinguishing problem addressed by a piece of research, and hence, they are not necessarily disjoint.

Test Oracle. While assertions are useful for specifying test oracles, writing and generating effective assertions are yet challenging [6]. Test oracle problem has been considered from different perspectives, including lack of specification, automatic generation of assertions statements, improving assertion oracles, and assertions based on specifications.

Specification of the intended behavior of the software under analysis is essential for assertion oracles. The *lack of such specification* has led to different techniques to capture the software behavior, and then generate assertions accordingly. Given an automatically generated test suite with no assertions, Ostra [86] collects objects' states, exercised by the test suite, and augments the test suite with new assertions specifying the behavior of a method. Zamprogno [91] propose to automatically generate assertions for a given test case, based on its previous executions and feedback of the developer. EvoSpex [52] uses genetic algorithms to automatically produce a specification of the method's current behavior, in the form of postcondition assertions. Mesbah et al. [48] use a crawler to infer a state-flow graph of user interface states and then identify AJAX-specific faults and DOM-tree invariants that can serve as oracles. TOGA [22] is a unified transformer-based neural approach to infer both exceptional and assertion test oracles for a focal method, that in particular handles units with ambiguous or missing documentation.

Assertion recommendation focuses on automatic generation of candidate assertion statements. Agitator [9] applies software agitation to facilitate test automation and recommends assertions based on observations of a code's behaviour. DODONA [44] ranks program variables based on the interactions and dependencies, and accordingly proposes a set of variables to be monitored within test oracles. Pham et al. [33] generate candidate assertions based on test cases and then apply active learning techniques to iteratively refine them. DSpot [18] takes developer-written test cases as input and synthesizes improved versions of them by triggering new behaviors and adding new assertions. Valueian et al. [79] employ an Artificial Neural Network to construct automated oracles for low observable software based on tests inputs and verdict. Abdi et al. [1] address test amplification for dynamically typed languages (e.g., Pharo), and exploit profiling information to infer the necessary type information creating special test inputs with corresponding assertions.

OASIs [34] is a search-based tool for improving oracle, using test case generation and mutation testing to reveal false positives and false negatives, respectively. Given a set of assertions and a set of correct and incorrect program states, GAssert [74] employs a co-evolutionary algorithm that explores the space of possible assertions to identify oracle with fewer false positives and false negatives. Xie et al. [87] propose a mutation analysis approach for strengthening the assertions of parameterised unit tests. Fraser and Zeller [28] present a mutation-based assertion generation, within EvoSuite [27], optimised towards satisfying a coverage criterion. ATLAS [80] is a deep learning (DL)-based approach to generate meaningful assert statements for test methods based on existing unit tests. Yu et al. [90] introduce an IR-based assertion retrieval technique and a technique to adjust the assertions based on the context, that are more effective in generating a long sequence of tokens comparing to ATLAS. Tufano et al. [77] propose an approach to generate accurate and useful assertions using transformer model finetuned on the task of generating assert statements for unit tests.

Specification-based assertions can effectively reveal faults, up to their limit [17], and hence have been employed in specifying test oracle. Xie and Memon [85] automate GUI test oracles by inserting "assert" statements in test cases based on the formal specifications, i.e., pre/postconditions of GUI events. Zhao and Harris [94] introduce an approach to generate assertions directly from the natural language specifications employing semantic analysis of sentences in the specification document. Franke et al. [26] propose a method that identifies life cycle dependent properties in the application specification, and derives test cases for validation. MeMo [8] automatically derives metamorphic equivalence relations from natural language documentation (given in Javadoc comments), which are then used as oracles in automatically generated test cases.

Runtime assertion checkers transparently ensure that the specification assertions hold during program execution [16]. JML (or an extension of JML) and its runtime assertion checker(s) are notably employed for testing in different context, such as testing conformance of safety-critical systems [73], specifying metamorphic relations [54], testing services in the Home Automation System [62], testing concurrent object-oriented software [5]. Cheon and Leavens [13,14] propose to use a specification language's runtime assertion checker (e.g., JML) to decide whether methods work correctly, and hence automating the test oracles. Pastore et al. [58] introduce CrowdOracles, exploiting CrowdSourcing idea in the context of test oracle problem, and demonstrate that CrowdOracles are a viable solution to automate the oracle problem, yet taming the crowd to get useful results is a difficult task.

> In summary, the studies in the *test oracle* category focus on how to generate assertions, what (kind of) information can be used for generating assertions, how to automate or augment the assertion generation process to have more effective assertions.

Test Generation. Assertions have been considered in the context of test generation addressing different challenges including generating either complete tests or part of a test, such as test data and input/output pair. Mirshokraie et al. [51] leverage existing DOM-dependent assertions in human-written UI-based test cases to automatically generate assertions for unit-level testing of JavaScript code. TESTILIZER [50] learns from existing human-written assertions to generate assertions for unchecked portions of the web application.

In *Assertion-based Testing*, program assertions are combined with automated test (data) generation in order to find assertion violations effectively. Zeng et al. [92], automatically convert program dynamic invariants into program assertions, which are then used to direct the test generation process. Mayer [47] develops an assertion-based testing framework and a tool to generate runtime checks based on the specification annotations, for the Go programming language.

Specification assertions are also used as the basis to automatically generate tests. Korat [10] uses a method precondition to automatically generate all test cases up to a given size and the method postcondition as a test oracle. Similarly, Jarteg [56] randomly generates test cases for Java classes specified in JML, which are used to eliminate irrelevant test cases and serve as a test oracle. Søndergaard et al. [73] use JML annotations to model conformance constraints – in a safety-critical system – in order to generate JUnit tests as well as runtime assertion checks. Higher-level specification languages (and their assertions) are also employed for test generation. Li and Sun [43] translate Z formal models into their UML/OCL counterparts and JUnit tests (containing assertions). TestEra [37] generates test inputs based on Alloy specifications using Alloy SAT solver. Stoyanova et al. [72] introduce a test generation process based on WS-BPEL, having assertions at different levels (HTTP, SOAP and BPEL variable), for testing web services. Drusinsky et al. [23] propose an automatic, JUnit-based, white-box testing of statechart prototypes augmented with statechart assertions.

Using more recent ML-based techniques, A3Test [2] presents a DL-based test case generation approach that uses a pre-trained language model of assertions to improve test case generation from language models (e.g., AthenaTest).

> In summary, different types of assertions have been basically employed to direct *test generation* in order to generate complete tests or part of them, such as test data and test oracle.

Specific Applications. *Specialised assertions* – in contrast to general-purpose assertions – have been introduced addressing special requirements in particular domains. For multi-agent system development, Tiryaki et al. [75] introduce a specialized assertion method for agent level verification. Delamare et al. [21] extend JUnit with new types of assertions to specify the expected joinpoints in aspect-oriented programming using AspectJ. Chang et al. [76] introduce visual assertions to verify whether certain GUI interaction generates the desired visual feedback. Koesnander et al. [40] introduce web macro assertions to encode the expectations and assumptions of a website developed by non-technical users.

Verification and validation of applications with inherent, uncertain outcomes (e.g., machine learning programs) requires new types of assertions. Dutta et al. [24] present FLEX which uses *approximate assertions* to compare the actual and expected values, while systematically identify the acceptable bound between the actual and expected output which minimizes flakiness. Kang et al. [36] introduce model assertions – that could be 'exact' or 'soft', which adapts the classical use of program assertions as a way to monitor and improve ML models.

Assertions are also adapted for *specific purposes*, in addition to typical testing, such as fault localisation, detecting merge conflicts, and test-suite reduction. Salehi Fathabadi et al. [64] use a formal model of the APIs of independently developed components to generate a set of assertions embedded in the implementation. Xuan and Monperrus [88] present spectrum-driven test case purification for improving fault localization, that generates purified versions of failing test cases, which include only one assertion per test. Sequeira [66] provide an automated technique to determine the DOM dependencies for each test assertion (on DOM), so that assertion failures are connected to the underlying JavaScript code which help finding the cause of failures. Pariente and Signoles [57] propose a method to trigger security counter-measures, based on static detection and run-time assertion checking of program weaknesses. Knauth et al. [39] recommend assertion-driven development instead of test-driven development and introduce meta-mutations at the code level to simulate common programmer errors. An assertion-aware test-suite reduction technique has been proposed by Chen et al. [12]. Messaoudi et al. [49] use assertion-based backward slicing to decompose complex system test cases into smaller, separate ones. Petke and Blot [60] suggest to consider the output of test case assertions in fitness functions for test-based program repair using genetic algorithms. Fang and Lam [95] introduce assertion fingerprint to identify suitable candidates in refactoring test suites. TOM [35] is a tool that detects merge conflicts with the help of assertions that are defined on the variables that have different values.

> In summary, the *specific applications* category demonstrates that assertions are useful for many different purposes. With specialised syntax and semantics, assertions may support specific problems more effectively.

Test Regression. Regression tests can fail not only due to faults in the program but also due to obsolete tests which do not reflect the behavior of the updated program. Moonen et al. [53] introduce "test-driven refactoring" in that general code refactorings are induced by (re)structuring tests, for example to remove assertion roulette. Sakakibara et al. [63] develop an assertion-based mechanism to eliminate unnecessary dependencies between test code and objects in order to decrease invalidated tests due to changes in a code. ReAssert [19] automatically repairs broken unit tests by for example changing assertion methods. ReAssert combines analysis of a test's dynamic execution with analysis and transformation of the static structure of test code. WATER [15] suggests repairs for web application test scripts (test assertions), employing differential testing in that the behavior of tests on two successive versions of the application are compared and analysed. Xu et al. [89] introduce TestFix to fix broken JUnit test cases by synthesizing new method calls. TestFix regards the assertion of a broken test as a constraint and relies on the information about changes between versions of the software to guide the search of method-call sequences that meet the constraint.

> In summary, the studies in *test regression* category largely address test obsolescence as the most known reason for test evolution, and introduce automatic test repair techniques that mostly focus on changing assertions and use assertion-based mechanisms.

Test Smells. Test smells, poorly designed tests, negatively affect the comprehensibility and the maintainability of the test code [7], and therefore, they have been investigated and considered in many studies, e.g., [20, 71]. Assertion Roulette (i.e., several assertions with no explanation within the same test method) is found as the most frequent and riskiest test smell [84]. RAID [65] provides automated detection of lines of code affected by test smells, namely Assertion Roulette and Duplicate Assert, and a semi-automated refactoring for Java projects using JUnit. Soares et al. [70] present a set of refactorings – exploiting specific features of JUnit 5 – that help to remove test smells. RTj [46] is a framework for detecting and refactoring rotten green test cases, i.e., tests that pass but contain assertions that are never executed, using static analysis and dynamic analysis. Vahabzadeh et al. [78] recognize incorrect and missing assertions as the dominant root cause of silent horror test bugs, i.e., those test that pass, while the production code is incorrect. Wei et al. [81] introduce an ML-based approach for labelling unit tests according to the AAA pattern (i.e., the

Arrangement, Action, and Assertion), as a best practice towards better code comprehension and less maintenance effort.

> In summary, the studies in the *test smells* category largely aim to prevent test quality degradation due to badly designed tests and hence, introduce techniques to automatically detect test smells, in particular assertion roulette.

Engineering Aspects. There are many studies that focus on, so-called, engineering aspects of using assertions in software development, including the impact of using assertions, comparison between different techniques or types of assertions, and good practices in using assertions. These studies consider assertions in a more general context in comparison to the aforementioned problems.

The application of assertions as test oracles is empirically investigated by Shrestha and Rutherford [68]. Li and Offutt [42] investigate the ability of test oracles (that vary in amount and frequency of program state checked) to reveal failures. The adequacy of assertions in test suite, particularly in the context of automated test generation has been investigated in several studies, e.g., [3, 67, 96]. Zhang and Mesbah [93] find a strong correlation between the number of assertions in a test suite with its effectiveness. The relation between developers' experience and assertion density is then investigated by Catolino et al. [11], showing that such experience is a significant factor in effective testing.

The effect of fluent assertions on comprehensibility of tests is investigated by Leotta et al. [41], demonstrating that adopting AssertJ (a fluent assertion library in JUnit) has no significant effect on the level of comprehension, though it significantly improves the efficiency in their comprehension. Ma'ayan [45] studied the quality of real world unit tests and reported that they don't follow the well-known good patterns (in particular using the right assertions) for writing tests.

> In summary, the studies of the *engineering aspects* category tend to empirically investigate the application of assertions in software development in order to provide rigorous evidence of the benefits developers gain by using assertions and/or discover the best practices in the context.

4.3 Solutions

In order to a have an expressive view over the proposals in our collection, the solution of each study is characterised by 1) the main *technique(s)* that specifies the essence of the proposal, 2) the target *domain/language* for that the solution is ultimately actualised and implemented (if applicable), and 3) the *tooling* support which could be either a prototype implementation or within an existing tool. Note that the studies considering the engineering aspects are excluded herein, since they inherently do not provide any particular solution, in the way it is investigated in this section, except very few of them. Also, the information was collected based on the papers as the only source of our survey, and is hence limited to what is explicitly provided.

Technique. By technique, the very core idea of the proposed solution is determined. While the technique(s) are (have to be) eventually implemented and hence, shaped within a context (e.g., language and domain) considering all of its restrictions and capabilities, herein we abstract from such details and tend to provide a high-level view of the techniques within limit. The main classes of techniques, identified throughout our survey, are summarised in this section.

Learning and evolutionary algorithms have been used in several studies, particularly among the ones on assertion generation. Pham et al. [33] use active learning techniques to generate assertions. A combination of evolutionary and learning based techniques have been applied in EvoSpex [52] to automatically generate specifications. GASSERT [74] applies a co-evolutionary algorithm that explores the space of possible assertions to improve test oracles. Valueian et al. [79] employ an Neural Network algorithm to construct automated test oracles for low observable software. A3Test [2] uses a pre-trained language model of assertions to generate assertions in test case generation process.

The application of *static analysis* is considered as a promising technique in the literature, in different context. Zeng et al. [92] automatically generate assertions based on program invariants. Pariente and Signoles [57] generate runtime assertions checks based on static detection of CWEs[1].

A number of studies *exploit test execution* in generating or improving test oracles. Xie [86] adds assertions based on the object states collected throughout previous test executions. Employing a search-based algorithm for improving assertions, Jahangirova [34] combine test case generation to reveal false positives and mutation testing to reveal false negatives. Test case execution logs are used in DS3 [49] to determine dependencies among test slices. Mutation analysis has been also used by Fraser and Zeller [28] to improve the fault detection capability of test oracles, by Knauth et al. [39] to assess the quality of the assertions, and by Xie et al. [87] for analyzing PUTs written by developers and identifying likely locations in PUTs for improvement.

In several studies, a *specific-purpose assertion* is introduced, that is typically defined on top of an existing assertion language/construct, through an extended syntax and semantics, and a novel assertion evaluation technique. Corduroy [54] introduces metamorphic assertions, built on top of Java Modelling Language (JML). Model assertions [36] adapt the classical use of program assertions, tailored to the specific needs of ML programs, in particular uncertainty in output.

Domain/Language. A wide range of domains and languages are considered by the collected papers, though with different density. In addition to solutions for general and typical programs, that are the target of many studies, the proposed solution in many studies are applicable to specific types of programs, e.g., Machine Learning programs [24,36], web/mobile applications [26], and GUI [85].

The solutions can also be characterised regarding the language for which the solution is introduced. While the most common language is Java (e.g., [33,

---

[1] Common Weakness Enumerations – https://cwe.mitre.org.

Table 1. Evaluation Methods vs. Assertion Problems

Problem	Evaluation Method			
	Limited	Many/Large	Benchmark	Empirical
Test Oracle	16	18	2	3
Test Generation	12	4	1	–
Specific Application	6	5	1	3
Test Regression	4	1	–	–
Test Smells	2	1	–	13
Engineering Aspects	3	1	1	17
Total	**43**	**30**	**5**	**36**

34, 52, 74, 86]), a variety of other general-/specific-purpose languages have been covered, including JavaScript/TypeScript [91], Go [47], and Pharo Smalltalk [1]. Other solutions (e.g., [49,79]) are not limited to a specific programming language and are applicable to programs in different languages. For example, Valueian et al. [79] demonstrate the application of their solution on programs in Java, C, C++, Verilog, and VHDL. There are also a number of studies that consider a higher level of abstraction and introduce their solutions for specific types of models, such as UML statecharts [23], Alloy models [37], Z Specification [43], WS-BPEL [72], and Machine Learning models [36].

Tool Support. Most of the solutions are embedded in and supported by *tool prototypes* that are typically available online. A number of studies use a chain of available tools to implement and demonstrate their solutions (e.g., [17,77]). One study [9] introduces its solution as part of a commercial tool (Agitator). Studies in the engineering aspects category and the empirical studies are exempted to have prototypes or any other implementation support and few papers (e.g., [60, 92]) have not explicitly mentioned how the solution is implemented.

4.4 Evaluation

Looking into how the proposals of the collected studies have been evaluated, we identified four main classes of the evaluation methods, namely *limited experiments, many/large experiments, benchmarks, and empirical & judgement,* that are described in the following. Note that most of the studies, excluding the ones looking into the engineering aspects, provide a proof of concept through developing a prototype of the tooling support for their proposed solutions, which is not considered herein as evaluation. There are few papers that do not present any evaluation which is however compatible to their types of study, such as short paper (e.g., [60]) or report on ongoing study (e.g., [87]). Table 1 summarises evaluation methods w.r.t. the assertion problems.

Limited Experiments. This type of evaluation provides preliminary and limited evidence of the application of the proposed techniques or tools, in that, for example, the effectiveness of the proposals and how the proposal meets its goal(s), is demonstrated throughout a limited number of case studies (e.g., up to 10 cases), e.g., [64,94], or by limited artificial experiments (e.g., by manually generating or adding required information [39,68]). In our collection of 119 papers, the evaluation of 43 studies fall into this category; the studies focusing on *test generation* and *test oracle/assertion generation* have the main portion among this group (28 studies in total).

Many/Large Experiments. Several studies provide more convincing evaluation results by assessing their solutions on many cases (e.g. > 10) or throughout one or more experiments in an industrial setting. Large, open-source or public projects or repositories, for example on GitHub, have been used in evaluation experiments (e.g., [12,33,86]), that is, mostly used in the studies that address *assertion generation*. Some of the studies use real systems/applications that are under operation to demonstrate the usefulness and/or the cost-effectiveness of their proposals, such as using an Aircraft e-Maintenance application [57].

Benchmarks. Few studies have used benchmarks to evaluate and demonstrate properties of their solutions. Different sets of benchmarks (e.g., regarding size, application, and domain) were used depending on the target and context of a study. Messaoudi et al. [49] use a proprietary benchmark of 30 complex system test cases to assess the effectiveness and efficiency of their solution in slicing system test cases. The quality of EvoSpex [52] was assessed on a benchmark of open source Java projects in SF110[2]. Alagarsamy et al. [2] use Defects4J repository to evaluate A3Test's performance. Ji et al. [35] firstly design the benchmark MCon4j and then use it to evaluate the effectiveness of their solutions.

Empirical & Judgement. Some of the studies investigate and demonstrate *empirical evidence* regarding a particular research question or of the use of a technique or tool in practice. They may use surveys or interview among a certain number of participants (e.g., [91]), or use more formal experimental methods (e.g., controlled experiment [41]). Most of the studies in this category, look into the *engineering aspects* of the use of assertions, that is however obvious considering their intention.

5   Discussion

This section summarizes the research findings following the same structure we used to review our collection of studies, and synthesise the results.

---

[2] https://www.evosuite.org/experimental-data/sf110/.

Assertion Problems. The dominant problem focus is the oracle problem. About 34% of the studies (41) address the substantial challenge of specifying the expected output or behaviour in tests using assertions. They largely investigate different types of information that can be used for generating or defining test oracle (assertions) and how to automate or augment the assertion generation process to improve effectiveness, efficiency, and practicality.

Engineering aspects is the second premier focus. About 20% of studies provide empirical evidence of the benefits to gain by using assertions and also point out challenges and obstacles in effective application of assertions in practice.

The third group of studies (about 15%) employ assertions to direct test generation tasks, such as generating test data. The use of assertions for specific applications, addressed in 16 studies, demonstrates that assertions are useful and could support specific problems more effectively. Among different specific domains, limited studies address uncertainty in outputs, which however, considering the emerging use of ML, require more research. The same of number of studies focus on poorly designed tests. Most of these studies investigate how test smells affect test quality, whereas few of them introduce techniques to detect and fix test smells. Finally, few studies address test regression due to program evolution which mostly introduce automatic test repair techniques.

Solutions. Most of the solutions are embedded in and supported by tool prototypes that are generally available online. About 85% of the studies excluding those considering the engineering aspects, since they inherently do not provide any particular solution.

As described in Sect. 4.3, many and various techniques have been previously introduced in the literature and therefore, they are not completely categorised. However, a number of techniques and ideas are more visible among others. Learning and evolutionary algorithms have been used as a promising technique in many recent studies (20 out of 119 papers), particularly among the ones focusing on test oracle and test generation. Nearly the same amount of papers suggest integrating static analysis and dynamic testing to improve the effectiveness of either testing and/or static program analysis. Defining a specific-purpose assertion language, including syntax, semantics, and possibly a new assertion checking method, is a common proposal among the studies, e.g., the studies addressing uncertainty in output.

While a wide range of domains and languages are considered in the collected papers, general software programs and C/C++ and Java programming languages are the target of the most of the studies (about 60%). While Java is a broadly used programming language, it is important for the assertions research to also take other languages into account. For example, in machine learning applications, Python is frequently used, which may be a specific target for assertions.

Evaluation. As demonstrated in Table 1, the largest set of studies have been evaluated throughout limited number of cases. The evaluation of 43 studies, out of 119 papers, fall into this category, where the studies focusing on test oracle and test generation have the main portion among this group (28 studies in total). Empirical and judgement is the next more common evaluation method, that is obviously used in the studies that focus on engineering aspects and also the studies on test smells. A quarter of the studies, largely on test oracle, evaluate their proposals using many experiments or within large–scale industrial cases. Benchmarks are used in five studies.

To ensure the relevance for practice, research has to go beyond small scale proofs of concept. Among the surveyed studies, one third are evaluated in more realistic cases, which is promising. However, for future research, we would like to see even more focus on the scaling and relevance aspects.

6   Limitations

The main issues related to threats to validity of this survey are incomplete set of studies in our collection and imprecise data extraction that are fundamentally because of the researcher bias in choosing search terms, the search engine, and the targeted databases, as well as, the exclusion/inclusion criteria. A very basic method to address these issues is to conduct a survey in a structured way; we accordingly carried out a semi-systematic review throughout four major steps, which were iterated in several cycles and carefully defined and reported.

To reduce the risk of incomplete set of primary sources, Google Scholar was used with a general search query which would render a large amount of studies, including grey literature, as the initial pool. To minimise researchers' bias, the second author took a validation role and double checked the work done by the first author. Design science paradigm was used as a lens for this survey, that was motivated by earlier research concluding that this frame is feasible for software engineering research. In order to ensure conclusion validity, the classification and synthesis were performed repeatedly, and the outcome of each turn was discussed between the authors to avoid any misunderstanding.

7   Conclusion

In this survey, we provide an overall picture of research work on assertions in software testing, within the last two decades of research. Using a term–based search, a collection of relevant papers was selected and then the papers were reviewed and synthesised with respect to the design science elements, namely the problem addressed, the solution proposed, and the evaluation method. The synthesis demonstrated that test oracle is the dominant problem focus, followed by engineering aspects of assertions and assertions in test generation. Solutions include a wide range of techniques and are typically embedded in tool proto-types. They are mostly consider general applications and languages, e.g., Java. This however, suggest to consider other languages that are getting attention more recently (e.g., Python). The proposals are by large evaluated within a lim-ited number of cases while using large–scale industrial settings is also visible. Nevertheless, in order to support practice, research has to go beyond small scale experiments since scaling up analyses to large code bases is an essential challenge. We conclude that assertions would be worth more attention in future research, particularly regarding the new and emerging demands (e.g., wide-spread applications of software, verification of applications with uncertain outputs), for effective, applicable, and domain-specific solutions, as well as more focus on the scaling and relevance aspects.

Acknowledgements. This work is funded by the ELLIIT strategic research area (https://elliit.se), project 'A19 – Software Regression Testing with Near Failure Assertions'.

References

1. Abdi, M., Rocha, H., Demeyer, S., Bergel, A.: Small-Amp: test amplification in a dynamically typed language. Empir. Softw. Eng. **27**(6), 128 (2022). https://doi.org/10.1007/s10664-022-10169-8

2. Alagarsamy, S., Tantithamthavorn, C., Aleti, A.: A3Test: assertion-augmented automated test case generation (2023). https://doi.org/10.48550/ARXIV.2302.10352

3. Almasi, M.M., Hemmati, H., Fraser, G., Arcuri, A., Benefelds, J.: An industrial evaluation of unit test generation: finding real faults in a financial application. In: IEEE/ACM International Conference on Software Engineering: Software Engineering in Practice Track, pp. 263–272 (2017). https://doi.org/10.1109/ICSE-SEIP.2017.27

4. Anand, S., et al.: An orchestrated survey of methodologies for automated software test case generation. J. Syst. Softw. **86**(8), 1978–2001 (2013). https://doi.org/10.1016/j.jss.2013.02.061

5. Araujo, W., Briand, L., Labiche, Y.: On the effectiveness of contracts as test oracles in the detection and diagnosis of race conditions and deadlocks in concurrent object-oriented software. In: International Symposium on Empirical Software Engineering and Measurement, pp. 10–19 (2011). https://doi.org/10.1109/ESEM.2011.9

6. Barr, E.T., Harman, M., McMinn, P., Shahbaz, M., Yoo, S.: The oracle problem in software testing: a survey. IEEE Trans. Softw. Eng. **41**(5), 507–525 (2015). https://doi.org/10.1109/TSE.2014.2372785

7. Bavota, G., Qusef, A., Oliveto, R., De Lucia, A., Binkley, D.: Are test smells really harmful? an empirical study. Empir. Softw. Eng. **20**(4), 1052–1094 (2015). https://doi.org/10.1007/s10664-014-9313-0

8. Blasi, A., Gorla, A., Ernst, M.D., Pezzè, M., Carzaniga, A.: MeMo: automatically identifying metamorphic relations in javadoc comments for test automation. J. Sys. Softw. **181** (2021). https://doi.org/10.1016/j.jss.2021.111041

9. Boshernitsan, M., Doong, R., Savoia, A.: From daikon to agitator: lessons and challenges in building a commercial tool for developer testing. In: ACM International Symposium on Software Testing and Analysis, pp. 169–180. ISSTA '06, ACM (2006). https://doi.org/10.1145/1146238.1146258

10. Boyapati, C., Khurshid, S., Marinov, D.: Korat: automated testing based on java predicates. ACM SIGSOFT Softw. Eng. Notes **27**(4), 123–133 (2002). https://doi.org/10.1145/566171.566191

11. Catolino, G., Palomba, F., Zaidman, A., Ferrucci, F.: How the experience of development teams relates to assertion density of test classes. In: IEEE International Conference on Software Maintenance and Evolution, pp. 223–234 (2019). https://doi.org/10.1109/ICSME.2019.00034, ISSN: 2576-3148

12. Chen, J., Bai, Y., Hao, D., Zhang, L., Zhang, L., Xie, B.: How do assertions impact coverage-based test-suite reduction? In: IEEE International Conference on Software Testing, Verification and Validation, pp. 418–423 (2017). https://doi.org/10. 1109/ICST.2017.45

13. Cheon, Y., Kim, M., Perumandla, A.: A complete automation of unit testing for java programs. Tech. Rep. UTEP-CS-05-05, University of Texas at El Paso (2005). https://scholarworks.utep.edu/cs_techrep/234

14. Cheon, Y., Leavens, G.T.: A simple and practical approach to unit testing: the JML and JUnit way. In: Magnusson, B. (ed.) ECOOP 2002. LNCS, vol. 2374, pp. 231–255. Springer, Heidelberg (2002). https://doi.org/10.1007/3-540-47993-7_10

15. Choudhary, S.R., Zhao, D., Versee, H., Orso, A.: WATER: web application TEst repair. In: ACM International Workshop on End-to-End Test Script Engineering, pp. 24–29. ETSE '11, ACM (2011). https://doi.org/10.1145/2002931.2002935

16. Clarke, L.A., Rosenblum, D.S.: A historical perspective on runtime assertion checking in software development. ACM SIGSOFT Softw. Eng. Notes 31(3), 25–37 (2006). https://doi.org/10.1145/1127878.1127900

17. Coppit, D., Haddox-Schatz, J.: On the use of specification-based assertions as test oracles. In: IEEE/NASA Software Engineering Workshop, pp. 305–314 (2005). https://doi.org/10.1109/SEW.2005.33, ISSN: 1550-6215

18. Danglot, B., Vera-Perez, O., Baudry, B., Monperrus, M.: Automatic test improvement with DSpot: a study with ten mature open-source projects. Empir. Softw. Eng. 24(4), 2603–2635 (2019). https://doi.org/10.1007/s10664-019-09692-y

19. Daniel, B., Gvero, T., Marinov, D.: On test repair using symbolic execution. In: ACM International Symposium on Software Testing and Analysis, pp. 207–218. ISSTA '10, ACM (2010). https://doi.org/10.1145/1831708.1831734

20. De Stefano, M., Pecorelli, F., Di Nucci, D., De Lucia, A.: A preliminary evaluation on the relationship among architectural and test smells. In: IEEE International Working Conference on Source Code Analysis and Manipulation, pp. 66–70 (2022). https://doi.org/10.1109/SCAM55253.2022.00013, ISSN: 2470-6892

21. Delamare, R., Baudry, B., Ghosh, S., Le Traon, Y.: A test-driven approach to developing pointcut descriptors in AspectJ. In: IEEE International Conference on Software Testing Verification and Validation. IEEE Computing Society. (2009). https://doi.org/10.1109/ICST.2009.41

22. Dinella, E., Ryan, G., Mytkowicz, T., Lahiri, S.K.: TOGA: a neural method for test oracle generation. In: IEEE/ACM International Conference on Software Engineering, pp. 2130–2141. ACM (2022). https://doi.org/10.1145/3510003.3510141

23. Drusinsky, D., Shing, M.T., Demir, K.: Creation and validation of embedded assertion statecharts. In: IEEE International Workshop on Rapid System Prototyping, pp. 17–23 (2006). https://doi.org/10.1109/RSP.2006.12, ISSN: 1074-6005

24. Dutta, S., Shi, A., Misailovic, S.: FLEX: fixing flaky tests in machine learning projects by updating assertion bounds. In: ACM Joint Meeting on European Software Engineering Conf. and Symposium on the Foundations of Software Engineering, pp. 603–614. ESEC/FSE 2021, ACM (2021). https://doi.org/10.1145/3468264. 3468615

25. Engström, E., Storey, M., Runeson, P., Höst, M., Baldassarre, M.T.: How software engineering research aligns with design science: a review. Empir. Softw. Eng. 25, 2630–2660 (2020). https://doi.org/10.1007/s10664-020-09818-7

26. Franke, D., Kowalewski, S., Weise, C., Prakobkosol, N.: Testing conformance of life cycle dependent properties of mobile applications. In: IEEE International Conference on Software Testing, Verification and Validation, pp. 241–250 (2012). https:// doi.org/10.1109/ICST.2012.104, ISSN: 2159-4848

27. Fraser, G., Arcuri, A.: EvoSuite: automatic test suite generation for object-oriented software. In: ACM SIGSOFT Symposium and European Conference on Foundations of Software Engineering, pp. 416–419. ESEC/FSE '11, ACM (2011). https://doi.org/10.1145/2025113.2025179

28. Fraser, G., Zeller, A.: Mutation-driven generation of unit tests and oracles. IEEE Trans. Softw. Eng. **38**(2), 278–292 (2012). https://doi.org/10.1109/TSE.2011.93

29. Garousi, V., Amannejad, Y., Betin Can, A.: Software test-code engineering: a systematic mapping. Inf. Softw. Technol. **58**, 123–147 (2015). https://doi.org/10.1016/j.infsof.2014.06.009

30. Garousi, V., Felderer, M., Kılıçaslan, F.N.: A survey on software testability. Inf. Softw. Technol. **108**, 35–64 (2019). https://doi.org/10.1016/j.infsof.2018.12.003

31. Garousi, V., Felderer, M., Mäntylä, M.V.: Guidelines for including grey literature and conducting multivocal literature reviews in software engineering. Inf. Softw. Technol. **106**, 101–121 (2019). https://doi.org/10.1016/j.infsof.2018.09.006

32. Garousi, V., Mäntylä, M.V.: A systematic literature review of literature reviews in software testing. Inf. Softw. Technol. **80**, 195–216 (2016). https://doi.org/10.1016/j.infsof.2016.09.002

33. Pham, L.H., Tran Thi, L.L., Sun, J.: Assertion generation through active learning. In: Duan, Z., Ong, L. (eds.) Formal Methods and Software Engineering, pp. 174–191. LNCS, Springer, Cham (2017). https://doi.org/10.1007/978-3-319-68690-5_11

34. Jahangirova, G., Clark, D., Harman, M., Tonella, P.: OASIs: oracle assessment and improvement tool. In: ACM SIGSOFT International Symposium on Software Testing and Analysis. ISSTA 2018, ACM, New York, NY, USA (2018). https://doi.org/10.1145/3213846.3229503

35. Ji, T., Chen, L., Mao, X., Yi, X., Jiang, J.: Automated regression unit test generation for program merges (2020). http://arxiv.org/abs/2003.00154

36. Kang, D., Raghavan, D., Bailis, P., Zaharia, M.: Model assertions for monitoring and improving ML models (2020). http://arxiv.org/abs/2003.01668

37. Khurshid, S., Marinov, D.: TestEra: specification-based testing of Java programs using SAT. Autom. Softw. Eng. **11**(4), 403–434 (2004). https://doi.org/10.1023/B:AUSE.0000038938.10589.b9

38. Kitchenham, B.A., Budgen, D., Brereton, O.P.: Using mapping studies as the basis for further research – a participant-observer case study. Inf. Softw. Technol. **53**(6), 638–651 (2011). https://doi.org/10.1016/j.infsof.2010.12.011

39. Knauth, T., Fetzer, C., Felber, P.: Assertion-driven development: assessing the quality of contracts using meta-mutations. In: IEEE International Conference on Software Testing, Verification, and Validation Workshops, pp. 182–191 (2009). https://doi.org/10.1109/ICSTW.2009.40

40. Koesnandar, A., Elbaum, S., Rothermel, G., Hochstein, L., Scaffidi, C., Stolee, K.T.: Using assertions to help end-user programmers create dependable web macros. In: ACM SIGSOFT International Symposium on Foundations of Software Engineering, pp. 124–134. SIGSOFT '08/FSE-16, ACM (2008). https://doi.org/10.1145/1453101.1453119

41. Leotta, M., Cerioli, M., Olianas, D., Ricca, F.: Fluent vs basic assertions in Java: an empirical study. In: International Conference on the Quality of Information and Communications Technology (QUATIC), pp. 184–192 (2018). https://doi.org/10.1109/QUATIC.2018.00036

42. Li, N., Offutt, J.: Test oracle strategies for model-based testing. IEEE Trans. Softw. Eng. **43**(4), 372–395 (2017). https://doi.org/10.1109/TSE.2016.2597136

43. Li, P., Sun, J., Wang, H.: Formal approach to assertion-based code generation. Int. J. Softw. Eng. Knowl. Eng. **27**(9), 1637–1662 (2017). https://doi.org/10.1142/S0218194017400162, publisher: World Scientific Publishing Co

44. Loyola, P., Staats, M., Ko, I., Rothermel, G.: Dodona: automated oracle data set selection. In: ACM International Symposium on Software Testing and Analysis, pp. 193–203. ISSTA 2014, ACM (2014). https://doi.org/10.1145/2610384.2610408

45. Ma'ayan, D.D.: The quality of Junit tests: an empirical study report. In: IEEE/ACM 1st International Workshop on Software Qualities and their Dependencies, pp. 33–36 (2018)

46. Martinez, M., Etien, A., Ducasse, S., Fuhrman, C.: RTj: a java framework for detecting and refactoring rotten green test cases. In: IEEE/ACM International Conference on Software Engineering: ICSE-Companion, pp. 69–72 (2020). publisher: ACM

47. Mayer, E.C.: Assertion-based testing of go programs. Master thesis, Technical University Munich (2020)

48. Mesbah, A., van Deursen, A., Roest, D.: Invariant-based automatic testing of modern web applications. IEEE Trans. Softw. Eng. **38**(1), 35–53 (2012). https://doi.org/10.1109/TSE.2011.28

49. Messaoudi, S., Shin, D., Panichella, A., Bianculli, D., Briand, L.C.: Log-based slicing for system-level test cases. In: Cadar, C., Zhang, X. (eds.) ACM SIGSOFT International Symposium on Software Testing and Analysis, pp. 517–528. ACM (2021). https://doi.org/10.1145/3460319.3464824

50. Milani Fard, A., Mirzaaghaei, M., Mesbah, A.: Leveraging existing tests in automated test generation for web applications. In: ACM/IEEE International Conference on Automated Software Engineering, pp. 67–78. ASE '14, ACM (2014). https://doi.org/10.1145/2642937.2642991

51. Mirshokraie, S., Mesbah, A., Pattabiraman, K.: Atrina: inferring unit oracles from GUI test cases. In: IEEE International Conference on Software Testing, Verification and Validation (ICST). IEEE Computer Society (2016). https://doi.org/10.1109/ICST.2016.32

52. Molina, F., Ponzio, P., Aguirre, N., Frias, M.: EvoSpex: an evolutionary algorithm for learning postconditions (artifact). In: IEEE/ACM International Conference on Software Engineering: ICSE-Companion, pp. 185–186 (2021). https://doi.org/10.1109/ICSE-Companion52605.2021.00080, iSSN: 2574-1926

53. Moonen, L., van Deursen, A., Zaidman, A., Bruntink, M.: On the interplay between software testing and evolution and its effect on program comprehension. In: Software Evolution, pp. 173–202. Springer, Heidelberg (2008). https://doi.org/10.1007/978-3-540-76440-3_8

54. Murphy, C., Shen, K., Kaiser, G.: Using JML runtime assertion checking to automate metamorphic testing in applications without test oracles. In: IEEE International Conference on Software Testing Verification and Validation, pp. 436–445 (2009). https://doi.org/10.1109/ICST.2009.19, ISSN: 2159-4848

55. Oliveira, R.A.P., Kanewala, U., Nardi, P.A.: Chapter three - automated test oracles: state of the art, taxonomies, and trends. In: Memon, A. (ed.) Advances in Computers, vol. 95, pp. 113–199. Elsevier (2014). https://doi.org/10.1016/B978-0-12-800160-8.00003-6

56. Oriat, C.: Jartege: a tool for random generation of unit tests for Java classes. In: Reussner, R., Mayer, J., Stafford, J.A., Overhage, S., Becker, S., Schroeder, P.J. (eds.) QoSA/SOQUA -2005. LNCS, vol. 3712, pp. 242–256. Springer, Heidelberg (2005). https://doi.org/10.1007/11558569_18

57. Pariente, D., Signoles, J.: Static analysis and runtime-assertion checking: contribution to security counter-measures (2017). https://zenodo.org/record/820856

58. Pastore, F., Mariani, L., Fraser, G.: CrowdOracles: can the crowd solve the oracle problem? In: IEEE International Conference on Software Testing, Verification and Validation, pp. 342–351 (2013). https://doi.org/10.1109/ICST.2013.13, publisher: IEEE

59. Patel, K., Hierons, R.M.: A mapping study on testing non-testable systems. Softw. Qual. J. **26**(4), 1373–1413 (2018). https://doi.org/10.1007/s11219-017-9392-4

60. Petke, J., Blot, A.: Refining fitness functions in test-based program repair. In: IEEE/ACM International Conference on Software Engineering Workshops, pp. 13–14. ICSEW'20, ACM (2020). https://doi.org/10.1145/3387940.3392180

61. Pezzè, M., Zhang, C.: Chapter one - automated test oracles: a survey. In: Memon, A. (ed.) Advances in Computers, vol. 95, pp. 1–48. Elsevier (2014). https://doi.org/10.1016/B978-0-12-800160-8.00001-2

62. Rajan, A., du Bousquet, L., Ledru, Y., Vega, G., Richier, J.L.: Assertion-based test oracles for home automation systems. In: ACM Int. Workshop on Model-Based Methodologies for Pervasive and Embedded Software, pp. 45–52. MOMPES '10, ACM (2010). https://doi.org/10.1145/1865875.1865882

63. Sakakibara, M., Sakurai, K., Komiya, S.: An assertion mechanism for software unit testing to remain unaffected by program modification - the mechanism to eliminate dependency from/to unnecessary object. Knowl.-Based Softw. Eng., pp. 125–134 (2008). https://doi.org/10.3233/978-1-58603-900-4-125

64. Salehi Fathabadi, A., Dalvandi, M., Butler, M., Al-Hashimi, B.M.: Verifying cross-layer interactions through formal model-based assertion generation. IEEE Embed. Syst. Lett. **12**(3), 83–86 (2020). https://doi.org/10.1109/LES.2019.2955316

65. Santana, R., et al.: RAIDE: a tool for assertion roulette and duplicate assert identification and refactoring. In: Brazilian Symposium on Software Engineering, pp. 374–379. SBES '20, ACM (2020). https://doi.org/10.1145/3422392.3422510

66. Sequeira, S.: Understanding web application test assertion failures. Ph.D. thesis, University of British Columbia (2014). https://doi.org/10.14288/1.0167024

67. Shamshiri, S., Just, R., Rojas, J.M., Fraser, G., McMinn, P., Arcuri, A.: Do automatically generated unit tests find real faults? an empirical study of effectiveness and challenges (t). In: IEEE/ACM International Conference on Automated Software Engineering, pp. 201–211 (2015). https://doi.org/10.1109/ASE.2015.86

68. Shrestha, K., Rutherford, M.J.: An empirical evaluation of assertions as oracles. In: IEEE International Conference on Software Testing, Verification and Validation, pp. 110–119 (2011). https://doi.org/10.1109/ICST.2011.50, ISSN: 2159-4848

69. Snyder, H.: Literature review as a research methodology: an overview and guidelines. J. Bus. Res. **104**, 333–339 (2019). https://doi.org/10.1016/j.jbusres.2019.07.039

70. Soares, E., Ribeiro, M., Gheyi, R., Amaral, G., Santos, A.: Refactoring test smells with JUnit 5: why should developers keep up-to-date? IEEE Trans. Softw. Eng. **49**(3), 1152–1170 (2023). https://doi.org/10.1109/TSE.2022.3172654

71. Spadini, D., Palomba, F., Zaidman, A., Bruntink, M., Bacchelli, A.: On the relation of test smells to software code quality. In: IEEE Intetnational Conference on Software Maintenance and Evolution, pp. 1–12 (2018). https://doi.org/10.1109/ICSME.2018.00010, ISSN: 2576-3148

72. Stoyanova, V., Petrova-Antonova, D., Ilieva, S.: Automation of test case generation and execution for testing web service orchestrations. In: IEEE International Symposium on Service-Oriented System Engineering, pp. 274–279 (2013). https://doi.org/10.1109/SOSE.2013.9

73. Søndergaard, H., Korsholm, S., Ravn, A.: Conformance test development with the Java modeling language. Concurr. Comput.: Pract. Exper. **29**(22), 32 (2017). https://doi.org/10.1002/cpe.4071

74. Terragni, V., Jahangirova, G., Tonella, P., Pezzè, M.: GAssert: a fully automated tool to improve assertion oracles. In: IEEE/ACM International Conference on Software Engineering: Companion Proceedings (ICSE-Companion), pp. 85–88 (2021). https://doi.org/10.1109/ICSE-Companion52605.2021.00042, iSSN: 2574-1926

75. Tiryaki, A.M., Öztuna, S., Dikenelli, O., Erdur, R.C.: SUNIT: a unit testing framework for test driven development of multi-agent systems. In: Padgham, L., Zambonelli, F. (eds.) AOSE 2006. LNCS, vol. 4405, pp. 156–173. Springer, Heidelberg (2007). https://doi.org/10.1007/978-3-540-70945-9_10

76. Tsung-Hsiang, C., Yeh, T., Miller, R.C.: GUI testing using computer vision. In: SIGCHI Conference on Human Factors in Computing Systems, pp. 1535–1544. ACM (2010). https://doi.org/10.1145/1753326.1753555

77. Tufano, M., Drain, D., Svyatkovskiy, A., Sundaresan, N.: Generating accurate assert statements for unit test cases using pretrained transformers. In: ACM/IEEE International Conference on Automation of Software Test, pp. 54–64. AST '22, ACM (2022). https://doi.org/10.1145/3524481.3527220

78. Vahabzadeh, A., Milani Fard, A., Mesbah, A.: An empirical study of bugs in test code. In: IEEE International Conference on Software Maintenance and Evolution, pp. 101–110 (2015). https://doi.org/10.1109/ICSM.2015.7332456

79. Valueian, M., Attar, N., Haghighi, H., Vahidi-Asl, M.: Constructing automated test oracle for low observable software. Scientia Iranica **27**(3), 1333–1351 (2020). https://doi.org/10.24200/sci.2019.51494.2219

80. Watson, C., Tufano, M., Moran, K., Bavota, G., Poshyvanyk, D.: On learning meaningful assert statements for unit test cases. In: ACM/IEEE International Conference on Software Engineering, pp. 1398–1409. ICSE '20, ACM (2020). https://doi.org/10.1145/3377811.3380429

81. Wei, C., Xiao, L., Yu, T., Chen, X., Wang, X., Wong, S., Clune, A.: Automatically tagging the "AAA" pattern in unit test cases using machine learning models. In: IEEE/ACM International Conference on Automated Software Engineering, pp. 1–3. ASE '22, ACM (2023). https://doi.org/10.1145/3551349.3559510

82. Weyuker, E.J.: On testing non-testable programs. Comput. J. **25**(4), 465–470 (1982). https://doi.org/10.1093/comjnl/25.4.465

83. Winkler, D., Urbanke, P., Ramler, R.: What do we know about readability of test code? - a systematic mapping study. In: IEEE International Conference on Software Analysis, Evolution and Reengineering (SANER), pp. 1167–1174 (2022). https://doi.org/10.1109/SANER53432.2022.00135, ISSN: 1534-5351

84. Wu, H., Yin, R., Gao, J., Huang, Z., Huang, H.: To what extent can code quality be improved by eliminating test smells? In: International Conference on Code Quality, pp. 19–26 (2022). https://doi.org/10.1109/ICCQ53703.2022.9763153

85. Xie, Q., Memon, A.M.: Designing and comparing automated test oracles for GUI-based software applications. ACM Trans. Softw. Eng. Methodol. **16**(1), 4-es (2007). https://doi.org/10.1145/1189748.1189752

86. Xie, T.: Augmenting automatically generated unit-test suites with regression oracle checking. In: Thomas, D. (ed.) ECOOP - Object-Oriented Programming, pp. 380–403. LNCS, Springer, Berlin, Heidelberg (2006). https://doi.org/10.1007/11785477_23

87. Xie, T., Tillmann, N., de Halleux, J., Schulte, W.: Mutation analysis of parameterized unit tests. In: IEEE International Conference on Software Testing, Verification,

and Validation Workshops, pp. 177–181 (2009). https://doi.org/10.1109/ICSTW.2009.43

88. Xuan, J., Monperrus, M.: Test case purification for improving fault localization. In: ACM/SIGSOFT International Symposium on Foundations of Software Engineering, pp. 52–63. ACM (2014). https://doi.org/10.1145/2635868.2635906

89. Xu, Y., Huang, B., Wu, G., Yuan, M.: Using genetic algorithms to repair JUnit test cases. In: Asia-Pacific Software Engineering Conference, vol. 1. IEEE Computer Society (2014). https://doi.org/10.1109/APSEC.2014.51

90. Yu, H., et al.: Automated assertion generation via information retrieval and its integration with deep learning. In: IEEE/ACM International Conference on Software Engineering, pp. 163–174 (2022). https://doi.org/10.1145/3510003.3510149, publisher: ACM

91. Zamprogno, L., Hall, B., Holmes, R., Atlee, J.M.: Dynamic human-in-the-loop assertion generation. IEEE Trans. Softw. Eng. **49**(4), 2337–2351 (2023). https://doi.org/10.1109/TSE.2022.3217544

92. Zeng, F., Deng, C., Yuan, Y.: Assertion-directed test case generation. In: World Congress on Software Engineering, pp. 41–45 (2012). https://doi.org/10.1109/WCSE.2012.16

93. Zhang, Y., Mesbah, A.: Assertions are strongly correlated with test suite effectiveness. In: ACM Joint Meeting on Foundations of Software Engineering, pp. 214–224. ESEC/FSE 2015, ACM (2015). https://doi.org/10.1145/2786805.2786858

94. Zhao, J., Harris, I.G.: Automatic assertion generation from natural language specifications using subtree analysis. In: Design, Automation Test in Europe Conference Exhibition (DATE), pp. 598–601 (2019). https://doi.org/10.23919/DATE.2019.8714857, iSSN: 1558–1101

95. Zheng, F., Lam, P.: Identifying test refactoring candidates with assertion fingerprints. In: ACM Principles and Practices of Programming on The Java Platform, pp. 125–137. PPPJ '15, ACM (2015). https://doi.org/10.1145/2807426.2807437

96. Zhi, J., Garousi, V.: On adequacy of assertions in automated test suites: an empirical investigation. In: IEEE International Conference on Software Testing, Verification and Validation Workshops. pp. 382–391 (2013). https://doi.org/10.1109/ICSTW.2013.49

FPGA-Based Encryption for Peer-to-Peer Industrial Network Links

Florian Sprang and Tiberiu Seceleanu[✉]

Mälardalen University, Västerås, Sweden
{Florian.Sprang,Tiberiu.Seceleanu}@mdu.se

Abstract. Securing company networks has become a critical aspect of modern industrial environments. With the recent rise of Industry 4.0 concepts, it became essential to extend IT security across increasingly connected factories. However, in the highly specialised field of operations technology and embedded systems, not every device can run additional security measures, as they are old or designed with sparse resources. We introduce here the concept of a "universal" encryption device that enables the securing of communication links in a direct peer-to-peer industrial setting by using the AES-128 encryption standard. We propose a design of such an encryption device by developing a modular system architecture with decoupled communication and cryptography. The resulting architecture is implemented as a proof of concept for Ethernet communication and tested through simulation as well as on an FPGA device. The impact of the encryption device is briefly investigated in a lab setup, followed by conclusions on system stability and performance.

Keywords: AES-128 · FPGA · encryption · industrial communication

1 Introduction

Cryptography has always been embedded into society. Encryption also brought along the first efforts to gain access to data, leading to approaches to forcefully decrypt messages and gain an advantage over the "adversary". In parallel with the development of newer technologies, more potent ciphers were developed.

In modern manufacturing environments, embedded devices are often used to control, monitor and supervise industrial processes. These enabled factories to become connected, enabling machines to be remotely controlled or monitored. Industrial processes no longer have to be supervised at the machine itself, instead this can be done from anywhere in the world. The current *Industry 4.0* concepts yield many benefits for companies, such as predictive maintenance or increased throughput. Yet from an economic standpoint, it is inefficient to rebuild and redesign all factories from ground up, due to a mix of technologies in production lines, with old control units and machines being connected to the modern manufacturing network. Legacy devices are notoriously known to have security vulnerabilities and thus being a weak point in many systems [12,17].

Modern industrial cyber security standards such as *IEC-62443* or *ISO-27001* call for different measures to protect those devices. One of them is to deploy encryption

© The Author(s), under exclusive license to Springer Nature Switzerland AG 2024
J. Kofroň et al. (Eds.): ECBS 2023, LNCS 14390, pp. 97–114, 2024.
https://doi.org/10.1007/978-3-031-49252-5_9

on important network links. However, these requirements cannot be met by all components, especially when it comes to protocols or legacy devices. The latter might lack the computing capabilities to incorporate new requirements, leaving security vulnerabilities opened to possible attack vectors [17].

This work investigates how communication of legacy devices can be secured in order to fulfill cryptography requirements of standards. We propose to add a signal encryption device, by deploying a field prgrammable gate array (FPGA) integrated circuit (IC), on a connection link, to provide the encryption/decryption of the respective data.

We address the feasibility of a generic approach to secure communication by applying cryptography shortly after the physical network layer. This idea's application is briefly considered for a small part of the Ethernet (IEEE 802.3) [10] standards family. To reach our goal, two ICs are introduced in front of each SCADA[1] device and are responsible for the encryption and decryption of the data link. Figure 1 depicts a high level of the proposed architecture, with each IC holding the key for data encryption and decryption.

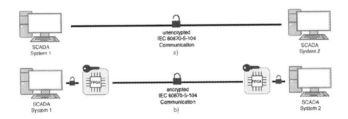

Fig. 1. High level representation of the proposed system architecture

2   Background

The ISO/OSI Model. The official ISO OSI specifications (1994), mostly known as ISO/OSI model - Fig. 2, describe how connections between two or more systems are handled. Typically, this model is used as a representation of internet connections, but it is a good generic representation of how connections work and it can be adapted to various kinds of transmission standards.

Encryption and decryption in the OSI model are handled at higher layers. Custom encryption can be implemented in layers 6 or 7, or existing protocols such as HTTPS or SFTP can be used at the session layer. Layer 3 can also introduce encryption in the IPsec context if communication is handled through standard internet protocols and both endpoints support IPsec. The model can be adapted. This often means layers are left out or combined for simpler transmission protocols, possibly removing capabilities of high-level encryption [2].

---

[1] Supervisory Control And Data Acquisition.

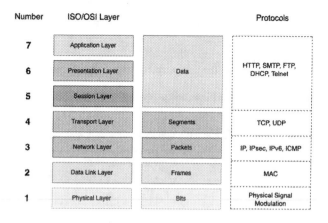

Fig. 2. ISO/OSI Model with associated protocols.

A digital signal between two compatible devices can be transmitted over an unshielded twisted pair (UTP) Ethernet cable, part of the physical layer. The modulation of the signal is handled by the so-called Ethernet Physical Layer (PHY) Chip. It is responsible for demodulating and modulating the signal and builds the bridge between the external electrical signal and a digital circuit. The PHY is further responsible for negotiating the link speed between two Ethernet devices and handling link establishment.

The media access control (MAC) controls the communication, defining the Ethernet frame: *header* - includes the destination and the sending MAC-address and the Ether Type, which either defines the size of the payload or the next layer protocol; *payload* - data; *checksum* - verifies the sent data integrity [1].

Figure 3 displays a model of a cryptosystem. The sender uses an encryption key to turn his original message/plaintext into an encrypted cipher text. A 3rd party that intercepts or copies the message can read the cipher text but cannot infer the original message, as it does not know the decryption key and the algorithm. The receiver knows those two components and can decipher the encrypted message.

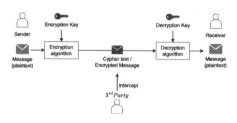

Fig. 3. Model of a cryptosystem

The advanced encryption standard (AES) [15] is a block cypher algorithm following the *symmetric encryption* approach. This means that it takes n-bits, forms them into a block, and encrypts them together. AES uses varying amounts of key lengths, most common being 128bit, 192bit or 256bit, with respective naming conventions of AES-128, AES-192, or AES-256. The algorithm can be divided into five steps (Fig. 4), to be applied multiple times based on the length of the keys: 10 iterations for AES-128, 12 for AES-192, and 14 for AES-256.

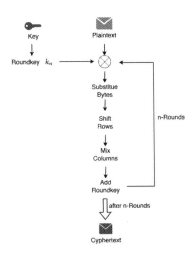

Fig. 4. Steps of the AES-Encryption Algorithm

After arranging the plaintext into the matrix format, a key is determined. The initial key serving as the pre-shared secret is created based on a true random generator that outputs a key in the desired length based on the algorithm. For each round, a different key is created by deriving it from the original pre-shared secret, with a technique called *key expansion*. Depending on the amount of performed rounds, n+1 keys with a length

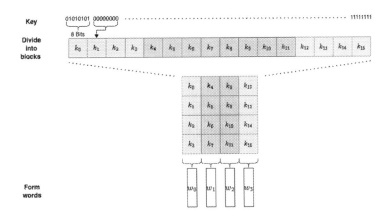

Fig. 5. Key-expansion: original key split into words.

of 128bit are needed. With each key containing four words, a total of $4 * (n + 1)$ words are needed [13] - Fig. 5.

3 Related Work

Currently, the problem of connecting old devices to the existing production network is ideally solved by deploying a firewall to protect them from malicious traffic. Two firewalls can be configured in a way that resembles the original problem solution: creating an encrypted site-to-site VPN, for sending the SCADA traffic. This works by taking the original protocol and packaging it into a standard TCP/IP package, encrypting it and sending it to the receiver. This task can be performed by small devices, such as a Raspberry Pi. Both firewall and VPN tunneling devices need to understand the original protocol [6]. This shows that securing industrial network connections and links is possible with lower-cost devices, yet encryption is applied on a higher layer. For Layer 2, encryption firewalls are necessary, coming with a premium in cost. Both solutions need to be maintained, patched, and licensed, bringing in additional costs.

Xue et al. are proposing a FPGA combined with a two-core ARM processor solution. Aiming to achieve a throughput of 1 GBit/s, a maximum of 700 Mbit/s was measured. The final design includes an additional chip that acts as a networking card accessing the Ethernet signal [18]. Ideally, the prototype that we propose here would not transfer the Ethernet frames back to a CPU, but only re-creates the digital signal in such a way that it is processable by the FPGA.

The approach of combining an FPGA with an Ethernet controller chip, such as the WIZnet W5500, is often used in designing Ethernet solutions for FPGA [5,16]. Such a design is proposed by Herrmann et al., focusing on UDP traffic [8]. It shows that Gigabit-Ethernet speeds can be achieved, by including RAM on both the transmitter and receiving side to buffer packets. The overall architecture and inclusion of the buffer RAM are relevant to us here. It would solve problems related to AES cypher rotation, as well as to clocking.

There is a relatively rich body of results on implementing AES on FPGAs. Naidu et al. are implementing FPGA by applying a fully pipelined architecture. They find a speed advantage over normal sequential encryption and further concluded that using low energy registers can also yield a lower power consumption [3]. This pipelining approach could be applied by us, as it allows the possibility to encrypt multiple (2) data lines at the same time.

Trang et al. [9] limited their approach to 128-bit length and focused on a low latency design, which was shown to depend on the used FPGA chip. Their longest encryption or decryption duration was done within 25 clock cycles, achieving an overall encryption throughput of 1GBit/s and 615 Mbit/s for decryption. The throughput related research is interesting, as it shows that lower-speed Ethernet standards 10Base-T, and 100Base-T are theoretically not limited by the encryption, resulting in no loss of network speed. Unfortunately, they do not provide any insights on the maximum usable clocking frequency.

Harb et al. [7] further show that, in a parallelized application, high speeds can be observed for hardware implementations of AES. In a video stream decoding implementation, they achieved 63 GBit/s, due to optimization techniques. In difference, though, they do not address networked system encryption, where data comes in continuous streams.

Caldas-Calle et al. [4] looked into the QoS, which can be achieved by small embedded devices that use site-to-site VPNs themselves. Applying encryption decreases the computational capacity of these devices, as the load can exceed the available resources, causing a slowdown of the overall system. Hence, not every device is capable of performing encryption with its provided resources, leading back to the solution of an additional device.

Park et al. [14] showed that in case of a continuous large data stream for video transmission, the deployment of VPNs increases the time needed to transmit the video between 20% of up to 60%. Measurements show that a significant latency is added to transmissions when encrypted.

The MAC security standard (*MACsec*) is defined by the IEEE 802.1AE standard, published in 2008. Despite its age, adoption has been slow with its addition to the Linux Kernel in 2016. The strength of MAC security is its application on all Layer 2 protocols and is independent of other higher-level security mechanisms [11]. At this moment, MACsec is the solution that implements important security mechanisms and uses key exchanges and common cryptography mechanisms. Nevertheless, its slow adoption will mean that legacy devices might not be able to support this standard, especially as two devices have to support it.

4   Implementation

An FPGA is ideal for prototyping and testing IC designs. As the design, construction, and validation of a deployment-ready custom PCB board cannot be performed in the limited available time, then *development boards* or *evaluation kits* are preferred. These contain the FPGA chip integrated into the necessary power circuitry, additional storage and communication interfaces, making them an ideal solution for evaluating the proposed implementation.

4.1   System Architecture

The overall idea of the implementation is that neither of the original systems is aware of the additional devices. The theory behind this is that it enables easier adaptability to other protocols in the future. Overall, the proposed architecture imitates the principle of a VPN. However, instead of using the entire TCP\IP stack, it uses only the MAC-Layer to communicate between the two crypto devices. In order to achieve this, the communication side towards the systems has to only implement the retrieval of the data stream of the original bus system. This is done in the PHY-chip, which has to be connected properly to the FPGA. The overall idea of the individual connection parts can be seen in Fig. 6.

The disadvantage of using a standard Ethernet connection between the two crypto devices is that it will add latency to the transmission. As the FPGAs do not come with a preset MAC address, it might be interesting to adapt the existing MAC core to address agnosticism. This would be a cost-saving measure with little impact on performance,

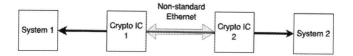

Fig. 6. MAC-tunneling between the crypto devices

as the area of deployment is directly connected peer to peer links. It is necessary to consider the usage of a non-standardized frame size, as adding an MMAC header might exceed the maximum standard size. Those frames are also called jumbo frames and cannot be routed easily through traditional network switches, hinting towards the direct network link limitation. The design of the crypto implementation, seen in Fig. 7, includes an abstract overview of the elements that must be implemented.

The interface consists of two data connections to the PHY chips, for receiving (RX) and for sending/transceiving (TX). On the open traffic side the FPGA needs to interface with the corresponding protocol PHY-chip but only directly forwards the bit-stream to the AES_encoder. After the message is encrypted, it is wrapped into a standard Ethernet frame and sent out through the other PHY chip. If that chip receives an encrypted message, it will unwrap it by removing the MAC header and then run it through the AES_decoder to retrieve the original signal. This is then forwarded to the PHY-chip to re-modulate the original signal.

The AES_encryptor and AES_decryptor will need the correct key for each round. Further, they will have to perform the key-expansion rounds and counting for the CTR operation mode of AES. The time within the FPGA should be decreased as much as possible to decrease the impact on latency.

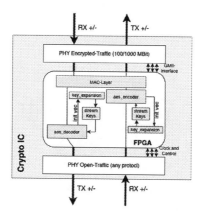

Fig. 7. The crypto IC with the dataflow and the sections in the FPGA.

4.2 System Implementation

A limitation of this project is that only a few protocols can be implemented, given the short time frame. Therefore the project will focus on providing an interface for Ethernet only, whose physical layer is utilized by many bus systems. As different physical mediums use different clock speeds it is essential to decouple the encryption from the communication side, providing more flexibility in terms of protocols and usable physical mediums.

For this, an approach is chosen which utilizes three different clocking zones. One for the open physical layer chip communication, one for encryption/decryption, and the last for the encrypted Ethernet communication. As proposed by the high-level system architecture in Fig. 7, the device can be divided into two independent data streams for deencryption. In order to connect the different clocking zones, two FIFO queues are used per data stream.

The encryption data stream consists of a minimal receiving interface and the "chunk generator" that combines the received data to be stored in chunks of 128 bits in the FIFO, alongside status information representing if it is the last chunk in the transmission and how many bits it contains. From there, the encryption controller takes out blocks of 128 bits and performs the encryption, after which it stores the cyphertext, with the status information, in the second FIFO of the data stream. This FIFO builds the bridge between clocking zones 2 and 3. From here, the FIFO is emptied continuously and its content is stored in a block of RAM until the original data frame is complete. This frame is then transmitted through the Ethernet PHY to the other crypto-IC.

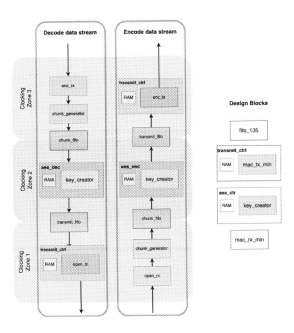

Fig. 8. Data streams combined with clocking zones and actual implemented modules

The decryption data stream works equivalent to the encryption stream, with the significant difference being that the output interface does not write any protocol-specific data, but only the decrypted data from memory which already includes the necessary control bits, such as the start of frame delimiter, in case of a standard Ethernet transmission.

Figure 8, shows the previously described concept of the streams. Each stream consists of the four major implemented design blocks, shown on the right of the picture. The actual schematic overview of the pipeline is available in Fig. 9.

In the following, each implemented module's pin assignments and programmed logic, will be discussed in detail. In many cases, the module will be implemented based on state machines. Finally, the actual flow of the program and implementation reasoning will be provided.

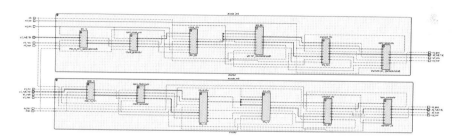

Fig. 9. Schematic drawing of the two data streams in a crypto device

4.3   Hardware Implementation

The resulting system was implemented in System Verilog, due to its benefits in data structures and lower complexity compared to VHDL. The used board is a custom communication board - Fig. 10. It provides the required network interfaces. The FPGA-chip is a Spartan 6 (xa6slx45) automotive chip that interfaces with two Ethernet PHYs through the MMII protocol. The Ethernet PHYs are Marvell 88E3018 chips. It further provides a Serial port through USB-A and JTAG to interface with the FPGA.

4.4   Test Methodology

The testing of the system is done in two steps, as follows.

A Simulation Approach That will Test for System Functionality. The simulation produces exact timings for signal propagation and models an ideal scenario with no delay within the developed circuit.

In order to evaluate the functionality of all developed modules, different test benches have been created, as unit tests for the **Chunk Gen Tester**, the **FIFO 135 Tester**, the **Transceiver Test**, the **Key Creator Tester** and the **AES Test**. A **Main test** testbench

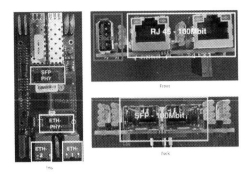

Fig. 10. Communication board.

was conceived to test *all* the components together, followed by a **Two device test**, where the **Main test** was extended to simulate communication on both endpoints.

The testbench structure is illustrated by Algorithm 1. It initializes one crypto core, and wires the output of the second Ethernet interface to its input. On the first interface, it injects a payload that resembles a real Ethernet package, consisting of the preamble, header, and payload. After encryption and decryption, the same data is written to the data out array. If the data matches, the simulation will halt, otherwise it will run indefinitely. With a clock of 25 MHz, it takes about 11 μs to complete for one frame.

Algorithm 1: Testbench FPGA simulation (*test_bench.v*)

clk = clk125MHz(); rst = resetSignal(); e1 = Eth.Port(); e2 = Eth.Port();
topMod testSub (.clk(clk), .reset(rst), .e1_rxc(e1.rxc), ..submodules..,
.e1_txer(e1.txer));   //Rewired eth2 to itself

1 *dataIN* = [h'5555 5555 55d5 abcd effe dcba fffe fdfc fbfa 0800]
2 + [h'656c 6c6f 2057 6f72 6c64 2054 6869 7320 6973 206d 65ff];
3 *dataOUT* = [];
4 **begin**
5 | $e1.rxdv = 1$ //Start transmission
6 | **foreach** *byte* in *dataIN* **do**
7 | | $@(posedgeclk)$; $e1.rxd = byte[3:0]$;
8 | |_ $@(posedgeclk)$; $e1.rxd = byte[7:4]$;
9 | **while** $e1.txen == 1$ **do**
10 | | $@(posedgeclk)$; $dataOUT = e1.txd$;
11 | | **if** $dataOUT == dataIN$ **then**
12 | |_ |_ $exit()$;

An Actual Real-World Deployment in a Test Environment. For testing the latency, a commonly used technique is the Internet Control Message Protocol (ICMP) echo, more commonly known as *ping*. An ICMP package containing a sequence number is sent to a device upon which it replies with the same sequence number back. The sender measures the time it takes from sending the package until an answer is returned. The package counts as lost if no reply is returned within two seconds. For establishing a baseline, 400 pings are sent without the encryption device. Later the encryption device is added, and the same amount of pings is repeated.

Figure 11 shows a picture of the test setup. The Pi connected to Ethernet interface 2 (left) and the MacBook connected to Ethernet interface 1 (right), via USB. Wireshark[2], a networking monitoring utility, and ping run on the laptop, to check and induce network traffic.

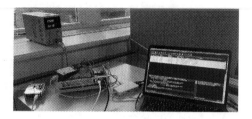

Fig. 11. Hardware test setup

A ping command measures the round trip time of a network link. The times are aggregated and stored for evaluation. At 25 MHz frequency, the expected throughput of the cryptography part is around 63 MBit/s. A frequency of 40 MHz is also tested, to see if the device can still function correctly. Testing the crypto core is done until 400 valid time samples have been gathered.

5   Evaluation and Results

We first perform a functional evaluation of all major components via simulation, and we follow up with tests run on the actual hardware.

5.1   Simulation

The introduction of different clocking zones is used to evaluate the functionality of the system based on simulation. As the FIFO does not contain important logic and works straightforwardly with data storing and reading, its functionality can be evaluated based on the output and input to the major modules. Further, we decided to go through one whole transmission of the main test bench, rather than looking into each module test.

Simulation Level. The simulated testbench runs a full execution until the output data matches the input. The duration of the entire transmission with full encryption and decryption is $8.88\,\mu s$. Sending of the open data takes $1.76\,\mu s$, and the transmission of

---

[2] https://www.wireshark.org/.

the encrypted data takes $3.32\,\mu s$. This increase in time is an additional overhead of 88% to the original time. In total, the actual sending of the data makes up $6.84\,\mu s$, or 77% of the added latency. Therefore the encryption, decryption, and additional control flows are $2.04\,\mu s$ long. These simulation timings reflect the sending of a 45 byte message (Fig. 12), where the last byte (ff) is for determining the data-streams end.

Frame part	Preamble	Mac-Header	Data
Data in Hex	5555 5555 5555 55d5	abcd effe dcba fffe fdfc fbfa 0800	4865 6c6c 6f20 576f 726c 6420 5468 6973 2069 7320 6d65 ff
Data in ASCII	-	-	"Hello World This is meÿ"

Fig. 12. Simulation test data.

One can test if the sent frame is correctly stored in the individual chunks: **Chunk 1:** 5555 5555 5555 $55d5$ | $abcd$ $effe$ $dcba$ $fffe$; **Chunk 2:** $fdfc$ $fbfa$ | 0800 | 4865 $6c6c$ $6f20$ $576f$ 72 $6c$; **Chunk 3:** 6420 5468 6973 2069 7320 $6d65$ ff | 00 0000.

Note that in the third stored chunk, the final three bytes are left blank, as they do not correspond to any message. This correlates to the previously established *size_last_frame* value. Thus the message is fully stored in the queue.

Encryption/Decryption. The encryption controller uses these 128 bit chunk data blocks for encryption. For the first message, the keys are not yet available as none has been set yet. The key generator starts generating keys once the *new_iv* signal is triggered, at approximately $3.5\,\mu s$. As of the end of the simulation, the write address of the RAM is located at $7a8_{16} = 1960_{10}$. The first generated 119 bit initialization vector is $f056638484d609c0895e8112153524_{16}$ with the static key being $2b7e151628aed2a6abf7158809cf4f3c_{16}$.

Once the controller has the data to encrypt and the keys, it creates the ciphertext blocks for the transmission. The stored header is: $00, 0, 01 f0$ $56638484d609$ $c0895e8112153524_{16}$, where the first byte of data $000000\ 01_2$ is the protocol flag for a new initialization vector. After that, the controller remains in an idle state until the first keys are created. Then, a XOR function is applied to the original message block and the key instance. This produces the output in Fig. 13 a), based on the created key instances and plain message blocks.

The input and output blocks are combined with the status flags of size and last frame, denoted by the comma-separated values at the beginning. After the plaintext is converted to the cyphertext, it is stored for transmission in the next FIFO-queue. The basic flow is the same when considering the decryption mode. It only differs upon reading the first data block from the queue, which is taken out right away, as it represents the protocol header. The decryption of each read data block, with the keys read from RAM are listed in Fig. 13 b).

Looking at the encrypted data output, it can be seen that it is equivalent to the data that is now inserted into the decryption. The read keys from the RAM are equivalent to the keys used for encryption, showing that the key generators create the same keys in both modules. The final output data to the transmit queue of the decryptor is also equivalent to the previously encrypted data blocks.

a) Encryption per input and the resulting ciphertext			
Data input	00,0, 5555 5555 5555 55d5 abcd effe dcba fffe	00,0, fdfc fbfa 0800 4865 6c6c 6f20 576f 726c	68,1, 6420 5468 6973 2069 7320 6d65 ff00 0000	...
Key instance	71d7 3c8e 03f0 1117 3dbe 55a1 a9d9 030b	ea63 cede 5428 426b 8a3e 5b14 9b2b 9b6d	a931 7854 1207 31ea 2eb2 cdf8 924b c1fb	...
Output	00,0, 2482 69db 56a5 44c2 9673 ba5f 7563 fcf5	00,0, 179f 3524 5c28 0a0e e652 3434 cc44 e901	68,1, cd11 2c3c 7b74 1183 5d92 a09d 6d4b c1fb	...

b) Decryption per input and the resulting message			
Data input	00,0, 01f0 5663 8484 d609 c089 5e81 1215 3524	00,0, 2482 69db 56a5 44c2 9673 ba5f 7563 fcf5	00,0, 179f 3524 5c28 0a0e e652 3434 cc44 e901	70,1, cd11 2c3c 7b74 1183 5d92 a09d 6d4b c1fb
Key instance	-	71d7 3c8e 03f0 1117 3dbe 55a1 a9d9 030b	ea63 cede 5428 426b 8a3e 5b14 9b2b 9b6d	a931 7854 1207 31ea 2eb2 cdf8 924b c1fb
Output	00,0, 5555 5555 5555 55d5 abcd effe dcba fffe	00,0, fdfc fbfa 0800 4865 6c6c 6f20 576f 726c	70,1, 6420 5468 6973 2069 7320 6d65 ff4b c1fb	...

Fig. 13. a) Encryption per input and the resulting ciphertext; b) Decryption per input and the resulting message.

The Transceiver. The transmit controller contains the control logic, the IP-RAM implementation, and the transmitter itself. The transmitter and the RAM are embedded within the controller. The controller is connected to the transmit FIFO. Therefore it needs inputs to the data, the status flag if a frame is complete, and the size of the last chunk. It also uses the status flags of the FIFO.

The block memory is able to store 2048 bytes, larger than the maximum transmission size of Ethernet. For this, it uses the state machine displayed in Fig. 14. The controller takes every data chunk from the FIFO until the last frame is detected. Each data frame can be fully stored in RAM. Upon detecting the last frame, it enables the transmitter to send out the full data frame.

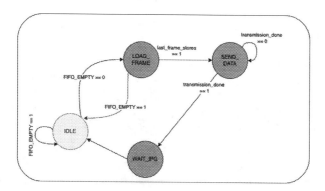

Fig. 14. State machine of the transmit controller

Upon a negative edge of a signal (*fifo_empty*), the controller changes from IDLE to LOAD_FRAME (state machine of Fig. 14), where it starts to write the data blocks of 128 bits to the RAM. It changes back and forth between these two states until another signal (*is_last_frame*) is triggered. After storing the last data block, the controller transitions to the SEND_DATA state, where the transmitter starts to work. Upon the transmitter finishing, the WAIT_IPG state is entered for waiting for the defined inter-packet gap and resetting all variables. After the waiting period, the controller moves back to IDLE and waits for the next frame. The transmit controller works for both operation modes the same.

Expected Signal Impact. It is possible to infer signal delays based on the simulation time from the first signal received to the last byte sent. A delay of approximately $8\,\mu s + 2 * modulation\_time_{encrypted} + 2 * modulation\_time_{plaintext}$ is added for the pipelined implementation. Looking at the slower low area implementation, the delay is significantly larger, with $\approx 242\,\mu s + 2 * modulation\_time_{encrypted} + 2 * modulation\_time_{plaintext}$. Both values represent a worst case, where no keys are stored in the key ram yet. Therefore, the modulation time has to be added and can be calculated based on the following formula for the encrypted packet and Fast Ethernet (100 MBit/s):

$$modulation\_time_{encrypted} = \frac{8 * (23 + plaintextLength)}{25 * 10^6\ Bits/s}$$

For the plaintext packet, the used length shortens by the added 23 bytes. These 23 bytes represent the additional preamble, mac-header, size, and encryption header. If keys are already available, the logic's added base delay for the low-area implementation equates to $127\,\mu s$ instead of the $242\,\mu s$.

It takes $\approx 20.4\,\mu s$ for a key to be generated in the low area implementation. Therefore a theoretical maximum throughput of $\frac{128bit}{20.4\,\mu s} = 62.74$ MBit/s is possible if the key generator is clocked at 25 MHz. For a 40 MHz clock this time is reduced to $\approx 12.6\,\mu s$, equating to a theoretical throughput of 101 MBit/s.

5.2   Hardware

Synthesis Results. The exact result of the synthesis is shown in Fig. 15, where the top result shows the non-fitting pipelined AES-core and the bottom one is the low area implementation for a single crypto device. With a more modern chip selection, a possible placement was reachable. Yet the amount of used LUTs, for the pipeline core, is significantly higher than the documentation-estimated 4000.

Performance Test. For performance evaluation, we develop an extensive testing routine and establish a performance baseline. For the link latency, we conducted 400 individual pings at different times, while no load is applied to either link, with a median latency of $700\,\mu s$ (Fig. 16). The highest measured latency is at $982\,\mu s$, and the quickest transmission was $302\,\mu s$. These values represent the round trip time between the devices, expecting half of them for one-way communication.

The same approach with the crypto device clocked at 25 MHz, resulted in a median round trip time of $715\,\mu s$. The highest measured round trip time is 1.97 s, compared to the $362\,\mu s$ of the lowest time. For the 40 MHz test, no data could be gathered. The

only AES-core	Device Utilization Summary (estimated values)		[-]
Logic Utilization	**Used**	**Available**	**Utilization**
Number of Slice Registers	5536	54576	10%
Number of Slice LUTs	10832	27288	39%
Number of fully used LUT-FF pairs	3535	12833	27%
Number of bonded IOBs	385	316	121%
Number of Block RAM/FIFO	29	116	25%
Number of BUFG/BUFGCTRLs	1	16	6%

a) Pipelined AES-Crypto Core (not mapable)

	Device Utilization Summary (estimated values)		[-]
Logic Utilization	**Used**	**Available**	**Utilization**
Number of Slice Registers	6224	54576	11%
Number of Slice LUTs	6317	27288	23%
Number of fully used LUT-FF pairs	4916	7625	64%
Number of bonded IOBs	28	316	8%
Number of Block RAM/FIFO	45	116	38%
Number of BUFG/BUFGCTRLs	5	16	31%

b) Synthesis results for hardware test

Fig. 15. Synthesis results.

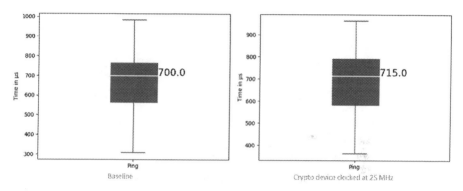

Fig. 16. Ping comparison in μs

increase of the clock speed seems to violate timing constraints within the process resulting in failure of correct decryption. Data is still received by the Pi but is omitted by the MAC layer.

The package loss due to instabilities is significant. In order to get 400 data points for the 25 MHz encryption, 2800 ICMP echo requests were sent, with 475 succeeded and another 38 slower than the required 2 s. This results in a package loss of 83%. In comparison, the median round trip time was increased by 100 μs, yet the overall spread increased. Also, more extreme highs were observed.

When running a quick throughput test, the measured transmission instance resulted in a measured throughput of 217 kbit/s.

6 Discussion

The overall functionality of the architecture was tested within a controlled simulation environment, in which the transfer of a fixed amount of Ethernet frames was successfully conducted. The simulation proved that both the synchronization as well as en-/decryption function according to the specifications. Using a stream cypher approach and the preparation of keys increases the system throughput and should theoretically support high bandwidth protocols such as Gigabit Ethernet. This could not be tested in a real-world scenario.

A downside of the conducted simulation is that it only looked into one-way communication and did not take simultaneous send and receive into account. Due to the separation of the encryption and decryption pipeline, the behaviour should be explored in additional simulations.

Depending on the choice of the FPGA, either a pipeline or a slower single-key generation approach can be chosen. The pipeline approach trades FPGA resources for speed and should be used for high throughput protocols. The low area single key implementation will significantly reduce the used resources, leaving more space for additional communication interfaces or other custom logic.

We also tested the impact of a crypto device on an actual network link, following a developed testing routine. The routine was first used without the cryptography device to establish a baseline. Given the amount of processed data, the used protocol proved highly stable and robust, with almost no re-transmissions.

The conducted tests provide a proof of concept. It is possible to encrypt a link's data independent of the protocol and maintain the original communication between the devices. This comes at the cost of latency, yet not a significant one. A more elaborate testing on the latency impact has to be pursued to get more definitive results, though.

In order to satisfy modern interfaces such as Gigabit Ethernet, a frequency of 25 MHz is insufficient. The performance should be increased, and the testing devices should be configured not to insert any additional traffic data.

Security Considerations. A lot has yet to be determined, when it comes to security. The devices themselves were not tested for implementation vulnerabilities. Due to the large volume of conducted work, errors and oversights are easily made that can lead to problematic outcomes.

One finding that came up, though, was that a potential leak of the key can be achieved by observing the data stream, and gaining the initialization vector while sending prepared payloads of continuous zeros. With a brute-force approach, it might be possible to identify the key. Another downside is that the message length can be inferred. This is especially important in industrial applications because messages and control signals are repeated multiple times. Depending on the protocol and deployment architecture, an attacker could potentially infer what message has been sent based on length.

Lastly, the remaining unencrypted link pieces have to also be secured physically. However, this is easier done for small sections of a long cable than physically securing the whole link.

7   Conclusions

We proposed here an architecture that takes extendability and flexibility into consideration, based on an FPGA design, for evaluation purposes. The architecture separates the communication from the actual cryptography part, by introducing FIFO queues to connect the communication and crypto core. We introduce a custom protocol header to synchronize the devices to the same initialization vector for key generation. We use state machines, resulting in simplified logic flows, increased readability, and code maintainability. In addition, dividing the architecture into different zones provides enhanced adaptability to multiple protocols, proven by the implementation of GMII and MII.

The implementation shows that encrypting any traffic on the network link and regaining the original signal can be a viable alternative to existing technologies. The result is a proof of concept to be seen as a complementary technology in case of non-accessibility to higher-layer solutions, with increased stability. It further indicates that a universal cryptography device interfacing with different physical layer chips can solve encryption requirements in industrial links.

Future Work. We present here a list of possible actions that will improve the quality and utility of the presented efforts.

- The approach should be scaled to cover different protocols (such as CAN) to enable the greater scheme of the protocol-independent encryption.
- The current design deals with direct network links. It is possible to extend the implementation to a one-hop distributed network by using the MAC addresses, assuming that the network is able to support larger frame sizes.
- Removing the buffering of the full frame in the transceivers and the FIFO queues. This alternative would only use the stream cypher approach, where the encryptor would no longer encrypt 128-bit blocks but rather apply a portion of the key on either the 4 bits of RGMII or the 8 bits of the GMII, to be sent out without waiting to rebuild a whole message. This may lead to time savings, but communication between the cryptography devices has to be solved differently, while also losing modularity.

References

1. IEEE Standard for Ethernet. Technical report. IEEE. https://doi.org/10.1109/IEEESTD. 2022.9844436, iSBN 9781504487252
2. OSI model, January 2023. https://en.wikipedia.org/w/index.php?title=OSI_model& oldid=1134681638, page Version ID: 1134681638
3. Anusha Naidu, A.P., Joshi, P.K.: FPGA implementation of fully pipelined advanced encryption standard. In: 2015 international Conference on Communications and Signal Processing (ICCSP), pp. 0649–0653 (2015). https://doi.org/10.1109/ICCSP.2015.7322568
4. Caldas-Calle, L., Jara, J., Huerta, M., Gallegos, P.: QoS evaluation of VPN in a Raspberry Pi devices over wireless network. In: 2017 International Caribbean Conference on Devices, Circuits and Systems (ICCDCS), pp. 125–128, June 2017. https://doi.org/10.1109/ICCDCS. 2017.7959718, iSSN 2165-3550
5. Choudhary, A., Porwal, D., Parmar, A.: FPGA based solution for ethernet controller as alternative for TCP/UDP software stack. In: 2018 6th Edition of International Conference on Wireless Networks and Embedded Systems (WECON), pp. 63–66, November 2018. https:// doi.org/10.1109/WECON.2018.8782050
6. Fattahi, A.: IoT Product Design and Development: Best Practices for Industrial, Consumer, and Business Applications. Wiley, Hoboken (2022)

7. Harb, S., Ahmad, M.O., Swamy, M.N.S.: A high-speed FPGA implementation of AES for large scale embedded systems and its applications. In: 2022 13th International Conference on Information and Communication Systems (ICICS), pp. 59–64, June 2022. https://doi.org/10.1109/ICICS55353.2022.9811140, iSSN 2573-3346

8. Herrmann, F.L., Perin, G., de Freitas, J.P.J., Bertagnolli, R., dos Santos Martins, J.B.: A gigabit UDP/IP network stack in FPGA. In: 2009 16th IEEE International Conference on Electronics, Circuits and Systems - (ICECS 2009), pp. 836–839, December 2009. https://doi.org/10.1109/ICECS.2009.5410757

9. Hoang, T., Nguyen, V.L.: An efficient FPGA implementation of the advanced encryption standard algorithm. In: 2012 IEEE RIVF International Conference on Computing and Communication Technologies, Research, Innovation, and Vision for the Future, pp. 1–4 (2012). https://doi.org/10.1109/rivf.2012.6169845

10. IEEE: IEEE 802.3 ETHERNET. https://www.ieee802.org/3/

11. Luber, S.: Was IST MACsec?, June 2022. https://www.security-insider.de/was-ist-macsec-a-e945e21bc26faeed7999ee600aa61d78/

12. National Cyber Security Centre: Obsolete products. https://www.ncsc.gov.uk/collection/device-security-guidance/managing-deployed-devices/obsolete-products

13. National Technical Information Service (NTIS): FIPS 197, Advanced Encryption Standard (AES). FIPS 197, November 2001

14. Park, S., Matthews, B., D'Amours, D., McIver Jr., W.J.: Characterizing the impacts of VPN security models on streaming video. In: 2010 8th Annual Communication Networks and Services Research Conference, pp. 152–159, May 2010. https://doi.org/10.1109/CNSR.2010.60

15. Lefmann, H.: AES - Advanced Encryption Standard (Rijndael) (2005). https://www.tu-chemnitz.de/informatik/ThIS/vlzits/aes.html

16. Shi, Y., Jin, C., Gao, F.: The solution of ethernet based on hardware protocol stack W5300 and FPGA. In: Proceedings of 2011 International Conference on Electronic and Mechanical Engineering and Information Technology, vol. 3, pp. 1328–1331, August 2011). https://doi.org/10.1109/EMEIT.2011.6023339

17. Stouffer, K., Pease, M., Tang, C., Zimmerman, T., Pillitteri, V., Lightman, S.: Guide to operational technology (OT) security: initial public draft. preprint, April 2022. https://doi.org/10.6028/NIST.SP.800-82r3.ipd, https://nvlpubs.nist.gov/nistpubs/SpecialPublications/NIST.SP.800-82r3.ipd.pdf

18. Xue, T., Pan, W., Gong, G., Zeng, M., Gong, H., Li, J.: Design of giga bit ethernet readout module based on ZYNQ for HPGe. In: 2014 19th IEEE-NPSS Real Time Conference, pp. 1–4, May 2014. https://doi.org/10.1109/RTC.2014.7097556

Formalization and Verification of MQTT-SN Communication Using CSP

Wei Lin[✉], Sini Chen, and Huibiao Zhu[ID]

Shanghai Key Laboratory of Trustworthy Computing,
East China Normal University, Shanghai, China
51265902028@stu.ecnu.edu.cn, hbzhu@sei.ecnu.edu.cn

Abstract. The MQTT-SN protocol is a lightweight version of the MQTT protocol and is customized for Wireless Sensor Networks (WSN). It removes the need for the underlying protocol to provide ordered and reliable connections during transmission, making it ideal for sensors in WSN with extremely limited computing power and resources. Due to the widespread use of WSN in various areas, the MQTT-SN protocol has promising application prospects. Furthermore, security is crucial for MQTT-SN, as sensor nodes applying this protocol are often deployed in uncontrolled wireless environments and are vulnerable to a variety of external security threats.

To ensure the security of the MQTT-SN protocol without compromising its simplicity, we introduce the ChaCha20-Poly1305 cryptographic authentication algorithm. In this paper, we formally model the MQTT-SN communication system using Communicating Sequential Process (CSP) and then verify seven properties of this model using Process Analysis Toolkit (PAT), including deadlock freedom, divergence freedom, data reachability, client security, gateway security, broker security, and data leakage. According to the verification results in PAT, our model satisfies all the properties above. Therefore, we can conclude that the MQTT-SN protocol is secure with the introduction of ChaCha20-Poly1305.

Keywords: MQTT-SN Protocol · Communicating Sequential Process (CSP) · Formal Methods · Modeling · Verification

1 Introduction

Wireless sensor nodes in wireless sensor networks (WSN) are characterized by their small size, ease of deployment, and low cost, making WSN widely used in various fields, such as real-time intelligent monitoring and hazardous zone operations [1,2]. MQTT-SN protocol (Message Queuing Telemetry Transport for Wireless Sensor Networks) is a topic-based publish-subscribe message transmission protocol designed by IBM specifically for WSN [3]. It is a lightweight and resource-efficient version of the MQTT protocol. Compared to the MQTT protocol, which requires the underlying protocol to provide ordered and reliable

© The Author(s), under exclusive license to Springer Nature Switzerland AG 2024
J. Kofroň et al. (Eds.): ECBS 2023, LNCS 14390, pp. 115–132, 2024.
https://doi.org/10.1007/978-3-031-49252-5_10

connections during data transmission, the MQTT-SN protocol eliminates these requirements. As a result, it is more suitable for sensor nodes in WSN with extremely limited energy, computing capacity, storage capacity, and bandwidth.

In addition, wireless sensor nodes are usually deployed in uncontrollable and open wireless environments where external security threats are inevitable [4]. At the same time, sensitive data that is not intended to be accessed by outsiders is often transmitted between wireless sensor nodes. Therefore, it is important to investigate whether MQTT-SN communication can meet the reliability and security requirements for data transmission in WSN.

Several studies have analyzed and tested the communication mechanism of the MQTT-SN protocol. For example, Park et al. [5] standardized the generation, distribution, and registration of security certificates. They then proposed a secure MQTT-SN protocol communication architecture and tested the performance of this architecture by building a simulation scenario. Roldán-Gómez et al. [6] constructed an MQTT-SN protocol communication network and simulated a series of attack behaviors to test the security of the protocol, comparing it with communication in an environment without attacks. Diwan et al. [7] used Event-B to propose an abstract model for the MQTT, MQTT-SN, and CoAP, and verified their common properties.

It can be seen that most studies have conducted experiments by building environments to simulate actual application scenarios or attacks, collecting experimental data, and analyzing the security of communication mechanisms based on the data. However, experiments may be affected by many external factors. Potential security issues in MQTT-SN communication may exist but have not been discovered.

As the MQTT-SN protocol itself does not specify any security mechanism to maintain its simplicity, this paper introduces a lightweight encryption and authentication algorithm, ChaCha20-Poly1305 [8–10], as a security guarantee for MQTT-SN. In this paper, we adopt a classical formal method, Communicating Sequential Process (CSP) [11], to construct models for entities involved in MQTT-SN communication. We also introduce the intruder which can intercept and fake messages to simulate real-world attacks. After that, we use the model checking tool Process Analysis Toolkit (PAT) [12,13] to verify seven properties with the interference of the intruder, including deadlock freedom, divergence freedom, data reachability, client security, gateway security, broker security, and data leakage. The verification results show that the reliability and security of the MQTT-SN protocol communication are ensured with the introduction of ChaCha20-Poly1305.

The structure of this paper is organized as follows. Section 2 provides a brief introduction to the communication mechanism of the MQTT-SN protocol, the process algebra CSP, and the verification tool PAT. In Sect. 3, we present the detailed modeling process for the main entities in our model. In Sect. 4, we implement the constructed model using PAT and verify seven properties. Section 5 concludes the paper and gives a discussion about further improvement.

2   Background

In this section, we start with the MQTT-SN architecture and a brief explanation of its communication mechanism. We also give a brief introduction to CSP and PAT.

2.1   MQTT-SN Architecture

The communication architecture of the MQTT-SN protocol is shown in Fig. 1. There are four main entities in MQTT-SN communication: clients, gateways, forwarders, and brokers [3].

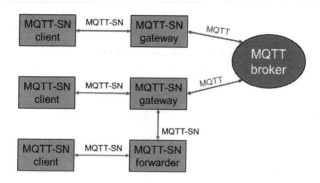

Fig. 1. MQTT-SN Architecture

- **Clients:** Clients can be divided into two types of roles, namely publishers and subscribers. Clients who publish messages with topics are called publishers, while clients who subscribe to topics are called subscribers.
- **Gateways:** The communication between clients and gateways follows the MQTT-SN protocol, while the communication between gateways and brokers adopts the MQTT protocol. The main function of the gateway is to adjust the format of data packets and forward them after protocol conversion between MQTT-SN and MQTT. The gateway may be integrated into the broker server or may exist independently. As the function of the gateway is independent of that of the broker, the gateway is assumed to be an independent module in the subsequent modeling part.
- **Forwarders:** When the gateway cannot directly connect to the network where the client is located, a forwarder is needed. The forwarder functions basically the same as the gateway. Therefore, it is omitted for simplicity in the subsequent modeling part.
- **Brokers:** All clients need to be connected to the broker via a gateway to achieve topic-based message exchange, rather than communicating with each other directly. The main function of brokers is to receive messages from publishers and distribute these messages to the appropriate subscribers.

2.2   Communication Mechanism of the MQTT-SN Protocol

The MQTT-SN protocol itself does not specify security mechanisms in order to maintain its lightweight characteristics. Since a majority of the MQTT-SN clients do not possess the ability to process and store complex data, there are higher efficiency requirements. Therefore, this paper adopts ChaCha20-Poly1305 [8–10], an efficient and lightweight cryptographic authentication algorithm, to ensure the security of MQTT-SN communication.

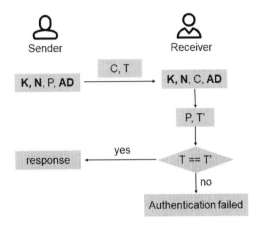

Fig. 2. Mechanism of ChaCha20-Poly1305

The workflows of ChaCha20-Poly1305 are shown in Fig. 2. The algorithm requires the secret key K, the interference term N, the plaintext P, and the associated data AD as input. As an assumption of this paper, the sender and the receiver need to generate the shared K, N, and AD that are kept confidential from others using a secure exchange algorithm. The sender computes the ciphertext C and the authentication tag T with the following two steps and sends them to the receiver:

– Use K and N to produce a stream of bytes that is XORed with P. The result of the XOR operation is C.
– Hash P with K, and then combine the hash value with N. The result is T.

After receiving these messages, the receiver needs to compute a new plaintext P and a new authentication tag T'. Only when the T and the T' are equal, the receiver considers that the sender can pass the identity authentication.

The two most important entity behaviors in MQTT-SN communication are publishing data with topics by publishers and subscribing to topics by subscribers. Because these two behaviors result in similar interaction behaviors, we will introduce the communication mechanism of MQTT-SN using the example of a publisher publishing data with topics. The whole process of a publisher publishing data with topics mainly consists of four stages, as illustrated in Fig. 3, including searching for a gateway, establishing a connection, registering a topic name and publishing a message.

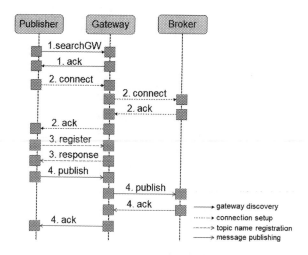

Fig. 3. MQTT-SN Communication Mechanism

In the first step, the publisher needs to find a gateway to assist in forwarding its requests and messages. This involves the following steps:

1. The publisher broadcasts an encrypted control packet to all other devices in the network to search for a gateway.
2. When a gateway receives the packet, it verifies the legitimacy of the publisher. If the publisher is legitimate, it replies to the publisher with a control packet containing its own information to inform the client of its address.
3. After receiving the packet containing the gateway's information, the client also needs to confirm the legitimacy of the gateway's identity. If the gateway is legitimate, the publisher stops searching for a gateway.

MQTT-SN is based on the publish-subscribe pattern and requires a broker to coordinate data between publishers and subscribers. In the second step, the publisher needs to establish a connection with the broker through the gateway to publish messages. The steps to establish a connection are as follows:

1. The client sends an encrypted packet requesting to set up a connection.
2. When the gateway receives the request, it verifies the legitimacy of the client. If the client is legitimate, it forwards the request to the broker.
3. When the broker receives the request, it also needs to verify the legitimacy of the gateway's identity. If the gateway is legitimate, it replies with a response message indicating that the broker agrees to establish a connection.
4. After the client successfully receives the response message agreeing to establish a connection, the connection is established successfully.

In the third step, the publisher needs to initiate a registration process with the gateway to obtain the *TopicId* corresponding to the topic name. When the publisher publishes a message, it needs to use a fixed-length 2-byte topic id (represented by **TopicId**) field to tell the broker which topic the message wants to be published to. Using a shorter *TopicId* to represent the topic instead of the topic name aims to reduce the length of the message, which is one of the adjustments made by MQTT-SN. Here are the steps to follow:

1. The publisher sends an encrypted registration request packet to the gateway.
2. When the gateway receives the request, it first checks the legitimacy of the publisher's identity. If legitimate, it assigns a unique *TopicId* and includes this *TopicId* in the response message to inform the client. The gateway ensures that different topic names have different *TopicIds*.
3. If registration fails due to network or other unexpected reasons, the publisher can initiate registration again.

The fourth step is that the publisher can send encrypted data to the gateway using the *TopicId* successfully registered in the third step. The message is then successfully published to the broker via the gateway. After the broker receives the message, it replies with a confirmation packet. When the publisher receives this confirmation packet, one successful publishing is complete.

2.3 CSP

Process algebra is a formal method that characterizes the communication between processes in concurrent systems. Communicating Sequential Process (CSP), proposed by C.A.R. Hoare [11], is a type of process algebra, which has been successfully applied to verify many parallel systems [14] and communication protocols [15,16]. Therefore, this paper uses CSP as the method to analyze and verify the security of the MQTT-SN protocol communication mechanism.

The syntax and definitions of CSP statements are briefly introduced below, where P and Q represent the processes, a means the atomic actions (also called events), b stands for a boolean expression and c denotes the name of channel:

$$P, Q ::= SKIP \mid a \rightarrow P \mid c\,?\,v \rightarrow P \mid c\,!\,x \rightarrow P \mid$$
$$P \lhd b \rhd Q \mid P \,\square\, Q \mid P \parallel Q \mid P\,;\,Q$$

- $SKIP$ represents that the process terminates successfully.
- $a \rightarrow P$ represents that the process performs the atomic action a first and then executes the process P.
- $c?v \rightarrow P$ represents that the process first receives a value a through the channel c, then assigns the value to the variable v, and finally continues to execute the process P.
- $c!x \rightarrow P$ represents that the process first sends a value x through the channel c to another process, and then continues to execute the process P.
- $P \lhd b \rhd Q$ represents that if b is true, process P is executed. Otherwise, process Q is executed.

- $P \ \square \ Q$ represents that it is uncertain whether process P or process Q is executed and the choice is made by the external environment.
- $P \parallel Q$ represents that processes P and Q are executed concurrently.
- $P; Q$ represents that processes P and Q are executed in sequence.
- $P\,[[a \leftarrow b]]$ represents that the atomic event a in process P is replaced by another atomic event b.
- $P\,[[c]]\,Q$ represents that processes P and Q are executed in parallel through the channels defined in set c.

3   Modeling MQTT-SN Communication

In this section, we formalize the MQTT-SN communication model based on the mechanism presented in the previous Sect. 2.2.

3.1   Sets, Messages and Channels

In order to formalize the behaviors of different entities in MQTT-SN, we first need to define the sets, messages, and channels used in our model.

First, we give the definition of the sets. **Entity** set contains all entities during message transmission, including the publishers, subscribers, brokers and gateways. **Req** set denotes all request messages during the communication process, such as topic registration requests, connection setup requests, etc. **Prk** set represents the set of private keys involved in communication transmission for implementing encryption and authentication algorithms. **Data** set is composed of plaintext data during communication. **Content** set contains all the other messages, which includes the **Ack** set for feedback messages, the **Tag** set for identity authentication and the **Identifier** set for various identifiers.

Next, we define the following messages based on the sets described above:

$$MSG = MSG_{req} \cup MSG_{data} \cup MSG_{ack}$$
$$MSG_{req} = \{msg_{req}a.b.E(k,t,req) \mid a,b \in Entity, k \in Prk,$$
$$t \in Tag, req \in Req\}$$
$$MSG_{data} = \{msg_{data}a.b.req.E(k,t,d) \mid a,b \in Entity, k \in Prk,$$
$$t \in Tag, req \in Req, d \in Data\}$$
$$MSG_{ack} = \{msg_{ack}a.b.E(k,t,ack),\ msg_{ack1}a.b.E(k,t,ack).id \mid$$
$$a,b \in Entity, ack \in Ack, id \in Identifier\}$$

MSG_{req} represents the set of request messages used in the interaction process for clients to find gateways and establish connections. MSG_{data} represents the set of messages involving topic registration, data publishing, topic subscribing, and data updating. MSG_{ack} represents all the confirmations and response messages. MSG includes all the messages above.

Take one message $msg_{ack1}a.b.E(k,t,ack).id$ as an example. It means that entity a sends an acknowledgment message to entity b with its identifier id.

$E(k,t,ack)$ indicates that ack is encrypted with the shared private key k by applying ChaCha20-Poly1305 algorithm and t is the generated tag value for identity authentication.

Finally, we define two sets of channels to simulate communications between entities. The set of channels used when there is no intruder is described as COM_PATH and it contains $ComPP$, $ComBP$, $ComSS$ and $ComBS$. The set of channels denoted as $INTRUDER\_PATH$ is used when an intruder is present and it contains $FakeA$, $FakeB$, $FakeC$, $FakeD$ and $FakeE$.

3.2   Overall Modeling

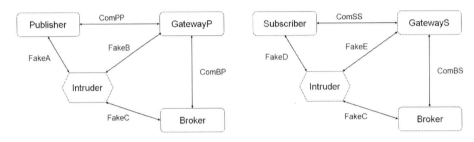

Fig. 4. Publisher Model   **Fig. 5.** Subscriber Model

Based on the communication model diagram for the publisher in Fig. 4 and for the subscriber in Fig. 5, we define two models $SystemP$ and $SystemS$. We divide gateways into two categories: $GatewayP$ to interact with the publishers and $GatewayS$ to interact with the subscribers.

$$SystemP = Pub\,[|COM\_PATH|]\,GatewayP\,[|COM\_PATH|]\,Broker$$
$$SystemS = Sub\,[|COM\_PATH|]\,GatewayS\,[|COM\_PATH|]\,Broker$$
$$System0 = SystemP\,[|COM\_PATH|]\,SystemS$$
$$SYSTEM = System0\,[|INTRUDER\_PATH|]\,Intruder$$

Then we formalize the MQTT-SN communication system without intruders $System0$ by combining $SystemP$ and $SystemS$. $SYSTEM$ stands for the complete system with the presence of intruders. In this paper, we assume that the intruders are able to eavesdrop on messages sent through normal channels, and are also capable of forging messages and sending them to other entities.

3.3   Publisher Modeling

It is the responsibility of the publishers to utilize gateways to transmit messages to the broker so that the broker can forward messages to other clients (i.e. subscribers). As we mentioned before in Sect. 2.2, the process of a publisher publishing data can be broken down into four main steps: searching for a gateway, establishing a connection, registering a topic id for each topic name and publishing messages. Based on this, we give the following definition:

$$Pub_0 = FindGWP; Connect; TopicReg; MsgPub; Pub_0$$

We define a recursive process Pub_0 that executes $FindGWP$, $Connect$, $TopicReg$ and $MsgPub$ in sequence, and finally executes itself. This definition indicates that Pub_0 can repeatedly execute itself so $FindGWP$, $Connect$, $TopicReg$ and $MsgPub$ will be continuously executed, which is in line with real-world scenarios where publishers can disconnect and reconnect to resume message publishing.

We define two special events to denote exception handling. We use **fail** to indicate that the request was not processed successfully due to various reasons while **drop** is adopted to represent that the response was sent by some invalid entities and should be discarded.

$$FindGWP = ComPP!msg_{req}A.B.E(k,t,search) \rightarrow$$
$$ComPP?msg_{ack1}B.A.E(k,t,ack).gwId \rightarrow$$
$$\begin{pmatrix} (\textbf{SKIP} \lhd (ack == true) \rhd (\textbf{fail} \rightarrow FindGWP)) \\ \lhd (\textbf{DV}(k,t',E(k,t,ack))) \rhd \\ (\textbf{drop} \rightarrow FindGWP) \end{pmatrix}$$
$$Connect = ComPP!msg_{req}A.B.E(k,t,connect) \rightarrow ......$$
$$TopicReg = ComPP!msg_{data}A.B.reg.E(k,t,name) \rightarrow ......$$
$$MsgPub = ComPP!msg_{data}A.B.pub.E(k,t,data) \rightarrow$$
$$ComPP?msg_{ack}B.A.E(k,t,ack) \rightarrow$$
$$\begin{pmatrix} (\textbf{MsgPub} \lhd (ack == true) \rhd (fail \rightarrow MsgPub)) \\ \lhd (DV(k,t',E(k,t,ack))) \rhd \\ (drop \rightarrow MsgPub) \end{pmatrix}$$
$$\Box \; ComPP!msg_{req}A.B.E(k,t,disconnect) \rightarrow$$
$$ComPP?msg_{ack}B.A.E(k,t,ack) \rightarrow ......$$

For instance, in the subprocess $FindGWP$, the publisher (**represented by A**) first sends an encrypted *search* request and then waits for a response from the gateway (**represented by B**). After that, it verifies whether the response is sent by a legal gateway entity using function **DV** (means **D**ecryption and **V**erification). The function **DV** will determine the legitimacy of the entity by comparing the tag values (i.e. t and t'). If the response is sent by an illegal entity, the publisher will drop the response (denoted as **drop**), resend the search request, and repeat the above steps. Otherwise, the publisher will judge whether the gateway allows a connection according to the value of the ack. If ack is true, it means that the gateway accepts communication from the publisher. The publisher can then stop searching for a gateway, which is denoted as **SKIP**, so the process Pub_0 can execute the next subprocess $Connect$ to establish a connection with the broker. However, the *search* request failed (denoted as **fail**) when *ack* is false.

Subprocesses *Connect*, *TopicReg* and *MsgPub* are similar to *FindGWP*, so we will only provide partial definitions for them. Especially, *MsgPub* will call itself instead of executing *SKIP* to continue the recursion when a *pub* request is successfully ended. This means that multiple messages can be published in a single connection until a *disconnect* request is made. The general choice symbol □ splits the handling of different requests, which are frequently used later.

The Pub_0 model above does not consider the presence of intruders. Based on the Pub_0 model, we define *Pub* model that takes intruders into account by the following renaming operations:

$$
\begin{aligned}
Pub = \ & Pub_0 \, [[ComPP!\{|ComPP|\} \leftarrow ComPP!\{|ComPP|\}, \\
& ComPP!\{|ComPP|\} \leftarrow FakeB!\{|ComPP|\}, \\
& ComPP?\{|ComPP|\} \leftarrow ComPP?\{|ComPP|\}, \\
& ComPP?\{|ComPP|\} \leftarrow FakeA?\{|ComPP|\}]]
\end{aligned}
$$

Here, $|c|$ represents the set of messages that can be transmitted on channel c.

The first two lines of the above *Pub* definition indicate that when Pub_0 sends messages on channel *ComPP*, *Pub* can also send the same messages on channel *FakeB*. This is to simulate the behavior of intruders faking messages. The last two lines indicate that when Pub_0 receives messages on channel *ComPP*, *Pub* can also receive the same messages on channel *FakeA*. This is to achieve the behavior of intruders eavesdropping on messages.

3.4 Gateway Modeling

The main function of gateways is to respond to search gateway requests and topic registration requests from clients. Gateways also need to forward other requests between clients and the broker. We divide and formalize the behaviors of gateways into two processes: *GatewayP* which interacts with publishers and *GatewayS* which interacts with subscribers.

The detail of modeling *GatewayP* is presented below. We omit the detail of modeling *GatewayS* due to their similarity. We set a variable **TpcTable** for *GatewayS* and *GatewayP* respectively, which records the corresponding relationship between each topic name and its *topicId*.

$$
\begin{aligned}
& GatewayP_0(\mathbf{TpcTable}) = \\
& \quad ComPP?msg_{req}A.B.E(k,t,search) \rightarrow \\
& \quad \begin{pmatrix} ComPP!msg_{ack1}B.A.E(k,t,true).\mathbf{gwId} \\ \lhd \, (DV(k,t',E(k,t,search)))) \rhd \\ ComPP!msg_{ack1}B.A.E(k,t,false).none \end{pmatrix} \rightarrow \\
& \quad GatewayP_0(TpcTable) \\
& \quad \square \, ComPP?msg_{data}A.B.reg.E(k,t,name) \rightarrow
\end{aligned}
$$

$$
\left(\left(\left(\begin{array}{c}
\begin{pmatrix}
SKIP \\
\lhd\,(\exists entry \in TpcTable \cdot entry.key == name)\rhd \\
\textbf{AddEntry}
\end{pmatrix}; \\
ComPP!msg_{ack1}B.A.E(k,t,true).\textbf{TpcTable}\,[\textbf{name}] \\
\rightarrow GatewayP_0(TpcTable)
\end{array}\right.\right.\right.
$$

$$
\lhd\,(DV(k,t',E(k,t,name)))\rhd
$$

$$
\left.\left.\begin{pmatrix}
ComPP!msg_{ack1}B.A.E(k,t,false).none \\
\rightarrow GatewayP_0(TpcTable)
\end{pmatrix}\right.\right)
$$

$\square\ ComPP?msg_{req}A.B.E(k,t,connect) \rightarrow \ldots\ldots$

$\square\ ComPP?msg_{data}A.B.pub.E(k,t,data) \rightarrow \ldots\ldots$

$\square\ ComPP?msg_{req}A.B.E(k,t,disconnect) \rightarrow \ldots\ldots$

In the first part, we describe how to handle gateway searching requests. Upon receiving a *search* request from a client, the gateway first uses the *DV* function to verify the legitimacy of the client. When the client is legal, the gateway replies with a message containing a value of *true* for *ack* and its own information represented by **gwId**, indicating its agreement to help the client forward messages. The reply messages also need to be encrypted.

In the second part, we describe how to handle topic registration requests. After receiving a registration request *reg* from the publisher, the gateway still needs to verify the legitimacy of the publisher's identity. Only when the publisher is a legal entity can the following steps be taken. The gateway searches in *TpcTable* for the topic *name*. If the *name* exists, it means that the *name* has been registered before and there is no need to allocate a new id. Otherwise, a unique id is assigned to the *name* and this record is added to *TpcTable*, which is marked as a function named **AddEntry**. Finally, we retrieve the corresponding id for *name* using **TpcTable[name]** and send it to the related publisher.

Since the definitions for the other requests are similar to the first part, their detailed modeling is omitted here.

As with the process *Pub*, we can define the process *GatewayP* that takes into account the existence of intruders by renaming operations based on the current process *GatewayP$_0$*.

3.5 Broker Modeling

The broker is mainly responsible for two functions: first, to respond to various requests from the gateway, and second, to coordinate messages from different topics. If the data related to a certain topic subscribed by a subscriber changes, the broker should push the updated data to the subscriber.

We formalize the model of the broker as below:

$$
Broker_0 = ComBS!msg_{data}C.D.update.E(k,t,data) \rightarrow
$$
$$
ComBS?msg_{ack}D.C.E(k,t,ack) \rightarrow
$$

$$\left(\begin{array}{l} (Broker_0 \lhd (ack == true) \rhd (fail \rightarrow Broker_0)) \\ \lhd \left(DV(k, t', E(k, t, ack)) \right) \rhd \\ (drop \rightarrow Broker_0) \end{array} \right)$$

$\Box\, ComBP?msg_{req}B.C.E(k, t, connect) \rightarrow$

$$\left(\begin{array}{l} ComBP!msg_{ack}C.B.E(k, t, true) \\ \lhd \left(DV(k, t', E(k, t, connect)) \right) \rhd \\ ComBP!msg_{ack}C.B.E(k, t, false) \end{array} \right) \rightarrow Broker_0$$

$\Box\, ComBP?msg_{data}B.C.pub.E(k, t, data) \rightarrow \ldots\ldots$

$\Box\, ComBS?msg_{data}D.C.sub.E(k, t, topic) \rightarrow \ldots\ldots$

$\Box\, \ldots\ldots$

In the first part, the broker (**represented by** C) sends an *update* request to the gateway (**represented by** D) interacting with the subscriber, in order to notify the subscriber that the data of topics he has subscribed to have changed. Then the broker waits for the response and uses the DV function to test the legitimacy of the gateway. After authentication, if the value of ack is true, the request is processed successfully, and vice versa. Failure to pass authentication means that the response is from an illegal entity. For simplicity, we allow the broker to send *update* requests at any time.

In the second part, the broker receives a connection setup request from the gateway. After verifying that the gateway is legitimate, the broker gives an answer with an *ack* value of *true*, indicating that the connection is allowed to be set up. The rest parts are similar to the second part, so we omit the details here.

As with the process *Pub*, we can define the process *Broker* under the existence of intruders by renaming *Broker0*.

3.6   Intruder Modeling

In this paper, we assume that intruders can intercept or fake messages via normal communication channels $ComPP$, $ComBP$, $ComSS$ and $ComBS$.

First, we define a set **Fact** as below, which includes all the facts the intruder can learn at its initial state. The intruder can know all the entities in the system, the intruder's own private key prk_i and its own tag value tag_i, as well as all the encrypted messages MSG during communication.

$$\textbf{Fact} = Entity \cup \{prk_i,\ tag_i\} \cup MSG$$

In addition, the intruder can deduce new facts based on the set of facts that it has already learned. And the specific deduction rules are as follows:

$$\{k, d\} \rightarrow E(k, d)$$
$$\{sk, E(sk, d)\} \rightarrow d$$
$$(F \rightarrow f) \wedge (F \subseteq F') \rightarrow (F' \Longrightarrow f)$$

The first rule states that the intruder can get the encrypted message $E(k,d)$ if it has the encryption key k and the data d. The second rule states that the intruder can get the plaintext d if it has the decryption key sk and the encrypted message $E(sk,d)$. The third rule states that if the fact f can be deduced from the fact set F, and F is a subset of F', then the intruder can also deduce f from the bigger set F'.

Then, we define the function $Info(msg)$ to describe the facts that the intruder can deduce from the different types of messages that are defined previously.

$$Info\,(msg_{req}a.b.E(k,t,req)) = \{a,b,E(k,t,req)\}$$
$$Info\,(msg_{data}a.b.req.E(k,t,d)) = \{a,b,req,E(k,t,d)\}$$
$$Info\,(msg_{ack}a.b.E(k,t,ack)) = \{a,b,E(k,t,ack)\}$$
$$Info\,(msg_{ack1}a.b.E(k,t,ack).id) = \{a,b,E(k,t,ack),id\}$$

The first rule indicates that the intruder can deduce from this kind of message that it was sent from entity a to entity b. Also, the message content is an encrypted packet $E(k,t,req)$. The remaining rules are similar to the first one.

Therefore, we introduce a channel called $Deduce$ for the intruder process to deduce new facts through this channel, which is defined as follows:

$$Channel\ \ Deduce : Fact.P(Fact)$$

Based on all the deduction rules and the channel definition above, the model of the intruder can be defined as follows:

$$Intruder_0(F) = {}_{m \in MSG}Fake?m \rightarrow Intruder_0(F \cup Info(m))$$
$$\Box\Box_{m \in MSG \cap Info(m) \subseteq F}Fake!m \rightarrow Intruder_0(F)$$
$$\Box\Box_{f \in Fact, f \notin F, F \rightarrow f}Init\,\{Data\_Leakage\_Success = false\}$$
$$\rightarrow Deduce.f.F$$
$$\rightarrow \left(\begin{array}{l} \left(\begin{array}{c} Data\_Leakage\_Success = true \\ \rightarrow Intruder_0(F \cup \{f\}) \end{array} \right) \\ \triangleleft\ (f\ ==\ data)\ \triangleright \\ Intruder_0(F) \end{array} \right)$$

In the above definition, $Fake$ represents the integrated set of all channels contained in $INTRUDER\_PATH$, and F is a set that contains the intruder's current known messages. The first line states that the intruder can eavesdrop on messages through all the channels in the $Fake$ set and add the deduced content to its known fact set F. The second line states that the intruder can fake messages based on known facts and send them to other entities. The remaining lines state that the intruder can deduce new facts based on known messages through the $Deduce$ channel, and then add these deduced new facts to its known fact set F. If the intruder can deduce the plaintext of a message (defined as $f==data$), it indicates a data leakage scenario.

Finally, we give the complete definition of the intruder process as below, where *IF* represents the set of facts the intruder can get initially:

$$Intruder = Intruder_0\,(IF)$$
$$IF = \{A, B, C, D, E, prk_i, tag_i\}$$

4   Implementation and Verification

In this section, we use the model checking tool PAT to implement the model we constructed in Sect. 3 and then verify seven properties of the model. The verification results are shown at the end of this section.

4.1   Implementation

First, we give a brief introduction of the syntax and definitions of PAT as below:

- #**define goal value** $==$ 1; It defines a proposition named *goal* that evaluates to true only when the variable named *value* is equal to 1.
- **var a** $=$ **1**; It defines a global variable named a and assigns it the value 1.
- **enum{a, b}**; It defines two enumeration constants named a and b.
- **channel c 0**; It defines a channel named c with a buffer size of 0, indicating that it is for synchronous communication. The buffer size of the channel must be greater than or equal to 0.
- # **assert P**() **deadlockfree**; It defines an assertion to check whether the process P will go into a deadlock state with a built-in primitive in PAT.
- # **assert P**() **reaches goal**; It defines an assertion to check whether the process P will go into a state, where the property named *goal* is satisfied.
- # **assert P**() $| = [\,]$! **F**; It defines an assertion to check whether the process P can never reach a state where the property F holds.

4.2   Properties Verification

Property 1: Deadlock Freedom
The deadlock state refers to the situation where the system is continuously blocked and unable to perform any actions. We can use the verification primitive provided by PAT to check this property. The verification primitive is as follows:

assert SYSTEM deadlockfree;

Property 2: Divergence Freedom
Divergence refers to the system being trapped in an infinite loop and continuously consuming resources secretly. We also use the primitive provided by PAT to check this property. The verification primitive is as follows:

assert SYSTEM divergencefree;

Property 3: Data Reachability

Data Reachability refers to the ability that all the messages published by the clients and all the requests sent by the clients can be successfully received and processed by the broker server. We define a state with a variable called *Data_Reachability_Success* to indicate that this property is satisfied and then use assert to check whether the model can reach this state.

> #define Data_Reachability_Success data_reachability == true;
> #assert SYSTEM reaches Data_Reachability_Success;

Property 4: Client Security

Client Security refers to the situation where intruders cannot impersonate publishers or subscribers to communicate with other entities in the system. We define a state called *Client_Fake_Success* to indicate that the system is in a state where intruders can successfully impersonate clients. Then we use an assert statement with the always symbol [] defined in PAT to check whether the model can ever reach this state.

> #define client_fake_success (pub_fake_success || sub_fake_success);
> #define Client_Fake_Success client_fake_success == true;
> #assert SYSTEM | = []! Client_Fake_Success;

Property 5: Gateway Security

Gateway Security refers to the state in which intruders are unable to pretend to be gateways. Similarly, we define a state called *Gateway_Fake_Success* and then check whether the system will never enter into this state.

> #define gateway_fake_success (gwp_fake_success || gws_fake_success);
> #define Gateway_Fake_Success gateway_fake_success == true;
> #assert SYSTEM | = []! Gateway_Fake_Success;

Property 6: Broker Security

Broker Security stands for the situation where intruders cannot impersonate brokers to communicate in the system. Similarly, we define a state called *Broker_Fake_Success* and check by using an assert statement.

> #define Broker_Fake_Success broker_fake_success == true;
> #assert SYSTEM | = []! Broker_Fake_Success;

Property 7: Data Leakage

Data leakage refers to the situation where intruders can obtain, use or share plaintext data during the communication process, which is not allowed in a safe system. Protecting data privacy and confidentiality is an important issue for WSN. We define a state called *Data_Leakage_Success* to indicate the state where intruders can access the plaintext data.

#define Data_Leakage_Success data_leakage_success == true;

#assert SYSTEM | = []! Data_Leakage_Success;

4.3   Verification Results

According to our definitions and assertions of different properties, we verify our model in PAT. The verification results are shown in Fig. 6. We can see that the seven properties are all valid.

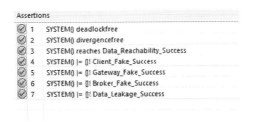

Fig. 6. Verification Results in PAT

This means that our system will never run into a deadlock or divergence state and all the clients can get the data they want. In addition, it indicates that the intruder cannot pretend to be a normal entity during communication and there is no risk of leaking data in our system.

5   Conclusion and Future Work

This paper analyzes and formalizes the main components of MQTT-SN communication. The MQTT-SN protocol does not specify security measures to maintain lightweight, so this paper introduces the ChaCha20-Poly1305 algorithm as a security guarantee. Then, we list seven properties that need to be verified including deadlock freedom, divergence freedom, data reachability, client security, gateway security, broker security, and data leakage. Moreover, we use the model checker PAT to verify the above properties. According to the verification results, we can summarize that all these properties are satisfied in our model.

When modeling the MQTT-SN protocol communication system, this paper considers the possible attack behaviors that may be encountered in the real environment, such as eavesdropping and forgery. However, in practical applications, there are more types of attacks that may weaken the security of the MQTT-SN communication, such as DDoS attacks and sinkhole attacks [4,17]. In the future, more attack behaviors can be introduced to enrich the intruder process.

Acknowledgements. This work was partially supported by the National Key Research and Development Program of China (No. 2022YFB3305102), the National Natural Science Foundation of China (Grant No. 62032024), the "Digital Silk Road" Shanghai International Joint Lab of Trustworthy Intelligent Software (No. 22510750100), and Shanghai Trusted Industry Internet Software Collaborative Innovation Center.

References

1. Kandris, D., Nakas, C., Vomvas, D., Koulouras, G.: Applications of wireless sensor networks: an up-to-date survey. Appl. Syst. Innov. **3**(1) (2020)
2. Sharma, S., Kaur, A.: Survey on wireless sensor network, its applications and issues. J. Phys: Conf. Ser. **1969**(1), 12042 (2021)
3. Stanford-Clark, A., Truong, H.L.: MQTT for sensor networks (MQTT-SN) protocol specification. Int. Bus. Mach. (IBM) Corporation version **1**(2), 1–28 (2013)
4. Avila, K., Sanmartin, P., Jabba, D., Gómez, J.: An analytical survey of attack scenario parameters on the techniques of attack mitigation in WSN. Wirel. Pers. Commun. **122**, 3687–3718 (2022)
5. Park, C.S., Nam, H.M.: Security architecture and protocols for secure MQTT-SN. IEEE Access **8**, 226422–226436 (2020)
6. Roldán-Gómez, J., Carrillo-Mondéjar, J., Castelo Gómez, J.M., Ruiz-Villafranca, S.: Security analysis of the MQTT-SN protocol for the internet of things. Appl. Sci. **12**(21), 10991 (2022)
7. Diwan, M., D'Souza, M.: A framework for modeling and verifying iot communication protocols. In: Larsen, K.G., Sokolsky, O., Wang, J. (eds.) SETTA 2017. LNCS, vol. 10606, pp. 266–280. Springer, Cham (2017). https://doi.org/10.1007/978-3-319-69483-2_16
8. Sadio, O., Ngom, I., Lishou, C.: Lightweight security scheme for MQTT/MQTT-SN protocol. In: 2019 Sixth International Conference on Internet of Things: Systems, Management and Security (IOTSMS), pp. 119–123. IEEE (2019)
9. Kao, T., Wang, H., Li, J.: Safe MQTT-SN: a lightweight secure encrypted communication in IoT. J. Phys: Conf. Ser. 012044. IOP Publishing (2021)
10. De Santis, F., Schauer, A., Sigl, G.: ChaCha20-Poly1305 authenticated encryption for high-speed embedded iot applications. In: Design, Automation and Test in Europe Conference and Exhibition (DATE), pp. 692–697. IEEE (2017)
11. Hoare, C.A.R.: Communicating Sequential Processes. Prentice Hall International, Upper Saddle River (1985)
12. National University of Singapore: PAT: Process Analysis Toolkit (2007). https://pat.comp.nus.edu.sg/
13. Sun, J., Liu, Y., Dong, J.S.: Model checking CSP revisited: introducing a process analysis toolkit. In: Margaria, T., Steffen, B. (eds.) ISoLA 2008. CCIS, vol. 17, pp. 307–322. Springer, Heidelberg (2008). https://doi.org/10.1007/978-3-540-88479-8_22
14. Xu, J., Yin, J., Zhu, H., Xiao, L.: Modeling and verifying producer-consumer communication in Kafka using CSP. In: 7th Conference on the Engineering of Computer Based Systems, pp. 1–10. ACM (2021)
15. Lowe, G., Roscoe, B.: Using CSP to detect errors in the TMN protocol. IEEE Trans. Softw. Eng. **23**(10), 659–669 (1997)

16. Chen, S., Li, R., Zhu, H.: Formalization and verification of group communication CoAP using CSP. In: Shen, H., et al. (eds.) PDCAT 2021. LNCS, vol. 13148, pp. 616–628. Springer, Cham (2022). https://doi.org/10.1007/978-3-030-96772-7_58
17. Abidoye, A.P., Obagbuwa, I.C.: DDoS attacks in WSNs: detection and countermeasures. IET Wirel. Sens. Syst. **8**(2), 52–59 (2018)

Detecting Road Tunnel-Like Environments Using Acoustic Classification for Sensor Fusion with Radar Systems

Nikola Stojkov[1]([✉])[iD], Filip Tirnanić[2], and Aleksa Luković[2]

[1] Faculty of Technical Sciences, Novi Sad, Serbia
nikola.stojkov@outlook.com
[2] Novi Sad, Serbia

Abstract. Radar systems equipped with Misalignment Monitoring and Adjustment (MM&A) face challenges in accurately functioning within complex environments, particularly tunnels. Standard radar system design assumes constant background activity of the MM&A throughout a host vehicle's ignition cycle, monitoring for misaligned radar sensors and mitigating issues associated with faulty radar measurements. However, the presence of tunnels and other unfavorable driving conditions can influence MM&A, thereby affecting its performance.

To address this issue, it is crucial to develop a reliable method for detecting tunnel-like environments and appropriately adjusting the MM&A system. This research paper focuses on the novel acoustic sensing system called SONETE (Sonic Sensing for Tunnel Environment) for classification of acoustic signatures recorded by pressure zone microphone to accurately identify tunnel environments.

The study aims to explore acoustic features and classification algorithms to distinguish between road and tunnel environment and using a sensor fusion with radar systems, suspend the MM&A system accordingly. By tackling this problem, the research contributes to the advancement of intelligent transportation systems by enhancing radar technology's robustness in complex environments and ensuring effective MM&A adjustments in tunnels.

Overall, this paper demonstrates the potential of using acoustic signatures as a complementary sensor for tunnel detection in vehicles where traditional sensors have limitations.

Keywords: Misalignment monitoring and adjustment · Acoustic signatures · Classification · Tunnel detection

1 Introduction

The presence of tunnel like environments might affect Advanced Driver Assistance Systems (ADAS). In this study we are focusing on radar systems. One

J. Kofroň et al. (Eds.): ECBS 2023, LNCS 14390, pp. 133–152, 2024.
https://doi.org/10.1007/978-3-031-49252-5_11

of the features in radar systems is MM&A, which performs a process of assessing and correcting the alignment of radar components to ensure optimal system performance. Signal reflections in tunnel like environments can result in overlapping or delayed signals reaching the radar system, leading to inaccuracies in target detection and localization. Misalignment in such scenarios can amplify the effects of signal reflections, making it challenging to distinguish between direct and reflected signals.

In this study we are exploring use of a complementary sensor for tunnel detection in order to compensate MM&A challenges in tunnel like environments. We will explore acoustic phenomena of the sudden change in an acoustic environment. In order to achieve this, an externally mounted acoustic pressure sensor proves to be suitable. Selected sensor configuration should remain unaffected by the tunnel's geometry, including wall curvature and internal infrastructure such as Heating, ventilation, and air conditioning (HVAC) systems and piping.

The driver, when listening to the aural landscape before and after the tunnel, may not be consciously aware of the tunnel's size or any specific internal characteristics. However, the presence of a tunnel is clearly perceivable throughout its entire length, with the driver's reaction time (i.e., resolution) determined by the capabilities of the human auditory system.

2   Related Studies

Numerous research studies have extensively explored different approaches and technologies for vehicle localization and tunnel detection. For instance, using LiDAR sensors and imaging technologies mounted on vehicles to acquire the geometry and structural information of tunnels while the vehicle is in moving [23, 24, 27].

Acoustic and vibration signals have also been effectively utilized for tunnel detection. Studies have examined the use of microphones to capture these signals and analyzed their distinct patterns or characteristics [13, 28].

Radar sensors integrated in vehicles could be used for tunnel detection by detecting changes in signal reflections. Researchers have explored diverse radar-based techniques, including Doppler radar, in order to assess their potential for tunnel detection [17, 21, 25].

Moreover, imaging systems have been deployed for tunnel detection, leveraging their capabilities to identify tunnel-like environments [1]. Certain research has focused on utilizing the object elevation property and applying Gaussian filtering techniques for detecting tunnel environments [7].

These comprehensive research studies highlight the diverse range of techniques and technologies being explored in the field of tunnel detection, effectively demonstrating the advancements made in this domain.

2.1   Discussion of Related Studies

This article shows use of pressure zone microphone (PZM) for tunnel detection through acoustic signature analysis, and offers some distinct differences compared to the previously mentioned detection methods.

Acoustic pressure variations are accurately captured by pressure zone microphones, which exhibit high sensitivity and can detect even subtle changes in sound pressure levels. On the other hand, LiDAR, imaging technologies, and radar sensors utilize different sensing modalities such as light, electromagnetic waves, or radio waves.

When it comes to tunnel environments, pressure zone microphones are primarily employed to analyze their acoustic signatures or characteristics. This analysis involves examining the frequency content, amplitude, and temporal patterns of sound signals collected by these microphones. In contrast, LiDAR, imaging technologies, and radar sensors focus on capturing the geometric or structural information of tunnels, rather than directly studying their acoustic properties. One notable advantage of pressure zone microphones is their ability to provide real-time monitoring of the acoustic environment while a vehicle is in motion. This allows for continuous detection and characterization of tunnel-like environments. Conversely, other detection methods often require periodic measurements or snapshots of the environment.

It's important to note that pressure zone microphones can be sensitive to internal infrastructure elements present in tunnels, such as HVAC systems or piping. These internal components may introduce additional noise or interfere with the analysis of acoustic signatures. Therefore, the implementation of noise filtering algorithms or physical isolation methods becomes necessary to minimize the unwanted effects caused by the internal infrastructure. In contrast, other detection methods like LiDAR or radar are generally less affected by these internal infrastructure elements.

Another advantage of pressure zone microphones is relatively low cost compared to specialized LiDAR or radar systems. They are also relatively easy to install and integrate into existing vehicles or monitoring systems, making them a cost-effective option for tunnel detection through the analysis of acoustic signatures.

3   Methodology

3.1   Selected Pressure Zone Microphone

Surface-mounted pressure microphone 147AX [6] was used as it is optimized for testing in the automotive industry. It combines the high precision and stability of a laboratory microphone with a high level of ruggedness, including the ability to function properly in the most challenging environment with vibrations, oil mists, water spray and dirt and dust - and high temperatures up to 125°C. Microphone design and other internal parts makes it resilient to shock and vibrations. It functions well under conditions with vibrations and g-forces from uneven road

Table 1. 147AX Specifications

Specification	Value
Frequency range (±1 dB)	5 to 12.5 kHz
Frequency range (±2 dB)	3.15 to 20 kHz
Dynamic range lower limit	19 dB(A)
Dynamic range upper limit	133 dB
Set sensitivity @ 250 Hz (±2 dB)	42 mV/Pa
Set sensitivity @ 250 Hz (±2 dB)	–27 dB re 1V/Pa
Output impedance	< 50Ω
Static pressure coefficient @250 Hz, typical	–0.02 dB/kPa

surfaces and other sudden directional shifts as encountered in real-life driving tests.

The provided Table 1 contains specifications of the pressure microphone suitable for tunnel detection.

The microphone has a wide frequency range from 5 kHz to 12.5 kHz (±1 dB) and 3.15 kHz to 20 kHz (±2 dB). Tunnels often exhibit specific acoustic characteristics within certain frequency ranges. By capturing and analyzing the acoustic signals within these ranges, the microphone can detect and differentiate tunnel environments from other surroundings.

Tunnels can have varying levels of ambient noise or signal strength. The microphone has a high dynamic range, with a lower limit of 19 dB(A) and an upper limit of 133 dB. This wide dynamic range allows the microphone to capture both low-level ambient sounds and high-intensity sounds within the tunnel environment.

Sensitivity level at 250 Hz is 42 mV/P which is important for detecting the acoustic signatures specific to tunnels, which may have characteristic frequencies and amplitudes. The microphone's sensitivity enables it to capture and analyze these signals effectively.

Output impedance of less than 50 Ω ensures that the microphone can provide a strong and stable output signal, allowing for accurate and reliable measurements of the acoustic environment.

Static pressure coefficient of –0.02 dB/kPa at 250 Hz indicates its ability to maintain consistent performance even in the presence of static pressure variations. This is important in tunnel environments, where air pressure may change due to factors such as ventilation or vehicle movement.

3.2   Recording Audio Signals

Microphone was placed on the vehicle (Škoda Karoq) at two positions. First position was on the right side of the vehicle where microphone was exposed to wind, and second position below back door handle making microphone less

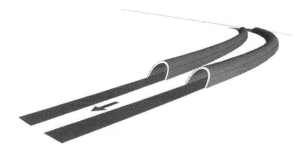

Fig. 1. Mišeluk tunnel model.

exposed to wind, see Fig. 5. Recordings of audio signals were done in Mišeluk tunnel, Novi Sad, Serbia showed in Fig. 1.

Recordings were made in two sessions, respectively to microphone positions, using a portable multi-channel sound analyzer Voyager at sample rate of 48 KHz [12]. Vehicle speed was in range between 70 Km/h and 80 Km/h. One set of recordings were in a quiet environment without traffic, and other in a quite busy environment with other vehicles on the road.

Audio samples were cut into 1 s length to be used in the signal processing algorithms showed in Fig. 5.

3.3   Time-Frequency Spectrum Analysis

The approach we used to identify tunnel-like environments is through the analysis of the time-frequency spectrum of acoustic signals. In our preliminary experiments, we determined that the presence of a dominant frequency component at around 1 kHz reliably indicates the presence of a tunnel-like environment.

We analyzed time-frequency spectrum to check the distribution of energy in the frequency domain over time, see Fig. 2. By capturing the variations in the spectral content of the acoustic signals, analysis revealed specific patterns and features associated with tunnel environments. When a vehicle enters a tunnel, analysis showed that there is a noticeable shift in the time-frequency spectrum of the acoustic signal. The sudden change in the acoustic environment shows a distinct shift in the energy distribution across different frequency bands. In particular, the presence of a dominant frequency component at around 1 kHz becomes more noticeable when entering a tunnel, see Fig. 2. This frequency component can be attributed to the interaction between the vehicle's motion and the tunnel's geometry, resulting in specific resonances or reflections that are characteristic of tunnel-like environments.

In Fig. 2 we see a dominant frequency component at around 1 kHz. This was used as a reliable indicator of tunnel presence. Algorithms and techniques can be developed to automatically detect and analyze the sudden changes in the time-frequency spectrum, allowing for real-time identification of tunnel-like environments. By focusing on the distinctive features of tunnel environments,

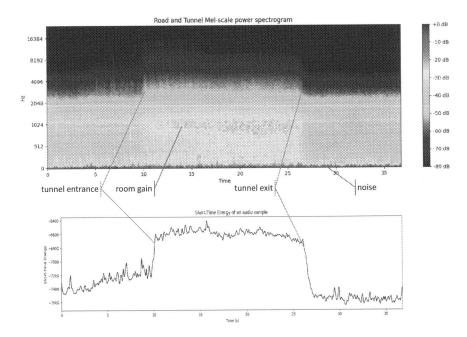

Fig. 2. Mel-scale power spectrogram and Short-Time Energy of raw audio sample.

such as the dominant frequency component at around 1 kHz, the research aims to develop accurate method for tunnel detection based on the analysis of the time-frequency spectrum of acoustic signals.

3.4 External Influences

Handling of external influences are crucial factors in designing an effective detection system for tunnel environments. One important aspect considered was the selection of an appropriate frequency range used. In the case of road and tunnel detection, it has been determined that the relevant frequency range for capturing the acoustic signatures is from 500 Hz to 2 kHz, see Fig. 6.

By focusing on this frequency range, the system can effectively capture and analyze the specific acoustic characteristics associated with roads and tunnels. These frequencies are known to contain vital information related to the road and tunnel environment, such as reverberations, echoes, and specific resonance patterns (Figs. 3 and 4).

To ensure accurate detection, frequencies outside of the relevant range were filtered out. Filtering out frequencies above and below the desired range helps to eliminate unwanted noise and interference that may arise from external sources, such as road traffic, wind, or other environmental factors.

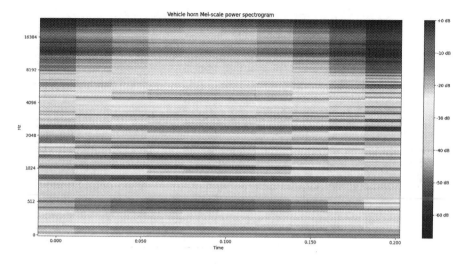

Fig. 3. Vehicle horn spectrogram.

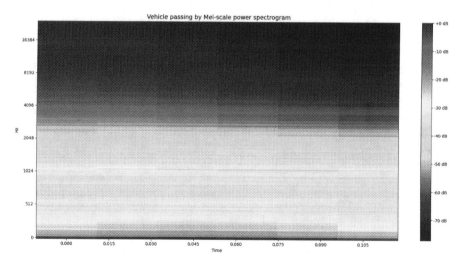

Fig. 4. Vehicle passing by spectrogram.

3.5   Data Collection Process

The audio processing pipeline for tunnel detection involved several steps. First, audio samples with a duration of 1 s were re-sampled from the original 48 kHz to 8 kHz, which had been found to yield good results, and also filter some noise out.

Next, Mel-frequency spectrograms (MELs) were computed from the re-sampled audio samples. The MEL spectrograms represented the spectral energy distribution of the audio signals across different frequency bands.

After generating the MEL spectrograms, a filtering operation was applied to isolate the frequency range of interest. The aim was to focus the analysis on the relevant frequency components. Specifically, the MEL coefficients outside the range of 500 Hz to 2 kHz were filtered out, see Fig. 6.

Once the filtering was completed, the resulting filtered MEL spectrograms served as the basis for extracting features using the Mel-frequency cepstral coefficients (MFCCs) technique. The MFCCs are calculated by taking the discrete cosine transform (DCT) of the logarithm of the filtered MEL spectrograms.

These steps were performed using the Python programming language [16], which provided a versatile and efficient environment for audio data processing.

Several Python libraries were used to streamline the various steps. The scikit-learn library [14] played a crucial role in providing powerful tools for data preprocessing, feature extraction, and machine learning algorithms.

The scipy library [20] proved invaluable for its comprehensive suite of signal processing functions. These functions were utilized for tasks such as Fourier transforms, filtering operations.

A key component of the data collection process was the utilization of the librosa library [11], which is specifically designed for audio and music signal analysis. Librosa provided a high-level interface and a wealth of functionality tailored for tasks such as audio loading, resampling, spectrogram computation, and feature extraction. Resulting data was shown via matplotlib library [8].

By following this pipeline, the system was able to preprocess the audio samples, extracting MFCC features from the filtered MEL spectrograms within the relevant frequency range of 500 Hz to 2 kHz, see Fig. 6 and Fig. 7. These MFCC features served as valuable inputs for subsequent analysis, classification, and detection algorithms, enabling the system to effectively differentiate tunnel-like environments based on their acoustic signatures.

These below formulas describe the mathematical operations involved in computing the MEL spectrogram and extracting the MFCC features:

– Computing the MEL Spectrogram:
   • Apply the Short-Time Fourier Transform (STFT) to audio signal $x(t)$:
     $X(n,\omega) = \sum_{m=0}^{N-1} x(m) \cdot w(m-n) \cdot e^{-j\omega m}$
     (This is a simplified equation which assumes that the audio signal is zero outside the range of 0 to $N-1$, where N is the length of the window. This is a frame-based approach, where the signal is divided into frames of fixed length.)
   • Compute the magnitude spectrum $|X(n,\omega)|$.
   • Apply a Mel filterbank to the magnitude spectrum:
     $S(m,t) = \sum_{\omega=0}^{N/2} H(m,\omega) \cdot |X(n,\omega)|^2$
   • Apply a logarithmic compression to the MEL spectrogram: $S(m,t) = \log(1 + S(m,t))$
– Extracting MFCC Features:
   • Apply the Discrete Cosine Transform (DCT)
     $S(m,t)$: $Y(p,t) = \sum_{m=0}^{M-1} C(m,t) \cdot \cos\left(\frac{\pi}{M}(m+0.5)p\right)$

(The equation calculates each MFCC coefficient $Y(p, t)$ by summing the product of the Mel-scaled filterbank energies or log-compressed spectrogram coefficients $C(m, t)$ and the cosine of a specific argument $\frac{\pi}{M}(m + 0.5)p$. The index m iterates over the filterbank or spectrogram coefficients, and M represents the total number of filters or coefficients.)

- Select a subset of the resulting DCT coefficients $Y(p, t)$ to represent the MFCC features.

4   Analysis and Results

In this section, we present the results of our study on road and tunnel acoustic signature classification combined with Principal Component Analysis (PCA). We begin by providing a detailed analysis of the obtained data, followed by a discussion of the implications and reliability of our findings.

The dataset used for this study consisted of audio spectrograms extracted from road and tunnel environments. Each spectrogram was processed to extract relevant features, and PCA was applied to reduce the dimension of the data. The resulting principal components represented the most informative aspects of the audio signals Fig. 5. A total of 280 samples were available, with 200 samples allocated for training and 80 samples reserved for testing the performance of the classification models.

Firstly, the data was scaled using the RobustScaler, which helps normalize the features and make them less sensitive to outliers. This step was crucial to ensure that all features have a similar scale and avoid biasing the classification models.

4.1   Principal Component Analysis

After scaling, PCA (Fig. 9) was applied to reduce the dimensionality of the feature space. PCA, short for Principal Component Analysis, is a widely used dimensionality reduction technique that transforms the data into a new set of uncorrelated variables called principal components [5]. This transformation is achieved by finding linear combinations of the original features that capture the maximum variance in the data. By doing so, PCA helps to extract the most important information while reducing the dimensionality of the dataset.

In the specific case of the PCA accuracy plot (Fig. 8), which depicts the performance of PCA for different numbers of components using k-fold cross-validation, an interesting observation can be made. Initially, as the number of components increases, there is a noticeable improvement in the accuracy of the PCA-based model. This suggests that the early principal components capture the essential information that contributes to accurate classification or prediction. However, as the number of components continues to increase, the improvement in accuracy becomes less substantial. Beyond a certain threshold, typically around 50 components in this case, the accuracy curve begins to flatten out,

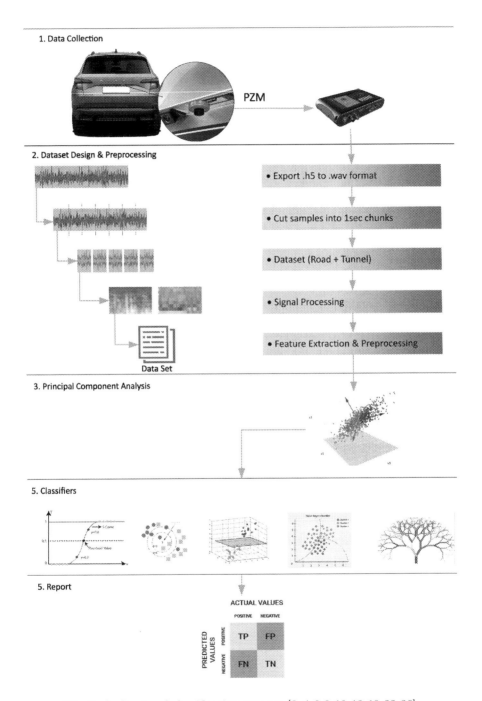

Fig. 5. Audio signal classification process. [2–4, 6, 9, 10, 12, 19, 22, 26]

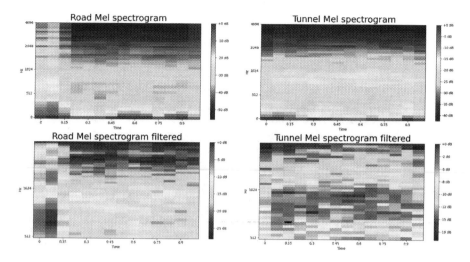

Fig. 6. Mel spectrogram for road and tunnel.

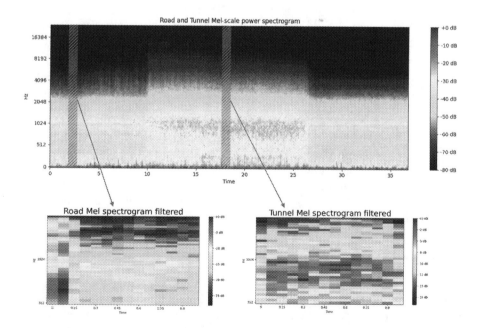

Fig. 7. Signals for classification.

indicating that additional components contribute less significantly to the overall performance. This suggests that a substantial portion of the discriminatory information is captured within the first 50 components, and incorporating more components provides diminishing returns in terms of accuracy improvement.

This finding reinforces the notion that PCA effectively captures the most relevant and informative aspects of the data, allowing for dimensionality reduction without sacrificing much accuracy. By retaining a subset of the most important principal components, we can achieve a compact representation that retains the discriminatory power necessary for accurate classification or prediction tasks.

4.2 Classification

Five different classification models were employed in this study: Logistic Regression, Support Vector Machine with c-support vector classification (SVM/SVC), K-Nearest Neighbors (KNN), Gaussian Naive Bayes (NB), and Random Forest. Each model was trained using the training dataset and evaluated on the test dataset.

The performance of each classification model was assessed using various evaluation metrics, including accuracy, precision, recall, and F1-score. Confusion matrices were also generated to visualize the classification results, see Table 2.

The Logistic Regression model achieved a high accuracy of 98.75% on the test dataset. The precision, recall, and F1-score for both road and tunnel classes were consistently high, indicating reliable classification performance.

The SVM model demonstrated a strong performance with an accuracy of 95.62%. It exhibited balanced precision, recall, and F1-score for both road and tunnel classes, suggesting effective discrimination between the two classes.

The KNN model yielded an accuracy of 70% on the test dataset. While it achieved a high recall for the tunnel class, its precision and F1-score were relatively lower for both road and tunnel classes, indicating some misclassifications.

The Gaussian NB model attained an accuracy of 83.75%. It demonstrated a higher precision and F1-score for the road class compared to the tunnel class. However, its recall for the tunnel class was notably higher, suggesting better identification of tunnel audio samples.

The Random Forest model achieved an accuracy of 80% on the test dataset. It exhibited balanced precision, recall, and F1-score for both road and tunnel classes, indicating reliable classification performance.

4.3 Results Overview

The results indicate that both Logistic Regression and SVM models outperformed the KNN, Gaussian NB, and Random Forest models in accurately classifying road and tunnel audio samples. Logistic Regression showed the highest accuracy, precision, recall, and F1-score, indicating its suitability for audio signature classification in road and tunnel environments.

The KNN model exhibited lower accuracy and precision, suggesting its limitations in effectively distinguishing between road and tunnel classes. The Gaussian NB and Random Forest models achieved moderate accuracies, with slightly varying precision, recall, and F1-scores for road and tunnel classes. These models may be suitable for specific applications or when a balanced performance is desired.

Overall, the findings presented suggest that audio signature classification for environments like road and tunnel can be effectively accomplished using Logistic Regression or SVM (Fig. 10) models. Further research could focus on refining and optimizing these models, as well as exploring additional feature extraction techniques to improve classification performance.

Analysis of PCA component cumulative variance (Fig. 9) shows an interesting trend. Initially, as the number of principal components increases, there is a rapid increase in the cumulative variance explained. This indicates that the early components capture the majority of the variability in the data.

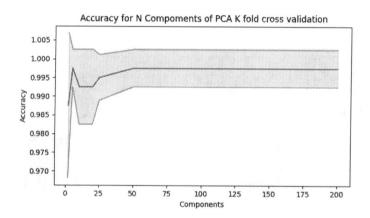

Fig. 8. PCA accuracy for N components.

However, we observed a diminishing rate of increase in the cumulative variance. We reach a point where adding additional components contributes only marginally to the cumulative variance explained. In fact, beyond a certain threshold, as shown in Fig. 9, the curve becomes nearly linear.

This suggests that a significant amount of information of the data is captured by a relatively small number of principal components. These components represent the most dominant and essential features that characterize the acoustic signatures of tunnel environments. As we incorporate more components beyond this critical threshold, the additional information gained becomes increasingly marginal.

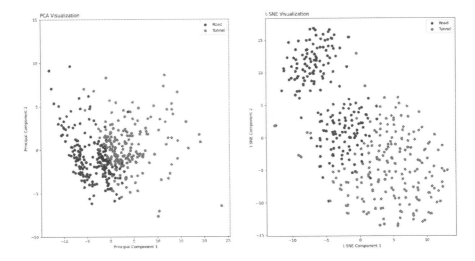

Fig. 9. Principal component analysis.

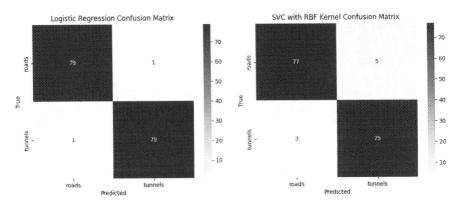

Fig. 10. Confusion matrix of Logistic Regression and SVM.

5   Misalignment Monitoring and Adjustment for Radar Systems

Monitoring and adjusting the alignment of radar systems is a critical process aimed at optimizing their performance. Radar systems consist of various hardware components, such as antennas, transmitters, receivers, and signal processing modules, all of which need to be properly aligned for accurate and reliable operation.

Misalignment in radar systems can result from mechanical vibrations, environmental conditions, installation errors, or component degradation over time. These misalignments can have detrimental effects on system performance,

Table 2. Model evaluation.

Sample	Model	Accuracy	Inference time
1 sec	LogisticRegression	98.75%	$\sim$ 1 ms
	SVC	95.625%	$\sim$ 15.6 ms
	GaussianNB	83.75%	$\sim$ 1 ms
	RandomForest	80%	$\sim$ 3 ms
	K-Nearest Neighbors	70%	$\sim$ 130.9 ms
0.5 sec	LogisticRegression	97.5%	$\sim$ 1 ms
	SVC	93.7%	$\sim$ 10.6 ms
	GaussianNB	86.8%	$\sim$ 1 ms
	RandomForest	81.8%	$\sim$ 2 ms
	K-Nearest Neighbors	73.1%	$\sim$ 80.9 ms
0.1 sec	LogisticRegression	94.3%	$\sim$ 1 ms
	SVC	88.1%	$\sim$ 5.6 ms
	GaussianNB	61.8%	$\sim$ 1 ms
	RandomForest	76.8%	$\sim$ 3 ms
	K-Nearest Neighbors	76.2.1%	$\sim$ 12.9 ms

including reduced detection range, inaccurate target localization, degraded signal quality, and increased false alarms.

Hence, it is essential to assess and correct misalignment in radar systems to ensure their effectiveness. This can be achieved through various techniques, such as sensor-based measurements, optical alignment systems, or signal analysis methods. These techniques enable operators or automated systems to analyze and identify the presence and extent of misalignment. The ultimate goal of this monitoring and adjustment process is to secure maximum accuracy, sensitivity, and reliability in radar system operations.

By employing rigorous analysis and assessment, radar system misalignment can be properly diagnosed and addressed. Findings from such analysis allow for informed conclusions and the development of effective alignment strategies. This comprehensive approach guarantees that radar systems operate at their highest potential, enabling them to fulfill their intended functions with optimal performance.

5.1   Environment Impact

When a vehicle is traveling trough a tunnel, several factors come into play that can affect the alignment and performance of radar systems such are: signal reflections and attenuation, electromagnetic interference etc.

Tunnels are enclosed environments with reflective surfaces, such as walls and ceilings, which can cause signal reflections and multi-path propagation. These reflections can result in overlapping or delayed signals reaching the radar system, leading to inaccuracies in target detection and localization. Misalignment in such scenarios can amplify the effects of signal reflections, making it challenging to distinguish between direct and reflected signals.

The presence of walls and other structures in tunnels can cause signal attenuation, leading to a decrease in signal strength. This attenuation can reduce the effective range and sensitivity of the radar system, making it more difficult to detect and track targets accurately.

Tunnels often have electrical infrastructure, such as lighting, ventilation systems, and power cables, which can generate electromagnetic interference (EMI). EMI can introduce noise and distortions into the radar signals, affecting the quality and reliability of the measurements.

5.2   Mitigate Issues of Misalignment in Tunnel Environments

One of the mitigation of issues with misalignment of radar systems in tunnel like environments, is to provide information of environment to the system in order to incorporate environmental compensation techniques. The radar system can adapt to the specific conditions inside the tunnel, compensating for signal loss and addressing the challenges posed by signal reflections and multipath propagation. This can help improve the quality of radar measurements and mitigate the impact of misalignment-induced errors.

We propose in this paper novel acoustic system called SONETE [18] (Sonic Sensing for Tunnel Environment) for automotive diagnostics.

Fig. 11. Sonete system. [15]

Assistance and driving functions, for example, lane keeping or automated driving, require information about the static and dynamic environment of a vehicle. Usually this information is available trough a sensor data fusion, where information about different environments is available. Here we add SONETE (Fig. 11) as a complementary sensor to a data fusion to ensure that information about vehicle tunnel entrance is available, thus using sensor data fusion to create a comprehensive view of the vehicle's surrounding.

Utilizing information of tunnel presence, Fig. 12, radar system can switch off MM&A feature while the vehicle is traversing trough the tunnel, thus not degrading performance of the system when vehicle exits the tunnel.

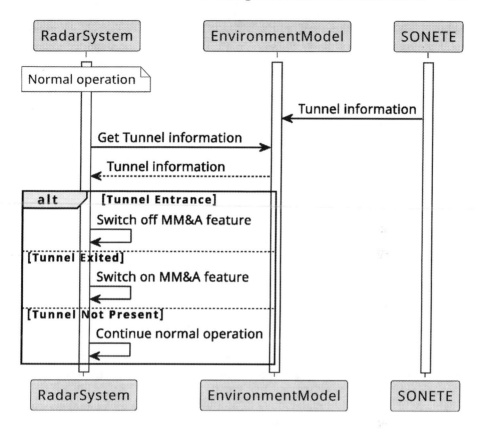

Fig. 12. Mitigate issues of MM&A in tunnel environments.

5.3 Limitations

The presented solution of using PZMs for tunnel detection through acoustic signature analysis has provided valuable insights and plausibility. However, it is important to acknowledge several limitations that should be taken into consideration when interpreting the results and guiding future research.

We analyzed acoustic signatures of a specific tunnel "Mišeluk", and in order to enhance the robustness of the SONETE system, it is crucial to gather recordings from more tunnels with varying characteristics. This would involve considering tunnels of different sizes, materials, traffic conditions, and geographical locations. With this, proposed approach can be better evaluated and its applicability to a wider range of tunnel environments can be assessed.

Placement of the PZM we believe can impact the overall system performance and classification. Optimal placement of the PZM might vary depending on factors such as the vehicle type. Therefore, further investigations will be needeed to explore the effects of different PZM placements to determine the most effective and reliable positioning for capturing tunnel acoustic signatures. This would involve systematically evaluating the influence of microphone location and orientation on the accuracy and consistency of the collected audio data.

The analysis and processing of the audio data in this study were performed on a Windows based machine (Windows PC) with Intel I7-11850H and 32GB of RAM memory, using Python and relevant libraries. However, it is crucial to assess the feasibility and performance of the proposed approach on embedded systems or real-time monitoring platforms. Evaluating the algorithm's implementation on resource-constrained devices would provide insights into its practical viability for on-board vehicle systems or embedded monitoring systems.

6   Conclusion

Time-frequency spectrum analysis of road and tunnel audio signals, showed the potential of utilizing acoustic signatures for classification of tunnel like environments, thus implying the use of PZMs for tunnel detection plausible.

In this paper we used information of the environment, gathered from a proposed novel SONETE system, to enhances the robustness of radar technology in complex environments and ensures effective MM&A adjustments in tunnels, where traditional sensors often encounter limitations.

Recordings from other tunnels with varying characteristics should be gathered in order to enhance the robustness of the SONETE system. This would involve considering tunnels of different sizes, materials, traffic conditions, and geographical locations. With this, proposed approach can be better evaluated and its applicability to a wider range of tunnel environments can be assessed.

In conclusion, this research paper highlights the significance of addressing the challenges faced by radar systems equipped with Misalignment Monitoring and Adjustment (MM&A) in complex environments, specifically tunnels.

References

1. Bertozzi, M., Broggi, A., Boccalini, G., Mazzei, L.: Fast vision-based road tunnel detection. In: Maino, G., Foresti, G.L. (eds.) ICIAP 2011. LNCS, vol. 6979, pp. 424–433. Springer, Heidelberg (2011). https://doi.org/10.1007/978-3-642-24088-1_44
2. Bhandari, A.: Understanding & interpreting confusion matrices for machine learning (2023). https://cdn.analyticsvidhya.com/wp-content/uploads/2020/04/Basic-Confusion-matrix.png
3. CarSized: Skoda karoq rear view image. (2023). https://www.carsized.com/resources/skoda/karoq/d/2017/ra_299000000_skoda-karoq-2017-rear-view_4x.png
4. Cheng, C.: Towards data science (2023). https://miro.medium.com/v2/resize:fit:596/1*QinDfRawRskupf4mU5bYSA.png
5. Pearson, K.: Liii. on lines and planes of closest fit to systems of points in space. London, Edinburgh, Dublin Philos. Mag. J. Sci. 2(11), 559–572 (1901). https://doi.org/10.1080/14786440109462720

6. GRAS: 147AX CCP rugged pressure microphone (2023). https://www.grasacoustics.com/products/measurement-microphone-sets/constant-current-power-ccp/product/806-147ax

7. Gupta, S., Debata, R.R.: Tunnel detection for automotive radar using object elevation trends and gaussian filtering. In: 2022 1st International Conference on Informatics (ICI), pp. 132–136 (2022). https://doi.org/10.1109/ICI53355.2022.9786874

8. Hunter, J.D.: Matplotlib: A 2d graphics environment. Comput. Sci. Eng. **9**(3), 90 (2007)

9. Javatpoint: logistic regression in machine learning (2023). https://miro.medium.com/v2/resize:fit:596/1*QinDfRawRskupf4mU5bYSA.png

10. KGP, K.I.: Naive bayes algorithm (2023). https://editor.analyticsvidhya.com/uploads/23385Capture6.PNG

11. McFee, B., et al.: Librosa: audio and music signal analysis in python. In: Proceedings of the 14th Python in Science Conference, vol. 8 (2015)

12. Microflown: Voyager portable measuring systems (2023). https://www.microflown.com/products/portable-measuring-systems/voyager

13. Nedelchev, K., Gieva, E., Kralov, I., Ruskova, I.: Investigation of the change of acoustic pressure in an element of acoustic barrier with an elliptical shape. Acoustics **5**, 46–56 (2022). https://doi.org/10.3390/acoustics5010003

14. Pedregosa, F., et al.: Scikit-learn: machine learning in python. J. Mach. Learn. Res. **12**, 2825–2830 (2011)

15. PngWing: Skoda karoq car (2023). https://w7.pngwing.com/pngs/355/475/png-transparent-volkswagen-%C5%A0koda-auto-%C5%A0koda-karoq-car-%C5%A0koda-fabia-vehicle-rim-metal.png

16. Python core team: python: a dynamic, open source programming language. Python software foundation (2020). https://www.python.org/, python version 3.9

17. Sim, H., Lee, S., Lee, B.H., Kim, S.C.: Road structure classification through artificial neural network for automotive radar systems. IET Radar, Sonar Navig. **13**(6), 1010–1017 (2019)

18. Stojkov, N.: Tunnel detection github repository (2023). https://github.com/nikolawinmaker/tunnel_detection

19. Vashist, A.: Random forest classification (2023). https://www.fromthegenesis.com/wp-content/uploads/2018/06/RanFore.jpg

20. Virtanen, P., et al.: SciPy 1.0: fundamental algorithms for scientific computing in python. Nat. Methods (2020). https://doi.org/10.1038/s41592-019-0686-2

21. Wang, K., et al.: An imaging algorithm for obstacle detection of tunnel horizontal transporter based on millimeter wave radar. In: 2022 4th International Academic Exchange Conference on Science and Technology Innovation (IAECST), pp. 1388–1393 (2022). https://doi.org/10.1109/IAECST57965.2022.10062270

22. Xilinx: Support vector machine (2023). https://www.xilinx.com/content/xilinx/en/developer/articles/exploring-support-vector-machine-acceleration-with-vitis/_jcr_content/root/parsys/xilinximage.img.png/1571676692198.png

23. Yanase, R., Hirano, D., Aldibaja, M., Yoneda, K., Suganuma, N.: Lidar- and radar-based robust vehicle localization with confidence estimation of matching results. Sensors **22**(9), 3545 (2022). https://doi.org/10.3390/s22093545, http://dx.doi.org/10.3390/s22093545

24. Yi, C., et al.: Hierarchical tunnel modeling from 3d raw lidar point cloud. Comput.-Aided Des. **114**, 143–154 (2019). https://doi.org/10.1016/j.cad.2019.05.033, https://www.sciencedirect.com/science/article/pii/S0010448519302064

25. Yoon, J., Lee, S., Lim, S., Kim, S.C.: High-density clutter recognition and suppression for automotive radar systems. IEEE Access **7**, 58368–58380 (2019). https://doi.org/10.1109/ACCESS.2019.2914267

26. Zhang, L.: K nearest neighbor illustration (2023). https://www.researchgate.net/profile/Le-Zhang-61/publication/261052898/figure/fig1/AS:613879138750464@1523371600052/K-Nearest-Neighbor-Illustration.png

27. Zhen, W., Scherer, S.: Estimating the localizability in tunnel-like environments using lidar and UWB. In: 2019 International Conference on Robotics and Automation (ICRA), pp. 4903–4908 (2019). https://doi.org/10.1109/ICRA.2019.8794167

28. Zhu, H.H., Liu, W., Wang, T., Su, J.W., Shi, B.: Distributed acoustic sensing for monitoring linear infrastructures: Curr. Status Trends. Sens. **22**(19), 7550 (Oct 2022). https://doi.org/10.3390/s22197550, http://dx.doi.org/10.3390/s22197550

Comparative Analysis of UPPAAL SMC, ns-3 and MATLAB/Simulink

Muhammad Naeem[✉], Michele Albano, Kim Guldstrand Larsen,
and Brian Nielsen

Department of Computer Science, Aalborg University, Aalborg, Denmark
{mnaeem,mialb,kgl,bnielsen}@cs.aau.dk

Abstract. IoT networks connect everyday devices to the internet to
communicate with one another and humans. It is more cost-effective
to analyse and verify the performance of the designed prototype before
deploying these complex networks. Network Simulator 3 (ns-3), MAT-
LAB/Simulink, and UPPAAL SMC are three industry-leading tools that
simulate communicating models, each with strengths and weaknesses.
NS3 is suitable for large-scale network simulations, MATLAB/Simulink
is suitable for complex models and data analysis, and UPPAAL SMC is
efficient for real-time probabilistic systems with complex timing requirements, This paper presents a comparative analysis of NS3 and MAT-
LAB/Simulink and UPPAAL SMC, based on a Sigfox-based case study,
focusing on the behaviour of a single Sigfox node. The comparison is
drawn on ease of use, flexibility, and scalability. The results can help
researchers make informed decisions when designing and evaluating simulation experiments. They demonstrate that the choice of tool depends
on the specific requirements of the simulation project and requires careful
consideration of the strengths and weaknesses of each tool.

Keywords: WSN · Network Simulators · Sigfox · Energy Model ·
Network Modelling · IoT

1 Introduction

The Internet of Things (IoT) has seen significant growth in recent years, leading
to the development of intelligent environments in areas like smart homes, energy,
and industry [8]. As IoT devices are often used in sensitive areas to collect
information and control the environment, designing an efficient model to reduce
the error risk and ensure system security is crucial. Simulating the prototype's
model during the design process is essential to analyse its performance, identify
flaws, and overcome potential vulnerabilities. Several network simulation tools
are available, but selecting the most suitable one can be difficult.

This paper presents a comparative analysis of three simulation tools: Network
Simulator 3 (ns-3), UPPAAL Statistical Model Checker (SMC) [3], and MAT-
LAB/Simulink [6], based on the simulation of an industrial case study aiming

© The Author(s), under exclusive license to Springer Nature Switzerland AG 2024
J. Kofroň et al. (Eds.): ECBS 2023, LNCS 14390, pp. 153–169, 2024.
https://doi.org/10.1007/978-3-031-49252-5_12

to develop an energy-efficient wireless network for monitoring water levels in drainage lines.

The choice to compare these three tools is driven by their distinct network simulation and analysis capabilities. ns-3 excels in scalability and efficiency, making it ideal for large-scale wireless network simulations. UPPAAL SMC's statistical model checking offers valuable formal verification capabilities, while MATLAB/Simulink's versatility in handling continuous and deterministic simulations adds another dimension to the comparison. This study aims to provide valuable insights into their performance and applicability for simulating energy-efficient wireless networks. The findings will help researchers and network administrators select the most suitable tool for their simulation needs.

The analysis involves the utilisation of these different tools to explore multiple aspects, including modelling complexity, simulation time, memory utilisation, and validation of the energy-efficient wireless network. The objective is to investigate the strengths and weaknesses of each tool and identify key considerations in selecting the most suitable tool for applications of this nature.

The rest of this paper is structured in the following manner: Sect. 2 provides an overview of the Related Work. Section 3 presents the tools overview used in this study. Section 4 presents the case study, focusing on the Sigfox sensor node. Subsequently, Sect. 5 describes the case study's modelling in ns-3, UPPAAL SMC, and MATLAB/Simulink. Section 6 presents a comprehensive comparative analysis of the tools. Finally, in Sect. 7, we conclude the paper and propose avenues for future research.

2 Related Work

In recent years, the availability of various network simulation tools has provided researchers and network administrators with numerous options to choose from. However, the diversity of tools can complicate selecting the most suitable one for specific applications [12].

Nayyar and Singh [12] provided a comprehensive review of 31 simulators, aiming to clarify the features and limitations of each simulator to help new researchers in selecting the most appropriate simulation tool for their applications. The authors discussed the architecture of WSN simulators and proposed evaluation criteria, including the type of simulator, license, platform, ease of coding, tracing, debugging, popularity, and graphical support. The simulators were classified into three categories: generic simulators, code-level simulators, and firmware-level simulators. Generic simulators use high-level programming languages to simulate networking models but are considered less reliable compared to code-level and firmware-level simulators.

Xian et al. [17] compared OMNet++ simulators against other simulators such as OPNET and ns-2. The study demonstrated that OMNet++ outperformed both OPNET and ns-2 in terms of functionalities, including debugging, tracing, hierarchical modelling, and a powerful simulation library. The authors evaluated the performance of the simulators by implementing a well-known WSN protocol called directed diffusion and measuring performance metrics like total run time, delivery rate, and memory requirement. The results showed that OMNet++ was the most powerful and efficient simulator.

In a study by Gnanaselvi [5], a survey was conducted to gain a better understanding of the current network simulation tools available and their features. Bakni et al. [1] presented a methodology for evaluating WSN simulators focusing on energy conservation. Kochhar and Kaur [7] proposed an approach to guide beginners in choosing an efficient simulator for designing a simulation environment based on their application area.

Our work presents the first comparative analysis of the network simulation tool ns-3 and MATLAB/Simulink with UPPAAL SMC. None of the prior research considers the use of the model checker, which is a distinct feature in UPPAAL SMC. The comparison is based on applying the three tools in an industrial case study.

3   Tools Overview

This section presents an overview of ns-3, UPPAAL SMC and MATLAB/Simulink.

3.1   ns-3

ns-3 is an open-source Discrete Event Simulator (DES) released in 2008 [13]. It offers C++ simulation language with optional Python bindings, making it highly adaptable. It includes models for wired technologies, such as Ethernet networks with CSMA/CD protocols, and wireless technologies, like 802.11 MAC-level and 802.11a physical layer models. Its simulation library focuses on realism and reusability, allowing researchers to create complex network scenarios. ns-3 also supports NetAnim software, allowing for real-time experiments via emulation. ns-3 is a comprehensive and widely used network protocol design and evaluation platform because it integrates various simulation tools. The ns-3 simulator's basic architecture is depicted in Fig. 1 [15]. The figure shows that users create simulation programs that define network behaviour, utilising a simulation library with built-in models for nodes, links, channels, and protocols (ns-3 core). The engine executes these scripts to simulate the network. Data analysis modules offer statistics and performance metrics. Simulation outcomes are generated in a text file that can be analysed using the external graphing tool.

3.2   UPPAAL SMC

Statistical model checking (SMC) advances the classic model checking technique [14]. SMC avoids the state-space exploration problem of the classic model checking, and it also comparatively consumes less time and memory in simulation. It simulates a model a number of times and uses statistical hypothesis testing for model checking. SMC technique can also estimate probabilistic systems' quantitative and qualitative properties.

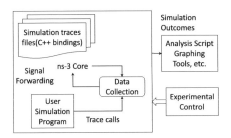

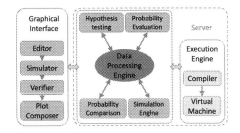

Fig. 1. Framework of NS-3 architecture [15]

Fig. 2. Architecture of UPPAAL SMC [4]

UPPAAL SMC is an extension of UPPAAL [3], and it models a system using priced timed automata. UPPAAL SMC's model is based on stochastic and non-linear dynamic behavioural properties. Figure 2 depicts the UPPAAL SMC's architecture [4]. The tool's interface allows users to create automata models in the editor and run simulations for the system's verification, validation and quantitative analysis. It supports visualising results as plots. The UPPAAL SMC execution engine exploits the stochastic semantics of interacting stochastic hybrid automata to evaluate the performance queries.

3.3   MATLAB/Simulink

MATLAB/Simulink is a robust simulation methodology, combining MATLAB for matrix-based computation and Simulink for dynamic system design and simulation [6]. It offers a graphical programming language, visualisation tools, and extensibility through MATLAB integration, enabling efficient modelling, simulation, and analysis of diverse systems.

This integration offers researchers and developers in the embedded systems domain an efficient platform to model, simulate, and analyse complex embedded systems scenarios. With a graphical programming language and visualisation tools, MATLAB/Simulink enables the creation of intricate embedded systems models, including various network topologies and sensor node behaviours.

4   Case Study

The aim of the Distributed ONline monitoring of the Urban waTer cycle (DONUT) project is to develop a cost and energy-efficient IoT-based network to monitor the water cycle (See Fig. 3). The Montem Company (a project partner of the DONUT project) has developed a prototype of a digital wireless sensor network based on the Sigfox transceiver. The prototype includes a Sigfox transceiver, Atmega controller, ultrasonic sensor, Digital accelerometer, EEP-ROM, Regulator, and Battery (10,000 mAh). The controller uses the ultrasonic sensor to measure the water height and then analyses the data to determine the water height for a cycle. The processed value is stored in the EEPROM before being transmitted to the base station through the Sigfox transmitter. The accelerometer is used to ensure the sensor node's position. Our project is focused on modelling the designed prototype's behaviour using a simulation tool to analyse the battery lifetime and investigate different transmission strategies to improve the overall node's lifetime.

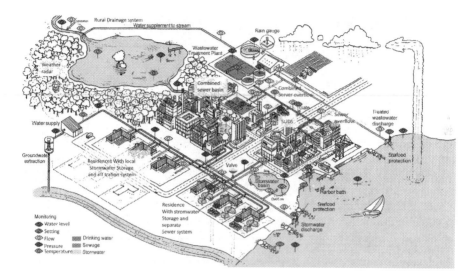

Fig. 3. DONUT-project's low cast sensor network provides holistic urban water system insights for better decisions. 200+ sensors monitor the water cycle, from groundwater to stormwater.

Sigfox is a low-power wide-area network (LPWAN) developed and operated by Sigfox, a company based in France. The basic structure of the Sigfox network is shown in Fig. 4. Sensor nodes use binary phase-shift keying modulation to communicate with the base station in a star topology. A Sigfox node broadcasts its message, which nearby base stations can receive, and these messages are then transferred to the Sigfox cloud. From there, they can be accessed by any IoT platform [16]. Sigfox specifications may vary depending on the region. The European part is the focus of this case study [16]. Sigfox restricts the messages a node can transmit to 6 per hour (144 per day) with a maximum payload of 12 bytes to reduce energy consumption. Additionally, nodes can receive up to 4 downlink messages per day.

5   Modelling the Case Study

In this section, we present the modelling of the DONUT case study utilising different tools, enabling us to conduct a comprehensive comparative analysis.

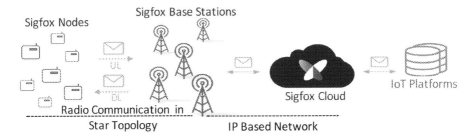

Fig. 4. Sigfox network Architecture

5.1   Implementation in ns-3

In [11], we have presented a Sigfox module for ns-3, and we also investigate the DONUT case study. The model is parametric concerning the hardware properties of the IoT device under research and includes all major energy-consuming states and actions of a Sigfox node. We built the energy model for the device based on data from the Sigfox radio specifications and power characteristics. We also used a novel battery model that considers the self-discharge current. Figure 5 depicts the class diagram of the C++-based designed Sigfox module, which includes the classes and functions that implement the core functionalities.

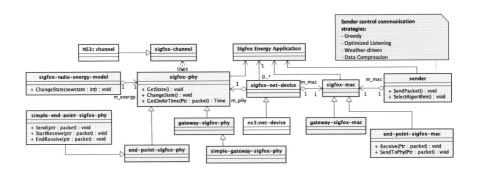

Fig. 5. Class Diagram of Sigfox Module in ns-3 [11]

Sigfox-phy: The `sigfox` module implementation features a PHY layer abstraction that models the interference between multiple colliding Sigfox transmissions to ensure appropriate behaviour when the simulation features large deployments. It also computes energy consumed by each state using subclass `sigfox-radio-energy-model` (See Fig. 5).

Sigfox-mac: The MAC protocol operates on top of the physical layer. As shown in Fig. 5, the implementation of this layer is divided into two classes, `EndPointSigfoxMac` and `GatewaySigfoxMac`, which model the MAC protocol for end node and Gateway separately. The behaviour of a node's MAC layer

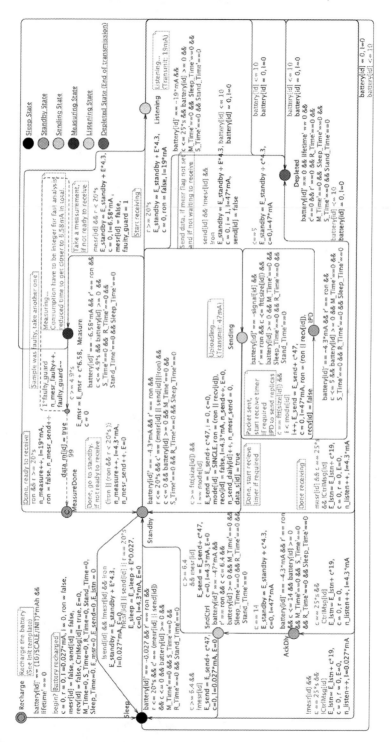

Fig. 6. Basic structure of the designed model in UPPAAL SMC [9]

implements the communication procedures (Uni-directional and Bi-directional), and it controls transmission strategies using subclass `sender` (See Fig. 5).

5.2   Implementation in UPPAAL SMC

In articles [9,10], we have presented the energy-aware analysis of this case study by designing and simulating its model in UPPAAL SMC. In the developed model, we only include the sensor node's behaviour, as the node's battery lifetime is unaffected by the remaining network elements following the Sigfox protocol. Unlike ns-3, we don't need to develop a complete network to simulate a node's behaviour but only a more abstract model capturing the system's behaviour.

The system's model includes four sub-process automaton models (`Initial`, `SensorNode`, `Self-Discharge`, and `Scheduler`), interconnected through shared variables and synchronisation channels to model the sensor node's energy behaviour effectively. `Initial` enables all other processes to an active state using a synchronisation channel, and the `Self-Discharge` model represents the battery's self-discharge behavior. The `SensorNode` automaton (shown in Fig. 6) models the behaviour of the Sigfox sensor node, and the `Scheduler` controls the actions of the `SensorNode`. The complete model is presented in paper [9].

The studies also investigate the different transmission strategies to optimise the battery lifetime. In UPPAAL SMC, as depicted in Fig. 6, users need to have proficiency in automaton modelling and a basic knowledge of the C language.

5.3   Implementation in MATLAB/Simulink

Figure 7 illustrates the behavioural model of the case study implemented in Simulink. We use the C Function block from the Simulink Library to build the Simulink model for the case study. It supports C programming to define the desired algorithm or functionality.

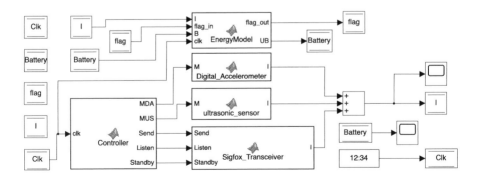

Fig. 7. Sigfox Sensor Node Energy Model in Simulink

The model comprises five main components: Controller, Sigfox_transceiver, Ultrasonic_sensor, Digital_Accelerometer, and EnergyModel. The Controller is responsible for managing the operations of the active components. A sum block adds the current consumption by the Sigfox_transceiver, Ultrasonic_sensor, and Digital_Accelerometer. The EnergyModel utilises the combined system's current to update the battery level for every time unit and manage the self-discharge mechanism. By using a scope block, we can observe the behaviour of combined current and battery discharge.

6   Comparative Analysis of UPPAAL and ns-3

This section presents the comparative analysis of ns-3, UPPAAL SMC, and MAT-LAB/Simulink, considering tool performance, simulation, validation, and usability. The research is based on the DONUT case study.

6.1   Classification of Network Simulation

Article [15] categorises simulations into different classes based on their application areas.

Continuous simulation: Continuous simulation is employed for models with dynamic state variables or parameters that change frequently over time. This type of simulation finds utility in diverse areas, such as military applications (e.g., simulating missile trajectories in WSN deployment).

DES: Discrete-event simulation is applied to systems with events occurring at discrete time intervals. Each change represents an event, with no expected changes between events.

Stochastic simulation: Stochastic simulation involves modelling probabilistic systems, such as evaluating telecommunication system latency, traffic flow in communication networks, and studying climatic changes. Monte Carlo simulation is a specific type of stochastic simulation.

Deterministic simulation: Deterministic simulation is employed in systems characterised by a lack of randomness. These systems possess pre-known inputs and yield unique sets of outputs.

UPPAAL **SMC:** UPPAAL SMC is a powerful tool that supports various simulations, including continuous, discrete, stochastic, and deterministic simulations [3]. It uses timed automata to model systems with precise timing and discrete events, allowing for continuous and discrete behaviour representation. With its support for continuous simulation, researchers can define clock variables to control the timing and duration of events. For stochastic simulation, UPPAAL SMC introduces random variables and probability distributions, making it suitable for modelling systems with uncertainty and probabilistic outcomes. Additionally, UPPAAL SMC can perform deterministic simulation, enabling researchers to precisely control the timing of events and verify the deterministic properties of real-time systems.

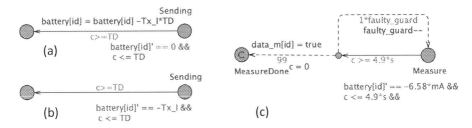

Fig. 8. Discrete and continuous behaviour (a,b) and Probabilistic choice (c) in UPPAAL SMC

Figure 8 depicts a segment of our UPPAAL SMC model. Figures 8(a,b) showcase discrete and continuous behaviours modelling. We update environment variables (Battery clock) after task completion to simulate discrete behaviour, considering the time spent at that location. UPPAAL SMC supports ordinary differential equations to model continuous variable evolution while staying at a specific location. Figure 8(c) illustrates the implementation of a probabilistic choice for stochastic simulation in UPPAAL SMC. The dotted line represents a probabilistic choice, where the model selects the next action based on probability. In our model, there is a 1% likelihood that the system measurement might be inaccurate. In this scenario, the model reverts to the measuring location. Otherwise, it will proceed to the following location.

Overall, UPPAAL SMC is a versatile tool that provides comprehensive capabilities for analysing a wide range of real-time systems with different behaviours and uncertainties. One limitation of UPPAAL SMC is that its continuous simulation is not as comprehensive as specialised tools like MATLAB/Simulink.

ns-3: ns-3 is a flexible and versatile network simulator that supports various types of simulation [13]. It can perform continuous simulation through event-based modelling, approximating continuous behaviour using small time steps. As a discrete-event simulator, ns-3 follows strict event scheduling for discrete simulation, making it suitable for modelling systems with specific time intervals for events.

In ns-3, we use Random Number Generator (RNG) (a built-in class) to model the probabilistic choice. It supports stochastic simulation by allowing researchers to introduce random variables and probability distributions. Additionally, ns-3 can perform deterministic simulation, where researchers can control the sequence of events and verify the deterministic properties of communication networks and protocols. It offers different algorithms to generate deterministic random variables.

While ns-3 offers a wide range of capabilities, it is important to note that continuous simulation in ns-3 is less comprehensive than in specialised continuous simulation tools, and stochastic simulation might require more manual intervention and configuration.

MATLAB/Simulink: Simulink is a robust simulation and modelling environment that extends the capabilities of MATLAB to support continuous, discrete, stochastic, and deterministic simulation [6]. It excels in continuous simulation by providing a graphical interface to model and simulate dynamic systems described by differential equations. Simulink's solvers can numerically solve these equations, allowing for the simulation of continuous behaviour over time. Additionally, researchers can use it to perform discrete simulations by specifying the sample time of blocks in the block diagram, enabling the simulation of systems with specific time intervals for events. It also supports stochastic simulation by allowing the introduction of random variables and probability distributions, and it can perform a deterministic simulation with precise control over the sequence of events. In this project, we use discrete modelling using an integer clock and schedule all events based on that, and we use a random variable to model stochastic behaviour. MATLAB/Simulink model is more abstract and simple in our case; however, the author [6] claims that building complex models in MATLAB/Simulink might require more time and effort than programming-based approaches.

6.2   Simulation Terms (Memory Consumption and Simulation Time)

The same model's memory consumption and simulation time can vary depending on the tool used. Figure 9 compares the tools regarding memory consumption and execution time while simulating the case study. ns-3 has less memory consumption, while UPPAAL SMC has the shortest execution time. MATLAB has the lowest memory consumption but the longest execution time.

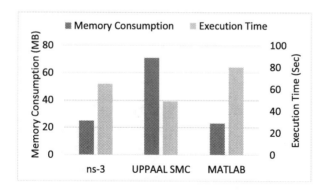

Fig. 9. Memory Consumption and Simulation time

System Configuration Details: The simulations for all models were conducted on a local machine with the following specifications: a MacBook Pro

(2019) workstation equipped with 16 GB 2133 MHz LPDDR3 memory and a 2.4 GHz Quad-Core Intel Core i5 processor. The machine ran macOS Monterey (Version 12.3.1) as the operating system.

6.3   General Comparison

This section provide a comprehensive comparison of the tools, with an abstract visual representation in Fig. 10 and a tabulated summary in Table 1. The Table presents how we categorise the different aspects of modelling a system in the tools focused on in this study; we've given them scores ranging from 0 to 10 (where 0 means challenging to use, and 10 means most accessible to use).

Expertise Required to Model: UPPAAL SMC focuses on formal modelling and verification, making it suitable for researchers with a strong background in formal methods and automata theory. It also required a basic level of C++ to model actions behaviour. On the other hand, ns-3 demands a higher level of programming expertise in C++ and the core architecture of the network and protocols for developing network simulations. MATLAB/Simulink, in contrast, provides a higher level of abstraction and requires less programming expertise.

Other Expertise: Modelling in ns-3 only requires only good programming expertise. UPPAAL SMC needs a good knowledge of automata models with the basic concept of programming to design a system model, and MATLAB/Simulink requires familiarity with Simulink's interface and its blocks.

Graphical User Interface (GUI) Support: UPPAAL SMC provides a user-friendly GUI that simplifies formal modelling and verification tasks, allowing users to design and visualise timed automata models. In contrast, ns-3 does not have a built-in GUI, and users must write network simulations using C++ or Python, which requires advanced programming expertise. MATLAB/Simulink provides a complete GUI environment allowing users to visually represent complex system models using blocks and connections. This user-friendly interface benefits researchers with an engineering or numerical analysis background.

Availability of Good Online Documentation: Online network analysis and simulation documentation for ns-3 and MATLAB/Simulink is more detailed and readily available than for UPPAAL SMC. The dedicated networking focus and their active community provide comprehensive tutorials and user guides. Many built-in libraries and baseline examples are also available to build the basic structure of the network and standard communication protocols. The specialised focus of UPPAAL SMC on formal modelling and verification may result in limited specific documentation for network analysis and simulation tasks. But it provides a good user guide and online support group for efficient model design.

Table 1. Comparison of Uppaal SMC (U/S), ns-3(N) and MATLAB/Simulink(M/S)

		U/S	ns-3	M/S
Programming Expertise				
No	10	7	3	7
Basic (Conditions, loops, function)	7			
Expert (Classes and structures, Pointers, Memory Management)	3			
Other Expertise				
Only programming skill required	10	3	10	3
Multiple languages required	7			
Other modelling technique	3			
GUI Support				
Advanced	10	10	0	10
Moderate	5			
No	0			
Availability of good online documentation				
BaseLine Examples	10			
Built-in libraries	8			
Strong Literature Review	6			
Week Literature Review	5			
Online Support Group	4	5	10	10
User Guide	2			
No Help	0			
Scalability				
Allowed large scale network simulations	10			
Allowed but simulation time increase more frequently	7	7	10	7
Partiacialy allowed	3			
Not allowed	0			
Limitations in model Design				
Allowed most of the operation in networks	10	5	10	10
Limited tool set	5			
Not allowed	0			
Result Visualisation				
Optimisation of graphs	10	7	3	10
Graphical Representation & Text Data output	7			
Text Data	3			
Model Verification				
Rich proper language	10			
Automatic analysis	8			
Model Validation for function requirements	6	10	4	4
Ad Hoc Test Cases as Script	4			
Verbose output log enabling extend analysis	2			
Documentation of model / Representation of model				
Graphical representation	10	10	5	10
Document in the form of blocks or class diagram	5			
Code based representation	3			

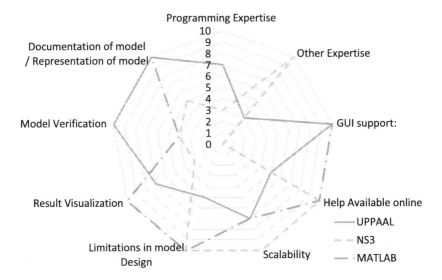

Fig. 10. General Comparison of UPPAAL SMC, ns-3 and MATLAB/Simulink

The Sigfox module wasn't available in ns-3 for this case study, so we modified and customised a LoRaWan module for Sigfox. We built the models for MATLAB/Simulink and UPPAAL SMC from scratch.

Scalability: Scalability was not within the scope of our case study, but in general, ns-3 is highly scalable and optimised for large-scale network simulations, making it an excellent option for simulations requiring much scalability. UPPAAL SMC is well-suited for small to medium-sized systems, but its scalability may be limited for large and complex systems. Scalability to the very large system can be achieved by exploiting the possibility in the newly released UPPAAL 5.0 of linking to external compiled C-code (this was successfully done for the simulation of a model of Nothern Jutland of COVID-19 comprising more than 1 million components) [2]. The scalability of MATLAB/Simulink is generally good for small to moderate-sized models, but it may have performance limitations for large-scale simulations involving complex mathematical computations.

Limitations in Model Design: Both ns-3 and MATLAB/Simulink exhibit versatility in network analysis, allowing for robust modelling without significant design limitations. On the other hand, UPPAAL employs clock variables in timed automata, which evolve continuously through time derivative rates. It only supports integer values in clock rates and clock conditional statements.

In this case study, the node takes 4.9 s to gather measurements in the measuring state. However, UPPAAL SMC doesn't support conditions with floating-point numbers, so we adjusted the base time clock from seconds to desi-seconds. This conversion allowed us to represent the condition as 49 desi-seconds instead of 4.9 s. Simulating the node becomes more complicated when the base clock needs to be reduced to micro or nanoseconds to avoid floating point numbers, and the simulation time is in multiple years.

Result Visualisation: UPPAAL SMC provides result analysis and visualisation through its built-in plot composer tool. However, it cannot zoom in on specific sections of the simulation graph for detailed analysis. In comparison, the ns-3 provides simulation results in a text data stream format that requires additional software like Gnuplot for graphical representations. We use MATLAB to visualise ns-3 simulation results and some simulation results from UPPAAL SMC to highlight a specific plot section. However, MATLAB/Simulink stands out with its extensive visualisation functions and exceptional versatility in handling diverse simulation types, making it highly suitable for a wide range of result analysis and visualisation tasks.

Model Verification: UPPAAL SMC is a specialised tool designed explicitly for formal model checking, making it a powerful choice for testing model correctness. It uses statistical model-checking techniques to verify if the system behaviour meets predefined requirements. This tool automatically checks for probabilistic systems' reachability, safety, and liveness properties, providing valuable insights into the model's correctness.

$$Pr[<=100*days](<> Sensors(0).Listening \&\& r>20) \tag{1}$$

Equation 1 illustrates a query in UPPAAL SMC, verifying the model's compliance with the requirement that it start listening (to receive a message) 20 s after sending an up-link. In this query, the clock variable r is a timer initiated upon transmitting the up-link frame. The query executes the model for hundred days to compute the possibility of reaching the state with the greater value of r. In this case, the calculated probability is zero, so the model is correct.

In contrast, ns3 and Simulink do not offer statistical model-checking capabilities like UPPAAL SMC. However, researchers can still create test cases, analyse simulation results, and validate the system's behaviour against expected outcomes.

Documentation of Model/Representation of Model: We need good documentation of a designed model to present in front of others for many reasons (Publishing, collaborating or proving). The documentation must be graphical and more generic to make it more understandable for people from all domains.

Comparatively, the model in UPPAAL SMC and MATLAB/Simulink has a graphical representation of the system's behaviour, and it is easy to convert into documentation in the form of states and actions.

7   Conclusions and Future Work

UPPAAL SMC is a powerful tool for verifying early-phase design and identifying vulnerabilities in distributed communication systems. Its statistical model-checking capabilities ensure the correctness and reliability of the model, particularly benefiting users with expertise in Automaton models. ns-3 stands out for large-scale network simulations. Its event-driven architecture and visualisation modules are ideal for extensive network simulations and analysis. It is particularly well-suited for users proficient in C++ programming with a solid understanding of communication networks and protocols, enabling them to perform comprehensive network analyses. MATLAB/Simulink is versatile for simulating and testing communication networks. It has powerful simulation capabilities and visualisation functions, making analysis and visualisation of results easy. It's flexible for different types of simulations and result analysis. It is more suitable for users who know basic C code function blocks.

Future work can explore the co-simulation of UPPAAL SMC, ns-3, and MATLAB/Simulink to leverage their strengths and enhance overall simulation capabilities. Integrating these tools can offer a more comprehensive approach to network simulation and analysis, allowing researchers to tackle complex scenarios more effectively.

References

1. Bakni, M., Chacón, L.M.M., Cardinale, Y., Terrasson, G., Curea, O.: WSN simulators evaluation: an approach focusing on energy awareness. arXiv preprint arXiv:2002.06246 (2020)
2. Bilgram, A., et al.: An investigation of safe and near-optimal strategies for prevention of covid-19 exposure using stochastic hybrid models and machine learning. Decis. Anal. J. **5**, 100141 (2022). https://doi.org/10.1016/j.dajour.2022.100141, https://www.sciencedirect.com/science/article/pii/S2772662222000728
3. David, A., Larsen, K.G., Legay, A., Mikučionis, M., Poulsen, D.B.: UPPAAL SMC tutorial. Int. J. Softw. Tools Technol. Transfer **17**(4), 397–415 (2015)
4. David, A., Larsen, K.G., Legay, A., Mikučionis, M., Poulsen, D.B., Sedwards, S.: Runtime verification of biological systems. In: Margaria, T., Steffen, B. (eds.) ISoLA 2012. LNCS, vol. 7609, pp. 388–404. Springer, Heidelberg (2012). https://doi.org/10.1007/978-3-642-34026-0_29
5. Gnanaselvi, S.: A study on various simulation tools for wireless sensor networks. Int. J. Eng. Res. Manag. (IJERM) **5**, 1–3 (2018)
6. Knight, A.: Basics of MATLAB and Beyond. CRC Press, Boca Raton (2019)
7. Kochhar, A., Kaur, P., Preeti.: Simulation platforms for wireless sensor networks: how to select?. In: Tuba, M., Akashe, S., Joshi, A. (eds.) Information and Communication Technology for Sustainable Development. Advances in Intelligent Systems and Computing, vol. 933, pp. 539–545. Springer, Singapore (2020). https://doi.org/10.1007/978-981-13-7166-0_54
8. Korala, H., Georgakopoulos, D., Jayaraman, P.P., Yavari, A.: A survey of techniques for fulfilling the time-bound requirements of time-sensitive IoT applications. ACM Comput. Surv. **54**(11s), 1–36 (2022)

9. Naeem, M., Albano, M., Larsen, K.G., Nielsen, B., Høedholt, A., Laursen, C.Ø.: Modelling and analysis of a sigfox based IoT network using uppaal SMC. IEEE Sens. J. **23**, 10577–10587 (2023)
10. Naeem, M., Albano, M., Larsen, K.G., Nielsen, B., Høedholt, A., Østergaard Laursen, C.: Battery aware analysis of sensor networks in uppaal SMC. In: 2021 10th Mediterranean Conference on Embedded Computing (MECO), pp. 1–6. IEEE Budva, Montenegro (2021)
11. Naeem, M., Albano, M., Magrin, D., Nielsen, B., Guldstrand, K.: A sigfox module for the network simulator 3. In: Proceedings of the WNS3 2022, pp. 81–88 (2022)
12. Nayyar, A., Singh, R.: A comprehensive review of simulation tools for wireless sensor networks (WSNS). J. Wirel. Netw. Commun. **5**(1), 19–47 (2015)
13. Riley, G.F., Henderson, T.R.: The ns-3 network simulator. In: Wehrle, K., Güneş, M., Gross, J. (eds.) Modeling and Tools for Network Simulation, pp. 15–34. Springer, Berlin (2010). https://doi.org/10.1007/978-3-642-12331-3_2
14. Sen, K., Viswanathan, M., Agha, G.: Statistical model checking of black-box probabilistic systems. In: Alur, R., Peled, D.A. (eds.) CAV 2004. LNCS, vol. 3114, pp. 202–215. Springer, Heidelberg (2004). https://doi.org/10.1007/978-3-540-27813-9_16
15. Sharma, R., Vashisht, V., Singh, U.: Modelling and simulation frameworks for wireless sensor networks: a comparative study. IET Wirel. Sens. Syst. **10**(5), 181–197 (2020)
16. Sigfox: Sigfox Radio specifications, February 2020. https://storage.googleapis.com/public-assets-xd-sigfox-production-338901379285/abaedf62-56de-402e-93c3-3a9c10a1cb49.pdf
17. Xian, X., Shi, W., Huang, H.: Comparison of Omnet++ and other simulator for WSN simulation. In: 2008 3rd IEEE Conference on Industrial Electronics and Applications, pp. 1439–1443. IEEE (2008)

Using Automata Learning for Compliance Evaluation of Communication Protocols on an NFC Handshake Example

Stefan Marksteiner[1,2]([✉]) [iD], Marjan Sirjani[2] [iD], and Mikael Sjödin[2] [iD]

[1] AVL List Gmbh, Graz, Austria
stefan.marksteiner@avl.com
[2] Mälardalen University, Västerås, Sweden
{stefan.marksteiner,marjan.sirjani,mikael.sjodin}@mdu.se

Abstract. Near-Field Communication (NFC) is a widely adopted standard for embedded low-power devices in very close proximity. In order to ensure a correct system, it has to comply to the ISO/IEC 14443 standard. This paper concentrates on the low-level part of the protocol (ISO/IEC 14443-3) and presents a method and a practical implementation that complements traditional conformance testing. We infer a Mealy state machine of the system-under-test using active automata learning. This automaton is checked for bisimulation with a specification automaton modelled after the standard, which provides a strong verdict of conformance or non-conformance. As a by-product, we share some observations of the performance of different learning algorithms and calibrations in the specific setting of ISO/IEC 14443-3, which is the difficulty to learn models of system that a) consist of two very similar structures and b) very frequently give no answer (i.e. a timeout as an output).

Keywords: NFC · Automata Learning · Protocol Compliance · Bisimulation · Formal Methods

1 Introduction

In this paper we describe an approach of very thoroughly evaluating the compliance of Near-Field Communications (NFC)-based chip systems with the ISO/IEC 14443-3 NFC handshake protocol [10] using formal methods, concretely automata learning and equivalence checking. We present a tool chain that is easy

---

This research received funding within the ECSEL Joint Undertaking (JU) under grant agreement No. 876038 (project InSecTT) and from the program "ICT of the Future" of the Austrian Research Promotion Agency (FFG) and the Austrian Ministry for Transport, Innovation and Technology under grant agreement No. 880852 (project LEARNTWINS). The JU receives support from the European Union's Horizon 2020 research and innovation programme and Austria, Sweden, Spain, Italy, France, Portugal, Ireland, Finland, Slovenia, Poland, Netherlands, Turkey. The document reflects only the author's view and the Commission is not responsible for any use that may be made of the information it contains.

J. Kofroň et al. (Eds.): ECBS 2023, LNCS 14390, pp. 170–190, 2024.
https://doi.org/10.1007/978-3-031-49252-5_13

to use - both the learning and the equivalence checking can run fully automatic. A complete automaton of the system-under-test (SUT) compared with a specification automaton modeled after the standard, provides a strong complement to conformance testing. The remainder of this paper structures as follows. First we provide its motivation and contribution. Section 2 gives an overview of basic concepts in this paper, including a formal definition of bisimulation for Mealy Machines as used in this paper. Section 3 describes the developed interface for automata learning of NFC systems, while Sect. 4 describes the learning setup including a comparison of different algorithms and calibrations to be most suitable for the specifics of the NFC handshake protocol. Section 5 shows real-world results, while Sect. 6 compare them to the works of others. Section 7, eventually, concludes the paper and gives and outlook on future work.

1.1   Motivation

As the NFC protocol is widely adopted in a broad variety of different, often security-critical, chip systems like banking cards, passports, access systems, etc., that use relatively weak hardware, a correct implementation is utterly important. While there are many works about security weaknesses in NFC (e.g., [14,30]), also specifically regarding the ISO/IEC 14443-3 handshake (e.g., [8,18]), there is few works on comprehensive testing (see Sect. 6). Assuring the correctness of the system is a principal step in the quest to trustworthy systems. As there is, to the best of our knowledge, no comprehensive works regarding assessment of the handshake protocols, as the fundament of secure protocols build atop, we aim for a strong verdict of ISO compliance for NFC systems. To make this verdict more scalable than manual modeling, yet strongly verified, we choose automata learning to automatically infer a formal model of the implementations under scrutiny. For the actual compliance checking, we use bisimulation and trace equivalence checks against a specification automaton from the ISO/IEC 14443-3 standard (a rationale is given in Sect. 2.2).

1.2   Contribution

Overall, this paper is on the interface between communications protocols, embedded systems and formal methods. This work provides the following contributions for people with scholarly or applied interest in this approach of strong compliance checking:

- Insights regarding the specifics of learning NFC using active automata learning
- An evaluation on the performance of different learning algorithms in systems with very similar structures
- Developing an NFC interface for a learning system
- An approach for automated compliance checking using bisimulation and trace equivalence

We saw the NFC handshake to be specific in two aspects: a) it consists of two parts that are very similar and hard to distinguish for Learners and b) the vast majority of outputs from a system-under-learning are timeouts. This has severe impact on the learning where we examined different algorithms and configurations. The maximum word length has an impact on correctly inferring an automaton: too short yields incomplete automata, too long seemed to have a negative performance impact. Surprisingly the L* algorithm [3] with Rivest/Schapire (LSR) closure [25] surpassed more modern ones in learning performance. For discovering deviations from the standard, the minimum word length was found to have an impact. Here, the TTT algorithm [12] performed best, also followed by LSR. We further created a concrete hardware/software interface using a Proxmark device and an abstraction layer for NFC systems. Lastly, we integrated bisimulation and trace equivalence checking into the learning tool chain, which enables completely automated compliance checking with counterexamples in the case of deviations from the standard.

2   Preliminaries

This section outlines the theoretical fundamentals of state machines and automata learning including a definition of equivalence and bisimilarity in the context of this paper. It further briefly describes the used framework and the basics and characteristics of the scrutinized protocol.

2.1   State Machines

A state machine (or automaton) is a fundamental concept in computer science. One of the most widely used flavors of state machines are Mealy machines, which describe a system as a set of states and functions of resulting state changes (transitions) and outputs for a given input in a certain state [20]. More formally, a Mealy machine can be defined as $M = (Q, \Sigma, \Omega, \delta, \lambda, q_0)$, with Q being the set of states, Σ the input alphabet, Ω the output alphabet (that may or may not identical to the input alphabet), δ the transition function ($\delta : Q \times \Sigma \to Q$), λ the output function ($\lambda : Q \times \Sigma \to \Omega$), and q_0 the initial state. The transition and output functions might be merged ($Q \times \Sigma \to Q \times \Omega$). An even simpler type of automaton is a deterministic finite acceptor (DFA) [19]. It lacks of an output (i.e. no Ω and no λ), but instead it has a set of accepted finishing states F, which are deemed as valid final states for an input word (i.e. sequence of input symbols), resulting in a definition of $D = (Q, \Sigma, \delta, q_0, F)$. The purpose is to define an automaton that is capable of deciding if an input word is a valid part of a language. A special subset of DFAs are combination lock automata (with the same properties) but the additional constraint that an invalid symbol in an input sequence would set the state machine immediately back into the initial state [22].

2.2 Transitions and Equivalence

An element of the combined transition/output function can be defined as 4-tuple $(\langle p, q, \sigma, \omega \rangle)$ with $p \in Q$ as origin state of the transition, $q \in Q$ as destination state, $\sigma \in \Sigma$ as input symbol and $\omega \in \Omega$ as output symbol. Generally, to conform to a standard, a system must display the behavior defined in that standard. The ISO 14443-3 standard [10] describe the states of the NFC handshake with their respective expected input and result. That means one can derive an automaton from this specification. The problem of determining NFC standard compliance can therefore be seen as comparing two (finite) automata. There is a spectrum of equivalences between Labeled Transition Systems (LTS) including automata. For being compliant with a standard, not necessarily every state and transition must be identical as long as the behavior of the system is the same. There might be learned automata that deviate from the standard automaton and still be compliant, e.g., if they are not minimal (the smallest automaton to implement a desired behavior). Figure 1 shows a very simple example of a three-state automaton and its behavior-equivalent (minimal) two-state counterpart.

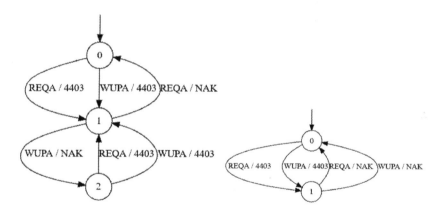

Fig. 1. Example for a partial automaton and its minimal counterpart.

To compare this type of equivalence between two LTS LTS_1 and LTS_2, commonly used are (various degrees of) simulation, bisimulation (noted as $LTS_1 \sim LTS_2$) and trace equivalence. Simulation means that one automaton can completely reproduce the behavior of the other, for the bisimulation, this relation becomes bidirectional (i.e. functional). Trace equivalence compares the respective output of automata. Just (uni-directional) simulation alone is not sufficient as this would only the presence *or* absence of a certain behavior with respect to the specification, while the standard compliance mandates both. Bisimilarity of two transition systems is originally defined for labeled transition systems (LTS), defined as $LTS = (S, Act, \rightarrow, I, AP, L)$, with S being the set of states, Act a set of actions, $\rightarrow$ a transition function, I the set of initial states, AP a set of atomic propositions and L a labelling function.

Definition 1 (Bisimilarity). *Bisimlarity of two LTS LTS_1 LTS_2 is defined as exhibiting a binary relation $R \subseteq QxQ$, such that [4]:*

A) $\forall s_1 \in I_1 \exists s_2 \in I_2 \cdot (s_1, s_2) \in R$ and $\forall s_2 \in I_2 (\exists s_1 \in I_1 \cdot (s_1, s_2) \in R$.
B) for all $(s_1, s_2) \in R$ must hold
    1) $L_1(s_1) = L_2(s_2)$
    2) if $s_1\prime \in Post(s_1)$ then there exists $s_2\prime \in Post(s_2)$ with $(s_1\prime, s_2\prime) \in R$
    3) if $s_2\prime \in Post(s_2)$ then there exists $s_1\prime \in Post(s_1)$ with $(s_1\prime, s_2\prime) \in R$

Condition A of Definition 1 means that all initial states must be related, while Condition B means that for all related states the labels must be equal (1) and their successor states must be related (2-3). Formally the succession ($Post$) is defined as $Post(s, \alpha) = \{s\prime \in S | s \xrightarrow{\alpha} s\prime\}$ and $Post(s) = \bigcup_{\alpha \in Act} Post(s, \alpha)$, meaning the union of all action successions, which again are again the result the transition function with a defined action and state as input. As this is recursive, a relation of the initial states implies that all successor states are related. Since all reachable states are (direct or indirect) successor states of the initial states, this definition encompasses the complete LTS. We interpret Mealy machines as LTS using the output functions as labeling functions for transitions and the input symbols as actions, similar to [28]. Based on this, we define Mealy bisimilarity (M_1 M_2) for our purpose follows:

Definition 2. Mealy Bisimilarity

A) $q_{0_1} \in Q_1, q_{0_2} \in Q_2 \cdot (q_{0_1}, q_{0_2}) \in R$.
B) for all $q_1 \in Q_1, q_2 \in Q_2 \cdot (q_1, q_2) \in R$ must hold
    1) $\sigma \in \Sigma \cdot \lambda_1(q_1, \sigma) = \lambda_2(q_2, \sigma)$
    2) if $q_1\prime \in Post(q_1)$ then there exists $q_2\prime \in Post(q_2)$ with $(q_1\prime, q_2\prime) \in R$
    3) if $q_2\prime \in Post(q_2)$ then there exists $q_1\prime \in Post(q_1)$ with $(q_1\prime, q_2\prime) \in R$

As the transition function is dependent on the input, we define $Post(q, \sigma) = \delta(q, \sigma)$ and $Post(\sigma) = \bigcup_{\sigma \in \Sigma} Post(q, \sigma)$, which is essentially the same as for LTS brought into the notation of Sect. 2.1. There are a couple of different bisimulation types that differentiate by the handling of non-observable (internal) transitions (ordinarily labeled as τ transitions), e.g. strong and weak bisimulation, and branching bisimulation to give a few examples. This distinction is, however, theoretical in the context of this paper. The reason is that we intend to compare a specification, which consists of an automaton that does not contain any τ transitions, with an implementation that is externally (black box) learned, rendering τs unobservable. Therefore, two automata without any τs are compared directly, which makes this distinction not applicable. More precisely, from a device perspective, the type of bisimulation equivalence cannot be determined, as the SUTs are black boxes. This means that internal state changes (commonly denoted as τ) are not visible, which determines the kind of bisimulation. From a model perspective, the chosen comparison implies strong bisimulation (i.e. the initial state is related (formally, $q_{0M_l} = q_{0M_s}$) and all subsequent states are related as well (formally $Q = Q_{M_l} = Q_{M_s}; n = |Q|; \forall n \in Q | q_{nM_l} = q_{nM_s}$).

Trace equivalence, on the other hand, means that two transitions systems produce the same traces for each same input.

Definition 3 (Trace equivalence). $Traces(LTS_1) = Traces(LTS_2)$

Although both bisimulation and trace equivalence might be principally capable of comparing a specification with an implementation automaton for determining the standard compliance, determining bisimulation is a problem to be solved in efficiently, whereas trace equivalence is PSPACE complete [2]. However, this might be negligible with a relatively low number of states and transitions. In any case, bisimulation implies trace equivalence ($LTS_1 \sim LTS_2$ implies $Traces(LTS_1) = Traces(LTS_2)$, but is finer than the latter [4]. For the purpose of this paper, we consider two automata equivalent if they are trace or bisimulation equivalent. In practice, we have obtained positive results with both bisimulation and trace equivalence (see Sect. 4.4). Therefore, trace equivalence is preferred as it is sufficient for standard compliance, but bisimilarity might be used in cases where more efficient checking algorithms are necessary.

2.3   Automata Learning

The classical method of actively learning automata of systems, was outlined in Angluin's pivotal work known as the L* algorithm [3]. This work uses a *minimally adequate Teacher* that has (theoretically) perfect knowledge of the SUT (in this case called System-under-learning – SUL) behind a *Teacher* and is allowed to answer to kinds of questions:

- *Membership queries* and
- *Equivalence queries*.

The membership queries are used to determine if a certain word is part of the accepted language of the automaton, or, in the case of Mealy machines, which output word will result of a specific input word. These words are noted in an observation table that will be made *closed* and *consistent*. The observation table consists of suffix-closed columns (E) and prefix-closed rows. The rows are intersected in short prefixes (S) and long prefixes ($S.\Sigma$). The short prefixes initially only contain the empty prefix (λ), while the long ones and the columns contain the members of the input alphabet. The table is filled with the respective outputs of prefixes concatenated with suffixes ($S.E$ or $S.\Sigma.E$). The table closed if for every long prefix row, there is a short prefix row with the same content ($\forall s.\sigma \in S.\Sigma \exists s \in S : s.\sigma = s$). The table is consistent if for any two equal short prefix rows, the long prefix rows beginning with these short prefixes are also equal ($\forall s, s\prime \in S \forall a \in \Sigma : s = s\prime \rightarrow s.a = s\prime.a$. A complete, closed and consistent table can be used to infer a state machine (set of states Q consists of all *distinct* short prefixes, the transition function is derived by following the suffixes). Even though this algorithm was initially defined for DFAs, it has been adapted to other types of state machines (e.g., Mealy or Moore machines) [15]. Alternatively, some algorithms use a discrimination tree that uses inputs as intermediate nodes, states as leaf nodes, and outputs as branch labels, with a similar method of inferring an automaton. One of these algorithms, TTT [12], is deemed currently the most efficient [29]. Other widely used algorithms include a modified version of the original L* with a counterexample handling strategy by Rivest and Schapire [25], or the tree-based Direct Hypothesis Construction (DHC) [21] and Kearns-Vazirani (KV) [17] algorithms.

Once this is performed, the resulting automaton is presented to the Teacher, which is called equivalence query. The Teacher either acknowledges the correctness of the automaton or provides a counterexample. The latter is incorporated into the observation table or discrimination tree and the learning steps described above are repeated until the model is correct. To allow for learning black box systems, the equivalence queries in practice often consist of a sufficient set of conformance tests instead of a Teacher with perfect knowledge [24]. Originally for Deterministic Finite Automata, this learning method could be used to learn Mealy Machines [26]. This preferred for learning black box reactive systems (e.g. cyber-physical systems), as modeling these as Mealy is comparatively simple.

2.4   LearnLib

To utilize automata learning we use a widely adopted Java library called LearnLib [13]. This library provides a variety of learning algorithms (L* and variants thereof, KV, DHC and TTT), as well as various strategies for membership and equivalence testing (e.g., conformance testing like random words, random walk, etc.). The library provides Java classes for instantiating these algorithms and interfaces systems under test. The interface classes further allow for defining the input alphabets that the algorithm routines uses to factor queries used to fill an observation table or tree. Depending on the used algorithms, the library is capable of inferring DFAs, NFAs (Non-deterministic finite acceptors), Mealy machines or VPDAs (Visibly Pushdown Automata).

2.5   Near Field Communication

Near Field Communication (NFC) is a standard for simple wireless communication between close coupled devices with relatively low data rates (106, 212, and 424 kbit/s). One distinctive characteristic of this standard (operating at 13.56 Mhz center frequency) is that it, based on Radio-Frequency Identification (RFID), uses passive devices (proximity cards - PICCs) that receive power from an induction field from an active device (reader or proximity coupling device PCD) that also serves as field for data transmission. There are a couple of defined procedures that allow for operating proximity cards in presence of other wireless objects in order to exchange data [11]. One standard particularly defines two handshake procedures based on cascade-based anti-collision and card selection (called type A and type B), one of which NFC proximity cards must be compliant with [10]. This handshake is the particular target system-under-learning (SUL) of this paper, with the purpose of providing very strong evidence for compliance. Due to the proliferation and the nature of the given system-under-learning, this paper concentrates on type A devices. Therefore, all statements on NFC and its handshake apply for type A only.

2.6   The NFC Handshake Automaton

ISO 14443-3 contains a state diagram that outlines the Type A handshake procedure for an NFC connection (see Fig. 2). This diagram is not a state machine

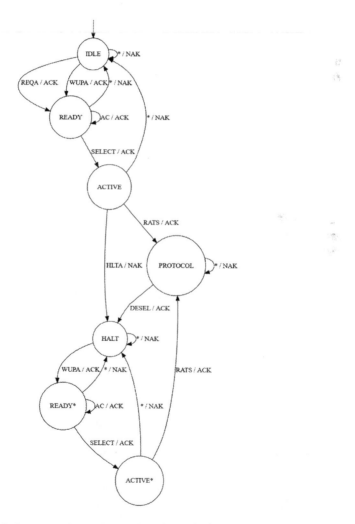

Fig. 2. NFC handshake automaton after ISO 14443-3 [10] augmented with abstract outputs. Note: star (*) as input means any symbol that is not explicitly stated in another outbound transition of the respective state.

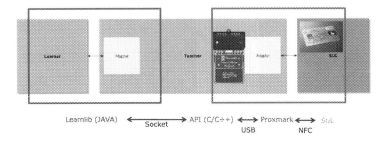

Fig. 3. NFC interface setup.

of the types described in Sect. 2.1, for it lacks both output and final states. As we learn Mealy machines, we augmented it with abstract outputs (see Sects. 4.2 and 4.4) to get a machine of the same type. The goal of the handshake is to reach a defined state in which a higher layer protocol (e.g. as defined in ISO 14443-4 [11]) can be executed (the *PROTOCOL* state). The intended way described in the standard to reach this state is: when coming into an induction field and powering up, the passive NFC device enters the *IDLE* state. After receiving a wake-up (*WUPA*) or request (*REQA*) message it enters the *READY* state. In this state, anti-collision (*AC*, remaining in that state) or card selection (*SELECT* going to the *ACTIVE* state) occur. In the latter state, the card waits for a request to answer-to-select (*RATS*), which brings it into said *PROTOCOL* state. In all of these states, an unexpected input would return the system to the *IDLE* state, no giving an answers (denoted as *NAK*). Based solely on ISO 14443-3 commands, the card should only leave this state after a *DESELECT* command, after which it enters the *HALT* state. Apart from a complete reset, it only leaves the *HALT* state after a wake-up (*WUPA*) signal (in contrast to the initial *IDLE* state, which also allows a *REQA* message). This brings it into the *READY** state, which again gets via a *SELECT* into the *ACTIVE** state that can be used to get to the *PROTOCOL* state again. The only difference between *READY* and *READY**, as well as *ACTIVE* and *ACTIVE** state is that it comes from the *HALT* instead of *IDLE* state. Similar to the first part of the automaton, an unexpected answer brings the state back to *HALT* without an answer (*NAK*).

Apart from the commands stated above that are expected by a card in the respective state, every other (i.e. unexpected) command would reset the handshake if its not complete (i.e. wrong commands from *IDLE, READY,* and *ACTIVE* states would lead back to the *IDLE* state, while *HALT, READY*,* and *ACTIVE** lead back to the *HALT* state and unexpected commands in the *PROTOCOL* state let it remain in that state. Even though this behavior of falling back into a base state resembles a combination-lock automaton or generally an accepting automaton, we model the handshake as a Mealy Machine for the following reasons:

a) As we observe a black box, input/output relations are easier to observe than not intrinsically defined accepting states

b) The states are easier distinguishable: a variety of input symbols with the corresponding output may represent a broader signature than just if a state is accepting (apart from the transition to other states)

c) The output may processed at different level of abstraction (see Sect. 4.2)

There is also one specific feature to the NFC handshake protocol: unlike most communication protocols, an unexpected or wrong input yield to no output. This has an implication to learning, as a timeout will be interpreted as a general error message.

3 NFC Interface

As Learner, we use the algorithm implementations in the Learnlib Java library (see Sect. 2.4), configured as outlined in Sect. 4. To interact with the NFC SUL, a Proxmark RFID/NFC device (see Sect. 3.1) is used that works with an adapter written in C++ (see Sect. 3.2). Figure 3 provides an overview of the setup.

3.1 Learner Interface Device

The interface with an NFC SUL is established via Proxmark3. Proxmark3 is a pocket-size NFC device capable of acting as an NFC reader (PCD) or tag (PICC), as well as sniffing device [7]. Proxmark3 can be controlled from a PC, as well as, allowing firmware updates. Thus it allows us to construct the NFC frames needed for learning and establishing a connection to the learning library via a software adapter (see Sect. 3.2).

3.2 Adapter Class

The actual access to the NFC interface runs over a C++ program, running on a PC, based on a provided application that comes with the Proxmark device. As this application is open source, it was possible to modify it in order to adapt it for learning. The main interface to the Java-based Learner is a Socket connection that take symbols from the Learner (see Sect. 4.2) and concretizes them by translating the symbols into valid NFC frames utilizing functions from the *SendCommand* and *WaitForResponse* families. These functions send and receive, respectively, command data (i.e. concrete inputs, symbol for symbol) to the Proxmark device where the firmware translates it into frames and sends them to the SUL and proceeds vice versa for the response. This, however, turned out to create an error prone bottleneck at the connection between the PC application and the Proxmark device running over USB. Due to round-trip times and timeouts, the learning was slowed down and occasional non-deterministic behavior was introduced, which jeopardized the learning process and made it necessary to repeat the latter (depending on the scrutinized system, multiple times, which hindered the overall learning greatly). Therefore, the Learner was re-implemented to send bulk inputs (i.e. send complete input words instead of single symbols), which improved the throughput significantly and solved non-determinism.

Firmware Modifications. In order to be able to transfer traces word-wise instead of symbol-wise, significant modifications of the device's firmware were necessary. The standard interface of the device is designed for sending a single packet at one time (via a provided application on a PC) and delivering the answer back to the application via a USB interface. This introduces latency, which through the sheer amount of symbols sent in the learning process, has a significant performance impact. To reach the device's firmware with multiple symbols at once, we modulate the desired inputs into one sent message in Type-Length-Value (TLV) format (implemented types are with or without CRC and a specialized type for SELECT sequences) and modify the main routine of the running firmware to execute a custom function if a certain flag is set. This custom function deserializes the sent commands and sends them to the NFC SUT. Answers are modulated into an answer packet in length-value format, followed by subsequent answer messages containing precise logging and timestamps, if used. As NFC is a protocol that works with relatively low round-trip times and time outs these modifications, eliminating a great portion of the latency times of frequently used USB connections, boost the performance of the learning using different learning algorithms significantly (for a performance evaluation see Sect. 4.1).

4   Learning Setup

One distinctive attribute of ISO14443-3 with respect to learning is that it specifies to not give an answer on unexpected (i.e. not according to the standards specification) input. Ordinarily, the result of such a undefined input is to drop back to a defined (specifically the IDLE or HALT) state. In this sense, the NFC handshake resembles a combination lock. A positive output on the other hand, ordinarily consists of a standardized status code or information that is needed for the next phase of the handshake, e.g., parts of a card's unique identifier (UID). The non-answer to undefined is a characteristic feature of the NFC standard. This directly affects the learning because it yields many identical answers and efficient time-out handling is essential. It is therefore necessary to evaluate different state-of-the-art learning algorithms for their specific fitness (see Sect. 4.1) well as determining the optimal parameter set (Sect. 4.1). We scrutinize the main algorithms supported by Learnlib: classical L*, L* with Rivest/Schapire counterexample handling, DHC, KV and TTT - the latter two with linear search (L) and binary search (B) counterexample analysis.

Table 1. Runtime (minutes) per algorithm and maximum word length.

Max. Word Length	Algorithm						
	L*-C	L*-RS	DHC	KV-L	KV-B	TTT-L	TTT-B
10	5.92	5.05	6.00	4.38	4.38	5.45	5.37
20	20.08	9.34	10.93	12.24	11.65	7.66	7.40
30	41.90	12.92	9.82	12.19	11.47	10.67	10.04
40	68.17	8.54	11.16	15.56	12.89	10.87	9.49
50	34.75	7.87	11.02	15.60	12.53	11.29	9.91
60	77.33	17.15	12.98	17.16	13.37	13.04	10.85
70	134.65	11.34	14.46	17.68	14.81	13.06	11.32

4.1 Comparing Learning Algorithms and Calibrations

All of the algorithms can be parameterized regarding the membership and equivalence queries. The former are mainly defined via the minimum and maximum word length, while the equivalence queries (lack of a *perfect Teacher*), is determined by the method and number of conformance tests. Generally speaking, a too short (maximum) word length results in an incompletely learned (which, if the implementation is correct, should contain seven states). The maximum length, however, has a different impact on the performance for observation and tree-based algorithms: table-based are quicker with a short maximum word length, whereas for tree-based ones there seems to be a break-even point between many sent words and many sent symbols in our specific setting. Table 1 shows a comparison of the runtime of different algorithms with different maximum word lengths (in red the respective algorithm's shortest runtime that learned the correct 7-state model). Some of the non-steadiness in the results can be explained by the fact that some calibrations with shorter word lengths required more equivalence queries and, thus, refinement procedures. Table 2 shows the results with the best performing (correct) run of the respective algorithm. This, however, only covers the performance of learning a correct implementation. The opposite side, discovering a bug, shows a different picture. We therefore used a SUT with a slightly deviating behavior (see Sect. 5.3). This system is much more error-prone, needing significantly higher timeout values, resulting in higher overall runtimes. One key property in this case seems to be the minimum word length. Some of the algorithms by their require a lower minimum word length to discover than others. This has a significant impact with the special setting of getting relatively many timeouts, which is greatly aggravated by the necessary long timeout periods. With a minimum word length of 10 symbols, again the original L* with the Rivest/Schapire closing strategy was performing quickest, but discovered only 7 out of 10 states of the deviating implementation. DHC yielded a similar result. Both needed a word length of 20 to discover the actual non-compliant model, which was significantly less efficient in terms of runtime.

Table 2. Performance evaluation of different algorithms for a compliant system with their respective fastest calibration in the given setting.

Algorithm	L*-C (20)	L*-RS (10)	DHC (30)	KV-L (30)	KV-B (30)	TTT-L (30)	TTT-B (40)
States	7	7	7	7	7	7	7
Runtime (min)	20.08	5.05	9.82	12.19	11.47	10.67	9.49
Words	1137	282	539	496	451	468	382
Symbols	10192	2588	5124	7932	7607	6628	6213
EQs	2	3	2	5	5	4	4

The TTT and KV algorithms needed a minimum length of 10, however with quite some deviation in efficiency. While TTT was the best performing algorithm to learn the SUT's actual behavior model, KV was performing worst. The runtimes roughly correspond with the amount of sent symbols, in this case the a very long timeout has to be set to avoid non-determinism. The classical L* is not in the list, as the algorithm crashed after more than 24 h of runtime. Table 3 provides an overview of minimum word lengths, run time, words, symbols and equivalence queries. Lower minimum word lengths yielded false negatives (i.e. the result showed a correct model with the deviation not uncovered).

4.2   Abstraction

Ordinarily, when applying automata learning to real-world systems, the input and output spaces are very large. To reduce the alphabets' cardinalities to a manageable amount, an abstraction function (∇), that transforms the concrete inputs (I) and outputs (O) to symbolic alphabets (Σ and Ω) using equivalence classes. Of all possible combinations of data to be send, we therefore concentrate on relevant input for the purpose of compliance verification. In the following we present some rationales for the chosen degree of abstraction through the input and output alphabets. These alphabets' symbols are abstracted and concretized via an according adapter class that translates symbols to data to be send (see Sect. 3.2).

Input Alphabet. For the input alphabet we use the one needed for successfully establishing a handshake (cf. Fig. 2), according to the state diagram for Type-A cards in the ISO 14443-3 standard [10]:

- Wake-UP command Type A (WUPA)
- Request command, Type A (REQA)
- Anticollision (AC)
- Select command, Type A (SELECT)
- Halt command, Type A (HLTA)
- Request for answer to select (RATS)

Table 3. Performance evaluation of different algorithms for a non-compliant system with their respective fastest calibration in the given setting.

Algorithm	L*-RS	DHC	KV-L	KV-B	TTT-L	TTT-B
Min Length	20	20	10	10	10	10
Runtime (min)	309.81	328.83	520.34	423.27	277.67	131.43
Words	575	855	952	679	688	616
Symbols	14637	15262	23867	19241	13353	11769
Eqs	5	3	6	6	5	5

- Deselect (DESEL)

The last two commands are actually defined in the ISO 14443-4 standard [11]. However, as the handshake's purpose is to enter and leave the protocol state, they are included in the 14443-3 state diagram and, consequentially, in our compliance verification.

Output Alphabets. In general, the output alphabet does not need to be defined beforehand. It simply consists of all output symbols observed by the Learner in a learning run. The Learner can derive the output alphabet implicitly. This means that if a system behaved non-deterministically, the output alphabet could vary – although when learning Mealy machines, which are deterministic by definition, nondeterminism would jeopardize the Learner. The output alphabet has obviously to be defined (in the abstraction layer) when abstracting the output. Therefore, using raw output has the benefit of not having to define the alphabet beforehand. The raw method has one drawback: there are cards that use a random UID (specifically, this behavior was observed in passports). Every anti-collision (AC) and $SELECT$ yields a different output, which introduces non-deterministic behavior. This is not a problem with abstract output, as the concrete answer is abstracted away. We therefore tried a heavily abstracted output consisting of only two symbols, namely ACK for a (positive) answer and NAK for a timeout, which in this case means a negative answer (see Sect. 2.5). This solves the problem, but degrades the performance of the Learner, since states are harder to distinguish if the possible outputs are limited to two (aggravated by the similar behavior of certain states - see Sect. 2.6). This idea was therefore forfeit in favor of raw output for the learning. We still maintained this higher abstraction for the equivalence checking (see Sect. 4.4 for the reasoning). Raw output, however, retains this problematic non-determinism. We therefore introduce a caching strategy to cope with this issue. Whenever a valid (partial) UID is received as an answer to an anti-collision or select input symbol, we put it on one of two caches (one for partial UIDs from AC and one for full ones from $SELECT$ sequences). The Learner will subsequently only be confronted with the respective top entries of these caches. We therefore abstract away the randomness of the UID by replacing it with an actual but fixed one. This keeps the learning deterministic while saving the other learned UIDs for analysis, if needed.

4.3   Labeling and Simplification

An implementation that conforms to the standard will automatically labeled correctly, as the labelling function follows a standards-conform handshake trace:

a) label the initial state with *IDLE*,
b) from that point, find the state, where the transition with *REQA* as an input and a positive acknowledgement as an output ends and label it as *READY*,
c) from that point, find the endpoint of a positively acknowledged *SELECT* transition and label it as *ACTIVE*,
d) from that point, find the endpoint of a positively acknowledged *RATS* transition and label it as *PROTOCOL*,
e) from that point, find the endpoint of a positively acknowledged *DESELECT* transition and label it as *HALT*
f) from that point, find the endpoint of a positively acknowledged *WUPA* transition and label it as *READY**
g) from that point, find the endpoint of a positively acknowledged *SELECT* transition and label it as *ACTIVE**

If the labeling algorithm fails or there are additional states (which are out of the labeling algorithm's scope), this is an indicator for the learned implementation's non-compliance with the ISO 14443-3 standard (given that only the messages defined in that standard are used as an input alphabet - see Sect. 4.2).

To simplify the state diagram for better readability and analysis, we cluster the transitions of each states for output/target tuples and label the input for that mostly traveled tuple with a star (∗). Normally that is the group of transitions that mark an unexpected input and transitions back to the IDLE or HALT state. This reduces the diagram significantly. Therefore, in those simplified diagrams, all inputs not marked explicitly in a state can be subsumed under the respective star (∗) transition.

4.4   Compliance Evaluation

Proving or disproving compliance needs a verdict if a potential deviation from the standard violates the (weak) bisimulation relation. We use mCRL2 with the Aldebaran (.aut) format for bisimilarity and trace equivalence checking (as described in Sect. 2.2) [5]. As the Learnlib toolset provides to possibility to store the learned automata in a couple of formats, including Aldebaran, setting up the tool chain is easy, even though some re-engineering was necessary. Learnlib's standard function for exporting in the Aldebaran format does not include outputs. This accepts transitions as equal that are in fact not (as they distinguish only through the output). We therefore rewrote this function to use the transition's in the label of an LTS as well. mCRL2 comes with a model comparison tool that uses, amongst others, the algorithm of Jansen et al. [16] for bisimilarity checking. We therefore simply model the specification in form of the handshake diagram (see Fig. 2) as an LTS with the corresponding Mealy's input and output as a label in the Aldebaran format and use the mCRL2 tool to compare it to automata of learnt implementations. The models of SUTs, although, could differ greatly event if the behavior is similar. Due to different UIDs the outputs to legit AC and SELECT commands would ordinarily differ between any two NFC cards. Also most other outputs might differ slightly. E.g., we observed some cards to respond to select with *4800*, others with *4400*. We therefore use the higher abstraction level as described above and use only NAK and ACK as output, circumventing this problem. This way, inequalities as detected by the tool indicate non-compliance to the ISO 14443-3 standard of the scrutinized implementation. If a non-compliance (i.e. a missing or additional state or transition actually countering the bisimulation relation) is found, all we need is to do a simple conformance test. A trace of the non-compliant state/transition is trivial to extract from the automaton (see the example in Sect. 5.3). If that trace is executed on the system-under-test and actually behaves like predicted in the model, we have found the actual specification violation in the real system, disproving the compliance.

Alternatively, an actual positive verdict of compliance of a learned model is simple. A full compliance proof can be made when doing identity equivalence, that is comparing the learned model state by state and transition by transition with the model manually derived from the ISO 14443-3 standard. If every state and transition is equal, we consider the system as compliant. More formally, the learned machine M_l must be fully equal the specification machine M_s, i.e. $M_l = M_s \wedge (M_l = M_s \models Q_{M_l} = Q_{M_s} \wedge \Sigma_{M_l} = \Sigma_{M_s} \wedge \Omega_{M_l} = \Omega_{M_s} \wedge \delta_{M_l} = \delta_{M_s} \wedge \lambda_{M_l} = \lambda_{M_s} \wedge q_{0_{M_l}} = q_{0_{M_s}})$. This, obviously, is a simpler but stronger relation that is not coersive for ISO protocol compliance. The probability of learning (with a sufficient amount of conformance testing) an incorrect model that is still compliant with the standard is negligible.

5   Evaluation

In this section we briefly outline the achieved results with the described tool chain. We used serveral different NFC card systems for testing, which are described below. All of these systems have shown to be conform to the ISO14443-3 standard, except for the Tesla key fob.

5.1   Test Cards and Credit Cards

We used five different NFC test test cards by NXP (part of an experimental car access system) to develop and configure the Learner. Furthermore, we used two different banking cards, a Visa and a Mastercard debit. All of these cards are conform to the standard, with only minor differences. One of these differences is replying with different ATQA to REQA/WUPA messages with 4400 and 4800

respectively. Overall, the results with these cards are very similar. Figure 4 shows
an example of a learnt automaton (left side).

Fig. 4. Automaton of an NXP test card (left) and a Tesla car key fob (right) learnt
with TTT.

5.2   Passports

We also examined two different passports from European Union countries: one
German and one Austrian. The main noticeable difference (at ISO 14443-3 level)
between the other systems is that these systems answer to AC and SELECT
inputs with randomly generated (parts of) UIDs. This implements a privacy
feature to make passports less traceable. Without accessing the personal data

stored on the device the passport should not be attributable. This, however, requires authentication.

5.3   Tesla Key Fob

Apart from significantly slower answers than the other devices, which required to adapt the timeouts to avoid nondeterministic behavior, the learned automaton slightly differs when learnt with the TTT algorithm. Figure 4 (right side) shows a model of a Tesla car key fob learnt with TTT. The (unnamed) states 3, 4 and 6 are very similar to the HALT, READY* and ACTIVE* states, respectively. Apart from the entry points (HALTA from the ACTIVE state for the first and DESEL from the PROTOCOL state, respectively) these two structures are identical and in the reference model, those two transitions lead to the same state. However, the ACTIVE* transition allows for issuing a DESELECT command that actually returns a value (i.e. an ACK in the higher abstraction), which does not correspond to the standard.

The mCRL2 comparison tool rightfully identifies this model not to be bisimilar and trace equivalent with the specification. Using the according option, the tool also provided a counterexample in the form of the trace ($\langle REQA/ACK \rangle$, $\langle SELECT/ACK \rangle$, $\langle RATS/ACK \rangle$, $\langle DESEL/ACK \rangle$, $\langle WUPA/ACK \rangle$, $\langle SELECT/ACK \rangle$, $\langle DESEL/ACK \rangle$). According to the specification, the last label should be $\langle DESEL/NAK \rangle$.

6   Related Work

There are other, partly theoretic, approaches of inferring a model using automata learning and comparing it with other automata using bisimulation algorithms. However, they target DFAs [6] or probabilistic transition systems (PTS) [9]. Neider et al. [23] contains some significant theoretic fundamentals of using automata learning and bisimulation for different types of state machines, including Mealys. It also contains the important observation that (generalized) Mealy Machines are bisimilar if their underlying LTS are bisimilar. Tappler et al. [28] used a similar approach of viewing Mealy Machines as LTS to compare automata regarding their bisimilarity. Similarly, bisimulation checking was also used to verify a model inferred from an embedded control software [27]. There is also previous work on using automata learning for inferring models of NFC cards [1], which concentrates on the upper layer (ISO/IEC 14443-4) protocol, dodging the specific challenges of the handshake protocol. Also there is no mentioning of automatic compliance checking in this approach. To the best of our knowledge, there is no comprehensive approach for compliance verification of the ISO/IEC 14443-3 protocol.

7   Conclusion

In this paper, we demonstrated the usage of automata learning to infer models of systems under test and evaluate their compliance with the ISO 14443-3 protocol by checking their bisimilarity with a specification. We described a learning interface setup, showed practical results and made interesting observations on the impact of the protocol specifics on learning algorithms' performances.

7.1 Discussion

Using our learning setup on real-world devices, we found little differences between the SUTs – all examined systems were compliant to ISO/IEC 14443-3. Observed differences were mainly in the privacy-related random UIDs sent by passports and the slow answers and a slightly different automaton of the Tesla key fob. However, the scrutinized NFC handshake protocol has two characteristics that are distinct from other communications protocols: a) it does not send an answer on unexpected input and b) the automaton has two almost identical parts (IDLE/READY/ACTIVE and HALT/READY*/ACTIVE*) that pose challenges in learning. Supposedly these characteristics are responsible for the somewhat surprising finding that the L* algorithm with the Rivest/Schapire improvement surpasses more modern tree-based algorithms for correct systems. However, TTT performed best in finding a non-compliant system, which is the actual purpose of the testing and that the minimum word length has an impact on the ability to find incompliances. This might give some hints for optimization of learning strategies for similar structures.

7.2 Outlook

The compliance checking is but a first step towards assuring correctness and, subsequently, cybersecurity for NFC systems. Concretely, further research directions include test case generation using model checking and using the model to guide an intelligent fuzzer to leverage cybersecurity validation and verification (V&V). The target of these V&V activities are on the one hand upper layer protocols and on the other hand NFC reader devices to search for faults that might lead to exploitable security vulnerabilities. To talk to readers, because of the low latency of NFC communications, it is crucial to already know what to send before a conversation, which is satisfied by the predefined input words in the automata learning process.

References

1. Aarts, F., De Ruiter, J., Poll, E.: Formal models of bank cards for free. In: 2013 IEEE Sixth International Conference on Software Testing, Verification and Validation Workshops, pp. 461–468 (2013). https://doi.org/10.1109/ICSTW.2013.60
2. Aceto, L., Ingolfsdottir, A., Srba, J.: The algorithmics of bisimilarity. In: Advanced Topics in Bisimulation and Coinduction, pp. 100–172. Cambridge University Press (2011)
3. Angluin, D.: Learning regular sets from queries and counterexamples. Inf. Comput. **75**(2), 87–106 (1987). https://doi.org/10.1016/0890-5401(87)90052-6
4. Baier, C., Katoen, J.P.: Principles of Model Checking. MIT Press, Cambridge (2008)

5. Bunte, O., et al.: The mCRL2 toolset for analysing concurrent systems. In: Vojnar, T., Zhang, L. (eds.) TACAS 2019. LNCS, vol. 11428, pp. 21–39. Springer, Cham (2019). https://doi.org/10.1007/978-3-030-17465-1_2

6. Chen, Y.F., Hong, C.D., Lin, A.W., Rümmer, P.: Learning to prove safety over parameterised concurrent systems. In: 2017 Formal Methods in Computer Aided Design (FMCAD), pp. 76–83 (2017). https://doi.org/10.23919/FMCAD.2017.8102244

7. Garcia, F.D., de Koning Gans, G., Verdult, R.: Tutorial: proxmark, the swiss army knife for RFID security research: tutorial at 8th workshop on RFID security and privacy (RFIDSEC 2012). Technical report, Radboud University Nijmegen, ICIS, Nijmegen (2012)

8. Hancke, G.: Practical attacks on proximity identification systems. In: 2006 IEEE Symposium on Security and Privacy (S&P 2006), pp. 6 pp.-333 (2006). https://doi.org/10.1109/SP.2006.30

9. Hong, C.-D., Lin, A.W., Majumdar, R., Rümmer, P.: Probabilistic bisimulation for parameterized systems. In: Dillig, I., Tasiran, S. (eds.) CAV 2019. LNCS, vol. 11561, pp. 455–474. Springer, Cham (2019). https://doi.org/10.1007/978-3-030-25540-4_27

10. International Organization for Standardization: Cards and security devices for personal identification - Contactless proximity objects - Part 3: Initialization and anticollision. ISO/IEC Standard "14443-3". International Organization for Standardization (2018)

11. International Organization for Standardization: Cards and security devices for personal identification - Contactless proximity objects - Part 4: Transmission protocol. ISO/IEC Standard "14443-4". International Organization for Standardization (2018)

12. Isberner, M., Howar, F., Steffen, B.: The TTT algorithm: a redundancy-free approach to active automata learning. In: Bonakdarpour, B., Smolka, S.A. (eds.) RV 2014. LNCS, vol. 8734, pp. 307–322. Springer, Cham (2014). https://doi.org/10.1007/978-3-319-11164-3_26

13. Isberner, M., Howar, F., Steffen, B.: The open-source LearnLib. In: Kroening, D., Păsăreanu, C.S. (eds.) CAV 2015. LNCS, vol. 9206, pp. 487–495. Springer, Cham (2015). https://doi.org/10.1007/978-3-319-21690-4_32

14. Issovits, W., Hutter, M.: Weaknesses of the ISO/IEC 14443 protocol regarding relay attacks. In: 2011 IEEE International Conference on RFID-Technologies and Applications, pp. 335–342 (2011). https://doi.org/10.1109/RFID-TA.2011.6068658

15. Jacobs, B., Silva, A.: Automata learning: a categorical perspective. In: van Breugel, F., Kashefi, E., Palamidessi, C., Rutten, J. (eds.) Horizons of the Mind. A Tribute to Prakash Panangaden. LNCS, vol. 8464, pp. 384–406. Springer, Cham (2014). https://doi.org/10.1007/978-3-319-06880-0_20

16. Jansen, D.N., Groote, J.F., Keiren, J.J.A., Wijs, A.: An $O(m \log n)$ algorithm for branching bisimilarity on labelled transition systems. In: TACAS 2020. LNCS, vol. 12079, pp. 3–20. Springer, Cham (2020). https://doi.org/10.1007/978-3-030-45237-7_1

17. Kearns, M.J., Vazirani, U.: An Introduction to Computational Learning Theory. MIT Press, Cambridge (1994)

18. Maass, M., Müller, U., Schons, T., Wegemer, D., Schulz, M.: NFCGate: an NFC relay application for Android. In: Proceedings of the 8th ACM Conference on Security & Privacy in Wireless and Mobile Networks, WiSec 2015, pp. 1–2. Association for Computing Machinery, New York (2015). https://doi.org/10.1145/2766498.2774984

19. McCulloch, W.S., Pitts, W.: A logical calculus of the ideas immanent in nervous activity. Bull. Math. Biophys. **5**(4), 115–133 (1943). https://doi.org/10.1007/BF02478259

20. Mealy, G.H.: A method for synthesizing sequential circuits. Bell Syst. Tech. J. **34**(5), 1045–1079 (1955). https://doi.org/10.1002/j.1538-7305.1955.tb03788.x

21. Merten, M., Howar, F., Steffen, B., Margaria, T.: Automata learning with on-the-fly direct hypothesis construction. In: Hähnle, R., Knoop, J., Margaria, T., Schreiner, D., Steffen, B. (eds.) ISoLA 2011. CCIS, pp. 248–260. Springer, Heidelberg (2012). https://doi.org/10.1007/978-3-642-34781-8_19

22. Moore, E.F.: Gedanken-experiments on sequential machines. In: Automata Studies, AM-34, vol. 34, pp. 129–154. Princeton University Press (1956). https://doi.org/10.1515/9781400882618-006

23. Neider, D., Smetsers, R., Vaandrager, F., Kuppens, H.: Benchmarks for automata learning and conformance testing. In: Margaria, T., Graf, S., Larsen, K.G. (eds.) Models, Mindsets, Meta: The What, the How, and the Why Not? LNCS, vol. 11200, pp. 390–416. Springer, Cham (2019). https://doi.org/10.1007/978-3-030-22348-9_23

24. Peled, D., Vardi, M.Y., Yannakakis, M.: Black box checking. In: Wu, J., Chanson, S.T., Gao, Q. (eds.) Formal Methods for Protocol Engineering and Distributed Systems. IAICT, vol. 28, pp. 225–240. Springer, Boston, MA (1999). https://doi.org/10.1007/978-0-387-35578-8_13

25. Rivest, R.L., Schapire, R.E.: Inference of finite automata using homing sequences. Inf. Comput. **103**(2), 299–347 (1993). https://doi.org/10.1006/inco.1993.1021

26. Shahbaz, M., Groz, R.: Inferring mealy machines. In: Cavalcanti, A., Dams, D.R. (eds.) FM 2009. LNCS, vol. 5850, pp. 207–222. Springer, Heidelberg (2009). https://doi.org/10.1007/978-3-642-05089-3_14

27. Smeenk, W., Moerman, J., Vaandrager, F., Jansen, D.N.: Applying automata learning to embedded control software. In: Butler, M., Conchon, S., Zaïdi, F. (eds.) ICFEM 2015. LNCS, vol. 9407, pp. 67–83. Springer, Cham (2015). https://doi.org/10.1007/978-3-319-25423-4_5

28. Tappler, M., Aichernig, B.K., Bloem, R.: Model-based testing IoT communication via active automata learning. In: 2017 IEEE International Conference on Software Testing, Verification and Validation (ICST), pp. 276–287 (2017). https://doi.org/10.1109/ICST.2017.32

29. Vaandrager, F.: Model learning. Commun. ACM **60**(2), 86–95 (2017). https://doi.org/10.1145/2967606

30. Vila, J., Rodríguez, R.J.: Practical experiences on NFC relay attacks with android. In: Mangard, S., Schaumont, P. (eds.) RFIDSec 2015. LNCS, vol. 9440, pp. 87–103. Springer, Cham (2015). https://doi.org/10.1007/978-3-319-24837-0_6

Towards LLM-Based System Migration in Language-Driven Engineering

Daniel Busch[(✉)], Alexander Bainczyk, and Bernhard Steffen

Department of Computer Science, Chair for Programming Systems,
TU Dortmund University, 44227 Dortmund, Germany
{daniel2.busch,alexander.bainczyk,bernhard.steffen}@tu-dortmund.de

Abstract. In this paper we show how our approach of extending Language Driven Engineering (LDE) with natural language-based code generation supports system migration: The characteristic decomposition of LDE into tasks that are solved with dedicated domain-specific languages divides the migration tasks into portions adequate to apply LLM-based code generation. We illustrate this effect by migrating a low-code/no-code generator for point-and-click adventures from JavaScript to TypeScript in a way that maintains an important property: generated web applications can automatically be validated via automata learning and model analysis by design. In particular, this allows to easily test the correctness of migration by learning the difference automaton for the generated products of the source and the target system of the migration.

Keywords: Software Engineering · Low-Code/No-Code ·
Language-driven Engineering · Large Language Models · Migration ·
Transformation · Automata Learning · Verification · Web Application

1 Motivation and Introduction

Many Large Language Models (LLMs) can be used for coding tasks [12]. They are used as programming assistants [16], reviewers [10], or even full-blown code generation tools [11]. In particular for small problems this works very well, but the quality and reliability of the code drastically degrades with growing context size and structural or conceptual complexity of the software projects. In [14], we have illustrated how this problem of scalability can be mitigated within a heterogeneous approach that comprises model-based and LLM-based code generation: We extended our Language-Driven Engineering (LDE) environment [7] for low-code/no-code development via dedicated Domain-Specific Languages (DSLs) to also support specification in natural language with the following benefits:

- The tasks to be solved via LLM-based code generation can be tailored in size and conceptual complexity and
- the overall heterogeneously constructed system can be directly validated at system level using automata learning and model analysis.

J. Kofroň et al. (Eds.): ECBS 2023, LNCS 14390, pp. 191–200, 2024.
https://doi.org/10.1007/978-3-031-49252-5_14

Our approach has been illustrated via a system to generate fully running, web-based point-and-click adventures from two specifications, (1) an easy graphical specification for the 'landscape' of the adventure, and (2) a natural language specification for the game logic. The corresponding system structure is depicted in the upper half of Fig. 1. In [14], we concluded that this approach is unique by placing this concept in the context of existing research.

In this paper, we illustrate an additional benefit of our approach to LDE-based natural language integration: The heterogeneous LDE-based structure also supports the *automatic migration* of entire heterogeneous LDE-based systems. In particular, we sketch a migration process that allows one to migrate the entire system generators we constructed for point-and-click adventures to different programming languages just using a simple user prompt specifying the target language. For illustration, we migrated the system generator from JavaScript to TypeScript which essentially requires the migrator to automatically insert the missing type information into the system code.

Like in [14], our approach applies natural language based code generation only for very dedicated, small-scale tasks. Other tasks can be solved using textual or graphical DSLs. For each task we apply the paradigm that is most suitable to solve it. In our example these tasks are:

1. Generating base code that implements the 'landscape' of the adventure using graphical models.
2. Generating a prompt frame that provides contextual information using the same graphical models.
3. Introducing game logic into the generated base code (from task one) utilizing the generated prompt frame (from task two) using an LLM.

This separation of tasks does not only addresses the scalability problem, but it also allowed us to maintain the second benefit mentioned above: The migrated system generator automatically supports validation at system level via automata learning and model analysis. In particular, this allows us to easily test the correctness of migration simply by learning the difference automaton for the generated products of the source and the target system of the migration.

Figure 1 explains the reason for this benefits: Migrating the original JavaScript system generator sketched in the top to the TypeScript generator in the bottom only requires very local adaptations. In our example, this means that we only have to provide a descriptive natural language prompt for the portion marked in red in Fig. 1.

This paper is organized as follows: In Sect. 2, we outline our previous work [14] and introduce fundamentals of learning-based evolution control. Section 3 covers our concept of LLM-based code generator migration. Next, Sect. 4 demonstrates this concept with a running example, and following that, Sect. 5 concludes this paper with a discussion and an outlook on future work.

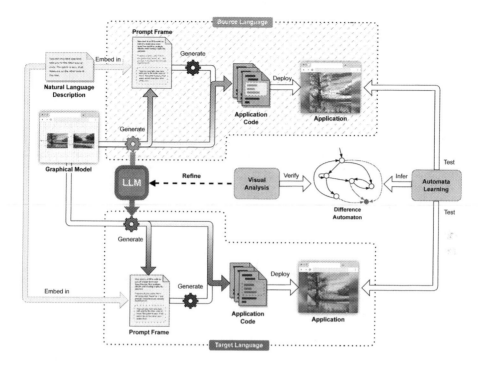

Fig. 1. LLM-based code transformation concept. (Color figure online)

2   Preliminaries

In this section, we recapitulate the core ideas of our work from our previous paper
[14] and outline the necessary basics of learning-based testing in the context of
our approach.

2.1   LLM-Based Code Generators and Language Decomposition

In [14] we presented a way to combine LDE with the generative power of LLMs.
This approach enables users to use both graphical modeling and natural language
descriptions, each applicable to whichever part of the domain is more suitable.
This also reduces overall complexity by splitting the domain into smaller, more
manageable aspects. We further demonstrated the approach on a web-based
point-and-click adventure: A sitemap of game screens is modeled graphically,
while the game logic is described in natural language.

Our approach generates code from graphical models and an accompanying
Prompt Frame that provides context to the LLM. The Prompt Frame contains
the expected target language, variables and functions that are available from
the code generated from the graphical model, as well as code stubs that provide
the function signatures for which the LLM needs to generate code to obtain the
resulting product. The combination of the code generated from the graphical

model, which we refer to as the base code, and the code generated by the LLM then results in the final product.

This divide-and-conquer approach aims to solve some problems of LLM-based code generation, such as too large contexts or loose task descriptions. Moreover, it allows us to benefit from the formal aspects of the LDE paradigms and informal natural languages and LLMs.

Further, our approach employs code instrumentation for the resulting product code which allows the automated inference of behavioral models for verification purposes, see Sect. 2.2. The instrumentation is part of the manually implemented code generator that generates code from the graphical model.

2.2   Learning-Based Evolution Control

Active Automata Learning. [1] has proven to be a viable solution for automated black-box testing of web applications in the past [2,4,9]. *Active learning* refers to the process in which a *learner* poses test queries over an input alphabet to a System Under Learning (SUL) in an automated fashion to infer a formal automaton model representing the SUL's behavior. Because web applications can be characterized as reactive systems, previous research relied on Mealy machines to capture their behavior.

To minimize manual effort, [13] introduces the iHTML DSL to instrument an application's HTML code in a way that enables the on-the-fly inference of system inputs by interacting with and analyzing the website's Document Object Model (DOM) automatically. We already exploited iHTML in [4] for our LLM-based code generation approach to generate instrumented, web-based point-and-click adventures that can be learned by simply providing their URLs.

Previous research [3,4] established that a stable alphabet abstraction is required to enable structural comparisons between models to detect behavioral changes. In this context, [8] introduces the notion of *difference automata*, i.e. Mealy machines inferred by testing two systems simultaneously. The resulting automaton will then show all traces that lead to the occurrence of divergent behavior, see e.g. Fig. 2. In this paper, we learn difference automata to detect and visualize behavioral differences between two software versions that are the result of LLM-based code migration.

3   Concept

Our goal is to use LLMs for code generator migration tasks. While in some cases this could be done for any code generator, we want to apply additional principles to be able to more easily handle the outcome of the code generated by the LLMs. The principles are based on the approach presented in [14] and are as follows:

1. Split the problem domain to minimize individual generation contexts and make code generation for LLMs easier to solve.
2. Instrument the generated code so that products can be verified which provides additional trust in the LLM-generated code.

3. Validate the product using automata learning and provide feedback to the user. Mismatches introduced by the migration can be detected using difference automata.

Splitting. We split the problem domain according to our approach of [14], as described in Sect. 2.1. The existing system generator (see the colored cogs in Fig. 1) consists of two sub-generators, one for the application code and another for the Prompt Frame (see Source Language in Fig. 1). Each sub-generator is migrated separately by being passed to an LLM, together with a supporting description to instruct the LLM with the migration task.

Instrumentation. Only the LLM-based migration of the application code generator may lead to violations of the iHTML syntax. However, such violations are automatically detected by the iHTML syntax checker and can be corrected manually by refining the prompt for the LLM-based migration.

Validation. Syntactically correct instrumented code can automatically be validated via difference automata provide via automata learning (see Fig. 2): Whenever there is a path ending in a behavioural discrepancy (see area marked in red) we can conclude that the LLM-based migration is erroneous. This information is then passed to a human expert for updating the prompt for the LLM-based migration in a similar fashion as before for eliminating iHTML syntax violations.

Figure 1 summarizes our setup. The upper half of the figure shows the approach as presented in [14]. In the middle, it is visualized that the generator used to generate the application code and the Prompt Frame is fed into an LLM (e.g. ChatGPT) to instruct it to migrate the sub-generators separately into the desired target language. The bottom half of the figure shows the same workflow as the top half, but using the migrated generator instead. Having two application instances, automata learning is used to create the difference automaton and feedback is passed to the user who refines the LLM-based migrator.

4   Example

To evaluate our concept described in Sect. 3, we have applied it to the example of the river crossing puzzle [14]. In this example, we developed a web-based point-and-click adventure using the Webstory DSL [5] of the graphical modeling suite CINCO [6]. Webstory has been modified so that graphical modeling is only used to model the available game screens and their reachability in a sitemap-like manner. From these graphical models a point-and-click adventure base code as well as a Prompt Frame with contextual information is generated (see Fig. 1). All game logic, such as win/loss conditions, is modeled using natural language descriptions that are embedded in the generated Prompt Frame.

Migration of the source generators that generate the base code and the Prompt Frame was done using ChatGPT in its GPT-4 version [15]. The source generators use JavaScript in the case of the base code and the code stubs in the Prompt Frame, or natural language referencing JavaScript and JavaScript objects in the case of the natural language part of the Prompt Frame. In this example, our goal is to migrate these generators to TypeScript, a typed scripting language.

Migration. Listing 1.1 shows the initial prompt that prepares ChatGPT to migrate the Prompt Frame generator. An excerpt of the target Prompt Frame generated by ChatGPT can be seen in Listing 1.2. Note that ChatGPT successfully migrated both the natural language contextualization and the code stubs to be implemented. All necessary functions were present and properly typed after the migration.

The base code generator was migrated using a separate conversation and prompts. Listing 1.3 is an excerpt of the target base code generator. Two things are noteworthy about this successful migration. First, the overall migration and typing was done correctly and quite extensively. Second, the instrumentation that is introduced with this base code is preserved. This second aspect is critical to the validation of the migration proposed in this paper.

```
You are provided with prompt frames. The prompt frame is
    wrapped into "BEGIN PROMPT FRAME" and "END PROMPT
    FRAME". The prompt frame includes ALL text AND code.
These prompt frames should be used for yourself to
    provide you with information to get a desired code
    output for an input scenario.

Your overall task will be to modify the given prompt
    frame so that you output a modified prompt frame for
    another programming language instead of the given
    prompt frame.

Answer only as follows in two interactions:
1. First, output only the programming language for which
    the given prompt frame seems to be made, and ask the
    user which programming language you should migrate the
    prompt frame to.
2. After receiving the user's answer, display only the
    migrated prompt frame and no additional text.
```

Listing 1.1. Priming prompt for Prompt Frame migration.

```
BEGIN PROMPT FRAME
Your task is to fill in code as part of a larger
    TypeScript code base.
[...]
The code blocks for you to implement:

function initVariables(): void {[...]}
function checkWin(): void {[...]}
function checkLoss(): void {[...]}
```

Listing 1.2. Excerpt of migrated Prompt Frame generator.

```
interface GameObject {
    name: string;
    currentScreen: string;
    transitions: Array<{ screen: string, function: () =>
        void }>;
}

function init(): void {
    this.currentState = states.first;
    this.states = states;
    this.gameObjects = [] as GameObject[];
    [...]
}
[...]
function addCustomClickAreas(): void {
    [...]
    items.forEach((item: GameObject) => {
    const itemElement: HTMLButtonElement =
        document.createElement('button');
    itemElement.classList.add('flex-item',
        'interaction-item');
    itemElement.setAttribute('data-lbd-action', 'Click');
    itemElement.setAttribute('data-lbd-name', item.name +
        '-' + this.currentState);
    itemElement.innerText = item.name;
    [...]
}
[...]
```

Listing 1.3. Excerpt of migrated base code generator.

Verifying the Migration. For illustrative purposes, we demonstrate how automata learning can be used to detect behavioral differences between two system iterations. The means for this are *difference automata* [8] (see Fig. 2),

which contain all observed traces that lead to a different input-output behavior
of the two systems in question. By default, difference automata are constructed
as Mealy machines, but in this paper we convert them to Moore machines to
reflect user-level interactions more accurately [14].

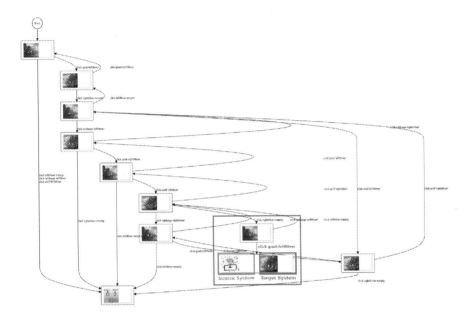

Fig. 2. Difference automaton for two learned WebStories.

To demonstrate the benefits of our migration approach, we manually introduced a bug into the generated code to simulate a possible flaw in the LLM when
translating the user specifications into TypeScript code. The changes affect the
part of the code responsible for checking the game's win condition. More specifically, it affects a function that returns **true** when the win condition is met, i.e.
when all items are on the right side of the river. For our example, however, we
have modified the function to return **false** in this case, resulting in the game
never reaching the winning screen.

We first learned the automaton of the original JavaScript application, transformed it to TypeScript using our presented approach, then manually introduced
the bug, and finally learned the automaton of the now erroneous application to
infer the difference automaton seen in Fig. 2. The behavioral difference is highlighted in red: If the farmer is on the left side of the river with the goat, while
the cabbage and wolf are on the right side of the river, the game would have
been won as soon as the user clicked on the goat, resulting in the display of the
winning screen in the source system. However, in our modified target system,
the game enters a state where instead of the winning screen, all three items are
displayed on the right side of the river, and therefore the game is never actually
won. This information is graphically displayed and can be used to fix the bug.

5   Conclusion

In this paper we have shown how our approach of extending Language-Driven Engineering (LDE) with natural language-based code generation presented in [14] supports system migration. Central to this extension is the LDE-characteristic decomposition into tasks that are solved with dedicated domain-specific languages, be they textual, graphical, or natural. This decomposition allows the division of the migration tasks into portions adequate to apply LLM-based code generation. We have illustrated the impact of our approach by migrating a low-code/no-code generator for web-based point-and-click adventures from JavaScript to TypeScript, showing that

- the LLM-based migration correctly introduces the types required for Type-Script and that
- also the point-and-click adventures generated with the migrated system can be validated via automata learning and model analysis by design. In particular, this allows to easily test the correctness of migration by learning the difference automaton for the generated products of the source and the target system of the migration.

Technically, we have used LLMs to automatically migrate all code generators involved in our presented example, those that follow classical model-driven approaches as well as those that were based on natural language descriptions. Currently, we are experimenting with more complex scenarios.

We are convinced that hybrid approaches as the one presented here are a good way to mitigate the weaknesses of LLM-based code generation: They provide means for decomposition-based scalability, and to safely position LLM-based code in an overall application.

References

1. Angluin, D.: Learning regular sets from queries and counterexamples. Inf. Comput. **75**(2), 87–106 (1987)
2. Raffelt, H., et al.: Dynamic testing via automata learning. Int. J. Softw. Technol. Transf. (STTT) **11**(4), 307–324 (2009). ISSN 1433-2779. https://doi.org/10.1007/s10009-009-0120-7
3. Windmüller, S., et al.: Active continuous quality control. In: Proceedings of the 16th International ACM Sigsoft Symposium on Component-Based Software Engineering, CBSE 2013, Vancouver, British Columbia, Canada, pp. 111–120. Association for Computing Machinery (2013). ISBN 9781450321228. https://doi.org/10.1145/2465449.2465469
4. Neubauer, J., Windmüller, S., Steffen, B.: Risk- based testing via active continuous quality control. Int. J. Softw. Tools Technol. Transf. **16**(5), 569–591 (2014). https://doi.org/10.1007/s10009-014-0321-6
5. Lybecait, M., Kopetzki, D., Zweihoff, P., Fuhge, A., Naujokat, S., Steffen, B.: A tutorial introduction to graphical modeling and metamodeling with CINCO. In: Margaria, T., Steffen, B. (eds.) ISoLA 2018. LNCS, vol. 11244, pp. 519–538. Springer, Cham (2018). https://doi.org/10.1007/978-3-030-03418-4_31

6. Naujokat, S., et al.: CINCO: a simplicity-driven approach to full generation of domain-specific graphical modeling tools. Int. J. Softw. Tools Technol. Transf. **20**, 327–354 (2018)

7. Steffen, B., et al.: Language-driven engineering: from general-purpose to purpose-specific languages. In: Computing and Software Science: State of the Art and Perspectives, pp. 311–344 (2019)

8. Bainczyk, A., Steffen, B., Howar, F.: Lifelong learning of reactive systems in practice. In: Ahrendt, W., et al. (eds.) The Logic of Software. A Tasting Menu of Formal Methods: Essays Dedicated to Reiner Hähnle on the Occasion of His 60th Birthday, pp. 38–53. Springer, Cham (2022). ISBN 978-3-031-08166-8. https://doi.org/10.1007/978-3-031-08166-8_3

9. Bainczyk, A., Boßelmann, S., Krause, M., Krumrey, M., Wirkner, D., Steffen, B.: Towards continuous quality control in the context of language-driven engineering. In: Margaria, T., Steffen, B. (eds.) Leveraging Applications of Formal Methods, Verification and Validation. Software Engineering, ISoLA 2022. LNCS, vol. 13702, pp. 389–406. Springer, Cham (2022). ISBN 978-3-031-19756-7. https://doi.org/10.1007/978-3-031-19756-7_22

10. Li, Z., et al.: Automating code review activities by large-scale pre-training. In: Proceedings of the 30th ACM Joint European Software Engineering Conference and Symposium on the Foundations of Software Engineering, pp. 1035–1047 (2022)

11. Vaithilingam, P., Zhang, T., Glassman, E.L.: Expectation vs. experience: evaluating the usability of code generation tools powered by large language models. In: Chi Conference on Human Factors in Computing Systems Extended Abstracts, pp. 1–7 (2022)

12. Xu, F.F., et al.: A systematic evaluation of large language models of code. In: Proceedings of the 6th ACM SIGPLAN International Symposium on Machine Programming, pp. 1–10 (2022)

13. Bainczyk, A.: Simplicity-oriented lifelong learning of web applications. [work in progress]. Ph.D. thesis. Dortmund, Germany: TU Dortmund University (2023)

14. Busch, D., et al.: ChatGPT in the loop - a natural language extension for domain-specific modeling languages. In: Lecture Notes of Computer Science, vol. 14380. Springer, Heidelberg (2023). https://doi.org/10.1007/978-3-031-46001-2_22

15. OpenAI. GPT-4 Technical Report. arXiv arXiv:2303.08774 (2023)

16. Tian, H., et al.: Is ChatGPT the ultimate programming assistant-how far is it? arXiv preprint arXiv:2304.11938 (2023)

Synthesizing Understandable Strategies

Peter Backeman$^{(\boxtimes)}$ ⓘ

Mälardalen University, Västerås, Sweden
`peter.backeman@mdu.se`

Abstract. The result of reinforcement learning is often obtained in the form of a q-table mapping actions to future rewards. We propose to use SMT solvers and *strategy trees* to generate a representation of a learned strategy in a format which is understandable for a human. We present the methodology and demonstrate it on a small game.

Keywords: Synthesizing Strategies · Reinforcement Learning · SMT

1 Introduction

Reinforcement learning has in the last decade gained enormous popularity for creating an AI agent learning an optimal strategy. The result is often obtained in the form of a q-table, mapping, for each state, every action to an expected future reward. While this is useful for a computer to execute it, for a human it is inconvenient. We propose to use SMT solvers to generate a representation of a learned strategy in a format which is *understandable*, by limiting the representation to a pre-defined format. Moreover, we introduce *strategy trees*, to enable a step-wise refinement process. Generating strategies is a well-researched problem, but In contrast to other recent work, e.g., [4], we emphasize trying to generate an understandable representation of a strategy. We demonstrate an approach on a simple example which we hope to extend to more challenging problems.

Running Example: Nim is a classic game with many variants. In this abstract we focus on a specific version for simplicity, where the game starts with 21 sticks being placed in a row. Each player takes turn removing *one or two sticks*, and the winning player is the one who removes the final stick.

2 Reinforcement Learning

Reinforcement learning is an approach where an optimal strategy is learned by interaction with an environment [3]. The programmer only provides a definition of the state-space, the possible actions and rewards for reaching certain states[1]. For our example, we consider a state space of a single variable $s \in [1, 21]$ indicating the number of remaining sticks. In each state there are two possible actions

---

[1] As well as a set of meta-parameters to the learning algorithm, e.g., learning rate.

J. Kofroň et al. (Eds.): ECBS 2023, LNCS 14390, pp. 201–204, 2024.
https://doi.org/10.1007/978-3-031-49252-5_15

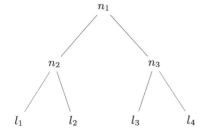

```
(assert (=> (= n2 0) (and
      (= n2val_0 (+ l1val_0 l2val_0))
      (= n2val_1 (+ l1val_1 l2val_1))
      (= n2val_2 (+ l1val_2 l2val_2))
      (= n2val_3 (+ l1val_3 l2val_3))
      (= n2val_4 (+ l1val_4 l2val_4))
)))
```

Fig. 1. AST for function template with three internal nodes $\{n_1, n_2, n_3\}$ and five leaf nodes $\{l_1, \ldots, l_5\}$

Fig. 2. Excerpt of SMT formula.

a_1, a_2, picking one or two sticks[2]. A reward of one is given when winning (i.e., reaching $s = 0$), and minus one when losing (i.e., opponent reaches $s = 0$).

By running a straightforward reinforcement learning algorithm, we can obtain a q-table as shown in Table 1, giving an optimal strategy for playing Nim. For example, it shows that when there are seven sticks left ($s = 7$), taking one stick ($a_1 = 0.90$) is preferable to taking two sticks ($a_2 = -0.90$).

Table 1. Q-table of Nim player.

s	1	2	3	4	5	6	7	8	9	10	11
a_1	1.00	−1.00	−1.00	0.95	−0.91	−0.95	0.90	−0.76	−0.90	0.86	−0.78
a_2	n/a	1.00	−1.00	−0.98	0.95	−0.95	−0.90	0.90	−0.90	−0.74	0.86
s	12	13	14	15	16	17	18	19	20	21	
a_1	−0.86	0.81	−0.76	−0.80	0.77	−0.70	−0.67	0.74	−0.47	−0.72	
a_2	−0.86	−0.75	0.81	−0.81	−0.62	0.77	−0.76	−0.70	0.74	−0.43	

3   SMT Synthesis

Satisfiability Modulo Theories (SMT) is a technique of finding models of formulas defined over a Boolean structure combined with theory literals [1]. In this section we present a method for searching functions, constrained by a template, to find a function which corresponds to a function relating inputs to outputs. A template is shown in Fig. 1. It is an AST with seven nodes. We restrict each internal node to be one of the operators $+, -, *, \%^3$, and each leaf to be set either the input value (x) or a constant ($c \in [-10, 10]$). The restrictions on the AST should be set in such a way to balance expressability and understandability.

---

[2] For simplicity, action a_2 is forbidden when $s = 1$, i.e., it is impossible to pick more sticks than remaining.

[3] Where % is the remainder operator.

Given an AST template and input/output-pairs, we can formulate an SMT query which yields a model with assignments to leaves and internal nodes such that the function computes as desired. We sketch the formulation here:

- Each internal node has an integer variable defining which operator it is,
- Each leaf has two variables: one indicating whether it is the input value or a constant; the second the value of the (potential) constant,
- For each input/output-pair, each node and leaf is given a integer variable which should equal the value of the node or leaf given the specific input.

For example, encoding that if node n_1 is addition (corresponding integer value is zero), then the value of n_2 should be equal to the sum of the values of l_1 and l_2 (with five input/output-pairs) is shown in Fig. 2.

We can encode the q-table in Table 1 (with symmetry-breaking constraints), and solve it using the SMT-solver Z3 [2]. After a long time (hours), it returns a model $\{n_1 = +, n_2 = +, n_3 = \%, l_1 = -1, l_2 = 0, l_3 = x, l_4 = 3\}$ which corresponds to the function $(-1 + 0) + (x\%3) = (x \% 3) - 1$.[4] This function condenses the strategy into a understandable format.

4   Strategy Trees

As finding the function takes a long time, we introduce an alternative approach: *strategy trees*. A tree over a set of input/output-pairs consists of a root r node with a set of children C, s.t. every edge from r to $c \in C$ is labelled with a function over the input variable, and every leaf is labelled with an output.

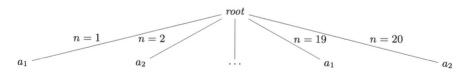

Fig. 3. (Partial) naive strategy tree for Nim game.

Intuitively, each child corresponds to a sub-strategy: its edge-label states *when* it should be applied, and the node-label states *what* action should be made. A naive strategy tree based on the q-table in our running example is obtained by creating one node for each row in the table, see Fig. 3. However, since such a tree is note very useful, we introduce a *merge*-operator, transforming a strategy tree into an equivalent one. We can merge two children if they have the same node label and we can find a edge label which identifies both sub-strategies and no other strategy. We can find functions using the approach presented in Sect. 3.

---

[4] The subtraction of one comes from the action space being defined as $\{a_1 = 0, a_2 = 1\}$ instead of the number of sticks removed ($\{a_1 = 1, a_2 = 2\}$).

For example, two children with identical node-labels and edge-labels $n = 1$ and $n = 2$ could be merged to a child with edge-label $1 \leq n \wedge n \leq 2$.[5]

We can apply the merge-operator repeatedly to obtain a reduced strategy tree. If we perform this strategy on the tree in Fig. 3, after a few seconds of merging, we obtain the tree shown in Fig. 4, a more succinct representation of the same information. Of course, in which order the operator is applied is important, currently a naive approach is used (enumerate all pairs of children with same node label, and try to merge in order).

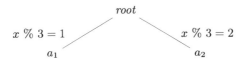

Fig. 4. Reduced strategy tree for Nim game.

5   Conclusions

We presented strategy trees and show we can use them to step-wise synthesize an understandable strategy representation. In future work, we want to flesh out the theory, e.g., considering more input variables and trees with greater depth. Moreover, we will look into different templates for the edge labels. We also wish to explore more use cases and compare different merging strategies and study the scaling of the approach. It is also interesting to introduce a splitting operator to allow the search to go in two directions (where a single split might allow for many merges).

Acknowledgements. This work was supported by the Knowledge Foundation in Sweden through the ACICS project (20190038).

References

1. Barrett, C., Tinelli, C.: Satisfiability modulo theories. In: Handbook of Model Checking, pp. 305–343. Springer, Cham (2018). https://doi.org/10.1007/978-3-319-10575-8_11
2. de Moura, L., Bjørner, N.: Z3: an efficient SMT solver. In: Ramakrishnan, C.R., Rehof, J. (eds.) TACAS 2008. LNCS, vol. 4963, pp. 337–340. Springer, Heidelberg (2008). https://doi.org/10.1007/978-3-540-78800-3_24
3. Sutton, R.S., Barto, A.G.: Reinforcement Learning: An Introduction, 2nd edn. The MIT Press (2018)
4. Wu, K., et al.: Automatic synthesis of generalized winning strategies of impartial combinatorial games using SMT solvers. In: Bessiere, C. (ed.) Proceedings of the Twenty-Ninth International Joint Conference on Artificial Intelligence, IJCAI-20, pp. 1703–1711. International Joint Conferences on Artificial Intelligence Organization (2020)

---

[5] Interval constraints are added on edges, limiting the functions domains for efficiency.

RePRoInspect: Framework for Reproducible Defect Datasets for Improved AOI of PCBAs

Ahmad Rezaei[1]([✉]) [ID], Johannes Nau[1] [ID], Detlef Streitferdt[1] [ID],
Jörg Schambach[2] [ID], and Todor Vangelov[1]

[1] Technische Universität Ilmenau, Helmholtzplatz 5, 98693 Ilmenau, Germany
{ahmad.rezaei,johannes.nau,detlef.streitferdt,
todor.vangelov}@tu-ilmenau.de
[2] GÖPEL electronic GmbH, Jena, Germany
j.schambach@goepel.com

Abstract. Today, the process of producing a printed circuit board assembly (PCBA) is growing rapidly, and this process requires cutting-edge debugging and testing of the boards. The Automatic Optical Inspection (AOI) process detects defects in the boards, components, or solder pads using image processing and machine learning (ML) algorithms. Although state-of-the-art approaches for identifying defects are well developed, due to three main issues, the ML algorithms and datasets are incapable of fully integrating into industrial plants. These issues are privacy limitations for sharing data, the distribution shifts in the PCBA industry, and the absence of a degree of freedom for reproducible and modifiable synthetic datasets.

This paper addresses these challenges and introduces "RePRoInspect", a comprehensive framework designed to meet these requirements. RePRoInspect uses fabrication files from the designed PCBs in the manufacturing line to automatically generate 3D models of the PCBAs. By incorporating various techniques, the framework introduces controlled defects into the PCBA, thereby creating reproducible and differentiable defect datasets. The quality data produced by this framework enables an improved detection and classification scenario for AOI in industrial applications. The initial results of RePRoInspect are demonstrated and discussed through detailed instances. Finally, the paper also highlights future work to improve the current state of the framework.

Keywords: Automated Optical Inspection · Machine Learning · 3D Rendering

1 Introduction

The global Printed Circuit Board (PCB) market size is currently growing from 72 billion USD in 2022 to an estimated 89 billion by 2028.[1] This rapid growth in

---

[1] MarketWatch, The Prospects of Printed Circuit Board (PCB) Market 2023: Industry Trends and Challenges till 2030.

J. Kofroň et al. (Eds.): ECBS 2023, LNCS 14390, pp. 205–214, 2024.
https://doi.org/10.1007/978-3-031-49252-5_16

Table 1. PCBA defect categories covered by AOI systems.

Category	Area	Short explanation
Incorrect placement (IP)	Component	The component is positioned in the false angle or place. The connection with the solder pad can be weak or lost
Missing component (MC)	Component	The component is not present in its specified place
Tombstone (T)	Component	Due to solder heat setting or placement the component loses solder connection on one side
Textual failure (TF)	Component	The text on the component refers to a false component or is distracted
Extra or insufficient solder (EIS)	Solder pad	The amount of solder is too low or too much
Not soldered (NS)	Solder pad	The soldering paste is removed before melting
Short circuit (SC)	Solder pad and Board	An undesirable electrical connection
Missing solder pad (MSP)	Board	Incorrect manufacturing of PCB solder pads
Open circuit (OC)	Board	The loss of connection between copper lines. which should be connected
Spurious or mouse bite on copper (SMC)	Board	damaged copper lines without loss of electrical connection
Pseudo defects (PD)	All areas	Environmental particles are observed

PCB production requires advancements for fast, reliable, and cost-effective production chains. A major challenge in production chains is the detection, repair, or elimination of defective components or boards.

AOI is a process for detecting defective PCBA boards (listed in Table 1) by processing the industrial camera images taken from the boards in the production line. AOI contains three factors; the camera and light setup, the image processing algorithm used for better highlighting the defects, and the machine learning (ML) techniques for decision-making. These factors are constantly studied and improved in the literature. For instance, defective areas and components are not observable without having the proper light setting and camera setup. Shadows or reflections of other components or solder pads should be tackled for a clear view of the defects. Authors in [3,8], and [9] cover these issues regarding capture angle and light settings, and they propose various settings for AOI systems. Moreover, the image processing techniques are mathematically well developed and intertwined with the need for ML techniques used for decision-making. For instance, the large industrial images should be re-scaled and divided into several smaller sets for faster decision-making [12,17]. Subsequently, ML techniques for the detection and classification of PCBA defects are constantly improving by using cutting-edge object detectors and Convolutional Neural Networks (CNNs); e.g. improved versions of the "You Only Look Once" (YOLO) algorithm for the detection of defects in PCBA surface [2,12] or CNN models used for component defect classification [8].

Although the state-of-the-art (SOTA) shows great improvement for AOI systems, three challenging factors (discussed in details in Sect. 2) in PCBA AOI datasets such as privacy-criticality, quality of synthetic data, and degree of freedom persist. Former datasets include a limited number of defect categories (due to privacy issue) without considering the distribution shifts present in the industry, and moreover, they produce synthetic or partly real data with constant light and camera setting for all images, which does not adhere to industry preferences and is not practical for detection of all defect types. In this paper, these factors are discussed and tackled with the proposal of a framework for reproducible PCBA AOI defect dataset. The framework adheres to industrial privacy constraints, and gives the users a degree of freedom in producing their own PCBA AOI datasets from 3D PCBA models with a degree of freedom in environmental settings, distribution shifts, and the quality of captured data.

The following sections in this paper are organized as follows. Section 2 elaborates on PCBA defects and covered defects in the former works. Next, the technical setup for the framework to produce synthetic data is covered in Sect. 2.2. The Sect. 3 presents our proposed framework and describes its architecture. Using this architecture, visual results for the captured data by the framework are discussed in Sect. 4.

2   Related Works

PCBA defects are abnormalities in the manufacturing process, which can lead to malfunction or complete breakdown of a PCBA. These defects in PCBA happen in three main areas such as electrical components, soldering pads, and board surface. More than 100 defects are categorized in National Physical Laboratory Industry Defects Database[2], which are structured into eleven categories (shown in Table 1) classified based on AOI system detection (categorized based on publications in [14,17]).

A summary on former datasets is provided in Table 2, which is used for the identification of research gaps discussed in Sect. 2.1. The literature consists of datasets for PCBA AOI for defect detection or normal board inspection [7,10,13]. The latter is out of scope for this paper; however, the ReProInspect framework can help enhance the datasets in the normal board inspections. In 2019, Deep-PCB [18] and synthesized PCB [6] datasets focused on five categories of defects on board or solder pads. The use case for these datasets is for the defect detection with object detectors, but they lack other common defects. Another issue in these datasets is the quality of synthetic data (manual insertion of defects) and the quality of captured data which does not conform to industrial settings. Moreover, in 2020, the authors in [10] used a nonpublic dataset, including real PCBA images captured in an industrial setting, that includes more defects focusing on solder pads. Furthermore, in 2021, CD-PCB [4] was published with 20 image pairs consisting of synthetic board and solder pad defects. In this dataset the manual synthesized data and lacking industrial capturing environment are persistent. Authors in [21] published PCBNet dataset (2022) that conversely to previous datasets focuses more on component defects. This dataset contains real images taken in an industrial setting, but it lacks other categories of defects. Subsequently, in 2023, the HU-Solder [20], capturing some of the defect categories on components and solder pads, is released. This dataset contains real images taken in a manual setting using a 13-megapixel camera. Finally, in the

---

[2] Available (last seen on 18.08.2023): http://defectsdatabase.npl.co.uk/.

Table 2. Summary on the datasets used in previous literature.

Dataset Name		DeepPCB [18]	Synthesized PCB [6]	Advantech Data [11]	CD-PCB [4]	PCBNet Data [21]	HU-Solder [20]	Vision Automobile [1]
Available		✓	✓	✗	✓	✓	✓	✗
Industrial Capture		✓	✗	✓	✗	✓	✗	✓
Real Data		✗	✗	✓	✗	✓	✓	✓
Covered Defects	IP	✗	✗	✗	✗	✓	✓	✗
	MC	✗	✗	✗	✗	✓	✗	✗
	T	✗	✗	✗	✗	✓	✓	✗
	TF	✗	✗	✗	✗	✓	✗	✗
	EIS	✗	✗	✓	✗	✗	✓	✗
	NS	✗	✗	✓	✓	✗	✓	✗
	SC	✓	✓	✓	✓	✗	✓	✓
	MSP	✓	✓	✗	✓	✗	✗	✗
	OC	✓	✓	✗	✓	✗	✗	✗
	SMC	✓	✓	✗	✓	✗	✗	✗
	PD	✓	✓	✓	✓	✗	✗	✗
#Defect images		1,500	1,386	834	20	-	655*	600*

(* snapshot images, -- no information given)

same year, a non-public dataset is used in [1] that includes real data taken under an industrial setting but with only a focus on some solder pad defects.

2.1 A Recap on the Privacy Issue

Privacy is the main culprit for the lack of unified and well-developed datasets in PCBA AOI domain. However, the privacy of companies' intellectual properties contributes to the reliability of the products, the companies' competition in open market, and resilience to security threats. In other domains, the authors try to leverage privacy by redefining privacy-preserving data exchange [15], but due to lack of viable solution for PCBA AOI, this paper proposes a solution adhering to the privacy constraints in the industry.

The quantity of produced images for PCBA defect datasets in [6,18] shows the great potential to create synthetic data from fewer actual PCBAs. However, the production of the synthetic data in former approaches is done manually and in an uncontrolled way. First, they include a subset of defect categories, which can be extended for a more realistic dataset. Second, the defects are manually inserted to a 2D image without adhering to their actual rationale (heat, physical fluid dynamics, and malfunction of pick-and-place arms) behind the formation of defects. Thus, larger quantity of higher quality data is producible with solving these two issues. Furthermore, in industrial AOI scenarios, the capturing angle and the light settings for images are adjustable. Henceforth, it is valuable to allow the researchers having the same degree of freedom while producing their synthetic dataset.

Subsequently, in realistic AOI scenarios, distribution shifts are available [19]. So the test data (PCBA images taken from the production line) can be different from training data (already-made defect dataset), which can degrade the performance of ML algorithms severely. In the PCBA AOI, the source of distribution shift is basically the difference in color of boards or in the components used during the assembly. The distribution shifts affect the defect detection greatly, although the PCBA possesses the same functionality. Creation of synthetic defects with distribution shifts for improving the AOI systems or evaluating the robustness of proposed AOI systems is beneficial.

Table 3. Ordered factors for selection of rendering software (highest priority first)

Priority	Factor	Description
1	Complexity Handling	Managing complex scenes efficiently
2	Speed	Rendering speed impacts dataset production timeline
3	GPU Rendering	Utilizing GPUs for fast rendering
4	Ease of Use	User-friendly interface for a smooth workflow
5	Cost-effectiveness	Balancing capabilities with costs
6	Render Farm Support	Integration with distributed rendering
7	Integration	Seamless collaboration with modeling tools
8	Light Control	Precise control over lighting settings/scenarios
9	Quality Control	Fine-grained adjustments for visual fidelity
10	Supported Platforms	Compatibility with multiple operating systems
11	Community Support	Active user community and resources
12	Updates and Development	Regular software improvements

In conclusion, the ReProInspect framework enables the users to reproduce a controlled defect dataset with a degree of freedom in modifying the image capture settings, distribution shifts, and adhering to industrial settings. The following sub-section explains the technical setup for generation of 3D defect data.

2.2   Technical Requirements and Setup

An important part of the ReProInspect framework is the rendering software which creates the PCBA 3D model from the fabrication data. In Table 3, twelve selection factors for producing sheer volume of high quality data are prioritized based on the authors' experiences and research.

After applying the first factor to the search for different rendering software packages, results were limited to 8 rendering softwares with similar characteristics for factors 6 to 12. These software packages are shown in Table 4 retaining high integration capacity, support for rendering farms, flexible control on light and quality, various OS support, and active maintenance and community support. Thus, Table 4 only lists the comparison factors of the subset between 2 to 5. Based on a comparison in this Table, Blender and LuxCoreRender allow a user-friendly, high speed, and open-source experience with GPU compatibility.

The 3D computer-aided design (CAD) data for components (in OBD++, DXF, and Blend formats) are usually accessible via open source libraries such as Kicad software package[3]. These 3D data enable manual user modifications, which are automated in ReProInspect framework with production of components with irregular shapes (due to manufacturing problems), broken parts, different colors or textures, and also, with simulated dust and other environmental particles as pseudo defects.

---

[3] Available: https://www.kicad.org/.

Table 4. Rendering software comparison for PCBA defect dataset production

Software	Speed	GPU Rendering	Ease of Use	Cost-effectiveness
Blender	Fast	Yes	User-friendly	Free
Autodesk Maya	Moderate	Yes	Moderate	Costly
Maxon Cinema 4D	Moderate	Partial	User-friendly	Costly
Chaos Group V-Ray	Fast	Yes	Moderate	Costly
Redshift	Fast	Yes	Less User-friendly	Reasonably Priced
LuxCoreRender	Fast	Yes	User-friendly	Free
Octane Render	Fast	Yes	Moderate	Reasonably Priced
Arnold	Fast	Yes	Less User-friendly	Costly

Furthermore, the fabrication data (Gerber files, PCB NC files, and Pick and placement files) are required for production and assembly of PCB and CAD components in the ReProInspect. Next section proposes the architecture of the ReProInspect based on the explained technical setup and requirements.

3   Proposed Framework

The architecture is based on an enhanced tool chain as described in [14]. The core architectural style of the tool chain is Pipes & Filters, to support several operations on each PCBA-element. As modelled in Fig. 1, the filters operate on a central repository. Thus, the original Pipes of the Pipes & Filters style had to be adapted, in favor of a data model supporting the later introduction of defects for the ML training, the ultimate goal of this paper.

As seen in Fig. 1, the input for the tool-chain are PCBA fabrication data (e.g. from Kicad) and the 3D component files for each of the PCBA components. In the diagram, the repository holds all the PCBA geometric layer data combined with the 3D component data items, which is essential for production of complete PCBA 3D model in the rendering step. Next, the Renderer is an independent component for final image production, and the tool-chain's filters are responsible for the introduction of defects (listed in Table 1) into the dataset. Eventually, the resulting and rendered image can contain correct or erroneous images of PCBA.

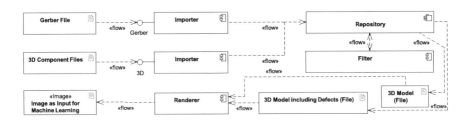

Fig. 1. Software Architecture, Tool Chain

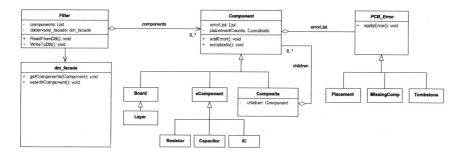

Fig. 2. Software Architecture, Data Model

Based on the detailed architecture of the repository (Fig. 2), each of the filters adhere to this software architecture. The filter has access to the complete data model of the PCBA and its components, which is modeled as a list of all *virtual* components. This list will be read and serialized back to the repository, e.g. a database.

The *virtual* components are the core part of the composite design pattern [5] for PCBA and its components, and it reflects the PCBA system structure and allows the introduction of defects at any layer or component of the structure. The *Board*, a leaf of the composite pattern, with its layers is the central building block of an electronic system, and the *eComponent* can then be placed on the board and have types like Resistor, Capacitor, or Integrated Circuit (IC). Based on this architecture a list of possible defects is held with any level of granularity, and these defects can be implanted sequentially as it results in different rendered output image (e.g. sequential order of a broken colored resistor or a colored broken resistor).

The main emphasis was put on the extensibility of the software architecture. The composite pattern allows to add any number of components for and layers of the PCBA. In addition, it would also be possible to derive classes from composite and introduce special composites, to allow a further grouping of components. The same argument holds for the PCBA defects which are also extensible. The method *applyError()* will be implemented in any new defect class. Thus, this method works on a component level and can change the components parameters (e.g. change the material, reflectiveness of the surface, or the written type on the component) or change its geometric form (e.g. to simulate mechanical damages or the simply move or misplace the component).

Although each filter will have to implement the architecture of Fig. 2, it will be specifically developed for a given defect use case/scenario. This allows to use the software framework within a command line scripting environment. Finally, we create the desired and fully labeled pictures for the following ML training. The scripts hold all the necessary information for the generated picture set and thus, will be stored in a versioning system.

Fig. 3. Correct PCBA Image   **Fig. 4.** PCBA Image With Defects

4   Results and Discussion

Produced images with *ReProInspect* framework underline the capabilities discussed in the last sections. In Fig. 3 an example PCBA[4] with black theme and without any defects is shown, whereas in Fig. 4, the same PCBA (green theme) has defects. Of course, in these views it is hard for humans to identify the defects on the board. Thus, an AOI system inspects components for the defect detection. Five defects are "implanted" on Fig. 4. Detailed pictures of four of them, generated with ReProInspect, are shown in Fig. 5.

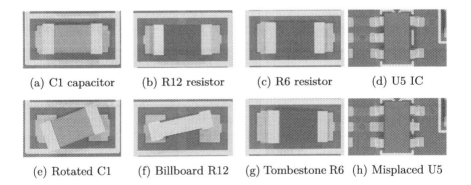

(a) C1 capacitor   (b) R12 resistor   (c) R6 resistor   (d) U5 IC

(e) Rotated C1   (f) Billboard R12   (g) Tombestone R6   (h) Misplaced U5

Fig. 5. Snapshots taken from normal and defective components.

First, a rotated capacitor in Fig. 5e with its correct positioning in Fig. 5a is shown. This defect might happen when the airflow in the soldering oven moves components with the liquefied soldering paste. Second, the resistor R12, correctly placed in Fig. 5b, has a billboard defect in Fig. 5f. This defect might be due to

---

[4] Available (last seen on 18.08.2023):https://github.com/dmitrystu/Nucleo2USB.

the placement of resistor upwards instead of its flat side. These two defects may result in fully functioning PCBA with probability of malfunctions, which is the reason for manufacturers to sort out such boards as *not ok*. Next defect is yet another resistor R6, placed correctly in Fig. 5c. The tombstone defect in Fig. 5g is hard to detect for humans from this above the component viewpoint. Tombstones are formed by a time delay of the liquefaction of the two solder paste sides. The right side liquefied earlier and its surface tension lifted the component. Fourth defect is a 180 degrees misplaced IC as in Fig. 5h (correct placement as in Fig. 5d). The last two defects cause malfunctioning PCBA in the end.

All in all the ReProInspect framework has been successfully set up a tool chain. It is capable of processing the original PCBA data as input and can generate the desired pictures as output and input for the following ML training. Its generality and scalability are given by the scalable architecture (any defects can be added). Across Operating systems only Python and the availability of the rendering engine (currently: Blender) are the requirements.

5 Future Works

Despite the current working state of the framework and its core software architecture, several of the architectural features have to be further enhanced.

As shown in the figures above, the soldering points, although available [14], need to be integrated into the picture generation process. Due to high computation and rendering time, the parallelization (discussed in Sect. 3) together with soldering computation could be further improved. Currently we experienced a speedup of 35 times from a four core CPU to a CPU + GPU setup.

The validation of PCBA dataset generated by ReProInspect will be done through a comparison with real industrial data. The important difference here is the validation on the premises of the picture owner. Thus, the actual data stays on owner's site and the privacy is ensured. The same applies for enhancement of AOI systems with distribution shifts so the ReProInspect can be used on sites for further enhancing and refining approaches (e.g. in [16]), again on the premises The same argumentation is taken for the defect in PCBAs which are different amongst PCBA production sites. Here, the defect classification as started in [16] can be further enhanced and refined, again on the premises of AOI systems.

Acknowledgments. Thüringer Aufbaubank (TAB, 2021 FE 9036) provided financial support for this study.

References

1. Chen, M.C., et al.: A PCBA solder joint defects inspection system based on deep learning technology. In: 2023 IEEE International Conference on Consumer Electronics (ICCE), pp. 1–3. IEEE (2023)
2. Du, B., Wan, F., Lei, G., Xu, L., Xu, C., Xiong, Y.: YOLO-MBBi: PCB surface defect detection method based on enhanced YOLOv5. Electronics **12**(13), 2821 (2023)

3. Du, Y., et al.: An automated optical inspection (AOI) platform for three-dimensional (3D) defects detection on glass micro-optical components (GMOC). Opt. Commun. **545**, 129736 (2023)

4. Fridman, Y., Rusanovsky, M., Oren, G.: ChangeChip: a reference-based unsupervised change detection for PCB defect detection. In: 2021 IEEE Physical Assurance and Inspection of Electronics (PAINE), pp. 1–8. IEEE (2021)

5. Gamma, E., Helm, R., Johnson, R., Vlissides, J.: Design Patterns: Elements of Reusable Object-oriented Software. Pearson Education (1994)

6. Huang, W., Wei, P.: A PCB dataset for defects detection and classification. arXiv preprint arXiv:1901.08204 (2019)

7. Jessurun, N., et al.: FPIC: a novel semantic dataset for optical PCB assurance. ACM J. Emerg. Technol. Comput. Syst. **19**(2), 1–21 (2023)

8. Kim, Y.G., Park, T.H.: SMT assembly inspection using dual-stream convolutional networks and two solder regions. Appl. Sci. **10**(13), 4598 (2020)

9. Lavrik, E., Panasenko, I., Schmidt, H.R.: Advanced methods for the optical quality assurance of silicon sensors. Nucl. Instrum. Methods Phys. Res., Sect. A **922**, 336–344 (2019)

10. Li, J., Gu, J., Huang, Z., Wen, J.: Application research of improved YOLO V3 algorithm in PCB electronic component detection. Appl. Sci. **9**(18), 3750 (2019)

11. Li, Y.T., Kuo, P., Guo, J.I.: Automatic industry PCB board dip process defect detection system based on deep ensemble self-adaption method. IEEE Trans. Compon. Packag. Manuf. Technol. **11**(2), 312–323 (2020)

12. Liao, X., Lv, S., Li, D., Luo, Y., Zhu, Z., Jiang, C.: YOLOv4-MN3 for PCB surface defect detection. Appl. Sci. **11**(24), 11701 (2021)

13. Lu, H., Mehta, D., Paradis, O., Asadizanjani, N., Tehranipoor, M., Woodard, D.L.: FICS-PCB: a multi-modal image dataset for automated printed circuit board visual inspection. Cryptology ePrint Archive (2020)

14. Nau, J., Richter, J., Streitferdt, D., Kirchhoff, M.: Simulating the printed circuit board assembly process for image generation. In: 2020 IEEE 44th Annual Computers, Software, and Applications Conference, pp. 245–254. IEEE (2020)

15. Pennekamp, J., et al.: Privacy-preserving production process parameter exchange. In: Annual Computer Security Applications Conference, pp. 510–525 (2020)

16. Richter, J., Nau, J., Kirchhoff, M., Streitferdt, D.: KOI: an architecture and framework for industrial and academic machine learning applications. In: MDIS 2020. CCIS, vol. 1341, pp. 113–128. Springer, Cham (2021). https://doi.org/10.1007/978-3-030-68527-0_8

17. Shi, W., Lu, Z., Wu, W., Liu, H.: Single-shot detector with enriched semantics for PCB tiny defect detection. J. Eng. **2020**(13), 366–372 (2020)

18. Tang, S., He, F., Huang, X., Yang, J.: Online PCB defect detector on a new PCB defect dataset. arXiv preprint arXiv:1902.06197 (2019)

19. Taori, R., Dave, A., Shankar, V., Carlini, N., Recht, B., Schmidt, L.: Measuring robustness to natural distribution shifts in image classification. Adv. Neural. Inf. Process. Syst. **33**, 18583–18599 (2020)

20. Ulger, F., Yuksel, S.E., Yilmaz, A., Gokcen, D.: Solder joint inspection on printed circuit boards: a survey and a dataset. IEEE Trans. Instrum. Meas. **72**, 1–21 (2023)

21. Wu, H., Lei, R., Peng, Y.: PCBNet: a lightweight convolutional neural network for defect inspection in surface mount technology. IEEE Trans. Instrum. Meas. **71**, 1–14 (2022)

Cyber-Physical Ecosystems: Modelling and Verification

Manuela L. Bujorianu[✉] ⓘ

University College London, Gower Street, London WC1E 6EA, UK
l.bujorianu@ucl.ac.uk

Abstract. In this paper, we set up a mathematical framework for the modelling and verification of complex cyber-physical ecosystems. In our setting, cyber-physical ecosystems are cyber-physical systems of systems that are highly connected. These are networked systems that combine cyber-physical systems with an interaction mechanism with other systems and the environment (ecosystem capability). Our contribution will be on two streams: (i) modelling the constituent systems and their interfaces, and (ii) local/global verification of cyber-physical ecosystems. We introduce a concept of basic model, whose skeleton is a Markov decision process and we propose a verification based abstraction methodology.

Keywords: cyber-physical ecosystem · Markov model · reachability · abstraction

1 Introduction

The Cyber-Physical System (CPS) paradigm was introduced by NSF in 2006 to define a new generation of systems that are built from, and rely upon, the coherent integration of computational algorithms and physical components. It is based on three technologies which are: embedded systems, sensor and actuation, and network and communication systems.

An ecosystem is a complex system, i.e. a group of interrelated things, working together to achieve a common objective. In system engineering, an ecosystem usually consists of components or subsystems, interacting via interfaces, which together satisfy a set of requirements. There exists also an external environment where the given system activates. Examples include the global financial infrastructure of banks and exchanges, transportation networks, cyber-physical systems, IoT networks and semiautomated manufacturing lines, and distributed databases.

Cyber-physical ecosystems (CPES) are ecosystems of networked CPS, meaning that they are systems of CPS (CPSoS) provided with an interaction activity between them and with their environment. Alternatively, we may call them cyber-physical infrastructures (CPI). Examples are smart grid, autonomous vehicles and maritime ships, autonomous swarm drones.

This work has been funded by the EPSRC project EP/R006865/1: Interface reasoning for interacting systems (IRIS).

© The Author(s), under exclusive license to Springer Nature Switzerland AG 2024
J. Kofroň et al. (Eds.): ECBS 2023, LNCS 14390, pp. 215–230, 2024.
https://doi.org/10.1007/978-3-031-49252-5_17

The aim of this paper is to set up a modelling framework for CPES based on the distributed system paradigm. The necessary shift to the ecosystem view means that we have to consider not only the construction of models of individual components but also the mechanism that allows them to interact with one another. The interaction mechanism is based on the concept of interface, which, in this paper, is defined in a very general way. From an engineering standpoint, the interfaces can be treated from different perspectives. It is important to note that in the architecture of an ecosystem, an interface may be itself a subsystem with its own interfaces.

In this paper, we consider that components have the possibility to connect with some free interfaces. The interfaces have separate structure and the link with specific components is realized via interface requirements.

We model the CPES components as Markov decision processes that encapsulate at a higher level of abstraction the interaction between physics and computation in the CPS model. The interaction between components will be done by means of specific interfaces, which will be modelled using again decision processes with constraints. This kind of interfaces is flexible enough to enable dynamic interactions and reconfiguration within the underlying CPES.

The novelty of our CPES modelling approach relies on the use of distributed systems paradigm combined with the dynamic behaviour of components described by suitable Markov models. In this setting, the component interaction is enabled by some independent interfaces that play the role of connectors. For this modelling framework, we propose a safety verification methodology based on abstractions.

The paper is structured as follows. In Sect. 2, we discuss our use of distributed systems as a metaphor for cyber-physical ecosystems of systems and show how we combine it with the dynamic system behaviours. In Sect. 3, we present the mathematical models for the CPES constituents using some suitable Markov models. In Sect. 4, we explain how to model the compositional structure of ecosystem models using a rather general notion of interface. Interfaces between models describe how they can be composed together to construct a model of an ecosystem. Conditions that ensure the soundness of the composition operation are also provided. Our notion of interface captures a wide range of the notions of interface that are in the literature on systems and modelling [6]. In Sect. 5, we define verification of CPES as a stochastic reachability problem. This reachability problem is specialised for models of components and interfaces. In Sect. 6, we introduce a specific concept of abstraction map that preserves the Markov property. Then this is used to obtain aggregations of models and interface models and to simplify the computation of the reach probabilities. The abstraction process is done in a modular way supporting the local reasoning. Modular reasoning involves breaking down a computational ecosystem into smaller, more manageable components, and to determine local properties of these components that guarantee desired properties of the global system. First, we check the local safety properties and then we combine them in order to deduce the global system safety. This modular safety approach is quite standard in the verification community [7]. We apply the philosophy of this approach in a new setting of CPES modelled as networks of Markov decision processes. The paper ends with some conclusions.

2 CPES - Conceptual Modelling

CPES are modelled as systems of systems, defined through the composition of their CPS constituents. The composition operation is done via specific subsystem interfaces. In this work, we combine the distributed system modelling approach with the behavioural approach for dynamical systems.

In a nutshell, a constituent can be viewed as a tuple

$$C = \langle Loc, X, I, Beh \rangle$$

where Loc represents its location, X is a finite set of variables (both computational and physical), $\mathcal{I}$ represents its interface thought of as a set of variables that can be observed by the other systems of the CPES. Finally, Beh denotes the set of the system behaviours that are thought as system traces (evolutions of its variables).

The interaction with other constituent systems and the environment may affect these parameters. For example, Loc can be modelled as a random graph, or the time evolution of X can be modelled as a stochastic dynamical system where the environment perturbation is captured as a contiguous noise (modelled as white noise in the structure of a stochastic differential equation), or as shot noise (modelled by a Poisson type process).

2.1 The Distributed Systems Metaphor

CPES are thought of as systems of systems, or systems with different (semi)-autonomous constituent systems, which interact, collaborate, inter-operate to achieve common goals. Each system may have a private activity with a specific structure, behaviour, decision mechanism or internal information encapsulated in a specific mathematical model.

We use distributed systems as a metaphor for describing CPES. Our modelling approach for ecosystems is component based, where each constituent system is modelled using a quite general basic model. A basic model is intended to capture the simplest convenient representation of a single constituent system.

There are three key ingredients upon which we draw.

- *Location.* Distributed systems naturally have a concept of distinct locations, which may be connected to one another. In the setting of computer systems, components are present at different locations and connected by a network. In the more general view, locations can be physical (e.g., a room, a container), logical (e.g., an address in computer memory), or abstract (e.g., the location where a semaphore exists).

– *Resource.* Resources exist at locations and can move between them according to the locations' connections. In general, they can represent physical objects, people, information, and more.
– *Process.* Processes manipulate resources—such as consuming, creating, and moving between locations—as they go.

These concepts can be used to build a representation of a system's structure and operation, but there is one more concept required: the environment in which the system operates.

– *Environment*—Environments capture the world outside of the system of interest and how the two interact.

Each basic model encapsulates the above primitives—locations, resources, processes, and environment.

2.2   Dynamic Behaviour

Each constituent system is characterized by a specific dynamic behaviour. We can model this behaviour as a deterministic dynamical system or a stochastic process. In [4], the behaviour of CPS subsystems has been modelled as a stochastic hybrid process to encapsulate the physical part and the digital part of a component.

In this paper, for simplicity, we will use an abstraction of this behaviour modelled by a simple Markov chain, viewed as graph whose states are the locations, which have associated some resources. To capture the processes that manage the resources, we add control actions to the Markov chain, transforming it into a Markov decision process. A CPES will be modelled as a network of Markov chains, and its safety verification will be based on some coarse-graining process implemented using specific abstraction morphisms. The continuous dynamics will be abstracted into control action, in the sense that an action could enable a continuous path from a discrete state to another. This technique has been successfully applied for different models of cyber-physical systems such piecewise deterministic Markov processes or stochastic hybrid processes [1]. An interesting CPES example is the water distribution network for which a modelling framework based on Markov decision processes has been developed in [12].

3   Mathematical Modelling of CPES

In this section, we set up a mathematical framework where the basic models and their composition are formally described. Our CPES model builds on some well-known formalisms as Markov chains and interface theory. A CPES, viewed as a system of systems, will be modelled as a composition of Markov chains.

3.1   Basic Model

The basic model is a representation of a single constituent system. In this paper, the basic model is defined as a discrete time Markov chain (MC) with a finite state space. The MC states represent the system locations. Resources exist in each state and their manipulation will be modelled using Markov decision processes.

A Markov Chain MC is a directed graph which consists of a set of states S as nodes, and a set of edges defined by a set of probabilistic transitions. An MC can be also specified as a (discrete-time) stochastic process (X_n) with values in S.

The relation between the states of the MC is defined by a set of transitions:

$$T = \{(s, s')|s, s' \in S\}$$

where each transition (s, s') is governed by a transition probability

$$p(s, s') = \mathbf{P}[X_{n+1} = s'|X_n = s].$$

The transition matrix $P = (p(s, s'))$ is a stochastic matrix (that means the sum of each row is equal to one).

Usually, to ensure the uniqueness of an MC, we need to have an initial state s_0 or an initial probability distribution μ_0. Sometimes, a deadlock or a cemetery state s_Δ to encounter for the case when the chain enters in a failure state or is dying (that is s_Δ is an absorbing state). Then, an MC is defined as a tuple:

$$MC = (S, T, s_0, s_\Delta).$$

The important advantage is that the infinitesimal generator has a matrix form, and the probability distributions are probability vectors. For a Markov chain, the generator is one-step increment of the transition matrix

$$\mathcal{L} = P - I \tag{1}$$

Each state of the MC is associated with some resources. We denote the set of resources by $\mathbf{R}$. We may add an algebraic structure to $\mathbf{R}$. The processes (which execute the resource management) will be modelled by using a Markov decision process (MDP). To introduce an MDP we need a set of actions $\mathcal{A}$, where each action $a \in \mathcal{A}$ will represent a resource operation decision or a resource control action. At each time step n, the corresponding decision is denoted by a_n.

Considering the decision process (a_n), the transition probabilities of the MDP is:

$$p^a(s, s') = \mathbf{P}[X_{n+1} = s'|X_n = s, a_n = a].$$

Therefore, we have a transition set T^a associated to each action $a \in \mathcal{A}$. For each $s \in S$, denote by $\mathcal{A}(s)$ the set of all actions $a \in \mathcal{A}$, which enable a transition from s.

For a $Q \subset S$, we use the notation $s \xrightarrow{a}_\mu Q$ whenever $a \in \mathcal{A}(s)$ and

$$\sum_{q \in Q} p^a(s, q) = \mu.$$

For an MDP, we may define also a reward function $\rho : S \times \mathcal{A} \to \mathbb{R}$, which specifies the gain and cost of being in a particular state and applying a particular action.

An MDP policy is a set of rules a controller would follow to choose the action to perform in each state. A Markov policy is a family of stochastic kernels $\pi_n : S \to \Delta(\mathcal{A})$, where $\Delta(\mathcal{A})$ is the space of probability distributions on $\mathcal{A}$:

$$\pi(s, a)(n) = \mathbf{P}[A_n = a | X_n = s]. \tag{2}$$

If a policy does not depend on time, it is called stationary. Under each policy, the MDP behaviour is described by an MC.

We define a basic model as follows:

$$\mathcal{M} = (S[\mathbf{R}], \mathcal{A}, (T^a)_{a \in \mathcal{A}}, s_0). \tag{3}$$

We can replace the initial condition s_0 with an initial probability distribution μ_0. A basic model is an MDP that models the resource dynamics. The basic model can be seen, as well, as a probabilistic automaton [11] where all the transitions are Markovian (we do not consider nondeterminism). We treat the basic model as graph with probabilistic transitions.

We can view an MDP or an MC as a dynamical system on the space of probability distributions of S, denoted by $\Delta(S)$. Let us call μ_n the probability distribution at time n; that is

$$\mu_n(s) = \mathbf{P}[X_n = s | X_0 = s_0]. \tag{4}$$

The distribution dynamics of an MC can be described the following *master equation*:

$$\mu_{n+1} = \mu_n P \tag{5}$$

where P is the associated stochastic matrix. Then (5) describes a semi-dynamical system with the initial condition equal to μ_0. For an MDP, to each action $a \in \mathcal{A}$, we have the corresponding dynamics:

$$\mu_{n+1} = \mu_n P^a, \tag{6}$$

where P^a is thought of as a matrix operator acting on the space of probability distributions. For simplicity we use the notation μ_n instead of μ_n^a.

We can adapt the master equation to capture also the resource dynamics:

$$\mu_n(s, R) = \mathbf{P}[X_n = (s, R) | X_0 = (s_0, R_0)].$$

Then the master equation describes a probabilistic modification function of the basic model graph. In the following, we consider the process dynamics contains the resource movement in an implicit way to ease the notation.

3.2 Probabilistic Modal Logic

We consider below a probabilistic modal logic (PML), which is a probabilistic version of the Henessy-Milner logic as defined in [8]

$$\phi := \neg\phi \mid \top \mid \perp \mid \phi \wedge \phi \mid \phi \vee \phi \mid \Delta_a \mid \langle a \rangle_\mu \phi$$

where $a \in \mathcal{A}$ and $\mu \in [0,1]$. The semantics of PML is given using a probabilistic labelled transition system, which is an MDP in our setting. The satisfaction relation between states and formulas $s \models \phi$ is defined as usual for $\neg\phi$, $\top$, $\perp$, $\phi \wedge \phi$ and $\phi \vee \phi$. $s \models \Delta_a$ holds whenever $a \notin \mathcal{A}(s)$.

The satisfaction of $s \models \langle a \rangle_\mu \phi$ holds when for some $Q \subset S$ we have $s \xrightarrow{a}_\nu Q$ for a $\nu \geq \mu$ and $q \models \phi$ for all $q \in Q$. Then

$$[a]\phi \equiv \langle a \rangle_1 \phi$$

A concept of probabilistic bisimulation can be defined on the state space S of an MDP which is characterized by the above logic (see [8] for definitions and characterizations).

4 Interfaces and Composition

To start thinking about system interaction, a concept that captures how these interactions happen is required. In this section, we introduce the notion of basic interface, and we equip our basic model with this concept.

4.1 Basic Interface

We define a basic interface for a basic model $\mathcal{M}$ as:

$$I = \langle S_I[\mathbf{R}], \mathcal{A}_I \rangle \tag{7}$$

where $\mathcal{A}_I$ is a set of actions specified by a transition function T_I. The transition function could be deterministic or stochastic. Such an interface will be connected with a basic model, and then we will define a model for a CPES subsystem.

With the above concept of interface, we define the model of a constituent system in the CPES architecture as $M = \langle \mathcal{M}, I \rangle$, where $S_I \subset S$, $\mathcal{A}_I \subset \mathcal{A}$ is a subset of observable actions and T_I coincides with T on S_I for all $a \in \mathcal{A}_I$.

For the soundness of the underlying mathematical model, we enforce the following assumption.

Assumption 1. *The state space S is partitioned into the union of a transient set and an absorbing set:*

- *$S \setminus S_I$ is a transient set for the underlying MC (that means the probability to leave this set is strictly positive);*
- *S_I contains an absorbing set for the underlying MC (it may contain also transient states).*

Moreover, the initial condition s_0 will belong to $S \setminus S_I$, otherwise the model will evolve only in S_I.

4.2   Composition of Models

The composition operation joins two models using a specified basic interface from each one. Let $M_1 = \langle \mathcal{M}_1, I_1 \rangle$ and $M_2 = \langle \mathcal{M}_2, I_2 \rangle$ be two models.

Assumption 2. *Suppose that* $S_{I_1} \cap S_{I_2} \neq \emptyset$, $\mathcal{A}_{I_1} \cap \mathcal{A}_{I_2} \neq \emptyset$ *and* $(S_1 \backslash S_{I_1}) \cap S_2 = \emptyset$, $(S_2 \backslash S_{I_2}) \cap S_1 = \emptyset$; $(\mathcal{A}_1 \backslash \mathcal{A}_{I_1}) \cap \mathcal{A}_2 = \emptyset$, $(\mathcal{A}_2 \backslash \mathcal{A}_{I_2}) \cap \mathcal{A}_1 = \emptyset$.

The two models need to match their transition structure on the intersection of their basic interfaces. So, the following assumption is necessary:

Assumption 3. *Let* $S_{I_{12}} = S_{I_1} \cap S_{I_2}$. *For any* $a \in \mathcal{A}_{I_1} \cap \mathcal{A}_{I_2}$, *we have:*

$$p_1^a(s, s') = p_2^a(s, s'), \ \forall s, s' \in S_{I_{12}}.$$

The composition $M_1 \circ_{I_1, I_2} M_2$ is defined as follows:

$$M = M_1 \circ_{I_1, I_2} M_2 = \langle S[\mathbf{R}], T, \mathcal{A}, s_0, I \rangle$$

where: $S = S_1 \times S_2$; $\mathbf{R} = \mathbf{R}_1 \otimes \mathbf{R}_2$; $T = T_1 \otimes T_2$; $\mathcal{A} = \mathcal{A}_1 \cup \mathcal{A}_2$; $s_0 = (s_{01}, s_{02})$, $I = I_1 \otimes I_2$.

The resource allocation for a state $s = (s_1, s_2)$ in the composed model M is defined as the union of component resources: $s(R) = s_1(R) \cup s_2(R)$.

The transition function T of model M is defined as follows:

- If $a \in \mathcal{A}_1 \backslash \mathcal{A}_2$, and $s = (s_1, s_2) \in S$ then $a \in \mathcal{A}(s)$ if and only if $a \in \mathcal{A}(s_1)$ with

$$p^a(s, s') = p_1^a(s_1, s_1')\delta_{s_2}(s_2'), \ \forall s' = (s_1', s_2') \in S.$$

- If $a \in \mathcal{A}_2 \backslash \mathcal{A}_1$, and $s = (s_1, s_2) \in S$ then $a \in \mathcal{A}(s)$ if and only if $a \in \mathcal{A}(s_2)$ with

$$p^a(s, s') = p_2^a(s_2, s_2')\delta_{s_1}(s_1'), \ \forall s' = (s_1', s_2') \in S.$$

The interface I of the model M has the following items:

- $S_I = S_{I_1} \times S_{I_2}$.
- The transition function T_I is defined similarly as T, the only difference is that we encounter an extra case:
  If $a \in \mathcal{A}_{I_1} \cap \mathcal{A}_{I_2}$, and $s = (s_1, s_2) \in S_{I_{12}} \times S_{I_{12}}$ then $a \in \mathcal{A}_I(s)$ if and only if $a \in \mathcal{A}_{I_1}(s_1) \cap \mathcal{A}_{I_2}(s_2)$ with

$$p^a(s, s') = p_1^a(s_1, s_1')p_2^a(s_2, s_2'), \ \forall s' = (s_1', s_2') \in S_I.$$

The synchronization of the two models is realized only on the overlapping region $S_{I_{12}}$. Outside of this region, the composed model inherits the structure (locations, resources, processes) of its components. The model composition is similar with the MDP composition, taking into account the interface separation. The following result is easy to establish.

Proposition 1 (Composition Soundness). *If* M_1 *and* M_2 *are models as above, then so is* $M_1 \circ_{I_1, I_2} M_2$.

Standard properties of composition as commutativity and associativity are straightforward.

When two models are composed using their basic interfaces it follows, by construction, that their basic structures fit together. But this is not always the case. The main observation is that for model, whenever it is composed with another model, it is necessary to specify which of the properties or functionalities must be preserved.

In this paper, we define a more general concept of interface which is defined as a model itself together with some constraints. These constraints may concern the states, the resources, the rewards or the cost functions associated to MDPs. To be more general, suppose we have given an appropriate logic for MDPs (for example, probabilistic modal logic defined in Subsect. 3.2).

4.3 Interface Model

An interface model is a pair $I = \langle M, \psi \rangle$ where M is a model, and ψ is a set of formulae that describe properties of the model that must be preserved under composition. We refer to these formulae as interface formulae.

The concept of an interface model strictly generalizes that of a model, as we can take the interface model as $\langle M, \{\top\} \rangle$, which has no constraint on M.

Our concept of interface model can be thought of as a connector with a model structure (locations, resources, processes and basic interfaces). The interface requirements are specified as logical formulas.

4.4 Admissibility

For the interface composition, some extra conditions are required to ensure the soundness of this operation.

Let $\langle M_1, \psi_1 \rangle$ and $\langle M_2, \psi_2 \rangle$ be interface models such that M_1 and M_2 are built on MDPs as in the previous section. Let $M_1 \circ M_2$ denote a composition of M_1 and M_2 using some choice of interfaces that satisfy the Assumption 2. Then the composition of $\langle M_1, \psi_1 \rangle$ and $\langle M_2, \psi_2 \rangle$, denoted

$$\langle M_1, \psi_1 \rangle \circ \langle M_2, \psi_2 \rangle := \langle M_1 \circ M_2, \psi_1 \wedge \psi_2 \rangle$$

is admissible if $\psi_1 \wedge \psi_2 \not\supset \bot$.

Proposition 2 (Composition Soundness). *If $\langle M_1, \psi_1 \rangle$ and $\langle M_2, \psi_2 \rangle$ are interface models, then so is their composition $\langle M_1, \psi_1 \rangle \circ \langle M_2, \psi_2 \rangle$.*

Proposition 3 (Commutativity and Associativity). *Commutativity of composition of interface model follows as for models. Associativity of composition of interface models $\langle M_1, \psi_1 \rangle$, $\langle M_2, \psi_2 \rangle$, and $\langle M_3, \psi_3 \rangle$ holds as for models provided also $\psi_1 \wedge \psi_2 \wedge \psi_3 \not\supset \bot$.*

In our setting, an ecosystem is modelled as a composition of interface models.

5   Verification

Verification of cyber-physical systems is a difficult, yet extremely important, problem. In this paper, we formulate the CPES verification as a reachability problem. Reachability analysis is a fundamental problem in verification that checks for a specific model and a set of initial states if the system will reach a specified set of unsafe states. Complementary, reachability analysis can check if the system will achieve its objective, that is if the system will reach a set of target states. For CPS, the reachability problem is challenging when we consider hybrid models that combine discrete transitions alternating with continuous dynamics. In this work, we abstract away the continuous behaviour of CPES, but the main difficulty is arising from the distributed nature of CPES.

In modular verification of distributed systems, the component verification is specified and solved independently (locally) for each module. Then the entire system verification is defined as a global property, whose solution is obtained as the composition of local solutions rather than using the global implementation of the system.

5.1   Reachability Problem for a Basic Model

Suppose that we have given a basic model $\mathcal{M}$ as described by (3).

Here, we define the state-constrained reachability, called sometimes reach avoidance problem. Let $U \subset S$ be an unsafe set, and $E \subset S$ be a target (or objective) set. Then the *reach avoidance problem* aims to compute the probability to reach the unsafe set U, before hitting the target E.

Formally, for the underlying MC, we have to compute the reach probability function, i.e.

$$q_{\mathcal{M}}(s) = q_{\mathcal{M}}(s, U, E) = \mathbf{P}\{\tau_U < \tau_E | X_0 = s\} \tag{8}$$

where we use the notation $\tau_Q = \min\{k > 0 | X_k \in Q\}$ for the first hitting time of a set $Q \subset S$. Then $q_{\mathcal{M}}$ is the solution of the following Dirichlet problem:

$$(\mathcal{L}q)(i) = 0, \forall i \in S \setminus U,$$

$$q(j) = 1, \forall j \in U,$$

$$q(l) = 0 \text{ if } l \in E,$$

which is a system of linear equations.

When the transition probabilities are triggered by the action $a \in \mathcal{A}$, we will use the notation $q_{\mathcal{M}}^a(s)$.

For an MDP, the reach probability can be computed for any policy π. Usually, the stochastic safety aims to compute the optimal policies for which the reach probabilities are bounded by an admissible threshold $p \in [0, 1]$. For the analysis and computational methods that characterize the reach avoidance problem for MDPs, we refer to [5, 13].

5.2   Reachability Problem for a Model

We adapt the reach probability function for a model that is equipped with a basic interface. In this case, we take $U \subset (S \setminus S_I)$ and $E \subset S$. Then we define:

$$q_M(s) = q_M(s, U, E) = q_{\mathcal{M}}(s, U, E \cup S_I) \qquad (9)$$

i.e.

$$q_M(s) = \mathbf{P}\{\tau_{(U)} < \tau_{E \cup S_I} | X_0 = s\}.$$

In this case, our objective is to compute the probability to reach either the unsafe set U before reaching the target E, or the basic interface space S_I. Then q_M is the solution of the following Dirichlet problem:

$$(\mathcal{L}q)(i) = 0, \forall i \in S \setminus (U \cup S_I); q(j) = 1, \forall j \in U; q(l) = 0, \forall l \in E \cup S_I. \qquad (10)$$

We assume that the basic interface is a safe region for the model. The problem of verification concerns only the unsafe states which are transient. As in the case of basic model, when the transition probabilities are controlled by the action $a \in \mathcal{A}$, we will use the notation $q_M^a(s)$.

5.3   Reachability for an Interface Model

Suppose now we have given an interface model $\langle M, \psi \rangle$. In order to verify safety of such a model, we need to check two conditions: (1) the logical constraints ψ are satisfied, and (2) the stochastic safety condition $q_M < p$, where $p \in [0, 1]$ is an admissible probability threshold. If the logical constraints ψ regard only the basic interface space S_I, the two conditions can be checked separately.

5.4   Reachability for Model Composition

Let $M_1 = \langle \mathcal{M}_1, I_1 \rangle$ and $M_2 = \langle \mathcal{M}_2, I_2 \rangle$ be two models that satisfy the Assumptions 2, 3 for composition. Let $M = \langle \mathcal{M}, I \rangle$ be their composition.
  Let

$$E = E_1 \times E_2 \subset S_1 \times S_2$$

be a target set, and

$$U = U_1 \times U_2 \subset (S_1 \setminus S_{I_1}) \times (S_2 \setminus S_{I_2})$$

be an unsafe set for M.

It is important to remark that the model composition does not change the behaviour on $S_1 \setminus S_{I_1}$ or $S_2 \setminus S_{I_2}$ of its constituents. Then the next result can be easily checked.

Proposition 4. *The reach probability function of M w.r.t. U and E is equal to the component reach functions as follows:*

– If $a \in \mathcal{A}_1 \setminus \mathcal{A}_2$ then

$$q_M^a(s, U, E) = q_{M_1}^a(s_1, U_1, E_1),$$

for all $s = (s_1, s_2) \in (S_1 \setminus S_{I_1}) \times (S_2 \setminus S_{I_2})$.
– If $a \in \mathcal{A}_2 \setminus \mathcal{A}_1$ then

$$q_M^a(s, U, E) = q_{M_2}^a(s_2, U_2, E_2),$$

for all $s = (s_1, s_2) \in (S_1 \setminus S_{I_1}) \times (S_2 \setminus S_{I_2})$.

The above proposition states that the computation of the reach probability for the composed model is done in a modular way, for each component. The reason is that outside of the interfaces, a control action a modifies only one component when it is enforced.

6   Abstractions

For MDPs, according to [9], there exist five types of abstraction functions. Here, we use the state abstraction function.

6.1   Abstraction of a Basic Model

Let $\mathcal{M}$ be a basic model defined by (3).

Formally, an *abstraction function* is defined as a surjective map $\varphi : S \to \overline{S}$, which maps the underlying MC into another MC. Then we define a matrix Φ of dimension $|S| \times |\overline{S}|$ by:

$$\Phi(s, \overline{s}') = \delta_{\overline{s}'}(\varphi(s)) = \mathbf{1}_{\varphi^{-1}(\overline{s}')}(s).$$

A sufficient condition for φ to be a Markovian abstraction function is the existence of a stochastic kernel $\Lambda : \overline{S} \to \Delta(S)$ such that $\mathrm{supp}\Lambda(\overline{s}, \cdot) = \varphi^{-1}(\overline{s})$ for all $\overline{s}$ in $\overline{S}$, i.e.,

$$\Lambda(\overline{s}, \varphi^{-1}(\overline{s})) = \sum_{y \in \varphi^{-1}(\overline{s})} \Lambda(\overline{s}, s) = 1, \forall \overline{s} \in \overline{S}.$$

This assumption implies that:

$$\Lambda\Phi = \mathbf{I}_{|\overline{S}|} \tag{11}$$

where $\mathbf{I}_{|\overline{S}|}$ is the identity matrix of order $|\overline{S}|$. Note this condition is more general than the one given in [9]. The condition is inspired by the seminal paper on Markov functions of Rogers and Pitman [10].

The kernel Λ will be called *concretization kernel*. The reason is that it maps the abstract model into the concrete one. The following relationship holds:

$$\mathbf{P}\{X_n = s | \varphi(X_m), 0 \leq m \leq n\} = \Lambda(\varphi(X_n), s), \forall s \in S. \tag{12}$$

This states a very prominent thing that the estimator of the state X_n that predicts the process from the abstractions is the same as the abstracted state. We denote by $\overline{X}_n = \varphi(X_n)$ the abstraction process, which is still Markov. The relationship between the infinitesimal generator of the abstraction process and the concrete one is as follows:

$$\overline{\mathcal{L}} = \Lambda \mathcal{L} \Phi.$$

We define an equivalence relation on S by:

$$s \sim s' \iff \varphi(s) = \varphi(s').$$

Let $[s]$ be the equivalence relation of s w.r.t. $\sim$, and $S/_\sim$ be the quotient space. A subset F of S is closed w.r.t. $\sim$ if whenever $s \in F$ then $s' \in F$ for all $s' \in [s]$.

In fact the abstract basic model is thought of as:

$$\overline{\mathcal{M}} = (\overline{S}[\mathbf{R}], \mathcal{A}, (\overline{T}^a)_{a \in \mathcal{A}}, \overline{s}_0), \tag{13}$$

where the underlying Markov chain is the quotient process. In fact, the equivalence relation $\sim$ is thought on the hybrid space $(S, \mathbf{R})$. Due to the limited room of this paper, we keep the implicit notation.

Let $U \subset S$ and $E \subset S$ be two closed subsets (w.r.t. $\sim$) of S. Denote $\overline{U} = \varphi(U)$ and $\overline{E} = \varphi(E)$. Then $\varphi^{-1}(\overline{U}) = U$ and $\varphi^{-1}(\overline{E}) = E$. The reach probability function $\overline{q_{\mathcal{M}}}$ for the abstraction process $\overline{X}_n$ the unsafe set $\overline{U}$ and target set $\overline{E}$ will be the solution of the Dirichlet problem associated to the generator $\overline{\mathcal{L}}$. The following result is straightforward:

Proposition 5. *The reach probability function $q_{\mathcal{M}}$ of the concrete basic model $\mathcal{M}$ w.r.t. the target set E and the unsafe set U is related with the reach probability function $\overline{q_{\mathcal{M}}}$ of the abstraction of the basic model $\overline{\mathcal{M}}$ w.r.t. the target set $\overline{E}$ and the unsafe set $\overline{U}$ by the following relation:*

$$q_{\mathcal{M}} = \overline{q_{\mathcal{M}}} \Lambda.$$

6.2 Abstraction of a Model

Let $M = \langle \mathcal{M}, I \rangle$ be a model defined as before. An abstraction function for M is defined as an abstraction function for the underlying basic model $\mathcal{M}$, which satisfies the following condition:

$$\varphi^{-1}(\overline{S}_I) = S_I, \tag{14}$$

where $\overline{S}_I = \varphi(S_I)$. Then, the interface space 'invariance' will lead to the following relations that connect the abstraction function and the concretization kernel:

$$\Lambda|_{\overline{S} \backslash \overline{S}_I} \Phi|_{S \backslash S_I} = \mathbf{I}_{|\overline{S} \backslash \overline{S}_I|}, \ \Lambda|_{\overline{S}_I} \Phi|_{S_I} = \mathbf{I}_{|\overline{S}_I|}.$$

For a model M, the reach probability function q_M w.r.t. U and E is a specialization of the reach probability function $q_{\mathcal{M}}$ of basic model $\mathcal{M}$ w.r.t. U and $E \cup S_I$. Then:

$$q_M = \overline{q_M} \Lambda. \tag{15}$$

6.3   Abstraction of an Interface Model

Let $I = \langle M, \psi \rangle$ be an interface model. An abstraction function $\varphi : S \to \overline{S}$ of the model M is an abstraction function for the interface model I if it is compatible with the constraints ψ. This will be explained below.

We impose the following compatibility assumption between $\sim$ and the constraints ψ:

Assumption 4. *If there exists $s' \in [s]$ such that $s' \models \psi$ then $s'' \models \psi$ for all $s'' \in [s]$.*

Therefore, the equivalence relation $\sim$ is consistent with the interface constraints. The computation of the reach probability function remains the same, the main difficulty in this case is to find an abstraction map that preserves the interface requirements.

6.4   Abstraction Composition

Suppose that we have given two interface models $\langle M_i, \psi_i \rangle$ with $i = 1, 2$ such that the Assumptions 2, 3 hold and the admissibility condition is satisfied.

Let φ_i, $i = 1, 2$ be associated abstractions functions, with their corresponding concretization kernels Λ_i, $i = 1, 2$ such that the Assumption 4 holds for both of them.

We have the underlying models defined as $M_i = \langle \mathcal{M}_i, I_i \rangle$, $i = 1, 2$. To make the composition of their abstractions we need a further assumption as follows.

Assumption 5. *The abstraction functions coincide on the basic interface overlapping $S_{I_{12}} = S_{I_1} \cap S_{I_2}$, i.e.*

$$\varphi_1(s) = \varphi_2(s), \; \forall s \in S_{I_{12}}$$

and $S_{I_{12}}$ is 'invariant' w.r.t. both abstraction maps:

$$\varphi_1^{-1}(\varphi_1(S_{I_{12}})) = \varphi_2^{-1}(\varphi_2(S_{I_{12}})) = S_{I_{12}}$$

Then $\varphi = (\varphi_1, \varphi_2)$ will play the role of an abstraction map for the composed model M.

We denote by $\overline{M}$ the composition of the abstract interface models $\overline{M}_1$ and $\overline{M}_2$.

The reach probability function q_M corresponding to the unsafe set $U = U_1 \times U_2$ and the target set $E = E_1 \times E_2$ will be the superposition of the component reach probabilities:

$$q_M = (q_{M_1}, q_{M_2}).$$

The reach probability function $\overline{q_M}$ corresponding to the unsafe set $\overline{U} = \overline{U}_1 \times \overline{U}_2$ and the target set $\overline{E} = \overline{E}_1 \times \overline{E}_2$ will be the superposition of the component reach probabilities:

$$\overline{q}_M = (\overline{q}_{\overline{M}_1}, \overline{q}_{\overline{M}_2}).$$

We introduce the notation:

$$\Lambda = (\Lambda_1, \Lambda_2)$$

where Λ_1 and Λ_2 are the concretization kernels associated to the component models M_1 and M_2. The following result holds:

Proposition 6. *The reach probability function q_M of the concrete model M and the reach probability $\overline{q}_{\overline{M}}$ of the abstraction model $\overline{M}$ are related as follows:*

$$q_M = \overline{q}_{\overline{M}} \circ \Lambda$$

where $\overline{q}_{\overline{M}} \circ \Lambda$ is the Hadamard product of matrices, i.e.

$$\overline{q}_{\overline{M}} \circ \Lambda = (\overline{q}_{\overline{M}_1} \Lambda_1, \overline{q}_{\overline{M}_2} \Lambda_2).$$

The main remark here is that the verification process is carried out in a modular way.

7 Conclusions

In this paper, we have presented an approach to modelling and verification of cyber-physical ecosystems based on concepts from distributed systems and Markov decision processes. We have developed the notion of a basic model based on the MDP skeleton, expanded it with basic interfaces to define a model. Then we have characterised an interface model as a model which has associated a set of formulae that characterize the composition requirements. We have defined the verification of CPES as a stochastic reach avoidance problem for all constituent models. Then, we have explored how to use modular abstractions to find simple computational solutions for the stochastic safety of CPES.

This paper provides the theoretical setting for CPES verification, when the system constituents are modelled as MDPs and they interact through some general interfaces. A case study of a cyber-physical ecosystem as a system of supply chains is under development. New results will be reported in a follow-up paper.

References

1. Bäuerle, N., Rieder, U.: Piecewise deterministic Markov decision processes. In: Bäuerle, N., Rieder, U. (eds.) Markov Decision Processes with Applications to Finance. Universitext, pp. 243–265. Springer, Heidelberg (2011). https://doi.org/10.1007/978-3-642-18324-9_8

2. Bujorianu, M.L., Caulfield, T., Ilau, M.C., Pym, D.S.: Interfaces in Ecosystems: Concepts, Form, and Implementation. Submitted to TARK

3. Bujorianu, M.L.: Stochastic reachability analysis of hybrid systems. In: Bujorianu, M.L. (ed.) Stochastic Reachability Analysis of Hybrid Systems. Communications and Control Engineering, pp. E1–E3. Springer, London (2012). https://doi.org/10.1007/978-1-4471-2795-6_12

4. Bujorianu, M.L., Caulfield, T., Pym, D.: Modelling and control of complex cyber-physical ecosystems. IFAC-PapersOnLine **55**(40), 253–258 (2022)

5. Bujorianu, M.L., Wisniewski, R., Boulougouris, E.: Stochastic safety for Markov chains. IEEE Control Syst. Lett. **5**(2), 427–432 (2021)
6. Caulfield, T., Ilau, M.-C., Pym, D.: Engineering ecosystem models: semantics and pragmatics. In: Jiang, D., Song, H. (eds.) SIMUtools 2021. LNICST, vol. 424, pp. 236–258. Springer, Cham (2022). https://doi.org/10.1007/978-3-030-97124-3_21
7. Kupferman, O., Vardi, M.Y.: Modular model checking. In: de Roever, W.-P., Langmaack, H., Pnueli, A. (eds.) COMPOS 1997. LNCS, vol. 1536, pp. 381–401. Springer, Heidelberg (1998). https://doi.org/10.1007/3-540-49213-5_14
8. Larsen, K.G., Skou, A.: Bisimulation through probabilistic testing. Inf. Comput. **94**(1), 1–28 (1991)
9. Li, L., Walsh, T.J., Littman, M.L.: Towards a unified theory of state abstraction for MDPs. In: Proceedings of the Ninth International Symposium on Artificial Intelligence and Mathematics (2006)
10. Rogers, L.C.G., Pitman, J.W.: Markov functions. Ann. Probab. **9**(4), 573–582 (1981)
11. Stoelinga, M.: An introduction to probabilistic automata. Bull. EATCS **78** (2004)
12. Misra, R., Wisniewski, R., Kallesøe, C.S.: Approximating the model of a water distribution network as a Markov decision process. IFAC-PapersOnLine **55**(20), 271–276 (2022)
13. Wisniewski, R., Bujorianu, M.L.: Probabilistic safety guarantees for Markov decision processes. IEEE Trans. Autom. Control (2023). https://doi.org/10.1109/TAC.2023.3291952

Integrating IoT Infrastructures in Industrie 4.0 Scenarios with the Asset Administration Shell

Sven Erik Jeroschewski, Johannes Kristan[✉], Milena Jäntgen, and Max Grzanna

Bosch.IO GmbH, Ullsteinstr. 128, 12109 Berlin, Germany
{sven.jeroschewski,johannes.kristan,milena.jantgen,max.grzanna}@bosch.io

Abstract. The Asset Administration Shell (AAS) specifies digital twins to enable unified access to all data and services available for a physical asset to cope with heterogeneous and fragmented data sources. The setup of an AAS infrastructure requires the integration of all relevant devices and their data. As the devices often already communicate with an IoT backend, we present three approaches to integrate an IoT backend with an AAS infrastructure, share insights into an implementation project, and briefly discuss them.

Keywords: IoT · Asset Administration Shell · I40 · digital twin

1 Introduction

The rising heterogeneity and complexity of their environments make it hard for manufacturers to adapt to changes, integrate new components, and prevent fast and sound decision-making, as relevant data may be theoretically available but practically not accessible where it is needed [8].

The Asset Administration Shell (AAS) [5,6] is a building block in achieving interoperability in Industrie 4.0 scenarios by specifying interaction models, formats, and abstractions for the handling and access of information as digital twins. Various domains already adopt the AAS for scenarios like Digital Calibration Certificates (DCC) [4], or accessing semantically and syntactically aligned data sets for training, and re-using higher quality AI models [8].

To benefit from the AAS, manufacturers link existing systems, services, and devices with an AAS infrastructure, which may result in high configuration efforts for each device and possibly long down times. Many connected devices already communicate with an Internet of Things (IoT) backend [1,7], which manages the device state, collects data, and routes messages. Often, it is thus easier to connect the AAS to an IoT backend and leave each device unchanged.

2 Integration Approaches

The AAS defines flows for data retrieval (Fig. 1) [6], which the presented integration approaches need to fit to. The flow starts by requesting an AAS ID from the

J. Kofroň et al. (Eds.): ECBS 2023, LNCS 14390, pp. 231–234, 2024.
https://doi.org/10.1007/978-3-031-49252-5_18

AAS discovery interface based on a (local) specific asset ID or a global asset ID. With the AAS ID, the application retrieves an endpoint for the AAS through the AAS Registry interface. The application then requests the Submodel (SM) ID from that AAS endpoint and uses this SM ID to get the SM endpoint from the SM Registry. From that SM endpoint, the user can request the SM Element (SME), which contains the required value.

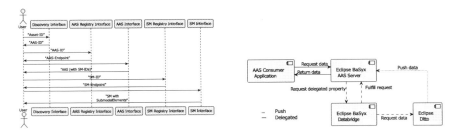

Fig. 1. Sequence of data flow through AAS infrastructure   **Fig. 2.** Implemented integration approaches

This generic flow shows that an IoT backend integration essentially boils down to making device data available via SMs and their SMEs as an SM Interface Endpoint. We identify three approaches for this: The IoT backend may *push* latest updates to an AAS SM server or the AAS SM server *pulls* the current state from the IoT backend either via a *wrapper* or via a *bridge*.

Push: Whenever the IoT backend receives an update from a device, a backend component transforms and pushes the data in the AAS format [5] to an SM server. This approach allows for re-using a generic implementation of the SM Server with the drawback of duplicate data storage in the IoT backend and the SM server, leading to potential synchronization and data consistency issues.

Pull via Bridge: Some AAS SM servers support delegating requests for specific SME values to other endpoints like a data bridge, which then retrieves the actual data from the IoT backend and applies transformation logic. With this approach, one can use a generic AAS server implementation and enable mixed scenarios where only a few requests get delegated to one or multiple IoT backends while the SM server stores all other SMEs. However, it requires the AAS server component to provide such functionality.

Pull via Wrapper: It is also possible to add a custom wrapper that implements the SM interface for the client and fetches the required data from the IoT backend. This approach does not require data duplication but may impose implementation efforts concerning identifier mapping and coupling between the wrapper and the IoT backend.

As part of the project GEMIMEG-II [4], which works on DCCs and better data orchestration, we implemented the approaches *push* (dotted) and *pull* via a bridge (dashed) as depicted in Fig. 2. We used Eclipse Ditto [3] as an IoT backend and Eclipse BaSyx as AAS infrastructure [2].

Eclipse Ditto is an IoT backend built of micro-services, which evolves around the concept of Things representing the state of a device. Each Thing has Properties grouped as Features, which may change over time (e.g. sensor values). One can express constant values, such as identifiers, as Attributes. Grouping of Things is possible by assigning them to a Namespace. Ditto comprises a Connectivity API for the integration with other systems, which allows to provide JavaScript code, which gets executed on events (e.g. changing a Thing).

Eclipse BaSyx is an open-source framework to realize an Industrie 4.0 middleware [2] based on the AAS Spec. [5,6].

For *push*, we configured a Ditto instance through the connectivity API to forward changes of a device and its corresponding Thing to a BaSyx SM Server. This results in duplicated data storage in Ditto and the BaSyx SM Server.

For *pull*, the BaSyx SM server supports delegation and calls the endpoint of a bridge component for each request for a corresponding SME. Since Ditto has the option to return the value without additional payload, the main task of the bridge is to perform the authorization flow of Ditto.

The *pull* via wrapper was not realized for AAS as it would require high implementation efforts, as demonstrated by the integration of the Web of Things (WoT) by the Eclipse Ditto Project [3].

The mapping between concepts of Ditto and AAS is depicted in Table 1.

Table 1. Concept mapping from Eclipse Ditto to the AAS

Eclipse Ditto	Asset Administration Shell
Namespace	Asset Administration Shell
Thing	-
Features	Submodel
Property	Submodel Element
Attribute	Submodel Element

3   Discussion

Based on our observations, the pull approach with a wrapper is a good trade-off for scenarios with a high and medium frequency of sensing and actuation updates. But the development and operation of new software artifacts lead to higher engineering costs and operation efforts in comparison to the other approaches. The push approach is a good solution for scenarios with many data reads and few data updates but it lacks a good way of pushing actuation information to the IoT backend and introduces risks regarding data inconsistency. Compared to the other presented approaches, the pull approach with data bridge seems to have lower engineering cost and is easier to operate allowing to get started a bit faster, but it is not so well-suited when the frequency of data access rises.

As we draw our conclusions about the three approaches solely from our observations in one project, it is worthwhile to extend the analysis and run some even quantifiable evaluations based on further projects or in controlled environments. We also have not yet looked further into executing AAS operations. Once BaSyx supports authenticating during requests for delegated data, we may also try to retrieve the raw data from Eclipse Ditto without using a data bridge.

4 Summary

We presented the architectural approaches, push, pull with wrapper, and pull with data bridge, to integrate existing IoT backends with the AAS. Based on the experiences gained in the GEMIMEG-II project, we discussed the approaches without identifying a preferred option since each alternative has different advantages and drawbacks for the sensing and actuating frequency or the engineering and operation cost.

Acknowledgements. The research has received funding from the Federal Ministry for Economic Affairs and Climate Action of Germany under the funding code 01MT20001J. The responsibility for the content of this publication lies with the author(s).

References

1. Banijamali, A., Heisig, P., Kristan, J., Kuvaja, P., Oivo, M.: Software architecture design of cloud platforms in automotive domain: an online survey. In: 2019 IEEE 12th Conference on Service-Oriented Computing and Applications (SOCA), pp. 168–175 (2019)
2. Eclipse BaSyx: Eclipse BaSyx - Industry 4.0 operating system (2023). https://www.eclipse.org/basyx/
3. Eclipse Ditto: Eclipse ditto (2023). https://www.eclipse.org/ditto
4. Hackel, S., Schönhals, S., Doering, L., Engel, T., Baumfalk, R.: The digital calibration certificate (DCC) for an end-to-end digital quality infrastructure for Industry 4.0. Sci **5**(1) (2023). https://doi.org/10.3390/sci5010011. https://www.mdpi.com/2413-4155/5/1/11
5. IDTA: Spec. of the Asset Administration Shell - Part 1: Metamodel, April 2023. https://industrialdigitaltwin.org/en/wp-content/uploads/sites/2/2023/04/IDTA-01001-3-0_SpecificationAssetAdministrationShell_Part1_Metamodel.pdf
6. IDTA: Spec. of the Asset Administration Shell - Part 2: Application Programming Interface, April 2023. https://industrialdigitaltwin.org/en/wp-content/uploads/sites/2/2023/04/IDTA-01002-3-0_SpecificationAssetAdministrationShell_Part2_API.pdf
7. Kristan, J., Azzoni, P., Römer, L., Jeroschewski, S.E., Londero, E.: Evolving the ecosystem: eclipse arrowhead integrates eclipse IoT. In: 2022 IEEE/IFIP Network Operations and Management Symposium, NOMS 2022, pp. 1–6 (2022)
8. Rauh, L., Reichardt, M., Schotten, H.D.: AI asset management: a case study with the asset administration shell (AAS). In: 2022 IEEE 27th International Conference on Emerging Technologies and Factory Automation (ETFA), pp. 1–8 (2022)

A Software Package (*in progress*) that Implements the Hammock-EFL Methodology

Moshe Goldstein[✉] ⓘ and Oren Eliezer ⓘ

Jerusalem College of Technology - Lev Academic Center, 9372115 Jerusalem, Israel
goldmosh@g.jct.ac.il

Abstract. This poster paper presents a software package (*in progress*) that implements the Hammock-EFL approach for Project Management and Parallel Programming, written in Python.

Keywords: Hammock-EFL · Project Management · Parallel Programming · Python Programming

1 Motivation

In sequential programming a problem is solved by decomposing it into sub-problems and by identifying the structural dependencies among them. In project design and management, the designer needs to identify not only all the activities (or sub-problems) that compose the whole project and their structural dependencies, but also their *temporal* dependencies. The identification of those temporal dependencies implicitly requires the application of parallel thinking. The same is required from a programmer when he tries to solve a problem by Parallel Programming. All those problem-solving-related observations induced us to realize that a project management methodology, like the Hammock Cost Techniques for Project Management [1], will contribute to better problem solving thinking in Parallel Programming.

EFL (Embedded Flexible Language) [2, 3] is a mini embedded language whose semantics are those of the Flexible Algorithms (FA) [4] approach to computation, which is applicable for parallel programming (as well as sequential programming) and ensures deterministic results without the need of locking. EFL was designed to make parallel programming independent of any specific parallel programming platform, making the programmer's task easier. To allow that independence, two EFL pre-compilers were implemented for the Python programming language as the host language.

Based on all the above, the Hammock-EFL methodology [5–7] was proposed. It combines the Hammock methodology and the FA approach to Computation. This combination allows developers to treat programs and project schedules as conceptually the same, at a higher level of abstraction, enabling them to deal with the complexity of computing systems engineering in a more reliable and easier way. This is *the* novelty of the Hammock-EFL methodology. We argue that this is the first research which makes a

J. Kofroň et al. (Eds.): ECBS 2023, LNCS 14390, pp. 235–238, 2024.
https://doi.org/10.1007/978-3-031-49252-5_19

symbiotic combination of methodologies taken from two different disciplines - (Parallel) Computing and Programming, and Project Management.

2   Proof of Concept

The Project Schedule diagram depicted in Fig. 1 was used as the Proof of Concept of the combined methodology.

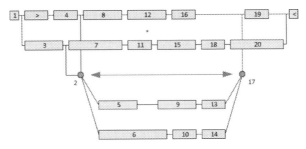

Fig. 1. The Project Schedule diagram (taken from [1]) used to try the software.

That schedule is composed by an appropriate combination of Regular, Compound and Hammock activities: two Compound activities are activated in parallel, the Regular activities that compose each of them, the activities no. 4, 8, 12, 16, and 19, and no. 3, 7, 11, 15, 18, and 20, are activated serially, and a Hammock activity H_1 whose Hammock members are organized in two groups, Regular activities no. 5, 9, and 13, and no. 6, 10, and 14. Each activity may include properties such as duration (D_i), earliest beginning (ES_i), latest beginning (LS_i), amount of resources (R_i), etc.

If the same diagram is intended to describe a program, a Regular activity represents a function with a relatively simple behavior, a Compound activity represents a function whose behavior is expressed by an appropriate combination of the behaviors of its sub-activities, a Hammock activity represents a function whose behavior is expressed by a randomly scheduled ensemble of sub-activities, executed in sequence. Based on the

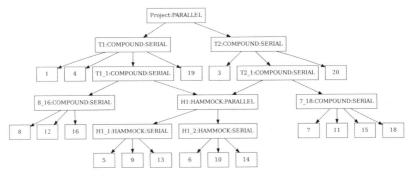

Fig. 2. The tree representation of the above project schedule

structural and temporal dependencies of the sub-activities of a Compound activity, the functions represented by them may be executed in parallel or in sequence.

The software presented here uses a tree data structure to represent project schedules like that in Fig. 1. Figure 2 shows the rendering of the tree representation of that schedule.

3 The Software

Figure 3 shows a graph of the modules that compose the software presented here, and their dependencies. Table 1 gives a brief description of each one of those modules.

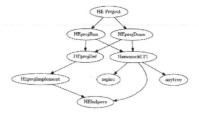

Fig. 3. The Dependency Graph of the Software.

Table 1. Description of modules that compose the software.

Program/Module	Description
anytree	A Python module implementing tree data structures
HammockEFL.py	*Schedule* and *Activity* are classes defined in this module. See [7]
HEhelpers.py	Helper functions are defined for general use, as needed
HEprojRun.py	Module used to actually run or simulate the schedule
HEprojDef.py	A tree data structure, representing a schedule (or program), will be defined by the designer (or programmer), using methods from the *Schedule* and *Activity* classes
HEprojDraw.py	A schedule's diagram is rendered using this module (see Fig. 2)
HEprojImplement.py	The behavior of each activity is expressed by a three-step (pre-processing → processing → post-processing) pipeline-like procedure. This module is intended to include their implementations
mpire	A module that substitutes Python's Multiprocessing module

4 Experiment

The software was successfully tried to run and simulate the above Proof of Concept schedule, restricted to the case that all the activities are defined to be executed in sequence. At the current moment, we are debugging the capability of running and simulating schedules that combine activities defined to be executed in sequence, with activities defined to be executed in parallel.

5   Conclusion and Further Work

The current state of a software package has been presented, which intends to be both, a framework for project management based on the Hammock Cost Techniques, and for developing parallel software based on the FA approach to Computation. Following [1], the impact of the presented tool should be expressed as a trade-off between project's makespan and total revenue. To check this, a comparative and experimental research must be done when D_i, ES_i, LS_i, R_i and cost, for each activity i, will be taken into account in the case of a planned project relative to an already executed project. A new version of the software should include (a) a shared-memory mechanism like PSTM [8] which will allow the implementation of shared-memory-based parallel programs, and (b) support of JSON files (or YAML files) which will allow a more readable and writable definition of a schedule (or program). Additionally, experimental analysis of Time and Space Complexity of a designed computing system will be possible by calculating actual run time and storage of programs described by graphs of the kind discussed above.

References

1. Csébfalvi, G., Csébfalvi, A.: Hammock activities in Project scheduling. In: Proceedings of the Sixteenth Annual Conference of POMS, POMS, Chicago, IL, USA (2005)
2. Dayan, D., et al.: EFL: implementing and testing an embedded language which provides safe and efficient parallel execution. In: Proceedings of ECBS-EERC 2015, Brno, Czech Republic, pp. 83–90. IEEE Press (2015). https://doi.org/10.1109/ECBS-EERC.2015.21
3. Goldstein, M., Dayan, D., Rabin, M., Berlovitz, D., Berlovitz, O., Yehezkael, R.B.: Design principles of an embedded language (EFL) enabling well defined order-independent execution. In: Proceedings of ECBS 2017, Larnaca, Cyprus, pp. 1–8. ACM (2017). https://doi.org/10.1145/3123779.3123789
4. Yehezkael, R.B., Goldstein, M., Dayan, D., Mizrahi, Sh.: Flexible algorithms: enabling well-defined order-independent execution with an imperative programming style. In: Proceedings of ECBS-EERC 2015, Brno, Czech Republic, pp. 75–82. IEEE Press (2015). https://doi.org/10.1109/ECBS-EERC.2015.20
5. Eliezer, O., Goldstein, M.: Implementing Hammock cost techniques using the parallel programming paradigm of EFL (embedded flexible language). In: Proceedings of ZINC 2018, Novi-Sad, Serbia, pp. 132–134. IEEE Press (2018). https://doi.org/10.1109/ZINC.2018.8448763
6. Eliezer, O., Goldstein, M., Dayan, D.: About the trade-off between time and space consumption when combining the Hammock-Cost model with the EFL (Embedded Flexible Language) parallel programming paradigm. In: Proceedings of the 16th International Conference on Civil, Structural and Environmental Engineering Computing, Riva del Garda, Italy (2019)
7. Goldstein, M., Eliezer, O., Dayan, D.: Implementing the Hammock-EFL methodology for project management and parallel programming. In: Proceedings of ECBS 2021, Novi-Sad, Serbia, pp. 1–5. ACM (2021). https://doi.org/10.1145/3459960.3459967
8. Popovic, M., Kordic, B.: PSTM: Python software transactional memory. In: 2014 2nd Telecommunications Forum Telfor, Belgrade, Serbia, pp 1106–1109. TELFOR (2014). https://doi.org/10.1109/TELFOR.2014.7034600

Dynamic Priority Scheduling for Periodic Systems Using ROS 2

Lukas Dust[✉] and Saad Mubeen

Mälardalen University, Västerås, Sweden
{lukas.dust,saad.mubeen}@mdu.se

Abstract. In this paper, a novel dynamic priority scheduling algorithm for ROS 2 systems is proposed. The algorithm is based on determining deadlines of callbacks by taking the buffer size and update rates of channels into account. The efficacy of the scheduling algorithm is demonstrated on an illustrative example, where the needed buffer size is reduced in comparison to the conventional single-threaded executor in ROS 2.

Keywords: Robot Operating System 2 · Scheduling · Executor

1 Introduction and Background

Robot Operating System (ROS) 2 is a middleware introducing real-time capabilities to its predecessor ROS [1]. With the end of support for ROS in 2025, researchers and practitioners are forced to transition their systems to ROS 2. Hence, increased research activities have been seen in the past few years. ROS 2 systems consist of so-called Nodes as main components distributed in a network, communicating via designated channels in the Data Distribution Service (DDS). As depicted in Fig. 1, each node consists of a scheduler, called an executor, that schedules the schedulable entities, called callbacks. Two types of trigger events release callbacks. Data-triggered callbacks are connected to a specified channel in the DDS. Time-triggered callbacks are connected to a system timer. Generally, there are four types of callbacks, namely, Timer, Subscription, Service, and Client callbacks. An input buffer with a configurable size for each callback collects the trigger instances, such as messages and timestamps. In order to explore the real-time capabilities of ROS 2, the inbuilt scheduling algorithm has been analyzed [2]. Alternative priority-based scheduling algorithm has been

Fig. 1. Schematic example of a ROS 2 Node and its essential components for scheduling.

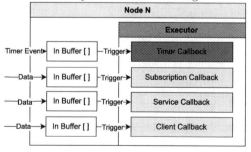

J. Kofroň et al. (Eds.): ECBS 2023, LNCS 14390, pp. 239–243, 2024.
https://doi.org/10.1007/978-3-031-49252-5_20

proposed [4], assigning static priorities to callbacks. In the default executor, only one instance of each callback, released before the scheduler interaction with the middleware (polling-point), is considered for scheduling. Polling is performed when the set containing one instance of every released callback has been emptied. Blocking of callbacks [3,6], and missing configuration options have been exposed as a weakness by [2,5]. In this paper, supported by the increased demand for enhanced scheduling options, we propose a new dynamic priority scheduling algorithm developed for periodic nodes. For the sake of simplicity, a periodic node is defined, where all n callbacks contained in a node execute periodically where the period P of each callback $P_{cb} > 0$. Each callback is released by the trigger events contained in the Buffer B_{cb}, where r^k is the kth trigger instance in the buffer and $t(r_{cb}^k)$ is the stored arrival time of the kth trigger instance of callback cb. This paper shows that the algorithm can reduce the needed buffer size compared to the native ROS 2 scheduling algorithm, while potentially reducing the number of resource-demanding interactions with the ROS Middle Ware (RMW) compared to the fixed-priority scheduling.

2   Algorithm

Algorithm 1:. Proposed Scheduling Algorithm

---

1 **foreach** *callback cb where nextrelease(cb) ≤ systime* **do**
2   collect entity(cb) from RMW
3   **if** *New Data available* **then**
4   add *cb* to *readyset*;
5   calculate T_{cb}^{min} and D_{cb};
6   **end**
7 **end**
8 **if** *readyset ≠ Null* **then**
9   cb = callback with shortest deadline
10   pop data from input buffer
11   **if** *buffer(cb) empty* **then**
12   remove cb from readyset
13   **end**
14   **else**
15   calculate new deadline
16   **end**
17   execute cb
18 **end**

The proposed algorithm, shown in Algorithm 1, assigns a deadline to every released callback collected in the so-called `readyset`. A scheduling decision is performed following the earliest-deadline-first metric. The deadline for a callback is determined by the predicted time the input buffer to overflow, following (2). Initially, the deadline is set to infinite. When new data arrives, the minimum time difference T_{cb}^{min} between two consecutive arrivals is determined using (1). Now, the deadline as the predicted time of a buffer overflow can be calculated by knowing T_{cb}^{min} and the buffer utilization $U(B_{cb})$. When running the algorithm, the scheduler updates the `readyset` by scanning the input buffers in the RMW. When newly arrived data is detected, the callback is added to the `readyset`. In order to reduce the needed interactions with the middleware, based on T_{cb}^{min}, the time for the next trigger instance arrival is predicted and stored as the `nextrelease` for every callback. An interaction with the middleware is performed only when the system time exceeds or equals the `nextrelease`. Initially, the `nextrelease` is set to zero, forcing a scan in the middleware until the first trigger instance has arrived. In the second step, the callback with the earliest deadline is selected for execution. In case of shared deadlines, the callback with the highest buffer utilization is given the highest priority, followed by the registration order in case of further shared priority. The data for the selected callback is removed from the buffer. A new deadline is calculated, or the callback is removed from the `readyset` when no trigger instance is left in the buffer.

$$T_{cb}^{min} = \begin{cases} t(r_{cb}^k), & if\ T_{cb}^{min} = 0 \\ min(T_{cb}^{min}, t(r_{cb}^k) - t(r_{cb}^{k-1})), & if\ T_{cb}^{min} > 0 \end{cases} \quad (1)$$

T_{cb}^{min} is the minimum time difference between two consecutive trigger events, and $t(r_{cb}^k)$ is the arrival time of the last trigger instance k.

$$D_{cb} = \begin{cases} inf, & if\ T_{cb}^{min} = 0 \\ T_{cb}^{min} * (S(B_{cb}) * (1 - U(B_{cb})) + t(r_{cb}^k), & if\ T_{cb}^{min} > 0 \end{cases} \quad (2)$$

D_{cb} is the deadline of callback cb, T_{cb}^B is the minimum time difference between two consecutive trigger instances, $S(B_{cb}$ is the input buffer size, $U(B_{cb})$ is the utilization of the buffer and $t(r_{cb}^k)$ is the arrival time of the latest (kth) message.

3   Illustrative Example and Comparison to ROS 2

In this section, the scheduling of the proposed algorithm is shown in an example and compared to the executor of ROS 2. Execution traces are carefully created by hand based on the algorithms. The following scenario is taken: A ROS 2 node consists of five callbacks that are triggered periodically. The callbacks are one timer callback `TI`, two subscriber callback `S1`, `S2`, and one service callback `SR`, all triggered every 400 ms and one client callback `CL` triggered every 100 ms. For the sake of simplicity, the input buffers have a size of five, and the execution time for each callback is 50 ms. Figure 2 shows the execution of the scenario by the proposed algorithm on the left and ROS 2 on the right plot. At the start, all callbacks have been triggered once at 0 ms. Therefore, each task's deadline is set to infinite. As all tasks have the same deadline and buffer utilization, execution is conducted after the registration order, leading to the execution of `TI` and `S1`. At *SI2*, `CL` is triggered a second time. The scheduler now determines T_{CL}^{min} as 100 ms and a Deadline of $D_{CL} = 400$ ms. Furthermore, the predicted next release time is 200 ms. As all other callbacks still do not have two consecutive releases, their deadline is still infinite. Therefore, the client callback is executed, and the deadline is calculated until the buffer is empty, as no other callback gains a lower deadline. At *SI8*, for `TI`, `S1`, `S2` and `SR`, T_{cb}^{min} is be determined as 400 ms and $D_{cb} = 2000$ ms. For `CL`, $D_{cb} = 800$ ms. Hence, `CL` is executed first. In comparison to the ROS 2 execution, `CL` is in all cases executed closer to the trigger event. The buffer utilization never exceeds 40%, while the maximum utilization in the ROS 2 system is 60%. If now `CL` has the smallest buffer size of all callbacks, even in the first 400 ms, there will never be more than one element in the buffer as `CL` would gain the highest priority.

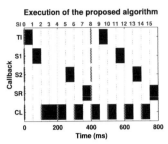 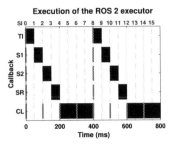

(a) Execution example of the proposed algorithm

(b) Execution example of the ROS 2 executor

Fig. 2. Execution traces using the proposed (left) and the ROS 2 executor (right). Red lines are trigger events and the blue numbers the scheduling iterations (SI). (Color figure online)

Table 1. Amount of RMW interactions

	Proposed Alg.	ROS 2	Static priority Alg.
First 400 ms SI 0–SI 7	37	20	40
Second 400 ms SI 8–SI 15	8	20	40

The number of needed interactions with the RMW is presented in Table 1. At the initial 400 ms, except for CL, the predicted next arrival time is 0. Therefore an interaction is performed during every scheduling iteration. After S2, the period of CL is known, and interactions with the middleware are only needed every second scheduling iteration. After 400 ms, the period for all callbacks is known, reducing the number of interactions with the RMW significantly. Therefore, fewer interactions with the RMW are needed than in the ROS 2 executor and static priority algorithms, that need to interact with the RMW at each scheduling iteration for each channel.

4 Discussion and Ongoing Work

The presented algorithm is created to give developers further configuration options while preventing buffer overflow. This work is in its infancy, and the proposed algorithm is at a conceptual level. Nevertheless, the given scheduling example showed the algorithm to have the potential to decrease the needed space of buffer size and give the developer more configuration options regarding priorities compared to the single-threaded executor in ROS 2. The needed interactions with the RMW are only increased at the first iterations. In the long run, the number of interactions can be decreased compared to the actual executor in ROS 2. Nevertheless, further analysis is needed to determine possible weaknesses of the proposed scheduling mechanism. Furthermore, the algorithm will be implemented in the ROS 2 stack and tested to be compared with the other existing algorithms on a real system. Adaptions of the algorithm might be needed to mitigate errors caused by offsets, changes in publishing rates, and message arrival jitter and make the algorithm usable in non-periodic systems.

References

1. OpenRobotics ROS 2: Docs (2023). https://docs.ros.org/en/humble
2. Blaß, T., Casini, D., Bozhko, S., Brandenburg, B.B.: A ROS 2 response-time analysis exploiting starvation freedom and execution-time variance. In: IEEE Real-Time Systems Symposium, pp. 41–53. IEEE (2021)
3. Casini, D., Blaß, T., Lütkebohle, I., Brandenburg, B.: Response-time analysis of ROS 2 processing chains under reservation-based scheduling. In: 31st Euromicro Conference on Real-Time Systems, pp. 1–23 (2019)
4. Choi, H., Xiang, Y., Kim, H.: Picas: new design of priority-driven chain-aware scheduling for ROS2. In: IEEE 27th Real-Time and Embedded Technology and Applications Symposium, pp. 251–263. IEEE (2021)
5. Dust, L., Persson, E., Ekström, M., Mubeen, S., Seceleanu, C., Gu, R.: Experimental evaluation of callback behavior in ROS 2 executors. In: 28th International Conference on Emerging Technologies and Factory Automation (2023)
6. Tang, Y., et al.: Response time analysis and priority assignment of processing chains on ros2 executors. In: IEEE Real-Time Systems Symposium, pp. 231–243 (2020)

Continuous Integration of Neural Networks in Autonomous Systems

Bruno Steffen$^{(\boxtimes)}$, Jonas Zohren , Utku Pazarci , Fiona Kullmann ,
and Hendrik Weißenfels

Technische Universität Dortmund, 44149 Dortmund, Germany
bruno.steffen@tu-dortmund.de
http://www.tu-dortmund.de/

Abstract. The perception of the autonomous driving software of the
FS223, a low-level sensor fusion of Lidar and Camera data requires the
use of a neural network for image classification. To keep the neural network up to date with updates in the training data, we introduce a Continuous Integration (CI) pipeline to re-train the network. The network
is then automatically validated and integrated into the code base of the
autonomous system. The introduction of proper CI methods in these
high-speed embedded software applications is an application of state-
of-the-art MLOps techniques that aim to provide rapid generation of
production-ready models. It further serves the purpose of professional-
izing the otherwise script-based software production, which is re-done
almost completely every year as the teams change from one year to the
next.

Keywords: ML Ops · Continuous Integration · Neural Networks

1 Motivation and Background

Since 1981 SAE international[1] hosts the Formula SAE, a student design competition where teams around the world design and manufacture formula-style
racing cars. The Formula SAE requires that major design decisions and implementations must not be made by professionals, but rather by students. This
paper is written by members of the German team of TU Dortmund University,
GET racing[2], who work on the autonomous driving capabilities of their vehicle
as the competitions have started featuring a driverless format.

In this paper, we discuss a solution within the software stack that is developed to enable the latest vehicle manufactured by GET racing (the FS223) to
autonomously participate in the racing events on Formula SAE-compliant racing

---

[1] SAE international is a standards developing organization for engineers, see: https://
www.sae.org/.

[2] GET racing participates annually in the events since 2005, see https://www.get-
racing.de/.

J. Kofroň et al. (Eds.): ECBS 2023, LNCS 14390, pp. 244–253, 2024.
https://doi.org/10.1007/978-3-031-49252-5_21

tracks. The software is designed to be safe and reliable but is also complex and requires a diverse set of software components. These components range from the perception of the environment to the processing of the recorded data and finally to the transmission of commands to the underlying actuators in the vehicle for steering and acceleration.

The presented solution is part of the perception component, where the challenge lies in the recognition of track-specific features. These are colored cones marking the edge of the track. To solve this issue, camera images are classified by a neural network as portraying blue, yellow, or orange cones, or alternatively, no cones at all. However, while the actual task of image classification is not particularly unique, the circumstances under which this network has to be developed, trained, and maintained are unusual.

On the one hand, GET racing as a student team does not have a lot of capital to invest in computational power that is crucial for the training of complex neural networks. As a consequence, the decision was made to use a fairly simplistic and lightweight neural network, building a framework around it that constantly uses the available computing power. On the other hand, the dataset used for the training of the network is not static, instead, it changes on a weekly basis. The original dataset does not generalize well to real life as it does not cover a wide variety of scenarios, resulting in the misclassification of many cones when testing on the field. Consequently, the team adds new data to the dataset after every test run. The network's performance can hence increase on a weekly basis, if and only if it is retrained or improved with the updated dataset.

Overall, to enable the work with limited computational power as well as an ever-changing dataset, we present a solution to continuously train and validate the neural network when one of the base components for the training of the network changes. The presented solution aims at the rapid generation of machine learning models through automation using CI-pipelines.

In Sect. 1.1 a discussion about related work takes place to put this paper in the context of the machine learning landscape. Section 2 introduces all concepts that are required for the understanding of the paper. In Sect. 3.1, the approach and important implementation details are explained. The solution is evaluated in Sect. 4 and future prospects are described in Sect. 5.

1.1   Related Work

Traditionally ML-based approaches are based on a data-centric design containing the data acquisition, analysis, and preparation for the ML models, also known as the CRISP-DM model [15], depicted in Fig. 1.

While the focus typically lies in the design and training of the models, a paradigm called MLOps coins the idea to improve and accelerate the process for providing production-ready software [5]. One recent and well-known application by Tesla is described by Andrej Karpathy's Ted Talk called "AI for Full-Self Driving at Tesla". Their approach uses continuous integration to constantly feed critical sensor data of vehicles into their supercomputer Dojo [9] for NN refinement. This approach aims at the improvement of the network for edge cases.

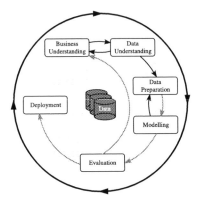

Fig. 1. Crisp-DM Process Model for Data Mining (edited from [15]).

While the project of Tesla vastly exceeds the complexity proposed in this paper, we also present an MLOps approach to continuously improve a neural network through automation. We do this by applying DevOps techniques such as continuous integration to the machine learning process, a workflow that was also presented and evaluated by Karamitsos et al. [4].

2   Preliminaries

This section introduces basic concepts and the overall software architecture for easier comprehension of the ideas and implementations shown in Sect. 3. In Sect. 2.1, we discuss the DevOps tools that are used to build our development framework. Section 2.2 introduces the theory behind image classification using neural networks. Finally, Sect. 2.3 presents the operational software pipeline that is used for autonomous driving.

2.1   DevOps Tools

To solve a difficult task such as autonomous driving, a certain level of software complexity is necessary. The complexity lies within individual tasks such as the perception of objects or control theory, but also results from the composition and connection of components.

DevOps tools and practices combat these difficulties. The methodology enforces development practices that ensure stable versioning and continuous delivery of software. This is typically accomplished using tools such as version control systems, but also Continuous Integration (CI), where staged builds (typically referred to as build pipelines) consisting of shell scripts are triggered once code is updated in order to test, build, and deploy software [1]. A prominent provider for such services is GitLab[3]. Within GitLab, the build pipelines have

---

[3] GitLab is a DevOps platform that aims to assist software developers with project management, versioning, etc. See https://about.gitlab.com/company/.

multiple capabilities that exceed simple scripts. It is possible to trigger other pipelines and to use (software-) artifacts from external pipelines and feedback can be portrayed through metrics and info texts.

Overall, build pipelines are perfectly suited to improve the quality of code through automated testing which enables developers to "Commit Daily, Commit Often" to introduce a culture which can greatly improve debugging capabilities [8].

2.2 Image Classification

Image classification is a fundamental problem in computer vision that has been prevalent for decades, and it has been used throughout history as one of the key instruments to benchmark the various approaches to artificial intelligence. There are many techniques that can be used to classify images into meaningful categories, namely support vector machines, fuzzy sets, genetic algorithms, or random forests [7,11]. However, with increasing computational power and availability of recorded data, the current state of the art is deep learning using neural networks (NNs).

While the state-of-the-art architectures of NNs evolve year by year, the training process has remained mostly the same. First, the given dataset is split into training, validation, and test sets. The neural network is trained and improved using the training set, while the validation set is used for further refinement of the model and its hyperparameters. Finally, the test set is used to check the performance of the neural network on unseen data.

During the training process, complex networks are prone to overfitting [16] generating perfect accuracy in prediction performed on the training data. However, at the same time, these models lose accuracy on the unseen test data. Consequently, the goal is to improve the performance of the neural network on unseen test data, rather than training data.

2.3 JARVIC

In order to understand how and why image classification is used, core principles of JARVIC, a self-developed software used for autonomous driving, must be introduced. In essence, perceived sensor data is processed and then used to generate commands for actuators that control the steering and throttle of the vehicle. This is done using a software pipeline that is depicted in Fig. 2 and is inspired by the pipeline of AMZ from 2019 [3]. Starting from the top, we have the Perception component, which takes in Lidar and camera data and processes these to allow for the detection of object location relative to the vehicle. This information and additional sensor data in the form of vehicle odometry (acceleration, wheel speed, etc.) is used by the Estimation component, to generate a map and localize the car within. The map is processed by the Planning component calculating a suitable trajectory for the vehicle to follow. Finally, the Controls component uses the trajectory to derive control commands for the steering and throttle of the vehicle.

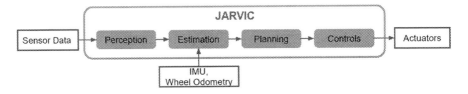

Fig. 2. Abstraction of JARVIC Software architecture.

The neural network described in this paper is found in the Perception component. As previously mentioned, the input for this component is Lidar point clouds and camera images. Both sources are used in a sensor fusion approach to combine the advantages of both sensors. Lidar is specialized in depth perception and camera images are great for the detection of objects and colors [14].

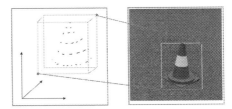

Fig. 3. Fusion of Lidar and Camera data (The figure is kindly provided by Leon Schwarzer[0000−0002−0882−3912].).

The fusion workflow is depicted in Fig. 3 and begins by matching the coordinate systems of both sensors. Once the Lidar detects a point cloud that resembles an object, the corresponding area in the video feed is cut out and then classified by color or as a no cone. This classification is done using a fairly simple neural network designed for image classification. Once the image is classified, the pose and color of the cones are forwarded to the Estimation component for further processing.

3   The Neural Network CI-Pipeline

The motivation section hinted at the unique characteristics of the use case regarding NN training. The NN of choice is the MobileNetV2 [10] which is fairly small with its 3.4 million adjustable parameters. This neural network is designed for usage on mobile and embedded devices.

A lightweight neural network was picked for two reasons. First, the task of image classification on a small (56×60 pixels) image does not require complex approximations. Choosing a more complex architecture such as the DenseNet with 46 million parameters, can perform worse since it has a higher runtime than smaller NNs [10] and is prone to overfitting due to high variance [6]. Second, the usage of a GPU was avoided to cut costs and power consumption. Instead, the NN is executed on an Edge TPU co-processor that is integrated into the hardware using a Coral PCIe Accelerator[4]. While the Coral setup is extremely efficient, it is also limited in its capacity to run complex neural networks.

An additional unique characteristic of our scenario is the frequently changing dataset of cone images used for training. The first iteration of the dataset was an adapted version of the Formula Student Objects in Context (FSOCO) dataset [13] which emerged through the collaborative efforts of multiple Formula SAE teams. Hence, the cone images vary in quality and a multitude of cameras were used for capturing. This is not necessarily bad, as a diverse dataset for training can lead to great generalization of the NN. However, the raw images from FSOCO did not exactly portray the characteristics found in real data. In an attempt to match the dataset closer to the real data, an augment of the FSOCO dataset is performed. A depiction of that step can be seen in Fig. 4. The augmentation focuses on imitating the size variance and cone position in captured images, even adding cropped cones to the augmented dataset. Analyzing, the average image shows that a cone is further zoomed out and less centered, compared to the original dataset. Using a CI-pipeline helps explore numerous configurations quickly, including augmentation setting and the integration of recorded data (from manual testing sessions) into the training dataset.

To ensure the usage of the best-performing NN, the following four requirements are used:

1. Train a new NN once the augmentation algorithm is changed
2. Train a new NN once images are added to the training dataset
3. Train a new NN once the training algorithm or NN architecture change
4. Validate the performance of any newly trained neural network

Section 3.1 will discuss the solution using CI-Pipelines to automate the training and validation process of the neural network.

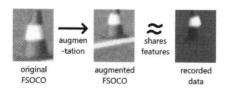

Fig. 4. Data augmentation of FSOCO dataset to resemble the real data.

---

[4] Coral offers hardware and software platforms for embedded systems. Our accelerator: https://coral.ai/products/pcie-accelerator.

3.1 Design and Implementation

Referring back to Fig. 1, we want to improve this paradigm through the use of MLOps techniques such as CI-pipelines. The goal is to fully automate the modeling, evaluation, and deployment steps (signified by the red arrows) for the rapid generation of models. This means that any changes triggered by the Data Preparation step automatically result in a trained model, an evaluation, and the deployment of production-ready software. The developer can then analyze the automatic evaluation, improve their Business or Data Understanding, and start the cycle again if expectations are not met.

To best explain the approach hands-on the focus will be kept on the workflow of the scenario when the data augmentation is updated since the other workflows are part of this case. The design, consisting of a pipeline, is depicted in Fig. 5. The process starts, once a developer changes the augmentation script *augment.py* inside the *prepare_dataset* project. The pipeline executes the script, preparing and augmenting the original FSOCO dataset. To accelerate feedback, a fraction of the FSOCO dataset is augmented, which serves as a sample.

The output is then combined with a set of self-recorded cone images called *self_train*, to train the NN with the corresponding *train.py* script. The resulting network is validated using the *validate.py* script with self-recorded data stored in *self_val*. If the validation shows an improvement to the previous version, the neural network is updated within JARVIC. As mentioned before, the cases of retraining of the NN when the dataset changed (meaning *self_train* increased) or when the training algorithm changed (*train.py*), are almost identical to the presented one. In both cases, the untouched pipeline steps can be skipped, resulting in a shortened overall pipeline.

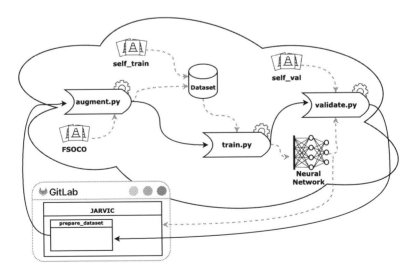

Fig. 5. Overall idea for the design of the continuous NN integration.

While the design above describes a single pipeline, the reality is a little bit more nuanced. Separate CI-pipelines are used for the dataset preparation, NN training, and for validation. These pipelines are then triggered in succession, automatically passing on the respective artifacts to continue validating the model. An additional detail is that it does not make sense to endlessly increase the amount of self-shot images for training. While adding data is beneficial, especially data that is captured using the real sensors, there is a point of diminishing returns with regard to the resulting NN performance [2]. Hence, the pipeline is used to test different combinations of datasets with varying sizes and characteristics, to ultimately find a suitable combination.

For demonstration purposes, we provide an exemplary simplified implementation of the proposed solution [12].

4 Conclusion

As hinted at throughout the paper, the aim of the presented solution is to save time and resources through the automation of training and validation of machine learning models. Using our solution, the pipeline does indeed provide a production-ready model that can be integrated into the JARVIC software stack.

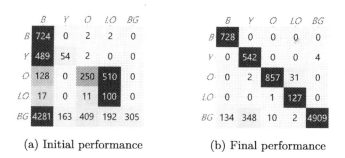

(a) Initial performance   (b) Final performance

Fig. 6. Confusion matrices of classification NNs. Green cells signify correct and red cells incorrect classifications. (Color figure online)

The CI-pipeline allows the user to assert the viability of NN training setups with the push of a button. This means that the hurdle to test ideas is almost diminished, meaning that a broad spectrum of ideas can be put into practice.

Even though manually running the scripts required for training and validation might not always take a lot of time, it does require human interaction every time the prior step is finished. In our use case, this sometimes meant the difference between 48 h and 8 h to retrieve a model, even though computation took the same amount of time.

To further assess the viability of the proposed solution, we regard the performance of the cone classifier NN used within JARVIC. The constant testing of new setups was primarily used to change the pre- and post-processing steps. This resulted in a significant increase in the performance of the neural network, as depicted in Sect. 4. These confusion matrices show the performance of the neural networks when classifying images of *blue, yellow, orange,* and *large orange* cones and *background* images. In the beginning, the neural network exhibited only an accuracy of 18.37% on the self-collected test dataset, with a significant number of misclassifications, as depicted in the confusion matrix of Fig. 6a. However, as seen in Fig. 6b, the classes are now predicted correctly with an accuracy of 91.83%. In this case, achieving further improvement is exceedingly challenging, as the test dataset was manually labeled, and some cases are impossible to classify even by humans.

While such an improvement of neural networks is not exclusive to cases where automated training and validation are in place, this mechanism motivated the developers to try out dozens of varying setups.

5   Future Work

The current architecture of the CI-pipelines already provides validation of the trained neural network with data that is captured on the same hardware as installed on the final vehicle. The quality of the NN can therefore be assessed by the number of correctly classified cones. However, it is not clear whether NNs with equally large test errors, perform equally well in an actual racing scenario. Depending on the algorithms used for the map generation or the boundary estimation of the track, different errors could lead to varying results. With a test error of 50%, one classification NN could be correct for one set of cones (blue or yellow) and completely wrong for the other, while a second NN could have the same error distributed over both kinds of cones equally. It is obvious that depending on the evaluation of the NN, either one of these errors could be better or worse.

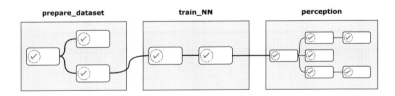

Fig. 7. Concept for extending the NN validation with the Perception CI-pipeline.

This is why validation of a newly trained NN in the already existing validation pipeline within JARVIC could result in a more accurate representation of the NN performance. The concept for this step is depicted in Fig. 7. Some of the validation techniques used in the CI-pipeline for the *Perception* component also include the execution of the *Estimation* and *Planning* components. Hence, deeper implications of the NN performance could be analyzed, and a final conclusion of the performance of the NN could be drawn.

References

1. Fowler, M., Foemmel, M.: Continuous integration (2006)
2. Goodfellow, I., Bengio, Y., Courville, A.: Deep Learning. MIT Press, Cambridge (2016)
3. Kabzan, J., et al.: AMZ driverless: the full autonomous racing system. J. Field Robot. **37**(7), 1267–1294 (2020)
4. Karamitsos, I., Albarhami, S., Apostolopoulos, C.: Applying DevOps practices of continuous automation for machine learning. Information **11**(7), 363 (2020)
5. Kreuzberger, D., Kühl, N., Hirschl, S.: Machine learning operations (mlops): overview, definition, and architecture. IEEE Access (2023)
6. Lever, J., Krzywinski, M., Altman, N.: N. model selection and overfitting. Nat. Methods (2016). https://doi.org/10.1038/nmeth.3968
7. Lu, D., Weng, Q.: A survey of image classification methods and techniques for improving classification performance. Int. J. Remote Sens. **28**(5), 823–870 (2007). https://doi.org/10.1080/01431160600746456
8. Meyer, M.: Continuous integration and its tools. IEEE Softw. **31**(3), 14–16 (2014). https://doi.org/10.1109/MS.2014.58
9. Salecker, J.: Whitepaper-tesla-floating-formats, November 2021
10. Sandler, M., Howard, A., Zhu, M., Zhmoginov, A., Chen, L.C.: Mobilenetv 2: inverted residuals and linear bottlenecks (2019)
11. Stathakis, D., Vasilakos, A.: Comparison of computational intelligence based classification techniques for remotely sensed optical image classification. IEEE Trans. Geosci. Remote Sens. **44**(8), 2305–2318 (2006). https://doi.org/10.1109/TGRS.2006.872903
12. Steffen, B., Zohren, J., Pazarci, U., Kullmann, F., Weißenfels, H.: Gitlab Demo Project for Paper "Continuous Integration of Neural Networks in Autonomous Systems", September 2023. https://doi.org/10.5281/zenodo.8370907
13. Vödisch, N., Dodel, D., Schötz, M.: Fsoco: the formula student objects in context dataset. arXiv preprint arXiv:2012.07139 (2020)
14. Wei, P., Cagle, L., Reza, T., Ball, J., Gafford, J.: Lidar and camera detection fusion in a real-time industrial multi-sensor collision avoidance system. Electronics **7**(6), 84 (2018). https://doi.org/10.3390/electronics7060084
15. Wirth, R., Hipp, J.: Crisp-DM: towards a standard process model for data mining. In: Proceedings of the 4th International Conference on the Practical Applications of Knowledge Discovery and Data Mining, vol. 1, pp. 29–39. Manchester (2000)
16. Ying, X.: An overview of overfitting and its solutions. J. Phys. Conf. Ser. **1168**, 022022. IOP Publishing (2019)

Building a Digital Twin Framework for Dynamic and Robust Distributed Systems

Tiberiu Seceleanu[⊠], Ning Xiong, Eduard Paul Enoiu, and Cristina Seceleanu

Mälardalen University, Västerås, Sweden
{Tiberiu.Seceleanu,Ning.Xiong,Eduard.Paul.Enoiu,
Cristina.Seceleanu}@mdu.se

Abstract. Digital Twins (DTs) serve as the backbone of Industry 4.0, offering virtual representations of actual systems, enabling accurate simulations, analysis, and control. These representations help in predicting system behaviour, facilitating multiple real-time tests, and reducing risks and costs while identifying optimization areas. DTs meld cyber and physical realms, accelerating the design and modelling of sustainable innovations. Despite their potential, the complexity of DTs presents challenges in their industrial application. We sketch here an approach to build an adaptable and trustable framework for building and operating DT systems, which is the basis for the academia-industry project *A Digital Twin Framework for Dynamic and Robust Distributed Systems* (D-RODS). D-RODS aims to address the challenges above, aiming to advance industrial digitalization and targeting areas like system efficiency, incorporating AI and verification techniques with formal support.

Keywords: digital twins · industrial automation · AI · verification and validation · resource utilization

1 Introduction

Industry 4.0 is the digital transformation (a.k.a. digitalization) in the industrial sector that includes automation, data exchange, cloud computing, robotics, Artificial Intelligence (AI), IoT, etc., all used to achieve industrial objectives and intelligent practices through the interaction of people, new technologies, and innovation. Modern industry is facing various complex challenges in adapting to Industry 4.0 contexts, covering the whole lifecycle of products. Further sources of challenges are identified as the inclusion of legacy systems and technologies, finding optimal deployment solutions, and achieving overall performance and robustness of complex systems.

One of the approaches that can provide a unified solution towards digitalization is arguably the exploitation of Digital Twins (DTs) - virtual representations (devices, data, properties, etc.) of actual systems that exist within their environment [4]. DTs use a set of models to describe the system and explore different

© The Author(s), under exclusive license to Springer Nature Switzerland AG 2024
J. Kofroň et al. (Eds.): ECBS 2023, LNCS 14390, pp. 254–258, 2024.
https://doi.org/10.1007/978-3-031-49252-5_22

types of actions on the system. Multiple "real" tests can be run before, during, and after product design. As standards in the DT domain are "barely emerging" [5], "reference architectures" and "DT-platforms"[1] are trying to provide the needed support for companies to cross into the digital world of DT.

The inherent complexity of the DT concept raises additional challenges with respect to industrial utilization [7]. D-RODS addresses problems related to system integration, performance, organization, data volume and quality, and challenges of distributed system automation: integration and compatibility of legacy systems, continuous improvement, lack of skilled labour, etc. D-RODS aims to advance the level of digitalization towards autonomous operations, validated via use cases coming from major Swedish companies in the domains of industrial automation: ABB, transportation: Alstom, and telecommunication: Ericsson.

The overall goal of D-RODS is to propose and validate a reference DT framework based on trustworthy artificial intelligence, supporting highly autonomous system testing and operation, optimal resource utilization and increased resilience to faults. D-RODS aims to support the development and operation of such a framework via modern and complementary approaches.

2 The D-RODS Approach

D-RODS solutions will offer verified and verifiable AI-based approaches, adapted to the size and features of system instances, continuously evolving through the operational stages, improving with respect to their targeted goals. The architecture is organized on several *contexts*, briefly described as follows.

Context: Physical (CP). This layer corresponds to the physical world, containing the plant, the system controlling it, etc.

Context: Learning (CL). This layer (Fig. 1 a)) focuses on the creation of the DT models corresponding to the relevant parts of the other layers. Unsupervised learning, validated by specific V&V methods (transparent, explainable, understandable results), extracts from a long data history a filtered set of data. Based on existing domain expertise and models from libraries, this creates the set of DT models to be employed in the other contexts. Once a complete version of the models is accepted, the **CL** can go offline, to reduce energy consumption.

Context: Functionality (CF) and **Context: Infrastructure (CI).** These similar layers (Fig. 1 b), c)) contain each an AI and a V&V block, which control and enhance the functionality of a complex DT (from **CL**). The DT execution is supervised by a collection of AI algorithms and a V&V procedures. Continuous learning, optimization and behavior evaluation are in place.

Targeted Results. D-RODS proposes a novel architectural set-up uniting DT, AI, and V&V technologies. It targets an increase in the trustfulness of AI approaches via formal analysis and online testing, optimizes operations, resource

---

[1] e.g. DIGITBrain. https://digitbrain.eu/.

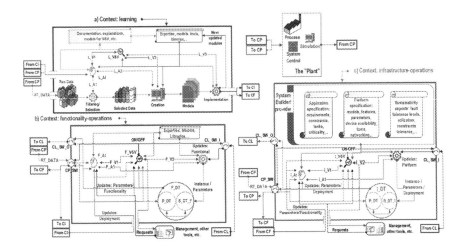

Fig. 1. Approach details.

usage and power consumption, and improves maintainability aspects. The D-RODS framework will cater to the accuracy and efficiency of employed models by continuous learning and verification, towards high levels of autonomy. The cross-domain validation is expected to innovate the content of "reference architectures" in the context of DT developments.

D-RODS also proposes, verifies and demonstrates a novel methodology to detect system faults and means to mitigate their impact, based on: a) new AI-based approaches to identify HW failures; b) a new and verified learning solution to acquire adaptation strategies to re-distribute resources in reaction to identified faults. This provides a novel dimension in the DT research, toward enhancing the resilience and robustness of digitalized systems.

Focusing on AI methods, D-RODS is set to refine system performance prediction and resource utilization optimization. For V&V, D-RODS is deriving from past work on passive testing, integrating formal verification and runtime testing. It ensures that the developed models, when incorporated into DT, are accurate and continuously monitor operational correctness. Techniques will include design verification, continuous monitoring, and metamorphic testing.

Related Work. In manufacturing and automation, several studies (e.g., [1]) show the usefulness of AI in monitoring, maintenance, error diagnosis and real-time optimization tools, at elevated costs in energy, though. If concepts such as DT and automated model creation exist, consumption may be reduced up to 20%, pending on computation efficiency and accuracy of models [6].

In the telecom, the non-incremental leap from 4G to 5G came with large implementation challenges. Existing assurance processes become inadequate, requiring new techniques and related procedures. Device and network DTs, using of AI and the correctness of results are critical for the industry as a whole [2].

Work on formal verification of AI components has been carried out, especially for neural networks [3]. The system-level simulation-based formal analysis of AI-based systems, performed by the VerifAI toolchain [8] is complementary. It comes close to D-RODS' envisioned verification approach, yet it does not apply game-theoretic model checking for AI verification, and it does not target distributed learning in networked environments, which we tackle in D-RODS.

AI and big data have played an important role in the development and training of production control optimization of DT models for industrial applications [9]. However, AI-related techniques have been only used for planning, scheduling and control of the operation of machines. They have not been exploited for monitoring and managing the sensing-computing system of DTs for enhancing their resilience, robustness and energy efficiency.

3   Conclusions

We introduced the D-RODS approach as a novel framework for the implementation of DT within Industry 4.0 paradigms. It is formulated to address existing challenges by creating a cohesive integration between AI methodologies, V&V techniques, and current DT concepts. This should foster enhanced system efficiency, reduced power consumption, and prolonged system component life. The inclusion of AI in D-RODS not only facilitates better simulation and prediction models but also offers advanced fault detection and mitigation mechanisms.

Acknowledgements. The authors are partly supported by Vinnova's *Advanced digitalization* programme in the project D-RODS (ID: 2023-00244).

References

1. Bambura, R., Šolc, M., Dado, M., Kotek, L.: Implementation of digital twin for engine block manufacturing processes. Appl. Sci. **10**(18), 6578 (2020)
2. Bhadada, K.: Enhancing innovation in telecom with digital twins. Harward Bus. Rev. Anal. Serv. (2022)
3. Gehr, T., Mirman, M., Drachsler-Cohen, D., Tsankov, P., Chaudhuri, S., Vechev, M.: Ai2: safety and robustness certification of neural networks with abstract interpretation. In: IEEE Symposium on Security and Privacy, pp. 3–18. IEEE (2018)
4. Jones, D., Snider, C., Nassehi, A., Yon, J., Hicks, B.: Characterising the digital twin: a systematic literature review. CIRP J. Manuf. Sci. Technol. **29**, 36–52 (2020)
5. Kung, A., Baudoin, C., Tobich, K.: Report of TWG digital twins: landscape of digital twins. EU Observatory for ICT Standardisation (2022)
6. Mawson, V.J., Hughes, B.R.: The development of modelling tools to improve energy efficiency in manufacturing processes and systems. J. Manuf. Syst. **51**, 95–105 (2019)
7. Perno, M., Hvam, L., Haug, A.: Implementation of digital twins in the process industry: a systematic literature review of enablers and barriers. Comput. Ind. **134**, 103558 (2022)

8. Tommaso, D., et al.: Verifai: a toolkit for the design and analysis of artificial intelligence-based systems. In: The 31st Conference on Computer Aided Verification (2019)
9. Zambrano, V., et al.: Industrial digitalization in the industry 4.0 era: classification, reuse and authoring of digital models on digital twin platforms. Array **14**, 100176 (2022)

A Simple End-to-End Computer-Aided Detection Pipeline for Trained Deep Learning Models

Ali Teymur Kahraman[1]([✉]) [iD], Tomas Fröding[2] [iD], Dimitrios Toumpanakis[3,4] [iD], Mikael Fridenfalk[5] [iD], Christian Jamtheim Gustafsson[6,7] [iD], and Tobias Sjöblom[1] [iD]

[1] Department of Immunology, Genetics and Pathology, Uppsala University, Uppsala, Sweden
ali_teymur.kahraman@igp.uu.se
[2] Department of Radiology, Nyköping Hospital, Nyköping, Sweden
[3] Neuroradiology, Karolinska University Hospital, Stockholm, Sweden
[4] Department of Surgical Sciences, Uppsala University, Uppsala, Sweden
[5] Department of Game Design, Uppsala University, Visby, Gotland, Sweden
[6] Department of Hematology, Oncology and Radiation Physics, Skåne University Hospital, Lund, Sweden
[7] Department of Translational Medicine, Medical Radiation Physics, Lund University, Malmö, Sweden

Abstract. Recently, there has been a significant rise in research and development focused on deep learning (DL) models within healthcare. This trend arises from the availability of extensive medical imaging data and notable advances in graphics processing unit (GPU) computational capabilities. Trained DL models show promise in supporting clinicians with tasks like image segmentation and classification. However, advancement of these models into clinical validation remains limited due to two key factors. Firstly, DL models are trained on off-premises environments by DL experts using Unix-like operating systems (OS). These systems rely on multiple libraries and third-party components, demanding complex installations. Secondly, the absence of a user-friendly graphical interface for model outputs complicates validation by clinicians. Here, we introduce a conceptual Computer-Aided Detection (CAD) pipeline designed to address these two issues and enable non-AI experts, such as clinicians, to use trained DL models offline in Windows OS. The pipeline divides tasks between DL experts and clinicians, where experts handle model development, training, inference mechanisms, Grayscale Softcopy Presentation State (GSPS) objects creation, and containerization for deployment. The clinicians execute a simple script to install necessary software and dependencies. Hence, they can use a universal image viewer to analyze results generated by the models. This paper illustrates the pipeline's effectiveness through a case study on pulmonary embolism detection, showcasing successful deployment on a local workstation by an in-house radiologist. By simplifying model deployment and making it accessible to non-AI experts, this CAD pipeline bridges the gap between technical development and practical application, promising broader healthcare applications.

Keywords: Computer-aided detection · grayscale softcopy presentation state · machine learning · deep learning · pulmonary embolism

© The Author(s), under exclusive license to Springer Nature Switzerland AG 2024
J. Kofroň et al. (Eds.): ECBS 2023, LNCS 14390, pp. 259–262, 2024.
https://doi.org/10.1007/978-3-031-49252-5_23

1 Introduction

In recent years, there has been a notable surge in both research and development pertaining to applications grounded in machine learning (ML) and deep learning (DL) models within the healthcare system [1]. This trend is aroused by the availability of extensive volumes of medical imaging data estimated at 4.2 billion annual diagnostic examinations worldwide [2], along with significant advancements in graphical computational capacities now measured in tera floating point operations per second [3]. Within these advances, researchers have demonstrated the potential of trained ML/DL models to support clinicians in a variety of medical image-processing tasks, including segmentation [4], classification [5]. However, adoption of these trained ML/DL models by clinicians for clinical validation purposes is hindered by two main factors. First, ML/DL models are trained on off-premises environments by ML/DL experts using Unix-like operating systems (OS) such as Ubuntu and macOS. Preparing the development environment for ML/DL model training on Unix-like operating systems requires proper installation of libraries, packages, and third-party components. Therefore, these challenging complex installations are not easy to do by non-AI experts such as clinicians. Second, the absence of a user-friendly graphical interface for trained ML/DL model outputs to maintain easy integration with a universal image viewer.

Cloud services that use Infrastructure as a Service (IaaS) architecture, such as Amazon Web Services (AWS), Microsoft Azure, and Google Cloud, are the common way of deploying trained ML/DL models by ML/DL experts [6]. While there have been advancements in the creation of cloud-based services for deploying DL models, the assessment of models on these platforms presents challenges, primarily because of regulations related to general data protection or local institutional policies. To address these challenges, we proposed a conceptual end-to-end Computer-Aided Detection (CAD) pipeline that can be easily implementable on the Windows OS, which does not require expert-level knowledge. The proposed conceptual pipeline enables non-AI experts such as radiologists and clinicians to perform trained ML/DL models offline within on-premises environments.

2 Objectives and Concepts

Our objective is to present a conceptual pipeline designed to simplify the offline installation of trained ML/DL models on local workstations, enabling non-AI experts, such as clinicians, to carry out this process with ease. To ensure this, the pipeline we propose involves two distinct parties: ML/DL experts and clinicians. ML/DL experts are responsible for both the development and deployment of the trained models, while clinicians are primarily tasked with utilizing these trained models. Unlike ML/DL experts, clinicians typically have greater familiarity with the Windows operating system [7].

As a result, it is imperative that trained ML/DL models are easily adaptable for use within the Windows OS environment. With the advent of containerization technology and the introduction of the Windows Subsystem for Linux (WSL), a new feature within the Windows OS, it has become notably straightforward to employ models developed on Unix-based operating systems on Windows platforms. Here, we have presented the pipeline, as explained below, by leveraging the capabilities of these two technologies.

First, we made a clear division of tasks between ML/DL experts and clinicians when utilizing deep learning models for medical image analysis. ML/DL experts are responsible for a series of complex tasks structured as follows: The DL model development and training, encompassing essential preprocessing steps to prepare the data for training, creating the model's inference mechanism, generating Grayscale Softcopy Presentation State (GSPS) objects for image annotations, saving the trained model in standard formats like HDF5 or pickle, packaging the model into a Docker container for deployment, crafting a bash script for automated setup of CUDA drivers, Docker, and Windows Subsystem for Linux (WSL), and finally, uploading all essential files, including the model, Docker configurations, and scripts, to platforms like GitHub for version control, collaboration, or storage purposes. As aimed, the clinicians have a less complex set of tasks. They just need to download and execute a single bash script uploaded to GitHub by the ML/DL experts. This script typically handles the installation of essential software and dependencies needed to run the DL model. Once the setup is complete, clinicians utilize a universal image viewer to analyze the results generated by the GSPS objects (Fig. 1).

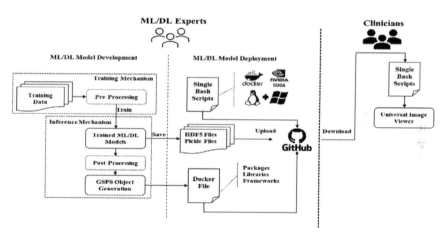

Fig. 1. The illustration of the end-to-end Computer-Aided Detection pipeline.

3   Case Pipeline: Pulmonary Embolism Detection

To assess the usability of the proposed pipeline, we followed the same procedures outlined in the previous section, using an in-house trained DL model for the detection of pulmonary embolisms [4]. First, the trained model was saved in the pickle file format. Second, a bash script file was generated to facilitate the proper execution of the DL model. As a final step, all files were uploaded to a file storage system for sharing. Our in-house radiologist was able to successfully deploy and test the trained DL model on 100 CT pulmonary angiography (CTPA) volume images at the local workstation without requiring expert assistance. The results of 97 of these 100 CTPAs were successfully analyzed in the universal image viewer.

4   Conclusion

In conclusion, our proposed CAD pipeline offers a practical solution to the challenges of deploying trained ML/DL models in on-premises environments. By streamlining the process and making it accessible to non-AI experts, such as clinicians, we bridge the gap between technical model development and practical application. Leveraging containerization technology and the Windows Subsystem for Linux, we've simplified the deployment of Unix-based models on Windows platforms, ensuring adaptability and usability. A successful case study in pulmonary embolism detection underscores the effectiveness of this approach, promising broader applications in healthcare.

References

1. Esteva, A., et al.: A guide to deep learning in healthcare. Nat. Med. **25**, 24–29 (2019). https://doi.org/10.1038/s41591-018-0316-z
2. UNSCEAR 2020/2021 Report Volume I. www.unscear.org/unscear/en/publications/2020_2021_1.html. Accessed 18 Sept 2023
3. Dally, W.J., Keckler, S.W., Kirk, D.B.: Evolution of the graphics processing unit (GPU). IEEE Micro **41**, 42–51 (2021). https://doi.org/10.1109/MM.2021.3113475
4. Kahraman, A.T., Fröding, T., Toumpanakis, D., Gustafsson, C.J., Sjöblom, T.: Deep learning based segmentation for pulmonary embolism detection in real-world CT Angiography: classification performance (2023). https://doi.org/10.1101/2023.04.21.23288861v2. https://doi.org/10.1101/2023.04.21.23288861
5. Esteva, A., et al.: Dermatologist-level classification of skin cancer with deep neural networks. Nature **542**, 115–118 (2017). https://doi.org/10.1038/nature21056
6. Nyarko, K., Taiwo, P., Duru, C., Masa-Ibi, E.: AI/ML systems engineering workbench framework. In: 2023 57th Annual Conference on Information Sciences and Systems (CISS), pp. 1–5 (2023). https://doi.org/10.1109/CISS56502.2023.10089781
7. Newaz, A.I., Sikder, A.K., Rahman, M.A., Uluagac, A.S.: A survey on security and privacy issues in modern healthcare systems: attacks and defenses. ACM Trans. Comput. Healthcare **2**, 27:1–27:44 (2021). https://doi.org/10.1145/3453176

Astrocyte-Integrated Dynamic Function Exchange in Spiking Neural Networks

Murat Isik[1]([⊠])[iD] and Kayode Inadagbo[2][iD]

[1] Stanford University, Stanford, CA, USA
mrtisik@stanford.edu
[2] Prairie View A&M University, Prairie View, TX, USA

Abstract. This paper presents an innovative methodology for improving the robustness and computational efficiency of Spiking Neural Networks (SNNs), a critical component in neuromorphic computing. The proposed approach integrates astrocytes, a type of glial cell prevalent in the human brain, into SNNs, creating astrocyte-augmented networks. To achieve this, we designed and implemented an astrocyte model in two distinct platforms: CPU/GPU and FPGA. Our FPGA implementation notably utilizes Dynamic Function Exchange (DFX) technology, enabling real-time hardware reconfiguration and adaptive model creation based on current operating conditions. The novel approach of leveraging astrocytes significantly improves the fault tolerance of SNNs, thereby enhancing their robustness. Notably, our astrocyte-augmented SNN displays near-zero latency and theoretically infinite throughput, implying exceptional computational efficiency. Through comprehensive comparative analysis with prior works, it's established that our model surpasses others in terms of neuron and synapse count while maintaining an efficient power consumption profile. These results underscore the potential of our methodology in shaping the future of neuromorphic computing, by providing robust and energy-efficient systems.

Keywords: Astrocytes · Spiking Neural Networks · FPGA Implementation · Dynamic Function Exchange · Fault Tolerance

1 Introduction

Fault tolerance has become a critical feature of today's increasingly sophisticated computational systems, which require not just high performance, but also continuous and reliable operation. This is especially true for neural networks that mimic the structure of the brain, pushing the limits of existing computing paradigms. Spiking Neural Networks (SNNs), a type of artificial neural network patterned after the brain's neuronal dynamics, are energy efficient, use time-dependent data processing, and have bio-plausible algorithms for learning. In spite of this, SNNs are susceptible to faults and failures, which could disrupt their functionality and reduce their efficiency. Therefore, fault-tolerant mechanisms within SNNs need to be explored. Recent research has demonstrated

J. Kofroň et al. (Eds.): ECBS 2023, LNCS 14390, pp. 263–273, 2024.
https://doi.org/10.1007/978-3-031-49252-5_24

that astrocytes play a crucial role in regulating neuronal activity and synaptic transmission in the brain. It has long been believed that neurons contributed significantly to the resilience and adaptability of biological neural networks, but astrocytes have now been found to play a much more important role which is shown in Fig. 1. Dynamically modulating neuronal activity based on state, they effectively support fault tolerance at the molecular level. The hypothesis of integrating astrocytic mechanisms into SNNs is an exciting prospect, potentially leading to dynamic adjustment for fault tolerance in these systems [2,5,6].

Field Programmable Gate Arrays (FPGAs) are reprogrammable silicon chips that can be customized to perform complex computations in parallel, making them ideally suited for implementing SNNs. FPGAs have been increasingly used for emulating SNNs due to their high degree of parallelism, energy efficiency, and low latency. Further, their inherent re-programmability makes them a prime candidate for implementing adaptive mechanisms, such as those inspired by astrocytes, to handle faults dynamically. This could potentially enable SNNs implemented on FPGAs to autonomously adapt in the face of faults, mimicking the resilience observed in biological neural networks [3,4].

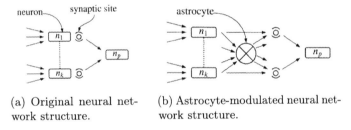

(a) Original neural network structure.

(b) Astrocyte-modulated neural network structure.

Fig. 1. Inserting an astrocyte in a neural network. [5]

In this paper, we explore how FPGA-implemented SNNs could benefit from astrocyte-powered dynamic adjustments to enhance fault tolerance. The purpose of this study is to investigate whether introducing astrocyte-inspired mechanisms could enhance network performance and reliability by reducing faults and failures. The rest of the paper is organized as follows: Sect. 2 discusses astrocytes' significance in SNNs and reviews related works. Section 3 describes SNN architecture and the integration of astrocytes. Section 4 details our astrocyte-augmented SNN model, emphasizing hardware implementations. Section 5 evaluates the model's fault tolerance and efficiency, comparing it with other models and introducing the Dynamic Function eXchange technology. Section 6 concludes with our key findings and suggests future research avenues.

2   Background

The principles of biological brains are reflected in SNNs, which are artificial neural networks. A key difference between them is the emulation of time-dependent spikes or 'action potentials', which are the primary means of communication between neurons in the brain. The SNN is a powerful computational model capable of handling complex tasks such as pattern recognition, sensory processing, and motor control in a highly energy-efficient, low-latency manner. Recent advances in neuromorphic engineering have propelled research in this field, which aims to create hardware and software solutions that mimic neuronal spike dynamics [11]. Fault-tolerance techniques are essential for ensuring robustness and reliability of complex systems like SNNs, particularly when uninterrupted functionality is critical. Several methods have been proposed and implemented, ranging from redundancy and error correction codes to adaptive mechanisms that enable dynamic fault recovery [18]. The disadvantages of these traditional techniques are often increased resource consumption and decreased performance. Therefore, innovative solutions are needed that minimize these trade-offs while ensuring robust fault tolerance. Astrocytes once considered mere supporting cells in the brain, are now recognized as key players in regulating neuronal activity. The ability of biological neural networks to detect and modulate neural activity contributes to their adaptability and resilience [13]. The idea of integrating these astrocytic mechanisms into artificial neural networks to enhance their resilience and adaptability is a novel and promising area of research. Previous works have explored the implementation of SNNs on FPGAs for their advantages in parallelism, energy efficiency, and re-programmability [15]. However, the integration of astrocyte-inspired fault-tolerance mechanisms in such systems has not been adequately explored. This research seeks to fill this gap, extending our understanding of fault tolerance in SNNs and paving the way for more robust and adaptive neural network architectures. By examining how astrocyte-powered dynamic adjustments could enhance fault-tolerance in FPGA-implemented SNNs, this study could provide a valuable contribution to the fields of computational neuroscience and neuromorphic engineering.

3   Astrocyte and Spiking Neural Networks

Astrocytes constitute about 20–40% of the total glial population in the human brain. Studies have revealed that these molecules play an active role in neuronal signaling and information processing. The astrocyte extends its processes near neurons, where it senses and modulates neuronal activity through gliotransmission [16]. This remarkable capability motivates the integration of astrocyte mechanisms into SNNs, providing an intriguing avenue to enhance their fault tolerance and adaptability. An SNN is an artificial neural network that mimics time-dependent and event-driven communication between biological neurons through spikes or 'action potentials'. High temporal resolution, high power efficiency, and bio-plausible mechanisms have made them a subject of keen interest [14]. It is possible to mimic the fault tolerance and dynamic adjustment of biological neural networks by incorporating astrocyte mechanisms into SNNs. A bidirectional communication system connects astrocytes to neurons. Neurotransmitters released by neurons can be detected and responded to by them, and the gliotransmitters released can modulate neuronal activity. Among the main mechanisms of astrocyte-neuron interaction is the tripartite synapse model, in which astrocytes actively contribute to neuronal synaptic transmission [1]. Among the diverse effects of this interaction are the modification of synaptic strength, the regulation of local blood flow, and metabolic support for neurons, thus enhancing network resilience and adaptability. SNNs based on astrocyte functionality can incorporate these aspects to enhance their resilience. Synaptic weights can be modulated by astrocytes to balance neuron firing rates across a network, thereby preventing neurons from 'dying out' or 'overfiring' as a result of neural network models. Moreover, astrocytes are able to sense and respond to changes in neuronal activity, enabling them to design fault-tolerance mechanisms that dynamically adjust to faults in networks [8,9]. The incorporation of astrocyte-neuron interactions into SNNs, especially those based on FPGAs, has yet to be explored in various computational neuroscience studies.

4   Method

4.1   Dataset

Our project is based on the DAVIS 240C Dataset, a unique collection of event-based data ideal for pose estimation, visual odometry, and SLAM. This dataset, generated using DAVIS 240C cameras by iniLabs, offers event-based images, IMU measurements, and motion-captured ground truth. Some datasets that utilized a motorized linear slider lack motion-capture or IMU data; however, their ground truth derives from the slider's position. The "calibration" dataset provides alternative camera models, with all gray datasets sharing identical intrinsic calibration. This dataset proves invaluable for image data analysis, particularly in SNNs and related domains [10]. For this project, we employ a subset of the DAVIS 240C dataset. Figure 2 showcases the DAVIS 240C event camera which was utilized to produce this dataset.

Fig. 2. DAVIS 240 DVS Event Camera

4.2   Training Details

In our implementation, the SNN is architected to emulate astrocyte functions using a subset of the DAVIS 240C Dataset that records astrocyte activity in response to neuronal behavior. The architecture is composed of:

- **Input Layer:** Simulates neuron-astrocyte interactions, customizable for specific neurological scenarios.
- **Astrocyte Layer:** Represents spiking astrocytes, processing inputs and relaying spike trains to the subsequent layer.
- **Output Layer:** Decodes the spike trains, producing responses analogous to biological outcomes from astrocyte activities.

During compilation, the aim is to synchronize the Output Layer's reactions with the anticipated responses in the training set. We employ the 'Adam' optimizer, recognized for efficiently addressing complex problems. Performance evaluation utilizes the 'accuracy' metric, with the 'EarlyStopping' callback integrated during training to mitigate overfitting. Following training, outcomes are juxtaposed with validation data, assessing accuracy, precision, and recall. This implementation paves the way for deeper explorations into astrocytic roles in SNNs. Subsequent iterations may further refine the model and incorporate additional cellular dynamics, with a recommendation to consider advanced SNN metrics such as spike timing and spiking rate accuracy.

4.3   Hardware Implementation

Hardware implementation is vital for real-world applications, particularly in computationally-intensive tasks. This section presents our methodology for physically implementing the astrocyte model using two different approaches: CPU/GPU and FPGA.

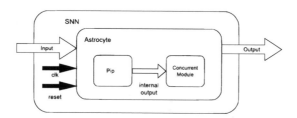

Fig. 3. Block Diagram of Implementation

CPU/GPU Implementations. We utilized Python to execute implementations on the CPU and GPU. The study leveraged the computational prowess of NVIDIA's GeForce RTX 3060 GPU and Intel's Core i9 12900H CPU, both of which are optimized for different tasks, ensuring an efficient execution of our implementations.

FPGA Implementation. Our FPGA implementation was executed on the XCVC1902 FPGA chip, equipped with 400 AI Chips, utilizing the 2021.1 software version of Vivado. Our central module, "Astrocyte", processes a 42-bit input and produces a 42-bit output. The internal operations of the PiP (Place-in-Place) module, which is a crucial component of this design, are depicted in Fig. 3. The efficiency of our astrocyte-augmented SNN, as presented through metrics, was evident in its low latency and theoretically infinite throughput, emphasizing its computational prowess. The presented metrics stem from an experiment involving an astrocyte-augmented SNN. Our aim was to evaluate how the astrocyte implementation impacts the network's robustness and computational efficiency. Initially, our SNN displayed a fault tolerance of 72.08% without astrocytes, signifying that a single artificially silenced neuron caused the network's output to diverge by this proportion from the original, fault-free state. Such a measure provided an estimate of the SNN's resilience to localized neuronal failures. When astrocytes were incorporated into the SNN, a remarkable reduction in latency was observed; the time required for an entire round of astrocytic updates was essentially zero as per the system clock. This extremely low latency indicated an impressive efficiency in the computational implementation. Moreover, this near-zero latency facilitated theoretically infinite throughput, implying instantaneous processing of all neurons in the network, which further emphasized the exceptional computational efficiency of our astrocyte-augmented SNN. The observed new fault tolerance was quantified as 8.96%, highlighting the degree of enhancement in SNN's fault tolerance as a direct result of astrocyte integration. Post astrocyte integration, the SNN demonstrated an improved fault tolerance of 63.11%. The fault tolerance FT of a SNN is conceptually defined as the proportionate deviation of the SNN's output from the original, fault-free state when subject to a fault condition.

1. FT_{initial}: Initial fault tolerance without astrocytes.
2. FT_{astro}: Fault tolerance after integrating astrocytes.
3. ΔFT: Improvement in fault tolerance due to astrocyte integration, given by $\Delta FT = FT_{\text{initial}} - FT_{\text{astro}}$.

The fault tolerance of the SNN, considering the given description, is represented as:

$$FT = \frac{O_{\text{fault}} - O_{\text{original}}}{O_{\text{original}}} \times 100\% \tag{1}$$

where:

- O_{original} is the output in the original, fault-free state.
- O_{fault} is the output when a fault (like a silenced neuron) is induced.

From our results:

$$FT_{\text{initial}} = 72.08\%$$

$$FT_{\text{astro}} = 8.96\%$$

$$\Delta FT = 63.11\%$$

This confirms the mathematical relationship:

$$\Delta FT = FT_{\text{initial}} - FT_{\text{astro}} \tag{2}$$

The reduced FT_{astro} implies that the network's output deviates less from the fault-free state when a fault condition is induced, indicating enhanced resilience of the SNN upon integrating astrocytes.

4.4 Adaptive Model Creation with Dynamic Function eXchange Technology

We utilize Dynamic Function Exchange (DFX) technology for an adaptable model construction. Central to this approach is on-the-fly hardware reconfiguration, allowing computational functions to map onto hardware according to emerging demands. Initially, the model engages in "Training & Predicting" using historical data, recognizing patterns for adaptation. It then proceeds to "Adjusting Hyperparameters" for performance refinement. Ultimately, in the "Execute DFX" phase, as illustrated in Fig. 4, DFX's real-time hardware reprogramming facilitates model functionality adjustments according to network state changes, optimizing computational resource allocation. This not only enhances adaptability to SNN variability but also fosters energy efficiency, pivotal for high-demand machine learning tasks. In essence, our DFX-integrated model offers enhanced performance and adaptability in astrocyte-based neuronal network implementations.

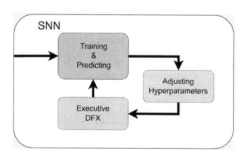

Fig. 4. DFX Diagram

4.5 Quantitative Analysis of the Hardware Accelerator

For computational tasks, especially in real-time scenarios, metrics like throughput and latency are vital. Throughput gauges the system's capability to handle data processing, whereas latency measures the delay before a transfer of data begins. These metrics play a pivotal role in understanding and optimizing the performance of our system.

$$\text{Throughput} = \frac{\text{No. of MACs}}{\text{Operational Latency}} \qquad (3)$$

The above equation delineates the throughput as a function of the number of Multiply-Accumulate (MAC) operations over the operational latency. The count of MAC operations is derived from specialized neural network libraries [12]. On the other hand, the operational latency, which is synonymous with simulation time in this context, predominantly emerges from the inherent characteristics and constraints of the underlying hardware architecture. This is mathematically captured by:

$$\text{Operational Latency} = \frac{\text{Time for Inference}}{\text{Dataset Loader Iteration}} \qquad (4)$$

This equation emphasizes the interdependence between the time taken for model inference and the iterations dictated by the dataset loader.

Table 1. Resource utilization summary

VC1902 Versal			
Resource	Utilization	Available	% Utilization
LUT	900	899,840	0.10%
FF	100	75,000	0.13%
BRAM	0	1,000	0%
IO	86	770	11.17%
AI Engine	0	400	0%
DSP	0	1,968	0%

Our FPGA implementation's efficiency can be further understood through the resource utilization summary provided in Table 1. The low percentages in the utilization column indicate efficient use of resources. However, there remains an opportunity to further leverage these resources for complex tasks or to enhance performance.

5   Results

Table 2 covers metrics such as manufacturing technology, operating frequency, and power consumption. Notably, the parallel execution of GPUs and FPGAs often surpasses CPUs in efficiency, even at lower frequencies. This is demonstrated by the Xilinx FPGA's 4.6 ms latency and its mere 2 W consumption. Emphasizing energy efficiency, the table indicates FPGA's throughput of 58.5

Table 2. Comparison between CPU, GPU, and FPGA

	i9 12900H	RTX 3060	VCK190
Vendor	Intel	NVIDIA	AMD-Xilinx
Tech (nm)	10	8	7
Freq (MHz)	5200	1320	100
MACs (G)	0.269	0.269	0.269
Latency (ms)	84	11.6	4.6
Power (W)	27	68	2
Throughput (GOP/s)	3.2	24.5	58.5
Efficiency (GOP/s/W)	0.11	0.36	29.2

GOP/s and an energy efficiency of 29.2 GOP/s/W, accentuating FPGAs' proficiency for energy-sensitive applications. This underscores the unique attributes
and potential applications of each technology. In Table 3, our FPGA-based astrocyte modeling on the advanced Xilinx VCK-190 chip is compared with prior
works such as [6,7], and [5]. Operating at a standard 100 MHz, our model encompasses 680 neurons and 69,888 synapses, outstripping other models in complexity.
Correspondingly, our model demonstrates robustness with a fault tolerance rate
of 9.96%, on par with [5], and a resilience improvement of 63.11%. Despite a
2W power demand, higher than certain FPGA models, our implementation's
extensive neuronal and synaptic counts justify this. This consumption reflects
our model's commendable energy efficiency amidst heightened complexity.

Table 3. Comparisons with previous implementations.

	[17]	[7]	[6]	[5]	Our
Platform	CPU	FPGA Virtex-5	FPGA Artix-7	FPGA VCU-128	**FPGA VCK-190**
Clock	3.1 GHz	100 MHz	100 MHz	100 MHz	**100 MHz**
Neurons	2	14	–	336	**680**
Synapses	1	100	–	17,408	**69,888**
Fault Tolerance Rate	30%	30%	–	39%	**8.96%**
Resilience Improvement	12.5%	70%	80%	51.6%	**63.11%**
Power	–	1.37 W	0.33 W	0.538 W	**2 W**

6 Conclusions

This work has presented a novel astrocyte-augmented spiking neural network
model implemented on CPU/GPU and FPGA platforms. The inclusion of astrocytes has shown significant improvements in the network's fault tolerance,

demonstrating the potential benefits of astrocyte integration in artificial neural networks. Additionally, the use of FPGA hardware for this model leverages the advantages of parallel computation and on-the-fly hardware reconfiguration offered by DFX technology. The comparison with different computational architectures and previous works highlighted the strengths of our approach in terms of computational efficiency and network robustness. Future research in this direction could yield more sophisticated and efficient neuromorphic systems, thus paving the way for advanced applications in diverse areas such as robotics, bioinformatics, and cognitive computing.

References

1. Covelo, A., Araque, A.: Lateral regulation of synaptic transmission by astrocytes. Neuroscience **323**, 62–66 (2016)
2. Haghiri, S., Ahmadi, A.: Digital FPGA implementation of spontaneous astrocyte signalling. Int. J. Circuit Theory Appl. **48**(5), 709–723 (2020)
3. Inadagbo, K., Arig, B., Alici, N., Isik, M.: Exploiting FPGA capabilities for accelerated biomedical computing. arXiv preprint arXiv:2307.07914 (2023)
4. Isik, M., Oldland, M., Zhou, L.: An energy-efficient reconfigurable autoencoder implementation on FPGA. arXiv preprint arXiv:2301.07050 (2023)
5. Isik, M., Paul, A., Varshika, M.L., Das, A.: A design methodology for fault-tolerant computing using astrocyte neural networks. In: Proceedings of the 19th ACM International Conference on Computing Frontiers, pp. 169–172 (2022)
6. Johnson, A.P., et al.: An FPGA-based hardware-efficient fault-tolerant astrocyte-neuron network. In: 2016 IEEE Symposium Series on Computational Intelligence (SSCI), pp. 1–8. IEEE (2016)
7. Johnson, A.P., et al.: Homeostatic fault tolerance in spiking neural networks utilizing dynamic partial reconfiguration of FPGAs. In: 2017 International Conference on Field Programmable Technology (ICFPT), pp. 195–198. IEEE (2017)
8. Karim, S., et al.: Assessing self-repair on FPGAs with biologically realistic astrocyte-neuron networks. In: 2017 IEEE Computer Society Annual Symposium on VLSI (ISVLSI), pp. 421–426. IEEE (2017)
9. Kumar, S.R., Singhal, S.: Implementation of neuron astrocyte interaction dynamics. In: 2023 IEEE 8th International Conference for Convergence in Technology (I2CT), pp. 1–6. IEEE (2023)
10. Mueggler, E., Rebecq, H., Gallego, G., Delbruck, T., Scaramuzza, D.: The event-camera dataset and simulator: Event-based data for pose estimation, visual odometry, and slam. Int. J. Robot. Res. **36**(2), 142–149 (2017)
11. Pfeiffer, M., Pfeil, T.: Deep learning with spiking neurons: opportunities and challenges. Front. Neurosci. **12**, 774 (2018)
12. PyTorch-OpCounter. https://pypi.org/project/thop/. Accessed 26 Aug 2023
13. Santello, M., Toni, N., Volterra, A.: Astrocyte function from information processing to cognition and cognitive impairment. Nat. Neurosci. **22**(2), 154–166 (2019)
14. Tavanaei, A., Ghodrati, M., Kheradpisheh, S.R., Masquelier, T., Maida, A.: Deep learning in spiking neural networks. Neural Netw. **111**, 47–63 (2019)
15. Venkataramani, S., et al.: Rapid: AI accelerator for ultra-low precision training and inference. In: 2021 ACM/IEEE 48th Annual International Symposium on Computer Architecture (ISCA), pp. 153–166. IEEE (2021)

16. Volterra, A., Meldolesi, J.: Astrocytes, from brain glue to communication elements: the revolution continues. Nat. Rev. Neurosci. **6**(8), 626–640 (2005)
17. Wei, X., Li, C., Lu, M., Yi, G., Wang, J.: A novel astrocyte-mediated self-repairing CPG neural network. In: 2019 Chinese Control Conference (CCC), pp. 4872–4877. IEEE (2019)
18. Zhang, S., Ji, W., Li, X., Huang, K., Yin, R.: Precise failure location and protection mechanism in long-reach passive optical network. J. Lightwave Technol. **34**(22), 5175–5182 (2016)

Correct Orchestration of Federated Learning Generic Algorithms: Formalisation and Verification in CSP

Ivan Prokić[1]([⊠])[iD], Silvia Ghilezan[1,3][iD], Simona Kašterović[1][iD], Miroslav Popovic[1][iD], Marko Popovic[2][iD], and Ivan Kaštelan[1][iD]

[1] Faculty of Technical Sciences, University of Novi Sad, Novi Sad, Serbia
{prokic,gsilvia,simona.k,ivan.kastelan}@uns.ac.rs,
miroslav.popovic@rt-rk.uns.ac.rs
[2] RT-RK Institute for Computer Based Systems, Novi Sad, Serbia
Marko.Popovic@rt-rk.com
[3] Mathematical Institute of the Serbian Academy of Sciences and Arts,
Belgrade, Serbia
http://www.ftn.uns.ac.rs/, http://www.mi.sanu.ac.rs/

Abstract. Federated learning (FL) is a machine learning setting where clients keep the training data decentralised and collaboratively train a model either under the coordination of a central server (centralised FL) or in a peer-to-peer network (decentralised FL). Correct orchestration is one of the main challenges. In this paper, we formally verify the correctness of two generic FL algorithms, a centralised and a decentralised one, using the Communicating Sequential Processes calculus (CSP) and the Process Analysis Toolkit (PAT) model checker. The CSP models consist of CSP processes corresponding to generic FL algorithm instances. PAT automatically proves the correctness of the two generic FL algorithms by proving their deadlock freeness (safety property) and successful termination (liveness property). The CSP models are constructed bottom-up by hand as a faithful representation of the real Python code and is automatically checked top-down by PAT.

Keywords: Decentralised intelligence · Federated learning · Python · Formal verification · CSP process calculus

1 Introduction

Originally, *federated learning* (FL) was introduced by McMahan et al. [13] as a decentralised approach to model learning that leaves the training data distributed on the mobile devices and learns a shared model by aggregating locally computed updates. Besides preserving local data privacy, FL is robust to the unbalanced and non-independent and identically distributed (non-IID) data distributions, and it reduces required communication rounds by 10–100x as compared to the synchronized stochastic gradient descent algorithm. Inspired by [13],

J. Kofroň et al. (Eds.): ECBS 2023, LNCS 14390, pp. 274–288, 2024.
https://doi.org/10.1007/978-3-031-49252-5_25

Bonawitz et al. [4] introduced an efficient secure aggregation protocol for federated learning, and Konecny et al. [10] presented algorithms for further decreasing communication costs. More recently, Bonawitz et al. [5] and Perino et al. [15] focused on data privacy.

Nowadays, there are many FL frameworks. The most prominent TensorFlow Federated (TFF) [12,23] and BlueFog [24,25] are well supported and accepted and they work well in cloud-edge continuum. However, they are not deployable to edge only, they are not supported on OS Windows, and they have numerous dependencies that make their installation far from trivial.

Recently, in 2021, Kholod et al. [9] made a comparative review and analysis of open-source FL frameworks for IoT, covering TensorFlow Federated (TFF) from Google Inc [23], Federated AI Technology Enabler (FATE) from Webank's AI department [2], Paddle Federated Learning (PFL) from Baidu [3], PySyft from the open community OpenMined [1], and Federated Learning and Differential Privacy (FL&DP) framework from Sherpa.AI [18]. They found out that application of these frameworks in the IoTs environment is almost impossible. So, developing a FL framework targeting smart IoTs in edge systems is still an open challenge.

More recently, in 2023, Popovic et al. proposed their solution to that challenge called Python Testbed for Federated Learning Algorithms (PTB-FLA) [16]. PTB-FLA was developed with the primary intention to be used as a FL framework for developing federated learning algorithms (FLAs), or more precisely as a runtime environment for FLAs. The word "testbed" in the name PTB-FLA that might be misleading was selected by ML & AI developers in TaRDIS project [22] because they see PTB-FLA as an "algorithmic" testbed where they can plugin and test their FLAs. Note that PTB-FLA is neither a system testbed, such as the one that was used for testing the system based on PySyft in [19], nor a complete system such as CoLearn [6] and FedIoT [26] (for more elaborated comparison with CoLearn and FedIoT see Sect. I.A in [16]).

PTB-FLA is written in pure Python to keep the application footprint small so to fit to IoTs, and to keep installation as simple as possible (with no external dependencies). PTB-FLA supports both centralised and decentralised FLAs. The former is as defined in [13], whereas the latter are generalized such that each process (or node) alternatively takes server and client roles from [13] or more precisely, it switches roles from server to client and back to server.

PTB-FLA enforces a restricted programming model, where a developer writes a single application program, which is later instantiated and launched by the PTB-FLA launcher as a set of independent processes, and within their application program, a developer only writes callback functions for the client and the server roles, which are then called by the generic federated learning algorithms hidden inside PTB-FLA.

So far, PTB-FLA usage has been illustrated and validated by three simple examples in [16], but PTB-FLA has not been formally verified. In this paper, we formally verify the correctness of two generic FL algorithms, a centralised and a decentralised one, using the Communicating Sequential Processes calculus (CSP)

[7] and the Process Analysis Toolkit (PAT) [21] model checker, in a process with two phases.

In the first phase, we construct by hand CSP models of the generic centralised and decentralised FLAs as faithful representations of the real Python code. We construct these models in a bottom-up fashion in two steps. In the first step, we construct processes corresponding to generic FL algorithm instances, and in the second step, we construct the system model as an asynchronous interleaving of n FL algorithm instances.

In the second phase, we formally verify CSP models constructed in the previous phase in two steps. In the first step, we formulate desired system properties, namely deadlock freeness (safety property) and successful FLA termination (liveness property). We formulate the latter property in two equivalent forms (reachability statement and always-eventually LTL formula). In the second step, we use PAT to automatically prove formulated verification statements.

The main contributions of this paper are: (i) the CSP models of the generic centralised and decentralised FLAs, (ii) the formulations of generic centralised and decentralised FLAs properties. To the best of our knowledge, this is the first paper that formally verifies decentralised FLAs.

The rest of the paper is organized as follows. Section 1.1 presents closely related work. Section 2 presents the PTB-FLA overview, Sect. 3 presents PTB-FLA formalization, Sect. 4 presents PTB-FLA verification, and Sect. 5 concludes the paper.

1.1 Short Discussion of Closely Related Work

While tools for decentralised ML (DML), especially FL, are starting to flourish, many are not flexible and portable enough to experiment with novel processors, not fully connected network topologies, and asynchronous schemes. To overcome these limitations, Mittone et al. use the formal language RISC-pb2l to describe distributed FL workloads and to map them to the FastFlow parallel programming library [14]. We consider this approach as orthogonal to our work because it targets parallel and distributed processing composition and optimization whereas our work targets formal verification of system correctness, i.e. proving desired system properties.

Multiparty Asynchronous Session Types (MPST) is a class of behavioural types tailored for describing distributed protocols relying on asynchronous communications. Hu and Yoshida extended MPST in [8] with explicit connection actions to support protocols with optional and dynamic participants. Although these extended MPST enabled modelling and verification of some protocols in cloud-edge continuum [20], we could not use them to model the generic centralised and decentralised FLAs, because we could not express arbitrary order of message arrivals that take place at an FLA instance.

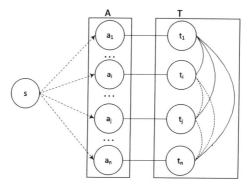

Fig. 1. Block diagram of the PTB-FLA system architecture. (The figure is an adaptation of a figure from [17]).

The design of robust protocols for coordination of peer-to-peer systems is difficult because it is hard to specify and reason about their global behaviour. Recently, Kuhn et al. presented an approach in [11] where a so-called swarm protocol is a global system specification, whereas swarm protocol projections to machines are local specifications of peers. They claim that swarms are deadlock free, but liveness is not guaranteed in their theory. We find this approach interesting and in our future work we plan to investigate whether it would be feasible for our generic FLAs. At present, we identify some of the differentiating points between [11] and our work: (*i*) in their approach communication of peers is conducted through a shared log instead of point-to-point message passing; (*ii*) they model peers using finite state automata, while we use (CSP) processes; (*iii*) they model protocols in the style of MPST via top-down approach (projecting global type onto peers to obtain local type specification) while we only write local processes specifications, that we ensemble together to obtain global protocol behaviour; (*iv*) they use TypeScript language and develop tools to check protocol conformance at runtime through equivalence testing, whereas our protocols are written in Python language, modeled in CSP, and we use PAT to prove deadlock freeness and liveness.

2   Generic Federated Learning Algorithms: PTB-FLA Overview

This section presents the PTB-FLA overview. The term *PTB-FLA system* refers to a system based on PTB-FLA. The next three subsections present the PTB-FLA system architecture, the PTB-FLA API, and the PTB-FLA system operation, respectively.

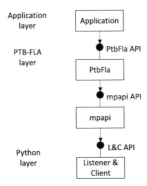

Fig. 2. UML class diagram of the PTB-FLA system architecture. (The figure is an adaptation of a figure from [17]).

2.1 PTB-FLA System Architecture

The PTB-FLA system architecture is composed of the application launcher process s, the distributed application $A = \{a_1, a_2, \ldots, a_n\}$, and the distributed testbed $T = \{t_1, t_2, \ldots, t_n\}$, see Fig. 1, where a_i is an application program instance, t_i is a testbed instance, and n is the number of instances in both A and T. The distributed application A uses the distributed testbed T to execute the distributed algorithm, which is specified by the callback functions within the application program. PTB-FLA supports both centralised and decentralised federated learning algorithms by providing the API functions that implement the generic centralised algorithm and the generic decentralised algorithm, named fl_centralised and fl_decentralised, respectively.

A particular distributed federated learning algorithm is executed as follows. Each instance a_i prepares its input data based on the command line arguments (including the identification i, the number of instances n, etc.) and then calls the desired generic API function on its testbed instance t_i.

The testbed instance t_i in turn plays its role in the generic algorithm by exchanging messages with other testbed instances and by calling the associated callback function at the right point of the generic algorithm. The communication graph of testbed instances either takes the form of a star in case of a centralised algorithm (see solid edges connecting the server t_1 and the clients t_2 to t_n in Fig. 1), or the form of a clique in the case of a decentralised algorithm (see solid and dashed edges connecting all the testbed instances in Fig. 1).

Figure 2 shows the simplified UML class diagram of a PTB-FLA system. The PTB-FLA system architecture comprises three layers: the distributed application layer, the PTB-FLA layer (comprising the class PtbFla in the module ptbfla and the module mpapi) in the middle, and the Python layer at the bottom. The application module uses the PtbFla to create or destroy a testbed instance and to conduct its role in the distributed algorithm execution by calling the API function fl_centralised or the API function fl_decentralised.

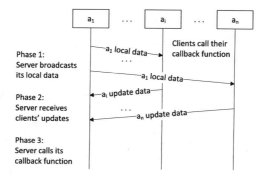

Fig. 3. The generic centralised one-shot FLA execution.

The API functions fl_centralised and fl_decentralised, within an instance t_i, use the module mpapi (mpapi is the abbreviation of the term *message passing API*) to communicate with other instances. The module mpapi in turn instantiates the Python multiprocessing classes Listener and Client to create the mpapi server and the mpapi client, which are hidden with the module mpapi and provide reliable TCP connections among testbed instances.

2.2 PtbFla API

There are many PTB-FLA APIs, and one of them is Ptb-Fla API. This is the only API intended for external usage. The PtbFla API offers the constructor, two generic FLAs, and the destructor:

- PtbFla($noNodes, nodeId, flSrvId = 0$)
- ret fl_centralised($sfun, cfun, ldata, pdata, noIters = 1$)
- ret fl_decentralised($sfun, cfun, ldata, pdata, noIters = 1$)
- PtbFla()

The arguments are as follows: $noNodes$ is the number of nodes (or processes), $nodeId$ is the node identification, $flSrvId$ is the server id (default is 0; this argument is used by the function fl_centralised), $sfun$ is the server callback function, $cfun$ is the client callback function, $ldata$ is the initial local data, $pdata$ is the private data, and $noIters$ is the number of iterations that is by default equal to 1 (for the so called one-shot algorithms), i.e. if the calling function does not specify it, it will be internally set to 1. The return value ret is the node final local data. Data ($ldata$ and $pdata$) is application specific.

Typically, $ldata$ is a machine learning model, whereas $pdata$ is a training data that is used to train the model. Normally, the testbed instances only exchange $ldata$ and they never send out $pdata$ (that is how they guarantee the training data privacy). The $pdata$ is only passed to callback functions within the same process instance to immediately set them in their working context.

2.3   PTB-FLA Operation

This subsection provides an overview of the PTB-FLA operation by presenting the two most important scenarios: the generic centralised and decentralised one-shot FLA executions, respectively.

The generic centralised one-shot FLA has three phases, see Fig. 3 (here a_1 is the server and a_i, $i = 2, \ldots, n$, are the clients). In the first phase, the server broadcasts its local data to the clients, which in their turn call their callback function to get the update data and store the update data locally. In the second phase, the server receives the update data from all the clients (in any order, caused by arbitrary delays), and in the third phase, the server calls its callback function to get its update data (i.e. aggregated data) and stores it locally. Finally, all the instances return their new local data as their results.

Unlike the generic centralised FLA that uses the single field messages carrying data, the generic decentralised FLA uses the three field messages carrying: the messages sequence number (i.e. the phase number), the message source address (i.e. the source instance network address), and the data (local or update).

The generic decentralised one-shot FLA has three phases, see Fig. 4. In the first phase, each instance acts as a server, and it sends its local data to all its neighbours. These messages have the sequence number 1, each instance sends $(n-1)$ such messages and is also the destination for $(n-1)$ such messages.

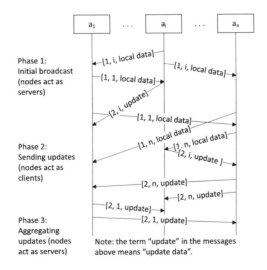

Fig. 4. The generic decentralised one-shot FLA execution.

In the second phase, each instance acts as a client, and it may receive either a message with the sequence numbers 1 or 2. In the latter case, it just stores it in a buffer for later processing in the third phase, whereas in the former case, it calls the client callback and sends the update data in the reply to the message source. Note that during the second phase, the instance does not update its local data, it just passes the update data it got from the client callback function.

Since messages are sent asynchronously, they may be received in any order. Figure 4 shows a scenario where the instance a_1 receives the messages in the messages sequence 1–2–1–2, which is out of the phase order, whereas the instances a_i and a_n receive the messages in the sequence 1–1–2–2, which is in the phase order. However, by using the abovementioned buffering, the instance a_1 postpones processing of the phase 2 messages until the third phase.

The second phase is completed after the instance received and processed all $2(n-1)$ message. In the third phase, each instance again acts as a server, and it calls the server callback function to get its update data (e.g., aggregated data) and stores it locally. Finally, all the instances return their new local data as their results.

3   CSP Formal Models

In this section we use the Communicating Sequential Processes calculus (CSP) [7] to obtain a formal specification of the communication layer of our PTB-FLAs. The CSP provides modeling of the concurrency primitives as follows:

- the system components are CSP *processes*;
- communication between the system components is performed through the *communication channels*;
- the system of parallel processes communicating asynchronously (i.e. without barrier synchronization) is assembled via *interleaving* of the CSP processes.

The rest of the section is organized as follows: Sect. 3.1 presents the model for our centralised algorithm and Sect. 3.2 presents the model for the decentralised algorithm.

3.1   Modeling Centralised Algorithm

Figure 5 shows a CSP model for our centralised algorithm. Lines 2–3 define number of nodes (NoNodes) (indexed with $0, 1, 2, \ldots$) with the server (FlSrvId) having the largest index, and other nodes being clients. We remark we could set here the index of the server node with the smallest index (as it is in Sect. 2.3), but this would in fact make our model less intuitive because of the channel manipulation (as explained bellow). Lines 4–5 define arrays of local data ldata and private data pdata—one per each node. The communication channels are defined in lines 8–9. The array of channels server2client - one per each client (hence, NoNodes−1 channels) are used for the server broadcast of their local data to the clients (one channel per client). Notice that the indexes of array elements are generated starting with 0, hence the channel index indicates the index of the client node. Since we consider one-shot algorithm the server sends their local data only once, hence the channels are specified to have FIFO buffers of size 1. Channel clients2server is used in the second phase of our algorithm, i.e.

```
1   // PTB-FLA
2   enum {False, True};
3   #define NoNodes 3;
4   #define FlSrvId 2;
5   var ldataArr[NoNodes];
6   var pdataArr[NoNodes];
7   var terminated;
8   channel server2client[NoNodes-1] 1;
9   channel clients2server NoNodes-1;
10
11  FlCentralised(noNodes, nodeId, flSrvId, ldata, pdata) =
12    if(nodeId == FlSrvId) {
13      CeServer(noNodes, nodeId, flSrvId, ldata, pdata)
14    } else {
15      CeClient(noNodes, nodeId, flSrvId, ldata, pdata)
16    };
17
18  CeServer(noNodes, nodeId, flSrvId, ldata, pdata) =
19    {terminated = False} ->
20    CeBroadcastMsg(0, noNodes, nodeId, ldata);
21    CeRcvMsgs(0, noNodes-1);
22    {terminated = True} -> Skip;
23
24  CeBroadcastMsg(id, noNodes, nodeId, ldata) =
25    if(id != nodeId) {
26      server2client[id]!ldata -> Skip
27    };
28    if(id < noNodes-1) {
29      CeBroadcastMsg(id+1, noNodes, nodeId, ldata)
30    };
31
32  CeRcvMsgs(i, noMsgs) =
33    if(i < noMsgs) {
34      clients2server?update -> CeRcvMsgs(i+1, noMsgs)
35    };
36
37  CeClient(noNodes, nodeId, flSrvId, ldata, pdata) =
38    server2client[nodeId]?srvLdata ->
39    clients2server!ldata+srvLdata ->
40    Skip;
41
42  SysCentralised() =
43    |||nodeId:{0..NoNodes-1}
44    @FlCentralised(NoNodes,
45                   nodeId,
46                   FlSrvId,
47                   ldataArr[nodeId],
48                   pdataArr[nodeId]);
```

Fig. 5. CSP model for centralised algorithm.

for clients replying to the server with the update data. The FIFO size of this channel is NoNodes−1, since all clients reply with a single update.

Lines 11–16 define a generic node as a CSP process with parameters of the number of nodes, identification of the node, index of the server, their local and private data. We remark that parameters $sfun, cfun$, and $noIters$, also present in fl_centralised (cf. Sect. 2.2), were considered out of the scope for this model. Based on the node index the process proceeds as the server node CeServer or as one of the client nodes CeClient.

The server node is modeled in lines 18–22. The process first sets its state to not terminated and then performs the broadcasting of the local data via CeBroadcastMsg (i.e. it enters the phase 1, cf. Fig. 3), then proceeds to phase 2 by receiving updates via CeRcvMsgs. The successful termination is modeled with Skip. The broadcasting of server's local data CeBroadcastMsg is defined in lines 24–30. The server sends ldata on channels server2clients[id] (if id is not their own index), and then recursively calls itself with index increased by 1 — if the index is less then noNodes−1. Since CeServer passes id to CeBroadcastMsg to be 0, the server will send the local data to all the clients exactly once. Once the broadcast is done, the server starts receiving clients' updates on channel clients2server as defined with CeRcvMsgs in lines 32–35.

The client process is defined with CeClient in lines 37–40. The client with index nodeId first receives server's local data on channel server2client [nodeId], and then replies updated server's local data with its own local data (here for simplicity modeled with addition) on channel clients2server, after which client process successfully terminates.

The system consisting of NoNodes−1 clients and a single server is then modeled as the interleaving of the FlCentralised processes (lines 42–48), since all processes but one indexed FlSrvId are instantiated as clients (and the one indexed FlSrvId is instantiated as a server).

3.2 Modeling Decentralised Algorithm

The CSP model for our decentralised algorithm is given in Fig. 6. Albeit more complex than the centralised one, the decentralised algorithm yields a slightly simpler CSP model. The reason is that all nodes in the system have the same behaviour. In phase 1 all nodes behave as servers broadcasting their local data to all other nodes, which in turn update the data and return an answer in phase 2 (corresponding to phases given in Fig. 4 in Sect. 2.3). All the nodes receive messages from all other nodes as they arrive, but first process the messages from phase 1 and only then deals with the messages from the phase 2. We model this behaviour with assigning two channels to each process (i.e. node). One channel is for receiving messages from other processes, called tonode, with buffer of size 2*(NoNodes-1) (line 7), since the node will receive messages from all other nodes from both phases. The other channel assigned to node, called buffer (line 8), serves only for storing messages from the second phase while all messages from the first phase are processed - later in phase 3 the same node will read those messages. Hence, the buffer size of these channels are NoNodes-1.

```
1   // PTB-FLA
2   enum {False, True};
3   #define NoNodes 3;
4   var ldataArr[NoNodes];
5   var pdataArr[NoNodes];
6   var terminated;
7   channel tonode[NoNodes] 2*(NoNodes-1);
8   channel buffer[NoNodes] NoNodes-1;
9
10  FlDecentralised(noNodes, nodeId, ldata, pdata) =
11    {terminated = False} ->
12    DeBroadcastMsg(0, noNodes, nodeId, ldata);
13    DeRcvMsgs(0, noNodes, nodeId, ldata);
14    DeRcvMsgs2(0, noNodes, nodeId);
15    {terminated = True} -> Skip;
16
17  DeBroadcastMsg(id, noNodes, nodeId, ldata) =
18    if(id != nodeId) {
19      tonode[id]!1.nodeId.ldata -> Skip
20    };
21    if(id < noNodes-1) {
22      DeBroadcastMsg(id+1, noNodes, nodeId, ldata)
23    };
24
25  DeRcvMsgs(i, noNodes, nodeId, ldata) =
26    if(i < 2*noNodes-2) {
27      tonode[nodeId]?phase.from.nodeldata ->
28      if(phase == 1){
29      tonode[from]!2.nodeId.ldata+nodeldata ->
30      DeRcvMsgs(i+1, noNodes, nodeId, ldata)
31      } else {
32      buffer[nodeId]!phase.from.nodeldata ->
33      DeRcvMsgs(i+1, noNodes, nodeId, ldata)
34      }
35    };
36
37  DeRcvMsgs2(i, noNodes, nodeId) =
38    if(i < noNodes-1) {
39      buffer[nodeId]?phase.from.update ->
40      DeRcvMsgs2(i+1, noNodes-1, nodeId)
41    };
42
43  SysDecentralised() =
44    |||nodeId:{0..NoNodes-1}
45    @FlDecentralised(NoNodes,
46                     nodeId,
47                     ldataArr[nodeId],
48                     pdataArr[nodeId]);
```

Fig. 6. CSP model for decentralised algorithm.

```
1  // ...
2  // CSP model for centralised algorithm
3  // ...
4
5  #assert SysCentralised() deadlockfree;
6  #define Terminated (terminated == True);
7  #assert SysCentralised() reaches Terminated;
8  #assert SysCentralised() |= []<> Terminated;
```

Fig. 7. Verifying centralised algorithm.

The node processes are defined with `FlDecentralised` in lines 10–15. Process first broadcasts their local data with `DeBroadcastMsg` (defined in lines 17–23) — which behaves in the same way as `CeBroadcastMsg` in the centralised algorithm (cf. Fig. 5), except that the sent messages now contain not only field for local data of the node, but also fields marking the phase (here 1) and the node's index (that the receiving node uses for the reply in phase 2). The node then proceeds with receiving messages from all other nodes with `DeRcvMsgs`, and finally (phase 3) process the messages from the second phase with `DeRcvMsgs2`.

`DeRcvMsgs` is given in lines 25–35. Here we deviate from the centralised algorithm: node receives all messages from both phases from the other nodes and then performs an analysis on the phase of the received message. If the phase is 1, the node replies updated data to `from` they received message in the first place, marking the phase of the message 2. If, on the other hand, the phase is 2, the node stores the message to their own channel `buffer[nodeId]`. Once the node process all messages from phase 1 (and buffers all messages from phase 2), `DeRcvMsgs2` (lines 37–41) is used to read from the `buffer[nodeId]`, which behaves in the same way as `CeRvcMsgs` from the centralised algorithm (cf. Fig. 5).

The system of `NoNodes` nodes is finally modeled as the interleaving of the `FlDecentralised` processes in lines 43–48.

4 Formal Verification in PAT

The correctness of our CSP models is automatically checked by Process Analysis Toolkit (PAT) [21], that supports the system analysis in two ways: simulation and model checker. We have used the latter one.

The correctness of our centralised and decetralised algorithms is verified by proving the deadlock freeness (safety property) and successful termination (liveness property). The properties about algorithms are stated in the form of queries, called *assertions*, which are checked by PAT. The assertions that formally verify the correctness of our centralised algorithm are shown in Fig. 7.

The assertion given in line 5 of Fig. 7 claims that the centralised algorithm is deadlock free. PAT model checker performs Depth-First-Search or Breath-First-Search algorithm to check if the assertion is true. It explores unvisited states

```
1  // ...
2  // CSP model for decentralised algorithm
3  // ...
4
5  #assert SysDecentralised() deadlockfree;
6  #define Terminated (terminated == True);
7  #assert SysDecentralised() reaches Terminated;
8  #assert SysDecentralised() |= []<> Terminated;
```

Fig. 8. Verifying decentralised algorithm.

until a non-terminated state with no further move—called a *deadlock state*, is found or all states have been visited.

The assertion given in line 7 of Fig. 7 claims that the centralised algorithm reaches a terminated state. This assertion is checked by performing Depth-First-Search algorithm. PAT model checker repeatedly explores all unvisited states until it finds a state at which the condition `Terminated` is satisfied or it visits all the states. The condition `Terminated` is a proposition defined as a global definition (line 6 in Fig. 7).

PAT supports the full syntax of the linear temporal logic (LTL), which is used in the last assertion of Fig. 7 that claims our centralised algorithm satisfies formula `[]<> Terminated`. The modal operator `[]` reads as "always" and the operator `<>` reads as "eventually", so statement asserts our centralised algorithm always eventually reaches the terminated state.

The proof of correctness of our decentralised algorithm is given in Fig. 8, and follows the same explanations given for the centralised one.

5   Conclusion

In this paper, we formally verified the correctness of two generic FL algorithms, a centralised and a decentralised one, using the CSP process calculus and the PAT model checker. The CSP models are constructed bottom-up by hand as a faithful representation of the real Python code and their correctness (safety and liveness) are automatically checked top-down by PAT.

The main contributions of this paper are:

– the CSP models of the generic centralised and decentralised FLAs,
– the formulations of generic centralised and decentralised FLAs properties. To the best of our knowledge, this is the first paper that formally verifies decentralised FLAs.

The main limitations of this paper are:

– we implicitly assumed that callback functions are terminating (i.e., have termination property),

- we did not model any ML&AI processing within the callback functions and therefore were unable to address the properties of the corresponding information flows and output results, such as privacy of information flows, understandability/interpretability of the resulting models, etc.

In our future work, we may try to address some of the latter limitations mentioned above.

Acknowledgements. ▇ Funded by the European Union (TaRDIS, 101093006). Views and opinions expressed are however those of the author(s) only and do not necessarily reflect those of the European Union. Neither the European Union nor the granting authority can be held responsible for them.

References

1. A world where every good question is answered. https://www.openmined.org. Accessed 15 Mar 2023
2. An industrial grade federated learning framework. https://fate.fedai.org/. Accessed 15 Mar 2023
3. An open-source deep learning platform originated from industrial practice. https://www.paddlepaddle.org.cn/en. Accessed 15 Mar 2023
4. Bonawitz, K.A., et al.: Practical secure aggregation for privacy-preserving machine learning. In: Thuraisingham, B., Evans, D., Malkin, T., Xu, D. (eds.) Proceedings of the 2017 ACM SIGSAC Conference on Computer and Communications Security, CCS 2017, Dallas, TX, USA, 30 October–3 November 2017, pp. 1175–1191. ACM (2017). https://doi.org/10.1145/3133956.3133982
5. Bonawitz, K.A., Kairouz, P., McMahan, B., Ramage, D.: Federated learning and privacy. Commun. ACM **65**(4), 90–97 (2022). https://doi.org/10.1145/3500240
6. Feraudo, A., et al.: CoLearn: Enabling federated learning in MUD-compliant IoT edge networks. In: Proceedings of the Third ACM International Workshop on Edge Systems, Analytics and Networking, pp. 25–30. EdgeSys 2020. Association for Computing Machinery, New York, NY, USA (2020). https://doi.org/10.1145/3378679.3394528
7. Hoare, C.A.R.: Communicating Sequential Processes. Prentice Hall, Englewood Cliffs (1985)
8. Hu, R., Yoshida, N.: Explicit connection actions in multiparty session types. In: Huisman, M., Rubin, J. (eds.) Fundamental Approaches to Software Engineering - 20th International Conference, FASE 2017, Held as Part of the European Joint Conferences on Theory and Practice of Software, ETAPS 2017, Uppsala, Sweden, 22–29 April 2017, Proceedings. LNCS, vol. 10202, pp. 116–133. Springer, Cham (2017). https://doi.org/10.1007/978-3-662-54494-5_7
9. Kholod, I., et al.: Open-source federated learning frameworks for IoT: A comparative review and analysis. Sensors **21**(1), 167 (2021)
10. Konečný, J., McMahan, H.B., Yu, F.X., Richtárik, P., Suresh, A.T., Bacon, D.: Federated learning: Strategies for improving communication efficiency (2017). http://arxiv.org/abs/1610.05492

11. Kuhn, R., Melgratti, H.C., Tuosto, E.: Behavioural types for local-first software. In: Ali, K., Salvaneschi, G. (eds.) 37th European Conference on Object-Oriented Programming, ECOOP 2023, 17–21 July 2023, Seattle, Washington, United States. LIPIcs, vol. 263, pp. 15:1–15:28. Schloss Dagstuhl - Leibniz-Zentrum für Informatik (2023). https://doi.org/10.4230/LIPIcs.ECOOP.2023.15

12. McMahan, B.: "Federated learning from research to practice", a presentation hosted by Carnegie Mellon University seminar series. https://www.pdl.cmu.edu/SDI/2019/slides/2019-09-05Federated. Accessed 15 Mar 2023

13. McMahan, B., Moore, E., Ramage, D., Hampson, S., y Arcas, B.A.: Communication-efficient learning of deep networks from decentralized data. In: Singh, A., Zhu, X.J. (eds.) Proceedings of the 20th International Conference on Artificial Intelligence and Statistics, AISTATS 2017, 20–22 April 2017, Fort Lauderdale, FL, USA. Proceedings of Machine Learning Research, vol. 54, pp. 1273–1282. PMLR (2017). http://proceedings.mlr.press/v54/mcmahan17a.html

14. Mittone, G., et al.: Experimenting with emerging RISC-V systems for decentralised machine learning (2023)

15. Perino, D., Katevas, K., Lutu, A., Marin, E., Kourtellis, N.: Privacy-preserving AI for future networks. Commun. ACM **65**(4), 52–53 (2022). https://doi.org/10.1145/3512343

16. Popovic, M., Popovic, M., Kastelan, I., Djukic, M., Ghilezan, S.: A simple Python testbed for federated learning algorithms. CoRR abs/2305.20027 (2023). https://doi.org/10.48550/arXiv.2305.20027

17. Popovic, M., Popovic, M., Kastelan, I., Djukic, M., Ghilezan, S.: A simple Python testbed for federated learning algorithms. In: 2023 Zooming Innovation in Consumer Technologies Conference (ZINC), pp. 148–153 (2023). https://doi.org/10.1109/ZINC58345.2023.10173859

18. Privacy-preserving artificial intelligence to advance humanity. https://sherpa.ai. Accessed 15 Mar 2023

19. Shen, C., Xue, W.: An experiment study on federated learning testbed. In: Zhang, Y.-D., Senjyu, T., So-In, C., Joshi, A. (eds.) Smart Trends in Computing and Communications. LNNS, vol. 286, pp. 209–217. Springer, Singapore (2022). https://doi.org/10.1007/978-981-16-4016-2_20

20. Simic, M., Prokic, I., Dedeic, J., Sladic, G., Milosavljevic, B.: Towards edge computing as a service: Dynamic formation of the micro data-centers. IEEE Access **9**, 114468–114484 (2021). https://doi.org/10.1109/ACCESS.2021.3104475

21. Sun, J., Liu, Y., Dong, J.S., Pang, J.: PAT: Towards flexible verification under fairness. In: Bouajjani, A., Maler, O. (eds.) CAV 2009. LNCS, vol. 5643, pp. 709–714. Springer, Heidelberg (2009). https://doi.org/10.1007/978-3-642-02658-4_59

22. TaRDIS: Trustworthy and resilient decentralised intelligence for edge systems. https://www.project-tardis.eu/

23. TensorFlow Federated: Machine learning on decentralized data. https://www.tensorflow.org/federated. Accessed 15 Mar 2023

24. Ying, B., Yuan, K., Chen, Y., Hu, H., Pan, P., Yin, W.: Exponential graph is provably efficient for decentralized deep training (2021)

25. Ying, B., Yuan, K., Hu, H., Chen, Y., Yin, W.: BlueFog: Make decentralized algorithms practical for optimization and deep learning. CoRR abs/2111.04287 (2021). https://arxiv.org/abs/2111.04287

26. Zhang, T., He, C., Ma, T., Gao, L., Ma, M., Avestimehr, S.: Federated learning for Internet of Things. In: Proceedings of the 19th ACM Conference on Embedded Networked Sensor Systems, SenSys 2021, pp. 413–419. Association for Computing Machinery, New York, NY, USA (2021). https://doi.org/10.1145/3485730.3493444

CareProfSys - Combining Machine Learning and Virtual Reality to Build an Attractive Job Recommender System for Youth: Technical Details and Experimental Data

Maria-Iuliana Dascalu[1]([⊠]), Andrei-Sergiu Bumbacea[1], Ioan-Alexandru Bratosin[1], Iulia-Cristina Stanica[1], and Constanta-Nicoleta Bodea[2,3]([⊠])

[1] National University of Science and Technology POLITEHNICA Bucharest, Splaiul Independenței 313, 060042 Bucharest, Romania
{maria.dascalu,iulia.stanica}@upb.ro
[2] Department of Economic Informatics and Cybernetics, Bucharest University of Economic Studies, Calea Dorobantilor 13-15, 010552 Bucharest, Romania
bodea@ase.ro
[3] "COSTIN C. KIRITESCU", National Institute for Economic Research, Romanian Academy, Calea 13 Septembrie 13, 050711 Bucharest, Romania

Abstract. The current article presents CareProfSys - an innovative job recommender system (RS) for youth, which integrates several emergent technologies, such as machine learning (ML) and virtual reality on web (WebVR). The recommended jobs are the ones provided by the well-known European Skills, Competences, Qualifications, and Occupations (ESCO) framework. The machine-learning based recommendation mechanism uses a K-Nearest Neighbors (KNN) algorithm: the data needed to train the machine learning model was based on the Skills Occupation Matrix Table offered by ESCO, as well as on data collected by our project team. This two-source method made sure that the dataset was strong and varied, which made it easier for the model to make accurate recommendations. Each job was described in terms of the features needed by individuals to be good professionals, e.g., skill levels for working with computers, constructing, management, working with machinery and specialized equipment, for assisting and caring, for communication collaboration and creativity are just a few of the directions considered to define a profession profile. The recommended jobs are described in a modern manner, by allowing the users to explore various WebVR scenarios with specific professional activities. The article provides the technical details of the system, the difficulties of building a stack of such diverse technologies (ML, WebVR, semantic technologies), as well as validation data from experiments with real users: a group of high school students from not so developed cities from Romania, interacting first time with modern technologies.

Keywords: Recommender System · Machine Learning · Virtual Reality on Web

1 Introduction

Career coaching is essential for preparing young individuals with the information and skills required to navigate a job market that is complicated and constantly evolving. Also, insufficient career advising resources in developing countries, such as Romania, have made the transition from education to job difficult for them. There are certain challenges encountered by young adults in developing countries that require our attention and discussion. Young adults in Romania, particularly those living in rural regions, have limited access to career counseling facilities. This lack of accessibility hinders their chances for long-term success in the job market by preventing them from making educated decisions on their education and future pathways [1]. At the same time, the job search process may be time-consuming, inefficient, and irritating for both job seekers and employers. To solve these difficulties, researchers have started creating RSs that employ deep reinforcement learning for online advertising. These systems strive to enhance the entire job search process by giving tailored job recommendations based on an individual's likes and talents.

This article presents a RS (RS) to enhance the efficacy and efficiency of job choosing for young individuals: the recommendations are made using a machine-learning (ML) technique and the provided results do not contain only a text-based description of a job, but a gamified virtual reality (VR) scenario of activities specific to that job, thus allowing the young users to better understand whether that job is suitable or not for them. To implement ML, accurate data about the features of practitioners of a certain job is needed. We used the Skills Occupation Matrix Table offered by European Skills, Competences, Qualifications, and Occupations (ESCO) framework [2], but also data provided by Romanian practitioners, thus we claim that the recommendations are useful in developing countries, such as Romania, but also aligned with the European landscape. Experimental data was collected from 27 technological high school students from Romania, participants at a summer school at National University of Science and Technology POLITEHNICA Bucharest. The young students, aged between 16 and 18 years old, decided to follow engineering, but were still undecided what engineering specialization to choose. Thus, they found the recommendations made by our system to be enlightening. Our article presents the ML-based recommendation technique, in the context of other RSs and underlines the efficiency of embedding WebVR in a career guidance system.

2   Job Recommender Systems

2.1   Recommender Systems: Usage and Typologies

A RS offers consumers customized on-line service or product tips to combat the expanding trouble of online information overload as well as to boost consumer connection monitoring. There are three main types of RSs: content-based, collaborative filtering, and hybrid ones. The purpose of content-based filtering systems is to recommend items based on the collected knowledge of users. This approach concentrates on matching individual interests with item attributes, so it is essential that the system includes one of the most essential item features. Concern number one prior to creating a system must be to determine each user's recommended features. This can be completed through a combination of the two strategies. Users are initially provided with a checklist of functions from which they can select those that most ignite their passion. Second, the recommendation algorithms keep a document of all items formerly chosen by the user, which acts as the premise for the customer's behavioral data. The customer's account is based on their preferences, inclinations, as well as options, which inevitably affect their rankings [3].

Collaborative filtering recommenders (CF RSs) require a set of things based on the individual's previous choices. Each object and user are described by an embedding or attribute vector, which places both the objects and the individuals in a similar embedding location. When suggesting a certain product to the primary user, the viewpoints of other customers are taken into consideration. It keeps an eye on the activities of all users to identify which item is the most popular. When suggesting an item to the main customer, it likewise relates comparable individuals based on their shared preferences and behavior toward a comparable product [3]. There are two types of collaborative filtering approaches. Memory-based Collaborative Filtering is an approach that determines the similarity between users or items by utilizing past user data, specifically rankings. The primary goal of this technique is to quantify the similarity between users or items, identify similar ratings, and recommend hidden items accordingly. Model-based approaches use ML models to predict and rank interactions between users and unengaged items. Using algorithms such as matrix factorization, deep learning, and clustering, etc., these models are trained utilizing the interaction information already available from the interaction matrix [4].

When making recommendations, a hybrid method mixes techniques from both collaborative and content-based filtering.

Understanding the differences between the types of RSs helps developers choose the best approach, as seen in Table 1.

Table 1. Criteria of choosing the RS type.

Criteria of choosing	Collaborative RSs	CB RSs	Hybrid RSs
Data used	User-item interaction data (e.g., clicks, purchases, ratings)	User-item interaction data (e.g., clicks, purchases, ratings)	Both user-item interaction data and item content data
User & Item cold start	Sensitive (new users & items have no interaction data)	Less sensitive (can use user preferences and item features to recommend new data)	Can handle cold start problems by leveraging content-based filtering component
Scalability	Can be computationally expensive for large user-item matrices	Can be computationally expensive for large user-item matrices	Depends on the specific combination of methods used
Diversity of provided recommendations	Can be high	Can be lower	Can be adjusted
Personalization	High	Moderate	Can be high if the combination of methods is optimized

CF RSs are used in music streaming, movies recommendation and e-commerce. CB RSs are also used in movies recommendations, but more in news articles' platforms and job portals, while hybrid RSs have a wide variety of exploitation cases.

2.2 Recommender Systems Used in Career Path Profiling and Jobs' Searching

In recent years, one may have witnessed a boom in the popularity of computer-based applications that assist individuals in the process of job searching. CareerExplorer by PathSource [5] uses ML algorithms to match users with careers based on their skills, interests, values, and work preferences. Users take an online assessment, and the platform generates personalized career suggestions along with relevant educational and job opportunities. The major limitation of the system is the fact that it depends on self-reported data, and the assessment process can be time-consuming. O*NET Interest Profiler [6] is a free tool that helps users identify their interests and match them to potential careers. Users answer questions related to their likes and dislikes, and the profiler suggests careers based on the user's interests. The system is limited to U.S. labor market data and may not be as engaging as other platforms. Pymetrics [7] uses neuroscience-based assessments, such as games and puzzles, to measure users' cognitive and emotional traits. The main drawbacks are: it is based on a relatively new and untested method, has a limited career database, and may not be suitable for all users due to the game-based assessment format. Jobscan [8] is primarily focused on optimizing resumes and LinkedIn profiles for specific job postings. However, it also offers a career path exploration feature by suggesting related job titles and industries based on the user's current resume or LinkedIn profile. Jobscan is limited in terms of career exploration, relies on existing resume or LinkedIn profile data, and may not cater to users seeking a significant career change. MyNextMove [9] allows users to search for careers based on keywords, browse careers by industry, or take an interest-based assessment (similar to O*NET Interest Profiler) to receive career suggestions. It is limited to U.S. labor market. Although all the systems have strengths and limitations, none is suitable for young people from European Union, especially from developing countries such as Romania. That is why CareProfSys, our recommended system, has a place in this plethora of career path guidance and job recommendation systems, by combining a ML hybrid recommender system with other emerging technology, very appealing to young people, VR on Web. VR technologies are increasingly used for developing professional capabilities, as required by jobs in different industries, e.g., in civil engineering [10], in medicine [11] or science [12].

3   CareProfSys: A Job Recommender System for Youth

Following registration and login, a user must answer a quiz about one's skills and then job recommendations are listed. After that, the user can access a WebVR scenario of basic activities typical for that job. By exploring this game-like scenario, the young user may better understand the details of a certain recommendation. Premium users have the possibility to browse the entire list of skills needed for a certain job, thus they can improve one's CV. In Fig. 1, snippets from CareProfSys system are provided: a list of recommended jobs and a scenario in VR for the profession of network specialist.

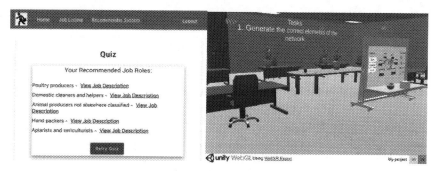

Fig. 1. Snippets from CareProfSys Recommender System.

3.1   Technical Details

Various technologies were used to make the recommender system work. The Angular framework was used to make the user interface for the recommender system. Angular is a strong tool for making dynamic, single-page web apps, and it helped make the user experience easy to use and responsive [13]. Flask is a simple, lightweight web platform for Python that was used to make a web server that the Angular application could talk to [14]. Python was used to build the core of the recommender system. The Python code was written so that it could read CSV files, preprocess the data, train the ML model, and then use this model to make job suggestions based on what the user said [15]. Specific packages of Unity Engine allowed us to execute a VR application directly from a web-browser: an application can be hosted on a web-browser if the build type of the application is WebGL [16]. WebGL is a Javascript API meant for rendering 3D graphics without the aid of additional plugins. WebXR Exporter is a Unity package that allows the development and build of VR applications in WebGL format compatible with multiple browsers such as Mozilla Firefox, Google Chrome, Microsoft Edge on Windows, Oculus Browser and Firefox Reality on Oculus Quest. The basic functionalities such as movement, rotation and interaction were handled using the VRTK Tilia packages which contain a collection of common functionalities meant for VR environments. Due to the WebGL format, the application is also compatible with multiple models of VR equipment as successful tests were done with HTC Vive Cosmos Elite, Oculus Rift and Oculus Quest. MongoDB, a JSON database, was also used: the Angular application sends user data to the Flask server in JSON format, which is further saved in the database and the Flask server responded with job recommendations in the same format [17] (Fig. 2).

3.2   Machine-Learning Based Recommendation Algorithm

To execute the ML algorithm, several steps had been taken, such as: data collection, data preprocessing and cleaning, feature extraction and engineering, ML model selection and training, ML model evaluation and fine-tuning.

Data Collection. Data gathering was a very important part of the work. The ESCO website [2] was the main place where the data was found. This platform offers a full

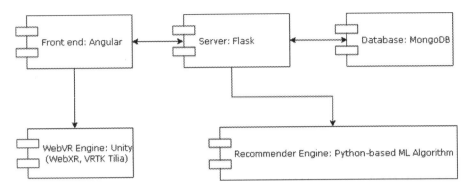

Fig. 2. Architecture of CareProfSys Recommender System.

grid of jobs and corresponding skills, which was used as the basis for training the ML model. ESCO is generally known as a reference for jobs and schooling in the European Union: it is like a dictionary for the European labor market. As the number of people who use ESCO grows, so does the number of ways the classification can be used. But not all users need the fine-grained information that ESCO skills or jobs provide. Some people like smaller, combined files that are easier to work with for their own reasons. To meet these needs, the European Commission has tried to make the ESCO dataset easier to understand by giving more active examples of how ESCO ideas can be linked together and used at more aggregated levels. The Commission has made matrix tables that link The International Standard of Occupations ISCO-08 work groups [18] to ESCO skills organizational groups. These tables, which come from the most thorough level of the ESCO classification, show what percentage of ISCO-08 work groups have ESCO skills. This method was very helpful in gathering data for our study: it made it possible to pull out relevant and doable data for the recommender system.

A Google Form poll was the second source of information. The goal of this survey was to get people's opinions about their skills and job choices: see Fig. 3. The answers were then put into a CSV file, thus building a complex model's testing data set. This two-source method made sure that the dataset was strong and varied, which made it easier for the model to make accurate recommendations. The fact that we used both the ESCO skills matrix table and other data assures that the job descriptions match also the local Romanian labor market status, as all our Google Form poll's respondents were Romanians. All jobs/ occupations were described in various precents (between 0 and 1) by the following skills: handling and moving, information skills, working with computers, constructing, management skills, working with machinery and specialized equipment, assisting and caring, communication, collaboration, and creativity. If several respondents declared to have a certain profession (e.g., accountant), then an average of their perceived need for a certain skill was made.

Data Preprocessing and Cleaning. Data preprocessing and cleaning is a crucial step in any data-driven project. For this research, both the training and testing datasets were cleaned using Excel. This process involved several steps: (1) any irrelevant or redundant information was removed to ensure the model was trained only on pertinent data; (2)

occupation	handlingAndMoving	informationSkills	workingWithComputers	constructing	managementSkills	workingWithMachineryAndSpecialisedEquipment	assistingAndCaring	communicationCollaborationAndCreativity
Accountants	0.8	0.9	0.9	0.8	0.9	0	1	0.9
Accountants	0.7	0.8	0.9	0.8	0.7	0.7	0.9	1
Accountants	1	0.8	0.9	0.8	0.8	0.7	0.6	0.6
Advertising and marketing	0.9	0.9	1	0.8	0.7	0.5	1	1
Advertising and marketing	1	1	1	1	1	1	1	1
Advertising and marketing	0.7	0.6	0.8	0.7	0.7	0.7	0.8	0.7
Agricultural and forestry p	0.4	0.2	0.4	0.2	0.4	0	0.8	1
Applications programmers	0.5	0.5	0.6	0.5	0.6	0.5	0.7	0.7
Applications programmers	0.8	0.8	1	0.7	0.7	1	0.9	0.7
Applications programmers	0.7	0.7	0.9	0.8	0.9	0.7	0.9	0.9
Bartenders	0.8	0.8	0.7	0.8	0.7	0.7	0.8	0.8
Building architects	0.7	0.8	0.8	0.9	0.8	0.7	0.9	1
Business services and adm	0.8	0.8	0.8	0.9	0.7	0.8	0.7	0.8
Chemical engineers	0.9	1	1	0.9	1	0.8	0.7	0.8
Coding, proof-reading and	0.9	0.9	0.8	0.9	1	0.7	1	1
Computer network and sy	1	1	0.8	0.8	0.9	0.8	0.9	1
Computer network and sy	0.8	0.9	0.7	0.7	0.8	0.6	0.8	0.8
Computer network and sy	0.7	0.7	0.6	0.5	0.7	0.5	0.9	0.6
Computer network and sy	0.8	0.8	0.9	0.8	0.8	0.9	0.7	0.7
Data entry clerks	0.8	0.8	0.6	0.7	0.9	0.3	1	0.9

Fig. 3. Snippet of the Matrix Job-Needed Skills of CareProfSys Recommender System.

missing or incomplete data was addressed to prevent any potential bias or inaccuracies in the model's recommendations; (3) the data was formatted appropriately to ensure compatibility with the ML algorithm. This meticulous cleaning process was essential in ensuring the integrity of the data and, by extension, the reliability of the model's recommendations.

Feature Extraction and Engineering. During feature extraction and engineering, the variables that the model would use to make its suggestions had to be found and worked on. In this case, the skills that go with each job were the variables, e.g., skill levels for working with computers, constructing, management, working with machinery and specialized equipment, for assisting and caring, for communication collaboration and creativity. These were taken from the datasets and then put on the same size to make sure they were all the same. Normalization is an important step because it makes sure that all features add the same amount to the distance calculation in the ML algorithm.

Model Selection and Training. The K-Nearest Neighbors (KNN) algorithm was picked for this study because it is good at making similarity-based recommendations. KNN is an instance-based learning algorithm that predicts the values of new instances based on how close their features are to the ones already known. In this case, it was used to suggest jobs based on how close the skills were. The model was trained with data from the ESCO page about jobs and skills and tested with the data provided by our poll. The number of neighbors was set to eight, so the model could suggest up to eight jobs that are most like the user's skills. This parameter was picked so that users would get a variety of job suggestions without having too many to choose from [19].

Model Evaluation and Fine-tuning. Model evaluation and fine-tuning is a fundamental part of building any maker discovering model. For this study, the screening dataset from our Google survey was used to analyze as well as modify the design. The design's success was evaluated by how well it could discover jobs that fit the preferences and abilities of the people that filled out the form. This indicated contrasting the model's tips with the jobs that the interviewees desired. To make the design of the job profile much better, changes were made to its features, such as the number of next-door neighbors. This process of evaluating and tweaking the model repeatedly ensured that it was as accurate as well as dependable as feasible.

3.3 Validation of CareProfSys System in Real-Life Settings

To validate the recommender system, we made a 2-weeks experiment with 27 high school students from Romanian technological schools, who participated at a summer school organized by University POLITEHNICA of Bucharest. The purpose of the experiment was to investigate whether the recommended jobs are considered appealing to young people and whether they see themselves practicing those professions. The students had the opportunity to test the VR scenarios of the recommended jobs, thus simulating some basic activities from a possible future working day: see Fig. 4. Almost half (51.9%) of the participants have used emergent technologies like VR before. All the students were offered the same explanations and the same testing conditions.

Some interesting experiment data are listed below: (1) 63% of the students have not done anything related to the activities of the recommended occupation before, especially the ones who were advised by CareProfSys to become computer networking specialists or civil engineers; nevertheless, just 7.4% of them found the tasks specific to that profession to be difficult and very difficult; (2) all participants enjoyed the tasks in VR for the recommended profession (70.4% of them very much); (3) 59.3% of participants understood what he/ she should do in the future profession; (4) 85.2% of participants saw the VR scenarios as learning experiences (not just entertainment); (5) 88.9% of students considered VR scenarios to be helpful for describing professional occupations to young people; (6) 92.6% of students considered the idea of CareProfSys Job Recommender

Fig. 4. Validation experiment of CareProfSys Recommender System.

to be useful, because they needed career guidance and explanations about the activities they would do whether choosing a certain occupation. Most of the participants were happy to discover the recommended professions and saw themselves practicing those jobs in the future.

Some validity threats for the positive response we obtained were: the fact that students were attracted by the gamification feature of the VR scenes, not by the activities specific to a certain profession, the fact that they wanted to be nice with us, as they were our guests and the fact that not all the recommended jobs has VR scenarios.

4   Conclusions

CareProfSys demonstrates how ML can be used to fix problems in real life: to implement a recommender system that can truly help young people discover their suitable jobs. The fact that CareProfSys does not offer only a textual description of the recommended profession, but a VR immersive experience, makes the recommender system to be especially useful for young people, a fact demonstrated by our experimental data. In the future, the hybrid recommended algorithm will be optimized by adding an ontological inference mechanism, the targeted ontology being the one reflecting the Romanian Classification of Occupations [20].

Acknowledgment. This work was supported by a grant of the Ministry of Research, Innovation and Digitization, CNCS–UEFISCDI, project number TE 151 from 14/06/2022, within PNCDI III: "Smart Career Profiler based on a Semantic Data Fusion Framework."

References

1. Stanica, I.C., Hainagiu, S.M., Neagu, S., Litoiu, N., Dascalu, M.I.: How to choose one's career? a proposal for a smart career profiler system to improve practices from romanian educational institutions. In: 15th annual International Conference of Education, Research, and Innovation Proceedings (ICERI 2022), pp. 7423–7432. IATED, Seville (2022)
2. ESCO: Skills-Occupations Matrix Tables. https://esco.ec.europa.eu/en/about-esco/publications/publication/skills-occupations-matrix-tables. Accessed 20 June 2023
3. Turing: How Does Collaborative Filtering Work in Recommender Systems? https://www.turing.com/kb/collaborative-filtering-in-recommender-system#user-item-interaction-matrix. Accessed 22 Oct 2022
4. Iterators: Collaborative Filtering In Recommender Systems: Learn All You Need To Know. https://www.iteratorshq.com/blog/collaborative-filtering-in-recommender-systems/. Accessed 28 Oct 2023
5. Career Explorer. https://www.careerexplorer.com/assessments/. Accessed 27 May 2023
6. *NET Interest Profiler. https://www.mynextmove.org/explore/ip. Accessed 25 June 2023
7. Pymetrics, https://www.pymetrics.ai. Accessed 25 June 2023
8. Job Scan. https://www.jobscan.co. Accessed 25 June 2023
9. My Next Move. https://www.mynextmove.org. Accessed 25 June 2023
10. Sampaio, A.Z., Martins, O.P.: The application of virtual reality technology in the construction of bridge: the cantilever and incremental launching methods. Autom. Constr. **37**, 58–67 (2014)

11. Tay, Y.X., McNulty, J.P.: Radiography education in 2022 and beyond - Writing the history of the present: a narrative review. Radiography **29**(2), 391–397 (2023)
12. Harknett, J., et al.: The use of immersive virtual reality for teaching fieldwork skills in complex structural terrains. J. Struct. Geol. **163**, 104681 (2022)
13. Angular. https://angular.io/. Accessed 25 June 2023
14. Flask. https://pythonbasics.org/what-is-flask-python/. Accessed 25 June 2023
15. Python. https://www.python.org/doc/essays/blurb/. Accessed 25 June 2023
16. WebG. https://developer.mozilla.org/en-US/docs/Web/API/WebGL_API. Accessed 25 June 2023
17. MongoDB. https://www.mongodb.com/. Accessed 25 June 2023
18. ISCO-08. https://www.ilo.org/public/english/bureau/stat/isco/isco08/. Accessed 17 Oct 2022
19. Guo, G., Wang, H., Bell, D., Bi, Y., Greer, K.: KNN model-based approach in classification. In: Meersman, R., Tari, Z., Schmidt, D.C. (eds.) OTM 2003. LNCS, vol. 2888, pp. 986–996. Springer, Heidelberg (2003). https://doi.org/10.1007/978-3-540-39964-3_62
20. Dascalu, M.I., et al.: CareProfSys – an ontology for career development in engineering designed for the Romanian job market. Rev. Roum. Sci. Techn.– Électrotechn. et Énerg. (RRST-EE) **68**(2), 212–217 (2022)

Author Index

J. Kofroň et al. (Eds.): ECBS 2023, LNCS 14390, pp. 299–300, 2024.
https://doi.org/10.1007/978-3-031-49252-5